Mary Frohlich

THE INTERSUBJECTIVITY OF THE MYSTIC

A Study of Teresa of Avila's *Interior Castle*

Scholars Press
Atlanta, Georgia

THE INTERSUBJECTIVITY OF THE MYSTIC
A Study of Teresa of Avila's *Interior Castle*

by
Mary Frohlich

Library of Congress Cataloging in Publication Data
Frohlich, Mary.
The intersubjectivity of the mystic : a study of Teresa of Avila's Interior castle / Mary Frohlich.
p. cm. — (American Academy of Religion academy series ; 83)
Includes bibliographical references and index.
ISBN 1-55540-931-8 (alk. paper). —ISBN 1-55540-932-6 (pbk. : alk. paper)
1. Teresa, of Avila, Saint, 1515-1583. Moradas. 2. Spiritual life—Catholic Church. 3. Mysticism—Catholic Church—History of doctrines—16th century. 4. Mysticism—Spain—History—16th century. 5. Intersubjectivity—Religious aspects—Catholic Church—History of doctrines—16th century. 6. Catholic Church—Doctrines—History—16th century. I. Title. II. Series.
BX2179.T4M7244 1994
248.4'82—dc20 93-40869
CIP

Printed in the United States of America
on acid-free paper

to the memory of my father,
Philip Earl Frohlich, Ph.D
1914--1991

TABLE OF CONTENTS

PART II: TOWARD VERIFICATION

CONCLUSION

APPENDICES

PREFACE

This book, it has been pointed out, could well have been two books. The first, consisting of Part I plus Chapter 7, would have as its agenda the working out of a theory of mystical transformation based in Bernard Lonergan's foundational theology. The second, consisting mainly of Chapters 8-11, would offer background for, and an example of, the use of applied psychoanalysis in the Self Psychology tradition to interpret religious literature.

On one level, these are indeed two quite distinct projects. Some readers will be primarily interested in only one of them, and may regard the other as somewhat of a distraction. In particular, readers with a more practical or pastoral interest may feel drawn to skip immediately to Part II, where the focus shifts away from the painstaking development of theory and gets on with the business of interpreting the experiences presented in Teresa of Avila's *Interior Castle*.

My hope, however, is that even readers who are predisposed to interest in only one part of the book will come away from their reading with at least an inkling of insight into why this is offered as one book, not two. The fundamental question that drives this project is: How can we explain God-experience in a way that both respects its non-reducible theological character *and* clearly indicates its integral relation with concrete psychological and social change? The goal of the detailed theoretical work of Part I is to sketch out such an explanatory viewpoint. Part II then picks up with the goal of testing and fleshing out the abstract explanation.

Reading Part II alone is valid, as long as one clearly understands its non-reductionistic context. This is not fundamentally a book about the psychology of mystical experiences--although one can learn something about that topic from reading it. It is, rather, a book about the mediation of the transcendent God in our psyches and in our community-building relationships. Its intent is to offer a theological model for articulating the experience that God both radically transcends us and, at the same time, is intimately involved in the concrete transformation of us and our world.

Such a model is necessarily complex in its theoretical foundations--hence the longwindedness of Part I. But it also potentially has much to offer to the thousands of ordinary folk who are struggling to be faithful both as people of prayer and as people called to build a just world. At an intuitive level, a lot of people already know very well that these two seemingly disparate agendas are really one. Our era cries out for a compelling theological articulation of that insight. I offer this book as a small contribution to that project.

As is always the case in the writing of books, the author's labor has been supported by the hidden labors of many others. A 1988-89 American Fellowship from the American Association of University Women was of immense help in completing the original dissertation. A partial tuition remission provided by the Training and Research Institute for Self Psychology (TRISP) in New York City greatly facilitated my studies there. The support and suggestions offered by TRISP candidates and faculty were invaluable; I especially note the contribution of my advisor, Dr. Charles B. Strozier.

During years of study and dissertation-writing, the faculty, students and staff of the School of Religious Studies at The Catholic University of America provided an atmosphere of support--both personal and intellectual--that greatly facilitated my work. The timely and astute insights of my major professor, Dr. James R. Price III, were essential to both the first and the last articulations of the ideas developed in this project.

The spiritual and practical caring of the members of the Association of Contemplative Sisters, the Carmelite Sisters of Baltimore, the Carmelite Sisters of Charity, and my present community, the Sisters of the Humility of Mary, is more deeply at the heart of this project than I can say. To all these, and to all my friends and family who have stood by me through the struggle, I am forever grateful.

Finally, this book is dedicated to my father, Philip Earl Frohlich, who died during the period of its final revision. Although he never understood or shared my Christian faith, he was an inspiration to me in his dedication to searching the depths of life and to seeking intellectual articulations for his findings. His life and death stand as a reminder to me that ultimately the heart of the matter is not explaining faith, but receiving faith as a gift. In his final childlike moments, defenses and theories of a lifetime were irrelevant. This, too, we must account for in our theories.

PART I

GENERATING THE CATEGORIES

INTRODUCTION

One of the characteristics of the modern age[1] has been an increasing isolation of contemplative practice and mystical experience from the mainstream of Christian life. In the preceding medieval period, contemplation and mysticism had been situated at the awe-inspiring peak of a hierarchical religious world view, and religious institutions were experienced as central pillars of human social life. In that context, individuals and groups wholly dedicated to contemplation were seen as incarnating the most profound religious and social values. With the rise of modernity and the dethroning of religious institutions, however, the walled-off contemplative life began to be seen as the epitome of religion's social irrelevance. Mysticism, likewise, came to be viewed with deep suspicion. It seemed to have no place within the emerging secular vision of free, self-directing human beings working together to build just and humane social structures. Within that context mysticism appeared, if not radically pathological, at least profoundly effete.

Today, in what is called the "post-modern" era, there is a plurality of views on the human, social, and religious value of contemplative practice and mystical experience. Some (including powerful forces within institutional Roman Catholicism) try to reinforce a hierarchical world view that, in the modern context, contributes to the theological and institutional isolation of contemplative practice. Others (including powerful forces within the reigning academic and intellectual communities) continue to disparage religion in any form--and mysticism

[1]The "modern age" is loosely defined here as the era between the time of Descartes (1596-1650) and the mid-twentieth century. The term "post-modern era" in the title of the chapter refers to the present period, in which many of the basic assumptions of the modern age are being questioned.

in particular--as illusory, oppressive, and anti-humanistic. Many Christian theologians, caught between these two forces both of which essentially deny that mysticism is intelligible within modern terms, abdicate the field and simply consign contemplation and mysticism to the vague margins of theological and human concern.

This inquiry takes up its position among the mediating group, whose members (in diverse ways) aim to deploy the considerable resources of contemporary science, philosophy and theology to grasp anew the fundamental intelligibility and value of contemplative practice and mystical experience. The goal will be to articulate an understanding of mystical transformation which will not only be conversant with the language and concerns of modern and post-modern thought, but will further indicate how such an understanding may contribute to the resolution of some of the dilemmas modernity presents to theology.

CHAPTER 1

MYSTICISM AND MODERNITY

This chapter schematically surveys modern thought and its dilemmas, as revealed in acute form when the modern thinker grapples with the question, "What is mysticism"? The method of this survey, which does not claim to be fully comprehensive, is to examine critically a series of major questions or sets of questions that emerge as modern thought confronts the phenomenon of mysticism. The goal will be to begin to derive the characteristics of the network of terms and relations which will be needed in order to move the conversation about mysticism to a new level of clarity and coherence.[1]

1. What patterns can be discerned in the mediation of mystical experience within the subjective forms of consciousness?

This set of questions comes first not because it is the most profound, but because it is typical of the way modern thought makes its first approach to a phenomenon it wishes to understand. Immanuel

[1]Those familiar with Bernard Lonergan's *Method in Theology* (London: Darton, Longman & Todd, 1971) will recognize here elements of his functional specialties of "history" and "dialectic." See ibid., especially pp. 175-266. Since the focus of the present project is on the subsequent step of intellectual inquiry, which Lonergan calls "foundations," this step is not pursued with the rigor that would be required in work focused within either of these functional specialities.

Kant's "critical turn," which has set the standard for modern intellectual inquiry, in essence demands that one recognize that there is no such thing as an unmediated experience; the structures of one's own subjectivity deeply form all the structures of one's experience. While pre-Kantian thought generally presumed the existence of the objects of experience and sought to know them, post-Kantian thought tended to abdicate judgment in regard to the existence of the objects of experience and instead to seek to know what certainly exists--that is, the knower.

The result has been the development of a powerful array of methods for the investigation of subjectivity. Applied to the subjective phenomena of mysticism, these have yielded rich results. The insights of a few of these methods are briefly surveyed here.

a. Psychology

Freud's groundbreaking exploration of the unconscious patterns structuring human experience has led to an "age of psychology" in which some minimal awareness of unconscious dynamics is widespread. Initial forays into a psychology of mystical experience began in the nineteenth century. The pioneering studies of William James[2] suggested that religious and mystical experiences represent the breakthrough of unconscious syntheses that have been in preparation for some time. During the early years of the twentieth century, many serious and in-depth studies of mysticism strove to develop more systematic insight into the psychological structures underlying mystical experience. Some of these sought primarily to show the pathological quality of mysticism,[3]

---

[2]William James, *The Varieties of Religious Experience* (New York: Modern Liberary, 1902).

[3]I.e., James H. Leuba, *The Psychology of Religious Mysticism* (New York: Harcourt, Brace, 1925); Henri J. Delacroix, *Études d'histoire et de psychologie du mysticisme: les grands mystiques chrétiens* (Paris: F. Alcan, 1908).

while others aimed to show a deeper religious potential underlying the psychological manifestations.[4]

More recently, psychologists have developed a variety of neurophysiological[5] and psychodynamic[6] explanations of mystical phenomena. Serious efforts to systematize the entire range of mystical phenomena have been made by Jungians[7] and transpersonalists.[8] A promising study by the German physician and psychologist Carl Albrecht,[9] not well-known in the English-speaking world, offers an alternative systematization that both explains the psychological phenomena of mysticism and leaves open its fundamental supra-worldly character.

---

[4]I.e., Joseph Maréchal, *Studies in the Psychology of the Mystics*, trans. Algar Thorold (London: Burns, Oates & Washbourne, 1927; reprint, Albany, NY: Magi, 1964); Friedrich Von Hügel, *The Mystical Element in Religion, as Studied in Saint Catherine of Genoa and Her Friends*, 2 vols. (London: J.M. Dent, 1908).

[5]I.e., Arthur J. Deikman, "Deautomatization and the Mystic Experience" and "Bimodal Consciousness and the Mystic Experience"; Robert E. Ornstein, "Two Sides of the Brain"; Roland Fischer, "A Cartography of the Ecstatic and Meditative States," all in Richard Woods, ed., *Understanding Mysticism* (Garden City, NY: Doubleday, 1980).

[6]I.e. Frank Barron, "The Creative Personality: Akin to Madness"; Kenneth Wapnick, "Mysticism and Schizophrenia"; Raymond H. Prince, "Cocoon Work: An Interpretation of the Concern of Contemporary Youth with the Mystical," all in Woods, *Understanding Mysticism*.

[7]I.e. Erich Neumann, "Mystical Man," *Eranos Jahrbuch* 30 (1968), pp. 375-415.

[8]I.e. Stanislav Grof, *Realms of the Unconscious* (New York: E.P. Dutton, 1976); the many books of Ken Wilber, including *The Spectrum of Consciousness* (Wheaton, IL: Quest, 1977), *The Atman Project* (Wheaton, IL: Quest, 1980), and *Up From Eden* (Garden City, NY: Doubleday, 1981); and Ken Wilber, Jack Engler, and Daniel P. Brown, eds., *Transformation of Consciousness: Conventional and Contemplative Perspectives on Development* (Boston: Shambhala, 1986).

[9]Carl Albrecht, *Psychologie des mystichen Bewusstseins* (Bremen, Germany: Carl Schuenemann Verlag, 1951) and *Das Mystische Erkennen* (Bremen, Germany: Carl Schuenemann Verlag, 1958). For summary, see Harvey D. Egan, *What Are They Saying About Mysticism?* (New York: Paulist, 1982), pp. 27-31.

b. *Phenomenology*

The phenomenological movement begun by Husserl strove to extend an empirical approach to the phenomena of consciousness. Its aim, then, was to apply the rigor of scientific method to subjectivity itself. Phenomenologists believed they would thus be able to discern the fundamental patterns and laws that govern all subjective experience.

Many of the best-known mid-twentieth century theories of mysticism employed a rather unsophisticated phenomenological approach. The advocates of the "perennial philosophy,"[10] for example, claimed that they could find similar patterns underlying the many diverse expressions in mystics of every religion and culture. R. C. Zaehner,[11] on the other hand, countered that at least three distinct types of patterns can be discerned.

The discussion moved to new levels of sophistication with the contributions of Ninian Smart,[12] who, while bringing to bear a vastly more nuanced awareness of the diverse forms and levels of interpretation manifested in mystical texts, still argues for an underlying cross-cultural similarity.[13] Meanwhile, many excellent phenomenological studies of specific mystical phenomena have contributed greatly to the store of data available on the subject.[14]

---

[10]I.e. Aldous Huxley, *The Perennial Philosophy* (New York: Harper & Bros., 1945; reprint, Harper Colophon Books, New York: Harper & Row, 1970).

[11]R.C. Zaehner, *Mysticism Sacred and Profane* (Oxford: Oxford University Press, 1961).

[12]Ninian Smart, *The Religious Experience of Mankind* (New York: Scribner, 1969); *The Phenomenon of Religion* (New York: Herder & Herder, 1973); "Understanding Religious Experience," in Steven T. Katz, ed., *Mysticism and Philosophical Analysis* (New York: Oxford University, 1978).

[13]Ninian Smart, "Interpretation and Mystical Experience," in Woods, *Understanding Mysticism*.

[14]To name only a few: R. Crookall, *The Interpretation of Cosmic and Mystical Experiences* (London, 1969); Mircea Eliade, *The Two and the One*, trans. J.M. Cohen (London: Harvill, 1965); R.C. Johnson, *Watcher on the Hills* (London, 1959); Marghanita Laski, *Ecstasy* (Bloomington, IN: Indiana University, 1962).

c. *The Linguistic Turn*

Wittgenstein effected a further deepening of the critical turn in philosophy by focusing intensively on the limitations and potential inherent in our use of language. His analysis of how every communicative sign is embedded in a specific "language game" has sharpened awareness of the immense potential for misinterpretation of others' communications. Wittgenstein's work has also served all contemporary thinkers with the warning that the attempt to use language in ways that subvert its actual potential will lead only to nonsensical expressions; in his view the majority of philosophical and theological expressions are riddled with such nonsense.

The impact of the linguistic turn upon studies of mysticism is best seen in the influential volumes edited by Steven T. Katz.[15] Katz and his colleagues argue that, since the expressions mystics use to describe their experiences are necessarily embedded in culturally-specific language games, we must presume that (as far as it is possible for us to know) the experiences themselves are likewise culturally specific. These thinkers argue that a rigorous and honest phenomenology must conclude with the affirmation of a fundamental and radical pluralism in the structure and content of mystical experience.

Many of the contemporary philosophical debates about mysticism are framed around the questions raised by this school. In simple terms, the question is whether there is a universal "common core" to mystical experience, or whether *all* mystical experience is necessarily linguistically contextualized. The most concerted challenge to Katz's contextualist view comes from Robert K.C. Forman and his colleagues, who argue for a "pure consciousness experience" that in and of itself

---

[15]Steven T. Katz, ed., *Mysticism and Philosophical Analysis* (New York: Oxford University, 1978); *Mysticism and Religious Traditions* (New York: Oxford University, 1983); and *Mysticism and Language* (New York: Oxford University,).

transcends linguistic construction--even though its instigation and expression may occur within a linguistic framework.[16]

d. Deconstruction

The critical turn culminates in the work of Derrida and the deconstructionists. Deconstruction relentlessly proclaims that "the emporer has no clothes." It deploys the resources of psychoanalysis and linguistic analysis to lay bare the fundamental incoherence at the roots of human mental constructions. The deconstructionist project highlights and celebrates the darkness and unintelligibility that, in its view, are more foundational than any light, order or intelligibility humans may impose upon reality.

Without explicitly developing a theory of mysticism, deconstructionist theologians point beyond language to the realm of the origination of meaning--a realm of pregnant "darkness."[17] There is a certain affinity between deconstructionist insights and the insights of the apophatic mystics, who likewise celebrate the basic inability of the human mind to comprehend reality. Yet unlike the mystics, who generally attribute this inability to an overwhelming superabundance of meaning, the stronger trend in deconstructionist thought seems to be toward a sense of ultimate meaninglessness.[18]

Pursuit of the first set of questions to its logical conclusion, then, results in a sort of "dead end." To focus entirely upon the subjective

---

[16]Robert K.C. Forman, ed., *The Problem of Pure Consciousness: Mysticism and Philosophy* (New York: Oxford University, 1990). See also the work of James R. Price, discussed in Chapter 5 below.

[17]See, for example, Charles E. Winquist, *Epiphanies of Darkness: Deconstruction in Theology* (Philadelphia: Fortress, 1986).

[18]For a different assessment of the value of deconstruction for understanding the role of mysticism in Christian theology, however, see Kevin Hart, *The Trespass ofthe Sign: Deconstruction, Theology and Philosophy* (New York: Cambridge University, 1989).

structures of the mediation of experience is to risk ending in darkness, incoherence and fragmentation, as the deconstructionists demonstrate. This conclusion can be interpreted positively in terms of the mystical "dark night,"[19] and the paradoxical rhetoric which it can generate can be powerfully transformative.[20] Yet in terms of the search for a coherent philosophical and theological understanding of the mystical experience and its value in human life, inquiries directed only by this set of questions are unsatisfactory.

2. How is mystical experience related to the dynamics of human intersubjectivity?

A major reason for the insufficiency of analyses that focus strictly on the subjective forms of the mediation of *individual* experience is that they fail to account adequately for the unique and central role that mediation through other persons and groups of persons plays in structuring human experience. While contemplative practice and mystical experience necessarily involve a profound dimension of solitude, the persons engaged in them are at the same time both formed by and forming of intersubjective mediation.

Under this set of questions, then, can be included sociological and social-psychological studies of mystics and their relations with others. The seminal 1967 article "Mysticism and Society" by Gershom Scholem raised the question of why the social context and social effectiveness of mystics has been so long ignored.[21] In the same year Philip H. Ennis set the agenda for sociological studies of the relationship between

---

[19]See Michael J. Buckley, "Atheism and Contemplation," *Theological Studies* 40 (1979): 680-99.

[20]See Frederick Streng, "Language and Mystical Awareness," in Katz, *Mysticism and Philosophical Analysis*, pp. 141-169.

[21]Gershom Scholem, "Mysticism and Society," *Diogenes* 58 (Summer 1967): 1-24.

transcendent experiences and social institutions.[22] A 1981 article by Roger A. Straus offers a sophisticated social-psychological view of experiences that transcend ordinary perceptual and conceptual structuring.[23] The numerous empirical studies of Ralph W. Hood continue to increase the data available in this field.[24]

An attempt to approach the question of intersubjectivity from the level of the mystical unitive experience itself has been made by transpersonalist Joseph Keller.[25] He employs the paradigms of quantum physics to speak of the mystic experience as "largely an unimpeded consciousness of the plenum in which all of us have our deepest being and whose potentialities unite us all, the unity to which our every particulate knowing implicitly refers and against which our knowing is profiled."[26]

The notion of intersubjectivity provides a bridge between the exploration of the structures of subjectivity and their placement within larger contexts. Sociological studies approach intersubjectivity from within the field of everyday life, while the transpersonal paradigm finds it at the foundation of mystical experience itself. Once the move has been made from an individual to a social paradigm, however, another

---

[22]Philip H. Ennis, "Ecstasy and Everyday Life," *Journal for the Scientific Study of Religion* 6 (1967): 40-48.

[23]Roger A. Straus, "The Social-Psychology of Religious Experience: A Naturalistic Approach," *Sociological Analysis* 42, no. 1 (1981): 57-67.

[24]Among Hood's many publications are: "Differential Triggering of Mystical Experience as a Function of Self Actualization," *Review of Religious Research* 18 (1977): 264-270; "Gender Differences in the Description of Erotic and Mystical Experiences," *Review of Religious Research* 21 (1980): 195-207; "Knowledge and Experience Criteria in the Report of Mystical Experience," *Review of Religious Research* 23 (1983): 76-84.

[25]Joseph Keller, "Mysticism and the Implicate Order," *Studia Mystica* 7, no. 4 (1984): 28-36, and "Mysticism and Intersubjective Creativity," *Studia Mystica* 8, no. 4 (1985): 36-46.

[26]Keller, "Mysticism and Intersubjective Creativity," p. 41.

set of questions soon becomes urgent: What about the political relevance of mysticism?

3. How is mystical experience related to the mystic's praxis?

Classically contemplation was understood in terms of the Greek notion of *theoria*, as "reflection upon eternal and unchanging, and to that extent divine, things."[27] The life of contemplation was seen as the highest good; it was its own justification. The corresponding notion of *praxis* had to do with action oriented to the human good within the contingent world. While highly valued, the "practical" or "active" life was clearly distinct from, and secondary to, the contemplative life. With the Renaissance and the Enlightenment, "theory" came to be identified with abstract systems of propositions on a mathematical model, while "practice" became identified with the technological application of such theoretical insights. In this model, contemplation and mysticism were almost totally marginalized.

The contemporary debate on these questions is largely influenced by the Marxist understanding of "theory" and "praxis." For Marx, the central human activity is revolutionary praxis, or action to change social structures toward greater justice. In this context, most theory is understood as false consciousness--it functions primarily to rationalize illusion and oppression. It is possible, however, to have a "critical theory" whose function is to critique existing structures so that one can see clearly what needs to be done to change them.

The classical identification of mysticism with an orientation to divine *theoria* or knowledge for its own sake is obviously very problematic in this context. If mysticism involves some form of "knowledge" isolated from or unconcerned with responsible human

---

[27]*Marxism, Communism and Western Society: A Comparative Encyclopedia*, ed. C.D. Kernig (NY: Herder and Herder, 1973), s.v. "Theory and Practice," by Nicholas Lobkowicz, 8:160.

action, it appears to the contemporary mind as at best a curious aberration and at worst a dangerous illusion.

Those sympathetic to mysticism generally try to soften the impression that this is the case, even when their own approach to mysticism finds in it no integral relation to praxis. Evelyn Underhill, for example, wrote that mysticism involves the whole self, not just the intellect, and true mystics will spend themselves in active love for others. Yet, she continued, the "aims [of mysticism] are wholly transcendental and spiritual. It is in no way concerned with adding to, exploring, re-arranging, or improving anything in the visible universe."[28]

Contemporary political and liberation theologies, which draw implicitly or explicitly upon a Marxist "primacy of praxis" orientation, find this account most unsatisfactory, and some of them have striven to develop alternative ideas about how mysticism is related to praxis.

Among Latin American liberation theologians, Segundo Galilea has addressed the question of mysticism most directly. He finds the mystics deeply at one with the struggle of Christians today to deepen their critical consciousness of sin, and he believes that the mystics were as committed to praxis--action to change structures toward the human good--as any militant today.[29] European political theologian Jürgen Moltmann even more forcefully rejects an oversimplifed, "activist" approach to praxis; he argues that Christian praxis requires first letting the self be taken over by the history of Christ's passion in meditation, then becoming aware of that history in one's self in contemplation, and finally letting go of self into union with God in mysticism.[30]

---

[28]Evelyn Underhill, *Mysticism: A Study in the Nature and Development of Man's Spiritual Consciousness* (New York: Meridian, 1958), pp. 81, 84.

[29]Segundo Galilea, *The Future of Our Past* (Notre Dame, IN: Ave Maria, 1985); idem, "Liberation as an Encounter with Politics and Contemplation," in Woods, *Understanding Mysticism*.

[30]Jürgen Moltmann, "Theology of Mystical Experience," *Scottish Journal of Theology* 32 (1979): 501-20.

Edward Schillebeeckx, another representative of the developing European tradition of political theology, provides a more developed theoretical framework for placing mystical experience within the context of emancipative praxis.[31] For him, the most authentic mystical experiences are "contrast experiences" in which the contrast between the deepest God-given reality of a thing and the present violation of that reality by oppressive forces comes forcefully to the fore, thus energizing liberating praxis. Schillebeeckx writes, "In the prophet Jesus, mysticism and the healing of men came from one and the same source: his experience of the contrast between the living God and the history of human suffering."[32] While such mystical "disclosure experiences" are essential to prevent reduction of emancipatory praxis to merely technical or ideological goals, the greater "density of reality" still lies in the ethical dimension.[33] In this, Schillebeeckx is faithful to the contemporary insistence on the primacy of praxis.

Galilea, Moltmann and Schillebeeckx each postulate a form of experience that momentarily lifts one's vision beyond the strictly political network of interaction, yet does not take one out of that network; rather, it amplifies one's clarity of vision, energy, and commitment. Where Marxist thought allows for the possibility of critical theory that can "stand above" praxis sufficiently to offer it guidance, these theologians go one step further and suggest that mystical experience may be a radicalization of that possibility of "transcendence."

These theologians, then, clarify how mystical transcendence can be highly valued from within the perspective of praxis. They have difficulty, however, when it comes to explaining the nature of this transcendence in itself, as well as exactly how it is both integral to, and

---

[31]For discussion, see: Mary Frohlich, "Politics, Mysticism and Liturgy: Schillebeeckx on Prayer," *Liturgy* 5, no. 3 (Winter, 1986): 35-39.

[32]Edward Schillebeeckx, *Christ: The Experience of Jesus as Lord* (New York: Crossroad, 1980), p. 821.

[33]Ibid., p. 61.

essentially distinct from, the kind of consciousness that operates in praxis.

4. How can the transcendent or supra-worldly claims of mysticism be accounted for?

The three sets of questions so far discussed all approach mysticism basically from within the perspective of modern secular thought, which is fundamentally hostile to the classical theological notion of "transcendence" as a distinct, supra-worldly, intrinsically superior realm. Yet a theology of radical transcendence appears to be central to the self-understanding of mystics. Dealing with this question of transcendence is pivotal for a contemporary theory of mysticism.

As Karl Lehmann notes, the very notion of transcendence contains a structural tension.[34] The tension seems to be generated by the human awareness of a gap between "what can be experienced" and "reality in itself." The classical approach tended to resolve this tension by leaning away from experience and toward a concept of ineffable, supra-temporal, transcendent Being. The modern approach tends to resolve the tension by leaning away from metaphysics and toward a concept of an evolving history that is permanently surpassing itself through human action. Though in a sense the tension is fundamentally irresolvable, theologians strive for a balanced view that can "combine a transcendence superior to history with a historical process of transcendence" while remaining sensitive to both the "critical differences" and the "harmony that is possible."[35]

In a philosophical discussion of "Justice and Mysticism," Ian F.G. Baxter made a distinction that helps to clarify the issues raised here and within the above discussion of praxis. Baxter argued that as long as

---

[34]*Encylopedia of Theology: The Concise Sacramentum Mundi* (NY: Crossroads, 1986), ed. Karl Rahner, s.v. "Transcendence," by Karl Lehmann, p. 1740.

[35]Ibid., p. 1741.

questions of ethics and social justice (human action in history) are viewed solely from within the field of what he calls "scientific" consciousness, they can only be seen as basically technical problems. A real vision of social justice requires recognition of the more fundamental, mystical drive of "intuitional" consciousness toward "perfection of being." Attention to both scientific and intuitional dimensions of consciousness, Baxter argued, is essential if a society is to move toward justice.[36]

Baxter's distinction of two dimensions of consciousness offers another perspective on what the praxis-oriented theologians are saying when they speak of mystical experience as (in Schillebeeckx's term) a "disclosure experience" that occurs within the field of ordinary experience and yet at the same time lifts one somehow beyond it. Baxter speaks of this in terms of his distinction between "scientific consciousness," which focuses on distinct objects, and "intuitional consciousness," which is the dynamism of the inner self. This distinction, developed in greater depth and in somewhat different terms, provides a basis for a resolution to the problem of understanding mystical transcendence.

The fundamental distinction is between "intentional consciousness" (consciousness of objects) and what Bernard Lonergan has sometimes called "implicit consciousness" (self-presence).[37] Intentional consciousness is the awareness of any kind of object. Examples would include physical objects, thoughts, dream images, moods or feelings, one's self-image, one's "sense of self." All of these are, so to speak,

---

[36]Ian F.G. Baxter, "Justice and Mysticism," *Revue Internationale de Philosophie* 17 (1963): 353-380.

[37]For discussion of this distinction, see: Karl Rahner, *Foundations of Christian Faith: An Introduction to the Idea of Christianity*, trans. William V. Dych (New York: Crossroad, 1982), pp. 14-23; and *On the Ontological and Psychological Constitution of Christ: A Supplement Prepared by Bernard Lonergan, S.J.*, for the Use of his Students, translation of *De Constitutione Christi ontologica et psychologica confecit Bernardus Lonergan, S.J* (Rome: Gregorian University 1956) by Timothy P. Fallon (University of Santa Clara, 1979), pp. 119-27.

the "images" (though not necessarily visual, or even particularly distinct) projected on the screen of the stream of consciousness. Intentional consciousness is "consciousness of" something.

Implicit consciousness, on the other hand, is the awareness that underlies intentional consciousness. Implicit consciousness is consciousness, not of any object (not even of one's self-image or sense of self), but of one's own subjectivity. It is the immediate self-presence that is the *sine qua non* of any experience of presence to an object. It can never be grasped by introspection, for any attempt to "look" at it turns it into an object of intentional consciousness; yet one can advert to its existence in any moment of consciousness. As Karl Rahner puts it, there are

> two factors in man's consciousness of himself: on the one hand an ultimate self-possession of the subject as free, i.e. a presence to himself which is never consciously explicated, a self-understanding on man's part which is never fully reflected upon; on the other hand man's objectified awareness of himself, his subjectivity and his capacity for free decision as objectified to himself.[38]

While intentional consciousness (consciousness of objects) is necessarily embedded in the network of this-worldly events, implicit consciousness (self-presence) can be said to "transcend" this network. It is the horizon within which any particular object or event is experienced, but it is limited by none of them. It is noteworthy that this distinction comes to the fore most clearly in the context of pressing the question about praxis. Praxis is mere activism unless it finds its grounding in something transcendent to the fields of technology and politics. Yet this transcendence must be intrinsic to human persons themselves, and integrally related to the dynamism of technological and political decisions in their own terms. The notion of implicit consciousness as

---

[38]Karl Rahner, "On the Theology of the Ecumenical Discussion," *Theological Investigations*, vol. 11, trans. David Bourke (London: Darton, Longman & Todd, 1974), pp. 37-38.

the "transcendent" ground of intentional consciousness can fulfill these qualifications.

Making this distinction, of course, does not immediately resolve the question of the relationship between ordinary forms of intentional consciousness and experience of transcendence. Theologians of the middle and later years of the twentieth century have proposed various answers to this question. Joseph Maréchal, for example, proposed that there is a "natural" mysticism which consists in an "empirical negativity"--an emptying or stopping of the mind so that it no longer engages in any intentional activity toward an object. Supernatural (i.e. Christian) mysticism fills this emptiness with an activity of God.[39] The weakness of Maréchal's theory is that while it asserts a unique supernatural activity in Christian mysticism, it leaves it essentially unexplained.

Karl Rahner went a step further, discussing the experience of "consciousness without an object" in terms of consciousness of the implicit horizon of all cognitive acts. He called it "the becoming conscious of the transcendence which is the necessary condition of all cognition and presupposed in all certitude; the foundation and ground of all these operations of the mind everywhere and always."[40]

For Rahner, such an experience even as "natural" necessarily is touched by "grace which supervenes to mould this natural unlimited receptivity and make of it a dynamic orientation toward participation in the life of God himself."[41] It is the "unlimited affirmation" that is the prerequisite to any delimited conceptualization in regard to the divine.[42]

---

[39]Joseph Maréchal, "Some Distinctive Features of Christian Mysticism," in *Psychology of the Mystics*, pp. 147-215.

[40]Karl Rahner, "The Logic of Concrete Individual Knowledge in Ignatius Loyola," in *The Dynamic Element in the Church* (New York: Herder & Herder, 1964), p. 149.

[41]Ibid., pp. 144-145.

[42]Ibid., p. 149.

Rahner did not claim to settle all the various controversial issues, such as whether this experience is strictly "miraculous" (requiring a special intervention of God in the natural order) and whether it occurs by gradual approach to a limit or by a sudden "quantum leap" of consciousness.[43] Nevertheless his conceptualization provides categories within which these questions can be framed in dialogue with the categories of modern philosophy.

5. Are there any criteria of objectivity that can be appropriately applied to mystical experience?

This final set of questions summarizes the issues raised by the other studies by asking two fundamental, interrelated questions: "Is the mystics' claim to be 'transcendental knowers' intelligible within a scientific worldview?" and "Is it possible to have objective, non-reductionistic knowledge of mystical transformation?"

Having largely abandoned hope of objective metaphysical knowledge, the modern mentality places great stock in methodical empirical study by which "facts" can be verified and made available as the building blocks of technological achievements. This redefinition of true knowledge as empirical science places the "transcendent" knowledge claimed by mystics in limbo. Indeed, the issues surrounding the study of mysticism are a radicalization of the issues surrounding all the human sciences.

Objectivity in the human sciences is a major problem because the knower and the known are not fundamentally separable; the researcher approaches any human psychological or sociological phenomenon from within his or her own psychosocial worldview. Mysticism radicalizes this problem in that it radicalizes the very notions of both "knower" and "known." The known is viewed as the fullness of ultimate reality ("God," "Being," etc.), while the knower is viewed as one capable of

[43]Ibid., p. 147.

knowing this fullness. The researcher, who approaches the mystic from within the researcher's own contingent psychosocial worldview, is by definition (from the point of view of the mystic) a knower of less than this fullness. The researcher has no place from which to "stand above" the mystic's transcendent knowledge, unless by joining the mystic as a mystic.

Empirical studies of mysticism, of course, have their place. Studies such as that undertaken by Marilyn Mallory,[44] who gave Christian contemplatives a battery of psychological and neurophysiological tests and analyzed the results both statistically and theoretically, are an essential component of a modern understanding of mystical experience.

Such studies, however, do not fully address the problem of finding criteria of objectivity appropriate to the reality of mystical transformation. Ordinary forms of empirical research carefully define and correlate combinations of intentional experience. Fundamentally, empiricism is measurement: a standard is established and other phenomena are understood in their relations to the standard. Both measuring standard and measured phenomena are, of course, necessarily within the world of contingent objects. Insofar as mystical experience has to do with something that transcends or sublates the standards being used to measure it, it is incompletely understood by these forms of empirical research.

The basic issue, then, is how to "measure" something that intrinsically transcends one's standard of measurement. One answer (often resorted to by religious adherents under attack by secular empiricists) is simply to agree that mysticism is ineffable, etc., and cannot possibly be understood by the human mind; in short, that it is fundamentally unintelligible within human terms.

Another approach, however, is to look in a different direction for one's "measure." Rather than looking to an "objective" standard outside

---

[44]Marilyn May Mallory, *Christian Mysticism: Transcending Techniques* (Amsterdam: Van Gorcum Assen, 1977).

the subject as the measure of knowledge, one looks to the standard of the knowing subject herself or himself. By developing a scientific knowledge of how the knowing subject knows, one may have a standard by which to "measure" both empirical knowing and mystical knowing.

Such a "knowledge of knowing" is what Lonergan means by interiority. It is the basis for his "generalized empirical method,"[45] which he asserts enables the knower to gain an objective knowledge and conscious mastery of underlying structures of knowing and so to discover the field within which all particular fields of knowledge intersect. The remainder of this inquiry will explore whether Lonergan's foundational methodology can provide the basis for a theory of mystical transformation that can enable the mystics to regain their position as central "conversation partners" for theologians and others who care about the future of humankind.

---

[45]For use of this term, see Bernard J.F. Lonergan, *Insight: A Study of Human Understanding*, 3rd ed. (New York: Philosophical Library, 1970), pp. 72, 243.

CHAPTER 2

LONERGAN AND FOUNDATIONAL METHODOLOGY

The goal of this project is to generate the categories and method through which mystical experience and transformation can be understood today. The preliminary methodological hypothesis of the inquiry is that Lonergan's foundational methodology is uniquely apt for this task. This chapter provides a preliminary overview of Lonergan's perspective on foundations, method, and the generation of categories.

A. Lonergan and the Generation of Categories

Lonergan's Foundational Methodology

Michael O'Callaghan has pointed out that even though Lonergan was a theologian, he concentrated more on developing the overall framework of "foundational methodology" than on theological issues per se.[1] Foundational methodology is the articulation of the foundations of

[1]Michael O'Callaghan, "Rahner and Lonergan on Foundational Theology," in Matthew Lamb, ed., *Creativity and Method* (Milwaukee, WI: Marquette University, 1981), pp. 123-40.

human knowing in general. It objectifies and develops general categories for all human experiencing, understanding and knowing, within which religious and mystical experience, understanding and knowing are specific forms.

O'Callaghan notes that Rahner, on the other hand, was clearly a specialist in "foundational theology." The foundational theologian's task is to develop specifically theological and Christian categories by reflecting on his or her own religious tradition in the light of experience of divine mystery. In regard to mystical experience, Lonergan himself noted the value of Rahner's exposition of the Ignatian "consolation that has no cause" within a modern philosophical framework.[2] What Lonergan's approach can add to Rahner's, however, is the placement of mystical experience within the differentiated framework of generalized empirical method. Thus, while Rahner went further than Lonergan in dealing with the explicitly theological issues of articulating the nature and implications of the experience of mystery, Lonergan's concentration in foundational methodology offers a much more adequate language and method for placing this experience in dialogue with modern science and with other religious traditions.

A method, in Lonergan's definition, is "a normative pattern of recurrent and related operations yielding cumulative and progressive results."[3] Lonergan's generalized empirical method or "transcendental method"[4] is based in the assertion that the human mind itself manifests a normative pattern of recurrent and related operations, and that a knower's objectification and appropriation of that pattern is the foundation of his or her capacity to attain cumulative, progressive, adequate knowledge in any field at all.

Lonergan's central assertion is that the very basis of the possibility of any knowledge is self-presence--that is, what was earlier termed

---

[2]Lonergan, *Method in Theology*, p. 106. See above, p. 21-22.

[3]Lonergan, *Method in Theology*, p. 4.

[4]Ibid., chap. 1.

"implicit consciousness."[5] Nevertheless, to know something also requires experiencing it, understanding it, and affirming it within the field of intentional consciousness. This is equally as true of "knowledge of knowing" as of knowledge of any other object. The standard that is to be established--the measure of objectivity--is an objective knowledge of oneself as a knower. Lonergan writes, "Genuine objectivity is the fruit of authentic subjectivity. It is to be attained only by attaining authentic subjectivity."[6]

This is how Lonergan describes the process from self-presence to activities of knowing to objective self-knowledge:

> In self-presence, then, we have the materials in which we can verify this idea of the knower . . . . Self-knowledge--the process from being present to oneself and finding typical activities in that self to understanding how these activities are combined, and from that combination to working out a theory of what it is to be a knower--is an objectification of oneself.[7]

On the basis of this objectification of the knowing process, Lonergan suggests that in the post-modern world, theology (and, indeed, any serious intellectual work) must proceed by developing eight "functional specialties."[8] The division of intellectual labor into functional specialties is a systematization of the processes intrinsic to the acquisition of knowledge. The first four functional specialties (research, interpretation, history, and dialectic) carefully and thoroughly establish the data concerning the object of the investigation. The fifth functional specialty, "foundations," focuses on the explicit objectification of the horizon within which the theologian will subsequently proceed to

---

[5]See above, p. 17-20.

[6]Lonergan, *Method in Theology*, p. 292.

[7]Bernard Lonergan, *Understanding and Being: An Introduction and Companion to Insight*, ed. Elizabeth A. Morelli and Mark D. Morelli (New York: Edwin Mellen, 1980), pp. 171, 172.

[8]Lonergan, *Method in Theology*, esp. pp. 125-45.

articulate a truth-claim in regard to the object under consideration. Finally, the truth-claim is actually articulated within the functional specialties of doctrines, systematics and communications.

As noted above, what Lonergan called "foundations" can be understood either in terms of the broader concerns of "foundational methodology" or in terms of the more focused concerns of "foundational theology." A major theme of Part I of this inquiry is exploration of the potential for employing Lonergan's method in making explicit the transition *from* foundational methodology *to* foundational theology. By employing the general categories which articulate the transcending dynamism of the subject as the basis for deriving the special categories for understanding mystical experience, it may be possible to build a bridge between the more general foundational concerns of the post-modern era and the specific concerns of foundational theology.

Foundations and the "Founding Act"

The root of foundations, Lonergan writes, is "a fully conscious decision about one's horizon, one's outlook, one's world-view."[9] The root, then, is an act of fully engaged human consciousness making an existential decision about where it finds truth. Such an act, obviously, cannot be totally and definitively captured in words, for the act necessarily sublates its own objectification and articulation. The functional specialty of foundations, however, strives to objectify and articulate the founding act to the degree that that is possible.

It is important to note that every human being has in fact implicitly made such a "founding act" of choosing an horizon. Within that basic horizon each person also has access to many differentiations of consciousness, ranging from the dreamy state on the verge of sleep to the varieties of concentrated attention given to different kinds of relationships and tasks. In speaking of a "fully conscious decision"

---

[9]Lonergan, *Method in Theology*, p. 268.

about one's horizon, however, Lonergan is referring to something quite rare; for such a decision requires being able to sort out the various specific contents and activities of consciousness and then to look beyond them to that which grounds all of them.

In Lonergan's view, such a founding act increases in consciousness, deliberateness, and coherence through "conversion"--a "vertical exercise of freedom" in which one makes a step from less authenticity to more authenticity. Ultimately, conversion involves a "total surrender to the demands of the human spirit: be attentive, be intelligent, be reasonable, be responsible, be in love."[10]

Lonergan views foundations, then, not as the first principles in an ordered set of propositions, but as grounding assent to the "immanent and operative set of norms"[11] that guide the ongoing, developing dynamism of the human spirit. Foundations is fully "subjective" in that it is rooted in the existential act of the free subject; but it is at the same time fully "objective" in that the norms to which the subject assents transcend the subject. Ultimately, foundations transcends and sublates the subject-object distinction. As we will see, this will be extremely important for the present project.

The "immanent and operative" norms of the human spirit are the transcendental notions, which make questions and answers possible; but questions and answers also must be determinate, and so the norms must generate categories.[12] The categories will be derived from the articulation of the founding act. They will objectify the structure of the human spirit in its self-transcending dynamism toward knowledge and love.

The "general categories" are those which are common to any intellectual endeavor. Additionally, the theologian will need to generate "special categories" through the objectification and articulation of that

[10]Ibid.

[11]Ibid., p. 270.

[12]Ibid., p. 282.

conversion which is specifically religious. This study, as noted, takes up its work on the threshhold between the generation of general categories (foundational methodology) and the generation of special categories (foundational theology). Our next task, then, will be to explore more thoroughly the processes by which the categories are generated.

The "Canons of Methodical Analysis"

It has been stated that the functional specialty of foundations has its root in a "founding act," an existential decision about where truth is to be found. That decision should not be arbitrary, but should be a rational affirmation of the experienced root of truth. This inquiry takes its stand with Lonergan in affirming that the root of truth is the affirmation of oneself as a knower capable of authentic acts of knowing.[13] The objectification of the founding act, then, will be the objectification of the authentic act of knowing.

The spelling out of this objectification will occupy much of Part I of this work. A preview of the implications of this particular founding act, however, can be gained by a brief review of what Lonergan once termed the "canons of metaphysical analysis."[14] These canons constitute the basic rules for the generation of categories. As the rules governing the movement from founding act to its objectification, they are the most schematic and general articulation of the founding act itself.

Within the total context of Lonergan's fully-developed methodical theology, there would seem to be less danger of confusion if these canons are called "canons of methodical analysis"; for in his later works Lonergan advocated "a transcendental doctrine of methods with

---

[13]See Lonergan, *Insight*, pp. 271-78. For further discussion, see the section entitled "The Subject as Objectified in Self-Appropriation" in Chapter 3.

[14]Lonergan, *Understanding and Being*, pp. 261-65.

the method of metaphysics just one among many."[15] In *Insight*, he had defined metaphysics as "the conception, affirmation and implementation of the integral heuristic structure of proportionate being";[16] and heuristic structure, he later wrote, is "the use of a set of analogies, where the analogies have a fundamental determination from cognitional process."[17] In this view, metaphysics as a set of categories or concepts becomes specifically the theory *of* the praxis of knowing and the theory that *fosters implementation* of the praxis of knowing. When transposed into the context of the functional specialties, "metaphysical analysis" becomes foundational methodology--that is, the foundational process of the derivation of categories.

The "canons of methodical analysis," then, are rules for any such derivation of categories. The canons are three: first, be concrete; second, be explanatory; third, focus on acts (operations) rather than on words. In this way, Lonergan transposes the classical scholastic metaphysical categories of "potency, form, and act" into a methodical framework.

"Because what exists is concrete, the first canon is concreteness: deal with the concrete."[18] The primary goal of the knower is not to know an abstraction or an idea or a generality; it is to know something that actually exists. As a canon for the derivation of categories, this injunction means that one must constantly refocus one's attention on actual instances. In deriving the general categories, attention is focused on the concreteness of oneself and one's praxis of knowing. In deriving the special categories, attention is focused on the concreteness of other existents in relationship to oneself.

---

[15]Bernard Lonergan, "Metaphysics as Horizon," in *Collection*, 2nd ed., ed. Frederick E. Crowe and Robert M. Doran (Toronto: University of Toronto Press, 1988), p. 204.

[16]Lonergan, *Insight*, p. 391.

[17]Lonergan, *Understanding and Being*, p. 254.

[18]Ibid., p. 263.

The second canon, "be explanatory," turns on the distinction between description and explanation, of which Lonergan wrote, "Description deals with things as related to us. Explanation deals with the same things as related among themselves."[19] Categories are, by definition, explanatory. In a certain sense, knowledge of the praxis of knowing always remains a knowledge "as related to us," since the object of this knowledge is our own subjectivity. Yet, Lonergan argues, "the subject is capable of an intentional self-transcendence, of going beyond what he feels, what he imagines, what he thinks, what seems to him, to something utterly different, to what is so."[20] Our knowledge of our own praxis of knowing must be pursued to the point of being explanatory, because only in doing so have we been faithful to the structure of the subject him/herself.

"One must go behind words to the experiences, the understanding, the rational judgment, through the analysis of the cognitional process at its root. . . . We are concerned with cognitional acts, not talk."[21] This final canon, the "canon of operations," is really the key to Lonergan's "methodological turn." The study of the human subject is the study of acts. Study of the subject is "the study of oneself insofar as one is conscious"; and, says Lonergan, the human person "is not conscious of himself except through his acts."[22] Consciousness itself is an infrastructure within the structure of cognitional activity; concepts and words are a product of such activity; but it is the activity itself which mediates between them, and thus constitutes the existing structure of the subject.

---

[19]Lonergan, *Insight*, p. 291.

[20]Lonergan, "The Subject," in *A Second Collection: Papers by Bernard Lonergan, S.J.*, edited by William F.J. Ryan and Bernard J. Tyrrell (London: Darton, Longman & Todd, 1974), p. 70.

[21]Lonergan, *Understanding and Being*, p. 264.

[22]Lonergan, *The Ontological and Psychological Constitution of Christ*, p. 126.

The Role of Theory

The present treatise is a work of theory--a work, that is, that specializes in obedience to the second canon, "be explanatory." Yet, according to the foundational stance taken here, theory only remains honest--and truly explanatory--when it is faithful to the other two canons as well. This means that in Lonergan's system theory is situated quite differently than it typically is in either classical or modern projects.

In the world of classical metaphysics, theory was to a large extent an end in itself. Achievement of a systematic, explanatory viewpoint was regarded as a knowledge of "highest causes," closely akin to contemplation of the divine. In the world of modern science, theory has been dethroned from this metaphysical pinnacle and instead is viewed as empirically-based, functionally-expressed hypotheses about concrete reality. Both of these, in Lonergan's view, are expressions of the pure "systematic exigence"--an intrinsic human drive to move beyond common sense, descriptive insight to systematic, theoretical, explanatory insight.[23]

Common sense and theory give completely different perspectives on actual phenomena. Which is real knowledge? Modern philosophy recognized this as problematic and sought the solution in closer attention to the structures of the subject, within whom both common sense and theory arise. This, says Lonergan, is the expression of the "critical exigence."[24] The modern philosophical project, however, has encountered numerous impasses: Descartes' objectivism, Kant's dichotomy of noumena and phenomena, Hegel's absolutization of the subject--none of these could resolve the essential problem of "How do we know?"

Dilthey's refocusing of the question in terms of the subject-as-subject and its concrete structures of knowing was a breakthrough. From Lonergan's perspective, however, Dilthey failed to complete the

---

[23]Lonergan, *Method in Theology*, pp. 81-83.

[24]Lonergan, *Method in Theology*, p. 83.

breakthrough, for he could not account for the real relationship of mediation between the subject-as-subject and its insights, judgments, and decisions. Lonergan himself did not draw directly upon Dilthey but, as Matthew Lamb has shown, Lonergan's own project can be seen as an effort to resolve what Dilthey left unfinished.[25] Simply put, Dilthey consolidated the modern move from a *metaphysical* context for theory to a *cognitional* context; Lonergan asserted the necessity of a further move from the cognitional context to a *methodical* context.[26]

Theory, in any context, is an expression of the systematic exigence; but in Lonergan's view the systematic exigence is sublated not only by the critical exigence, which insists upon attention to the concrete ground of knowledge in the subject, but also by the methodical exigence, which demands that this ground of knowledge be differentiated as conscious, structured praxis.[27] It is, therefore, necessary, but not sufficient, for theory to be systematically coherent (i.e., obedient to the canon of explanation). In deference to the critical exigence, it must also be coherent with the concrete structure of the cognitional acts from which it is born (canon of concreteness); and, in deference to the methodical exigence, it must furthermore be situated as one moment within a more encompassing praxis of knowing (canon of operations).

A work of theory, then, is not its own justification. It stands as a particular moment in an ongoing process which begins with attention to data and bears fruit in praxis. The methodological perspective recognizes that it is not possible or desirable to isolate any of these moments, so as to have "pure" attention to data, "pure" theory, or "pure" praxis. What is desirable, rather, is to have conscious awareness

---

[25]See Matthew L. Lamb, *History, Method and Theology: A Dialectical Comparison of Wilhelm Dilthey's Critique of Historical Reason and Bernard Lonergan's Meta-Methodology*, AAR Dissertation Series #25 (Missoula, MT: Scholars Press, 1978), pp. 249-54.

[26]Ibid., esp. pp. 115-210.

[27]Lonergan, *Method in Theology*, p. 83; Lamb, *History, Method, and Theology*, p. 176.

of the norms of the interplay among these moments so as maximize the authenticity of the process.

The Structure of Theory

The root of foundations is the founding act. An act, by definition, is both concrete and operational. What is generated by the act, in this case, is the categories--the explanatory constructs that constitute theoretical knowledge. The categories emerge from the act in an organic structure; that is, the most basic categories are more radically grounded in the act, with other categories in turn grounded in those most basic categories. The following is a brief overview of the structural generation of the categories.

The most encompassing category of categories is the "theorem." For Lonergan, a theorem is a "set of coordinates" or a "mental perspective"[28] that eliminates false or problematic ways of construing a particular set of data, thus enabling inquiry to proceed and questions to be answered. A theorem is neither the discovery of new data, nor an argument from known data to necessary conclusions; it is simply new insight into the data already known.[29] Synonyms or closely related terms include insight, definition, law, function, correlation, hypothesis.[30] Theorems are highly abstract, and they are likely to be either totally uncomprehended or badly misconstrued unless one's consciousness is theoretically differentiated and one is consciously operating within the theoretic realm.[31]

A theorem is more basic than a "term" or a "concept"; it is the

[28]Bernard J.F. Lonergan, *Grace and Freedom: Operative Grace in the Thought of St. Thomas Aquinas*, ed. J. Patout Burns (New York: Herder and Herder, 1971), p. 16.

[29]Lonergan, *Grace and Freedom*, pp. 88, 143.

[30]Cf. Lonergan, *Insight*, p. 759.

[31]Cf. Lonergan, *Method in Theology*, pp. 81-83.

insight that grasps what the terms and concepts must be and how they must be related to one another. The theorem, then, sets up a network or "nest"[32] of terms and the relations among them. The terms and relations are organically and structurally related to one another and to the underlying theorem, so that "the terms fix the relations, the relations fix the terms, and the insight fixes both."[33] No term, relation, or theoretical concept can be properly understood without reference to its "nest"--its organic and structural relations with its fellow terms and relations as expressions of an underlying theorem.

Networks of terms and relations, as thus articulated, can form "models." Models are "interlocking sets of terms and relations" that direct the investigator's attention in a determinate direction. Whether ultimately verified or overturned, models are extremely useful "in guiding investigations, in framing hypotheses, and in writing descriptions."[34]

As a work of theory, the present treatise strives to be faithful to the structure of theory as outlined here. We begin with a brief statement of a theorem. Its position at the beginning of the project marks this theorem as a hypothesis, articulated on the basis of previous work[35] but not yet refined or verified. The major work of the project will be working out, refining, and verifying the networks of terms and relations that articulate the theorem. If this work is successful, its net result will be a full-fledged model of mystical transformation that can serve as the basis for future work in theology and religious studies.

---

[32]Ibid., p. 286.

[33]Lonergan, *Insight*, p. 12.

[34]Lonergan, *Method in Theology*, pp. 284-5.

[35]As is common in scholarly work, the "previous work" in this case has largely been done by thinkers other than the present writer. In particular, the hypothesis presented in the following section builds on and carries forward the theoretic work of Bernard Lonergan.

B. Mysticism, Intersubjectivity, and Foundations: An Hypothesis

In his discussion of theological models in *Blessed Rage for Order*, David Tracy asserted that the most basic terms and relations of each model are its "self referent" (that is: what sort of "subject" is the theologian?) and its "object referent" (that is: what sort of "object" is the theologian primarily concerned with?).[36] The hypothesis that is going to be developed here is that, if mystical experience is to be taken seriously as the originating source of theology, a yet more basic--indeed, "transcendent"--dimension must be included in one's model.

Chapter 1, "Mysticism and Modernity," noted that it is within the context of searching for a ground for praxis that the question of transcendence emerges most clearly.[37] Praxis is defined here as the free, committed engagement of the human subject in morally significant action. Such praxis requires a profound "founding act" of judgment and commitment on the part of the subject. Is such an act essentially the arbitrary grasping of some subjective possibility or other, as classical existentialism asserts? Or is it the equally arbitrary conjunction of essentially impersonal, objective "causes," as an empiricist worldview assumes? The dilemma of modern and post-modern thought is that it enshrines committed praxis as central, yet fears that the founding act of praxis really has no ground transcendent to the subject and/or its objects.

As Chapter 1 noted, the most viable way to resolve this dilemma is to reframe it. The key to the reframing is to let go of the basic theorem that experience is constituted in "subject-object" terms. Instead of beginning with a subject who is either determining of or determined by objects, begin with a subject constituted by a structure of self-transcendence. Then a transcendent ground for praxis can be found in

---

[36]David Tracy, *Blessed Rage for Order: The New Pluralism in Theology* (New York: Seabury, 1978), pp. 22-23.

[37]See above, p. 20-21.

the subject her/himself; "implicit consciousness" or "the subject-as-subject," which is radically non-reducible to subject-object terms, is the ground of all acts of intentional consciousness. The "founding act," then, can be an act of claiming and affirming one's own ground and its implications.

Mysticism becomes an issue as soon as one begins to talk about "transcendence" or "transcendent ground." A preliminary definition of mystical experience is "an experience of the transcendent ground of consciousness." Mystical experience, as defined here, is a radicalization or "limit experience" of the self-transcending structure of the subject.

Once one has raised the question of mysticism it is easy to become embroiled in disputes such as whether the "transcendent ground" is essentially beyond and other than the subject or is essentially a subset of the subject. In more ordinary language, the dispute is over whether there is a divine "Other" (dualism) or whether there is only the "higher Self" (monism). Obviously, many complex philosophical and theological issues are involved in such disputes. The claim being made here, however, is that in many cases such disputes are specious, because they are predicated on a misconception of what is meant by "transcendent ground."

Again, a basic reframing away from a subject-object model is the essential step that is rarely taken or, if taken, is rarely rigorously adhered to. With that reframing it becomes evident that there can be no question of a subject who exists either as over-against, or as inclusive of, an object called "the transcendent ground." There is no such object--and, therefore, no such subject. What is meant by "subject" has to be radically re-envisioned.

As long as one is working with an explicit or implicit subject-object model, the subject will be envisoned in one of three ways: 1) as an object-among-objects, essentially determined by impersonal cause-and-effect forces; 2) as a solipcistic subject, essentially incapable of knowing anything other than itself; 3) as a subject defined by its relationships with objects. Our assertion that the subject is a structure of self-transcendence with a ground in implicit consciousness clearly excludes the first and third models noted above, since both of these explicitly define the subject in terms of objects. But how does our chosen definition differ from the model of the solipcistic subject, for whom objects are the shadowy reflections of its own subjectivity? The answer to this question will be central for our project.

The key to a correct insight continues to be making a definitive move away from a notion of a "subject-with-objects." The transcendent ground of consciousness is not adequately spoken of as an object, nor is it a "subject" in the sense of that term derived from the basic subject-object model. The claim being made here is that a more adequate articulation of the essential nature of the subject begins with a notion of a "subject-with-other subjects." The best "prime analogue"[38] for the nature of the transcendent ground of consciousness, in this view, is "a state of intersubjectivity."

What is being suggested is that the ground and *telos* of self-transcendence is more like a communion--ultimately, a union--of subjects than it is like anything else that we can name. The structure of self-transcendence that constitutes the subject, then, ultimately is more like self-transcendence toward union with another subject than it is like self-transcendence toward knowledge of an object. In plain language, it is more like love than like science.

The subject-object structure of intentional knowing is sublated within this basic structure of self-transcendence. In the analogy of a human love relationship, a form of objectivity arises as an essential part of the process because fully to be present with, to know, and to respond to another subject requires full recognition of that one as other than

---

[38]Language about the transcendent is necessarily analogous. On the notion of the "prime analogue," see David Tracy, *The Analogical Imagination: Christian Theology and the Culture of Pluralism* (New York: Crossroad, 1981), p. 408, where he says that analogy "is a language of ordered relationships articulating similarity-in-difference. The order among the relationships is constituted by the distinct but similar relationships of each analogue to some primary focal meaning, some prime analogue." The nuances of this designation within this inquiry will be considered again in the concluding Chapter.

oneself. The small child's experience of life has been called a "love affair with the world";[39] this phrase captures the basically personal structure out of which more impersonal forms of objectivity--appropriate for knowledge of, and interaction with, non-personal dimensions of reality--are differentiated.

It was said above that the re-envisioning of the subject in terms of a structure of self-transcendence necessarily implicates the question of mysticism, because mystical experience is a "limit form" of self-transcendence. If, as suggested here, the ground and *telos* of self-transcendence is a state of intersubjectivity, mystical experience must be a "limit form" of the state of intersubjectivity.

Without reducing mysticism to its contingent effects, this approach provides new opportunities for clarity about the relationship between transformation that is properly mystical and positive transformations of intersubjectivity on the interhuman level. A preliminary definition of mystical transformation is "those horizon shifts and/or new differentiations of consciousness within which a mystical experience of the ground of consciousness is mediated." The above discussion has explained mystical experience in terms of a process of self-transcendence whose ground and *telos* is analogously described as a state of intersubjective union. If the analogy is a true one, careful unpacking of its meaning will point to what mystical transformation means on the level of interhuman intersubjectivity.

To spell out the analogy: the contingent forms of intersubjectivity experienced in human relations are incomplete mediations of a "full" state of intersubjectivity which is their ground.[40] This "full" intersubjectivity, unlike its mediations in interhuman intersubjectivity,

---

[39]P. Greenacre, "The Childhood of the Artist: Libidinal Phase Development and Giftedness," *Psychoanalytic Study of the Child* 12 (1957).

[40]This way of understanding the analogy depends upon development of the notion of "mediation," which relies on a model of ground-and-expressions, as a more adequate theoretical framework than notions of "causality," which rely on the basic subject-object model. These concepts will be explicated in Chapter 4.

transcends all "twoness" and all subject-object structure. If mystical experience is in some sense a breakthrough of the *grounding* intersubjective state, it makes sense to say that the *expressions* of that ground will be affected. It also makes sense to say that the trajectory of any such effect will be toward greater coherency, fullness, virtue, etc., since it is a result of a lessening of any disjunction between the expression and its own ground.

In short, this hypothesis suggests that "mystical transformation" will be isomorphic with other forms of human development toward intersubjective fulfillment and responsibility. The gist of the hypothesis presented here, then, is that a model of mystical transformation as the mediation of experience of the transcendent ground of consciousness, for which the prime analogue is "a state of intersubjectivity," may be an essential part of the foundations of a theology that is fully responsive to the modern and post-modern concern with the human person as the author of responsible praxis in history.

C. Overview of Method in this Inquiry

So far we have established the context of the present inquiry, laid out in preliminary form the terms and relations of a foundational methodology, and outlined an hypothesis regarding "Mystical Transformation, Intersubjectivity, and Foundations" which the remaining chapters will strive to refine and verify. The steps taken to carry out that refinement and verification are explicitly based on Lonergan's articulation of "generalized empirical method."

In his chapter in *Method* on "Foundations," Lonergan wrote:

> The genesis of the special theological categories occurs . . . with explicit commitment in foundations. The commitment, however, is to the categories only as models, as interlocking sets of terms and relations. The use and acceptance of the categories as hypotheses about reality or description of reality . . . occurs in interaction with

> the data. They receive further specifications from the data. At the same time, the data set up an exigence for further development of the categories and for their correction and development.
>
> In this fashion there is set up a scissors movement with an upper blade in the categories and a lower blade in the data.[41]

In essence, Part I of this work corresponds to the derivation of what Lonergan here calls the "upper blade in the categories," while Part II corresponds to the work with the "lower blade in the data." The image of the "scissors movement" conveys how the two "blades" are not being developed for their own sake, but for the sake of the ongoing activity of "doing theology." In other words: the interplay between the categories and the data is fruitful if it enhances our capacity to experience, understand, judge, and act in response to God's presence in the world.

Part I begins with the data of consciousness and seeks to articulate its formal intelligibility. In this way the general categories are generated by an analysis of cognitive process. Chapter 5, the concluding chapter of Part I, explicitly makes the transition from the general categories to the special categories for mystical experience and transformation. The work of Part I, then, corresponds to the steps of generalized empirical method that focus on "experience" (attention to data--in this case, the data of consciousness) and "understanding" (an articulation of formal intelligibility; the generation of categories).

The work of Part II corresponds to the step of generalized empirical method that focuses on "judgment." It involves the refinement and verification of the formal categories through their interaction with concrete data. The concrete data, in this case, derive from the articulation of her own mystical transformation which St. Teresa of Avila presents in her masterwork, the *Interior Castle*.

The first analysis in Part II (Chapter 7, "An Interiority Analysis of the *Interior Castle*") applies the formal categories developed in Part I directly to this data, looking for evidence as to whether they enable us to make a plausible, coherent, and elegant interpretation of the data. If

[41]Lonergan, *Method in Theology*, p. 293.

so, the categories are--in a quite provisional sense--"verified": that is, we have evidence that they actually correspond in some way to the structure of reality. At the same time, the categories will also receive additional development and "fine tuning" from their interaction with the data.

Interiority analysis provides only a provisional verification, however, because it correlates the categories only with data very similar to that from which they were derived--that is, the data of cognitive process. Our hypothesis that the prime analogue of mystical experience (the transcendent ground of consciousness) is "a state of intersubjectivity," so that mystical transformation involves a transformation of all dimensions of human intersubjectivity, requires verification in a broader context. While the categories used in the interiority analysis can illuminate those dimensions of intersubjectivity that are involved in cognitive process, they speak only very indirectly of the larger human reality of intersubjectivity: namely, its affective, interpersonal, and social dimensions. If mystical experience is truly transformative, the evidence will have to be found in that larger forum as well as in the rarified forum of interiority analysis.

Detailed consideration of these more comprehensive dimensions of intersubjectivity on their own terms is beyond the scope of this inquiry. The present project, however, does require that we find a perspective that in some way bridges the gap between interiority analysis and the larger reality of intersubjectivity. Chapters 8 and 9 present the case that the psychoanalytical work of Heinz Kohut aptly provides such a bridge. The remaining chapters of Part II, then, carry out a second analysis of the text of the *Interior Castle* in terms of this psychoanalytical perspective.

The concluding chapter reviews the results of the two analyses of the *Interior Castle* and discusses what evidence they provide for the verification of the hypothesis just presented. It also briefly considers potential implications of this work for the fields of theology, spirituality, and religious studies.

CHAPTER 3

LONERGAN'S PHENOMENOLOGY OF THE SUBJECT

The brief overview of Lonergan's foundational methodology in Chapter 2 has provided an introduction to the perspectives he regarded as central for a responsible contribution to modern and post-modern inquiry. This chapter sets out in greater detail the warrants for this approach.

In his "Notes on Existentialism" lectures in 1957, Lonergan made a statement that summarizes the nub of his argument for the methodological turn. Speaking of what is prior or prerequisite to any experience at all, he said:

> The argument is: that the prior is not object as object or subject as object; there only remains subject as subject, and this subject as subject is both reality and discoverable through consciousness. The argument does not prove that in the subject as subject we shall find the evidence, norms, invariants and principles for a critique of horizons; it proves that unless we find it there, we shall not find it at all.[1]

---

[1]Bernard Lonergan, "Existentialism" (Notes on lectures given at Boston College, July 1957; unpublished mimeographed edition, Montreal: Thomas More Institute, 1957), p. 29.

Lonergan's argument, then, is both modest and radical. It is modest in that he does not claim the possibility of "proof"; for proofs rest on the possibility of setting up an invincible logical system, and Gödel's theorem has shown that no such system can ultimately be "closed."[2] Yet his argument is radical in that he asserts that "the subject as subject is both reality and discoverable through consciousness." The subject-as-subject is "real"--it constitutes a foundation for our experience and knowledge of reality and truth; and, it is discoverable through consciousness--it is not just a matter of "taking it on faith," but a matter of committing oneself to a painstaking process of coming to know oneself as one really is. Lonergan's approach is, in the words of Martin Matustik, "a genuine and legitimate *ad hominem*";[3] that is, it is an appeal to one's own conscious experience as the ground of all knowing.

The concrete data to which Lonergan calls us to attend, then, is the data of consciousness. The study of the subject, says Lonergan, is "the study of oneself inasmuch as one is conscious."[4] Western thought before Kant neglected the subject, Lonergan believed, in favor of notions of both the soul and truth as existing "objectively" and independent of the subject.[5] Kant's "Copernican revolution . . . brought the subject into technical prominence while making only minimal concessions to its reality."[6] That is: Kant recognized that the

---

[2]On Gödel's theorem, see Lonergan, *Insight*, pp. xxiv-xxv, 574; idem, *Philosophy of God and Theology* (London: Darton, Longman & Todd, 1973) pp. 6-7, 47. For further discussion, see Martin J. Matustik, *Mediation of Deconstruction: Bernard Lonergan's Method in Philosophy: The Argument from Human Operational Development* (Lanham, MD: University Press of America, 1988), pp. 162-64, 177-78.

[3]Matustik, *Mediation of Deconstruction*, p. 162. See also Mark Morelli, "Reversing the Counter-Position: The *Argumentum Ad Hominem* in Philosophic Dialogue," in Fred Lawrence, ed., *Lonergan Workshop* (Atlanta, GA: Scholars Press, 1986) 6:195-230.

[4]Lonergan, "The Subject," p. 73.

[5]Lonergan, "The Subject," pp. 69-73.

[6]Ibid., p. 70.

subject (human consciousness) is at the center of all experience and knowledge, but he continued to assign the fullness of "realness" and "truth" to what exists independently of the subject.

Subsequent modern thinkers have struggled to complete what is missing in Kant's turn to the subject. The "post-modern" conclusion of the deconstructionists is that fundamentally there are no grounds whatsoever for any claims of knowing "reality" or "truth"; the subject-as-subject is unknowable, and the pursuit of knowledge of any sort eventually comes face to face with that abyss.[7] Lonergan's counter-assertion is that only by radically claiming the subject-as-subject as the foundation of all experience and knowledge is it possible to arrive at an objective "knowing of knowing" and, on that basis, to develop a method for arriving at true conclusions about reality.

A. The Subject-as Subject

"The key to method," says Robert Doran, "is the subject-as-subject."[8] A grasp of the implications of Lonergan's notion of the subject-as-subject is crucial for understanding every dimension of his contribution. This notion was at the center of both *Insight* (first published 1957) and the Latin notes *De Constitutione Christi ontologica et psychologica* (first published 1956),[9] although the terminology and forms of explication became more lucid in later works.

The subject-as-subject is the subject simply as self-aware, as

---

[7]On deconstruction, see Matustik, *Mediation of Deconstruction*, pp. 28-32; on Lonergan's "mediation of deconstruction," see Matustik's entire book, especially pp. 32-37.

[8]Robert Doran, *Subject and Psyche: Ricoeur, Jung, and the Search for Foundations* (Washington, DC: University Press of America, 1977), p. 114.

[9]*De Constitutione Christi ontologica et pyschologica supplementum confecit Bernardus Lonergan, S.J.* (Rome: Gregorian University, 1956). For translated version, see above, Chapter 1, footnote 37, p. 17.

conscious. Explicit concern with the subject is modern; the ancients were concerned with the objective soul, or with human nature as it is always and everywhere, apart from accidental variations. Study of the subject, however, prescinds from everything that is not given in consciousness.[10] Once this choice is made, it becomes crucial to be able to distinguish the subject-as-subject from the subject as intentional knower.

Perhaps the clearest way to begin to grasp that distinction is by distinguishing three types of "presence."[11] There is the presence of an object in space, without regard to the presence of any subject; for example, "There is a chair in my room at home." There is the presence of the subject to an object, as in "I see a chair." This type of presence results from the intending activity of the subject. Finally, there is the presence of the subject to him/herself.

This self-presence, according to Lonergan, is not of the same order as the presence of the subject to an object; it is not just a more subtle, reflexive variety of intentional activity. Lonergan did a *reductio ad absurdum* argument on the latter suggestion, showing how the assumption that consciousness of self is of the same structure as consciousness of an object would mean that one could only know oneself as a being without consciousness.[12]

In his early works Lonergan named this self-presence "consciousness as experience in the strict sense,"[13] meaning that it is the "prior and rudimentary" awareness that is presupposed in any intentional act. In later works he clarified this by speaking of it as an

---

[10]Lonergan, "The Subject," p. 73.

[11]See Bernard Lonergan, "Cognitional Structure," in *Collection*, pp. 226-7. For discussion, see Matustik, *Mediation of Deconstruction*, pp. 60-71.

[12]Lonergan, "Christ as Subject: A Reply," in *Collection*, pp. 175-6.

[13]Lonergan, *On the Ontological and Psychological Constitution of Christ*, pp. 119f.

"infrastructure" within the suprastructure of cognitional knowing. Of this infrastructure he said:

> It is pure experience, the experience underpinning and distinct from every suprastructure. As outer experience it is sensation as distinct from perception. As inner experience it is consciousness as distinct not only from self-knowledge but also from any introspective process that goes from the data of consciousness and moves towards the acquisition of self-knowledge.[14]

As this quotation indicates, "consciousness as experience in the strict sense" is not, in itself, self-knowledge; for knowledge of self, as of any object, requires the operation of the full series of cognitional acts. Consciousness, however, is "not merely cognitive, but constitutive"[15]--it constitutes the very possibility of any cognitive knowing. What is fundamental is not consciousness as knowing an object, but consciousness-as-consciousness--the subject-as-subject.

It is equally important to emphasize, on the other hand, that this "consciousness-as-consciousness" is not a realm or an inner space that can be "experienced" in the "common sense" sense of that term. A clear distinction must be maintained between "experience in the strict sense" and intentional experience of objects. The data provided by inward introspection, like that provided by outward sensing, is a result of experience as intentional. "Experience in the strict sense" "is an awareness, not of what is intended, but of the intending."[16] As the awareness that makes intending possible, it cannot be made an object of human intending. We can heighten our awareness of it, but we cannot "know" it.

---

[14]Bernard Lonergan, "First Lecture: Religious Experience," in *A Third Collection: Papers by Bernard J.F. Lonergan, S.J.*, ed. by Frederick E. Crowe (New York: Paulist, 1985), pp. 116-7.

[15]Lonergan, "Christ as Subject," p. 176.

[16]Lonergan, *Method in Theology*, p. 15.

Thus, Lonergan's way of reframing Kant's distinction between the"inner sense" and the "transcendental unity of apperception"[17] is to speak of a distinction between the data appearing in consciousness and the underlying self-presence which this data presupposes. Though he agrees with Kant that strictly speaking this underlying consciousness cannot become an object within the scope of the inner sense, Lonergan rejects the position of the deconstructionists who conclude that therefore self-presence has no foundational relevance. As Matustik summarizes:

> While the post-structuralists, such as Derrida, deny a privileged place to "presence" in the subject as subject, Lonergan argues that the center of immediacy, which the subject *as* conscious is, cannot be served on a silver platter for a direct, unmediated grasp, and if one tried for such a naive "presence-in-itself," there would be *nothing* to deal with in terms of both "being" and the "I."[18]

Thus, Lonergan strives for a position that mediates between the deconstructionist denial of all foundations and a naive affirmation of consciousness as foundational. His "foundational methodology" relies on the affirmation of a relationship of mediation between an infrastructure of consciousness or self-presence and a suprastructure of cognitional operations.[19] Understanding and appropriation of the suprastructure converge upon the affirmation of such a relationship. If this affirmation is rejected the possibility of objective self-knowledge is lost, because it is implied that self-knowledge can only consist of an infinite regression of reflexive acts.

Lonergan, however, affirms that objective self-knowledge is possible through the development of a method "for going back and forth

---

[17]Immanuel Kant, *Critique of Pure Reason*, trans. Norman Kemp Smith (New York: St. Martin's, 1965), pp. 131-38.

[18]Matustik, *Mediation of Deconstruction*, p. 59.

[19]The significance of the term "relationship of mediation," which is central for the present exposition of Lonergan's theory, will be discussed in detail in Chapter 4.

between experience which has been given form by understanding and conception[,] and experience in the strict sense."[20] This method, which is the basis of what Lonergan calls "interiority," is the key to foundational methodology.[21]

B. The Subject as Self-Transcending

The subject-as-subject is the *sine qua non* of any experience or knowledge whatsoever; but experience and knowledge are also intentional, that is, they involve objects. Kant's "turn to the subject" introduced a quandary: what bridges the gap between the subject and its objects? How can the wholly subjective subject have any knowledge of what exists objectively? Lonergan resolved this quandary with an "inverse insight."

An inverse insight is the realization that a given set of data actually has no intelligibility according to the terms in which one is demanding it. As an example of inverse insight Lonergan cites Newton's discovery of the first law of motion.[22] It appears obvious on the common sense level that bodies move because they are pushed by external forces. The inverse insight is that motion is not intelligible as the resultant of a series of external forces, but as a state of rest: a body continues in uniform motion until it is stopped by an external force.

Lonergan's inverse insight into the subject-object problem was the realization that there can be no intelligibility so long as one begins from the common-sense assumption that there are subjects, and there are objects, and somehow they have to find one another. Attention to the concrete data of consciousness, Lonergan asserts, reveals that knowing

---

[20]Lonergan, *On the Ontological and Psychological Constitution of Christ*, p. 131.

[21]This method will be discussed in greater detail below in the section on "The Subject as Objectified in Self-Appropriation."

[22]Lonergan, *Insight*, pp. 21-23.

is fundamentally not a matter of a subject encountering objects, but of a subject operationally transcending itself as it intends objects.

If the nature of the subject-as-subject is to transcend itself in its cognitional operations, the place to begin our inquiry into the subject-object problem is with the question "What are we *doing* when we are knowing?" This is the question which is in accord with the canons of concreteness, explanation, and operationalism. It begins from what is concretely given in consciousness--namely, cognitional operations--and moves toward an explanatory account of the activity of cognitional process.

When one attends to what one is doing when one is knowing, it quickly becomes evident that knowing is a directional process. The subject in search of knowledge does not just meander around aimlessly; it tirelessly undertakes a repeated series of operations until it is satisfied that it has reached its goal, namely, knowledge of what is the case. The directionality of this process, says Lonergan, is self-transcendence. The subject has an intrinsic dynamism toward objectivity--toward knowledge of what is really so.

Lonergan, then, resolves the dual problem of how one can know oneself and how one can know an object by the discovery of the single foundational reality of self-transcending consciousness. Before knowledge, whether of subject or object, there is, first, consciousness-as-consciousness and, second, intentionality. Self-transcendence is not a matter of "going beyond a known knower, but [of] heading for being within which there are positive differences and, among such differences, the difference between object and subject."[23] It is the arc of operational self-transcendence that "creates" both subject and object as known entities.[24]

---

[23]Lonergan, *Insight*, p. 377.

[24]See Lonergan, *Method in Theology*, p. 8; see also idem, "Christ as Subject," p. 177.

Knowing is not only directional; it is also structured. Lonergan defined a structure thus:

> Each part is what it is in virtue of its functional relations to other parts; there is no part that is not determined by the exigences of other parts; and the whole possesses a certain inevitability of its unity, so that the removal of any part would destroy the whole, and the addition of any further part would be ludicrous.[25]

A structure is "dynamic" if its parts consist of activities, as, for example, in a dance or a drama. A structure is "formally dynamic" if these activities are self-assembling, that is, if the structure "puts itself together, one part summoning forth the next, till the whole is reached."[26] Human knowing, says Lonergan, is a formally dynamic structure--it consists of a functionally interrelated set of operations that are self-assembling, that is, they build upon one another and call one another forth until the whole is reached.[27]

The infrastructure of all cognitional operation is "experience in the strict sense," that is, experience not as intentional but simply as conscious.[28] The first act of the self-transcending conscious subject produces experience in the "common sense" sense, that is, experience as relatively undifferentiated, prelinguistic awareness of something-out-there. In technical terms, if the intended "something" is interior it appears in experience as the "data of consciousness," while if it is exterior it appears as the "data of sense."

If one remains only at the level of experience, however, one's "knowing" remains at an essentially animal level. "In fully human knowing," Lonergan wrote, "experience supplies no more than materials

---

[25]Lonergan, "Cognitional Structure," p. 222.

[26]Ibid., p. 223.

[27]Ibid., pp. 222-24.

[28]Lonergan, *Method in Theology*, p. 8.

for questions."[29] The next movement of self-transcendence is to ask questions about one's experience: "What is it?" "Why does it work that way?" "How can we make that happen again?" An answer to such a "question for intelligence" comes in the form of an insight--the act of understanding, in which the self-assembling process of knowing assembles the data provided by experience into a schema of coherent intelligibility.

Understanding is an exciting, sometimes even awesome, achievement; yet it is not the culmination of "fully human knowing." The dynamism of self-transcendence raises more questions: "Is it so?" "Is that *really* the way it is?" Adequately answering such a "question for reflection" requires carefully considering all relevant data and all potentially coherent understandings, until the conviction of an act of judgment emerges: "It is so." This is the point at which the self-assembling process of knowing reaches its apogee in an affirmation of fact.

The act of judgment is a pivot-point for Lonergan's notion of the subject as self-transcending. In the act of judging, says Lonergan, the subject goes beyond what appears, what is experienced, what is desired, what "makes sense," to what *exists*.[30] The metaphor "apogee" has been employed intentionally at this juncture to indicate that, on the one hand, self-transcendence as cognitional culminates in the act of a judgment of being while, on the other hand, self-transcendence as the dynamism of the subject has not yet completed its course. We will return to a further discussion of the pivotal role of judgment after considering the fuller reality of the subject.

---

[29]Lonergan, *Insight*, p. 252.

[30]See Lonergan, "The Subject," p. 70.

C. The Subject as Intersubjective

The self-transcendence that has been discussed so far is primarily cognitive, that is, it has to do with the dynamic orientation of the subject toward objective knowing. For Lonergan, this is the necessary starting point of the generation of categories. Yet as his thought developed, he became more and more sensitive to how the "canon of concreteness" demanded attention to the larger context within which subjects actually exercise this dynamic orientation. Ultimately, he was able to clarify how the full trajectory of human intentionality sublates even the drive to objective knowledge.

Concretely, the human subject is not a monad, but a person who lives in a complex world of interpersonal and social relations. Lonergan's understanding of intersubjectivity is analogous to his understanding of the relation of subject and object. Just as one must begin one's analysis of knowing at a point prior to the distinction of subject and object, so one must begin one's analysis of human relatedness at a point prior to the distinction of subject and subject. Just as the subject does not begin with a differentiated awareness of objects, but arrives at that awareness by the mediating activity of knowing, so the subject does not begin with a differentiated awareness of other subjects. The subject begins, rather, with a primordial intersubjectivity.

This notion of a primordial intersubjectivity, then, is a corollary of Lonergan's notion of the subject-as-subject. What is prior is neither the subject as object, nor the subject as over against objects, but the subject-as-subject--in other words, the subject as sheer "self-presence-in-world."[31] This presence of the subject-as-subject is not that of a monad, isolated (i.e., absent) from all other realities, but that of an undifferentiated consciousness which is present-with all other realities prior to having differentiated, objective consciousness of them.

---

[31]Lamb, *History, Method, and Theology*, p. 360.

Most fundamental of all the other realities which the subject-as-subject is present-with are other subjects-as-subjects. This primordial manifestation of intersubjectivity is on a vital, spontaneous level. Human beings, Lonergan wrote, "are social animals and the primordial basis of their community is not the discovery of an idea but a spontaneous intersubjectivity."[32] This innate sociability is grounded in the depths of human psychology, for

> Prior to the 'we' that results from the mutual love of an 'I' and a 'thou,' there is the earlier 'we' that precedes the distinction of subjects and survives its oblivion. . . . It is as if 'we' were members of one another prior to our distinctions of each from the others.[33]

This intense, completely undifferentiated level of intersubjectivity in the "world of immediacy," Lonergan suggests, is experienced by infants, and is perhaps approached by adults in such moments as mass hysteria, sexual orgasm and mystical ecstasy. The more usual adult experience of primordial intersubjectivity, however, is in what Lonergan called "incarnate meaning." He wrote,

> The bodily presence of another is the presence of the incarnate spirit of the other; and that incarnate spirit reveals itself to me by every shift of eyes, countenance, color, lips, voice, tone, fingers, hands, arms, stance. Such revelation is not an object to be apprehended. Rather it works immediately upon my subjectivity . . .[34]

Here the subject has already moved from the "world of immediacy" to a "world mediated by meaning," although mediation remains

---

[32]Lonergan, *Insight*, p. 212.

[33]Lonergan, *Method in Theology*, p. 57.

[34]Lonergan, "Dimensions of Meaning," in *Collection*, p. 264; cf. also idem, *Method in Theology*, pp. 59-61.

prelinguistic.[35] The self-transcending dynamism inherent in human existence, however, pushes onward. Interpersonal communication through incarnate meaning in direct bodily presence is intrinsically limited; the urge to communicate more completely and with more people drives humans to differentiate myriads of ways to mediate meaning through complex sign-systems. The relatively simple social structures of families and small tribes, which can rely heavily on spontaneous intersubjectivity and face-to-face communication, have to give way to intelligently devised social orders that sublate and transcend individuals' spontaneous desires and understandings. It is into such communities, constituted by complex networks of sign-systems and value-choices, that human beings are born.

Although the subject-as-subject is ontologically the primordial dimension of the human being, existentially community is primordial. Speaking of the human person, that is, the subject as concretely existing in the world, Lonergan wrote, "the person is not the primordial fact. What is primordial is the community. It is within community through the intersubjective relations that are the life of community that there arises the differentiation of the individual person."[36]

D. The Existential Subject

The concretely existing subject, then, is not only a knower, but a citizen and a lover; she or he operates not only cognitively, but intersubjectively. Lonergan's insight into the constitutive integration of these dimensions in the existential subject deepened over the course of his life.

When Lonergan wrote *Insight*, he tended to identify the vital,

---

[35]This distinction will be discussed in greater detail in Chapter 4 in the subsection entitled "Meaning and Intersubjectivity."

[36]Lonergan, *Philosophy of God, and Theology*, pp. 58-59.

intersubjective level with the primitive dynamism of psychic desire, in which "the good" is whatever the individual spontaneously desires.[37] He viewed social order as deriving from another dynamism, "the detached and disinterested stand of intelligence,"[38] for which the good is intelligently and rationally devised order. Taken to its culmination, this dynamism would result in "cosmopolis"--the perfect realization of the good of order.[39]

The difficulty with this formulation is that it too closely identifies the highest human good with the goals proper to intelligence and rationality. Intelligence and rationality are fulfilled in arriving at a knowledge of being through a judgment of fact. While this is one dimension of the human good, it leaves out other equally essential dimensions. What was needed was a clearer articulation of the entire trajectory of human intentionality, from vital intersubjectivity to cognitive objectivity to responsible community-building, as a unified dynamism.

The key to this clarification was Lonergan's insight that "detached and disinterested" intelligence, which is oriented toward factual knowledge of being and which sublates spontaneous desire, is in turn sublated by an existential orientation toward the total human good.[40] Every action, then--including cognitive operations oriented toward theoretical or factual knowledge--takes place in an existential context which has been constituted by concrete judgments about the human good.

The human good, says Lonergan, is "at once individual and social,"[41] and it involves a complex structure of interaction between

---

[37]See, for example, Lonergan, *Insight*, pp. 211f.

[38]Ibid., p. 215.

[39]Ibid., pp. 238-42.

[40]Cf., for example, Lonergan, "Cognitional Structure," p. 237.

[41]Lonergan, *Method in Theology*, p. 47.

these two dimensions. The central aspect of the individual dimension is human choice: the individual's capacity and responsibility to decide freely what one is to make of oneself. The central aspect of the social dimension is community: an "achievement of common meaning"[42] in which in these choices "individuals do not just operate to meet their needs but cooperate to meet one another's needs."[43]

Underlying this complex interaction between individual choice and communal meaning is the radical intention of the good. This "notion of value" is the deepest motivating force of human self-transcendence. Lonergan wrote,

> As the notion of being is dynamic principle that keeps us moving toward ever fuller knowledge of being, so the notion of value is the fuller flowering of the same dynamic principle that now keeps us moving toward ever fuller realization of the good, of what is worth while.
>
> . . . It is the intention of the good in this sense that prolongs the intention of the intelligible, the true, the real, that founds rational self-consciousness, that constitutes the emergence of the existential subject.[44]

As Robert Doran has put it, "to the extent that one is existentially self-transcendent, one's response is to values, to the effective promotion of that concrete historical process that is the human good."[45]

The supreme criterion for the existential subject, then, is

---

[42]Lonergan, "*Existenz* and *Aggiornamento*," in *Collection*, p. 245; idem, *Method in Theology*, p. 79.

[43]Lonergan, *Method in Theology*, p. 52.

[44]Lonergan, "The Subject," pp. 82, 84. Note that Lonergan's way of overcoming the disjunction that tends to arise in a Kantian system between "pure" and "practical" reason is to include them both within the single movement of self-transcending consciousness. "Practical" reason (the existential judgment and commitment to a course of action) sublates "pure" reason (the judgment of objective fact) but is not of an essentially different order.

[45]Robert M. Doran, *Psychic Conversion and Theological Foundations: Toward a Reorientation of the Human Sciences*, AAR Studies in Religion, no. 25 (Chico, CA: Scholars Press, 1981), p. 64.

authenticity: the openness continually to follow the call of self-transcendence as it moves one to go beyond experiencing to understanding, reasoning, responsibility, and action. The criterion of authenticity is a criterion of praxis; it replaces the criterion of speculative reason, which took "necessity" as its norm and regarded practical issues as secondary.[46] Praxis differs from speculative reason in that one must take a stand--make an existential, self-constituting choice--on the basis of a grounding judgment of value, even prior to the point in time when it is possible to make a completely adequate judgment of "fact."

Another way of putting this is to say that praxis recognizes that the "facts"--the data of experience--may be the products of inauthenticity, in which case their intelligibility may not be straightforward. Praxis therefore begins from "above downwards," by first making a discernment of authenticity--a judgment of value--through a "hermeneutic of suspicion as well as a hermeneutic of recovery." In this it differs from empirical method, which moves from "below upwards, from experience to understanding, and from understanding to factual judgment."[47]

Praxis also differs from modes of consciousness oriented toward theory and "facts" in that it operates primarily out of a narrative framework. Existential subjects operate in what Lonergan called the "dramatic pattern of experience,"[48] experiencing themselves as actors in a developing drama complete with plot, stock characters, tragedy and comedy, etc. As John Haught writes, "Human consciousness seems to have something like a narrative *a priori* that compels us communally to experience events, places and persons in the context of some story or

---

[46]Lonergan, "Third Lecture: The Ongoing Genesis of Methods," in *Third Collection*, p. 160.

[47]Lonergan, "Ongoing Genesis," p. 160. For a more complete discussion of Lonergan's usage of the terms, see the subsection entitled "'Below Upward' and 'Above Downward' Operations" in Chapter 4.

[48]Lonergan, *Insight*, pp. 187-91.

other. . . . The story by which we live is the integrative element determining the specific tone not only of sentient and interpersonal, but also of aesthetic and (in a sense) even theoretical awareness."[49]

This is a dimension that was not well developed by Lonergan himself; his specialty was using the theoretic mode to develop an explanatory understanding of human subjectivity. Others, however, notably Doran and Haught, have shown how the affirmation of the grounding narrative context is implied by Lonergan's affirmation of the centrality of praxis. The existential subject, oriented toward concrete action in history to construct the human community, must have an identity rooted in the creative, future-oriented narrative mode. Haught writes, "Story-telling relates us to reality by conjoining our givenness, accessible to us through memory, with our possibility anticipated in imagination. . . [It] is so linked to our communality that it is revelatory of the world's and others' possibilities as well."[50]

What is crucial is to recognize that narrativity, rather than invalidating the systematic and critical imperatives of the mind, actually calls them forth. The story is, in fact, the first manifestation of the systematic imperative--the story is the primal mode of finding coherence in experience, and it will continue the task even when theory has abandoned it.[51] As for the critical imperative, its task is to emerge when the personal or communal story becomes inauthentic, when it is bogged down in a dead end, when it is in danger of being abandoned altogether. As Johann Metz put it, the place of rational argument in theology is "to protect the narrative memory of salvation in a scientific

[49]John F. Haught, *Religion and Self-Acceptance: A Study of the Relationship Between Belief in God and the Desire to Know* (Washington, DC: University Press of America, 1980), p. 37.

[50]Haught, *Religion and Self-Acceptance*, p. 91.

[51]Ibid., chap. 6.

world, to allow it to be at stake and to prepare a way for a renewal of this narrative, without which the experience of salvation is silenced."[52]

Lonergan's specialty was in the development of categories for implementing the systematic, critical, and methodical exigencies within the modern and post-modern world. With increasing clarity as his thought developed, this project was contextualized within the more fundamental project of fostering the good of existential subjects. For existential subjects, the struggle to develop just social structures and to preserve the "narrative memory of salvation" has a more immediate claim of value than does the search for objective knowledge. Yet Lonergan's assertion is that, concretely, the path to the fulfillment of these urgent concerns passes through a rigorous discipline of self-objectification.

E. The Subject as Objectified in Self-Appropriation

In Chapter 2, it was stated that Lonergan's fundamental assertion is that in order to attain adequate knowledge in any field, a knower must objectify and appropriate the normative pattern of operations as manifested in his or her own consciousness. This subsection deals with what happens as the process of objectification and appropriation progresses.

At first glance the words in the above paragraph may appear to describe a process undertaken only by a relatively elite group of rather introspective, theory-obsessed persons. It is important to remember, however, that for Lonergan the orientation toward objectivity is intrinsic in the human subject as existential. The dynamism toward objectivity is the same dynamism that is elsewhere referred to under the names of self-transcendence, intentionality, and orientation toward intersubjective presence. Differentiation of this dynamism through an intensive focus

---

[52]Johann Baptist Metz, *Faith in History and Society: Toward a Practical Fundamental Theology*, trans. David Smith (New York: Seabury, 1980), p. 213.

on objectification and appropriation of one's own conscious operations is, indeed, a project that is unlikely to gain mass appeal. It is, nevertheless, isomorphic with the processes of self-objectification and self-appropriation that are intrinsic to the existential subject in everyday life.

For Lonergan, the subject is intrinsically intentional--that is, it is oriented toward dynamic self-transcendence in the activity of knowing that which exists.[53] This activity--the formally dynamic structure of human knowing--is knowable. The operations as intentional can be applied to the operations as conscious,[54] and an objective, explanatory account of the structure of the subject-as-knower can be attained. This "knowing of knowing" involves a "reduplication of the structure,"[55] that is, an application of the ordered, self-assembling activities of knowing to the study of the activities themselves.

This account, Lonergan asserted, "has all the advantages of the concreteness of the descriptive type insofar as the elements and the unity are verifiable in consciousness. It has all the advantages of the explanatory type insofar as the different elements are of their very nature interdependently linked together in the process."[56] It is this account that forms the basis of a consciously methodological approach.

It is important to remember, however, that Lonergan's claim is that a consciously methodological approach is simply an enhancement of what is already taking place in any instance of human knowing. What is important, then, is not the explanatory account as a set of concepts and ideas, but its role in increasing the authenticity of praxis. Explanation, when it is explanation of the subject him/herself, is for the sake of self-appropriation. The canons--"Be concrete; Be explanatory;

---

[53]Cf. Lonergan, "Cognitional Structure," pp. 228f.

[54]Lonergan, *Method in Theology*, p. 14.

[55]Lonergan, "Cognitional Structure," p. 224.

[56]Lonergan, *Understanding and Being*, p. 175.

Focus on acts, not words"--point us always back toward concrete existence and praxis, not toward abstract knowing for its own sake.

Subsection B above, "The Subject as Self-Transcending," described the basic microstructures of the dynamism toward objectivity. Analysis of any single act of knowing reveals the pattern of experience, understanding, and judging; in judgment, with the affirmation of the "virtually unconditioned," objectivity is attained. The existential subject, however, rarely (if ever) experiences such pure, single acts of knowing. Rather, he or she is engaged in a variety of sustained inquiries. These inquiries, no matter what their specific content, are "existential" in that they are embedded in the total practical life-context and self-transcending dynamism of that particular individual.

Each such inquiry involves hundreds and thousands of repetitions and variations on the basic microstructure of knowing. Yet over time, a sustained inquiry will also tend to exhibit a macrostructure: a movement through a series of realms of meaning, corresponding to the consolidation and systematization of insights according to the norms of each operation of the microstructure. These realms are: common sense (corresponding to experience); theory (corresponding to understanding); interiority (corresponding to judgment); and praxis (corresponding to decision).[57]

It is important to re-emphasize at this point that the entire pattern of operations is completely manifested in each realm of meaning. Common sense knowing involves just as much understanding, judgment and decision as praxis does. One moves into a new realm, however, when one has thoroughly objectified and appropriated one of these steps of the knowing process.

The person operating only in the common sense realm of meaning does not have an objective awareness of what it means to understand, to judge, and to decide, although she or he is perfectly capable of actually carrying out these operations. Likewise, the person operating only in

[57]See Lonergan, *Method in Theology*, pp. 81-85.

the realms of common sense and theory does not have an objective awareness of what it means to judge and to decide, even though she or he does in fact judge and decide; and the person operating only in the realms of common sense, theory, and interiority does not have an objective awareness of what it means to decide--to take an existential stand--even though in fact she or he is doing so.

The movement from one realm to the next is driven by what Lonergan calls the "exigences."[58] The exigences are the specific manifestations of the dynamism of self-transcendence as it works to consolidate and place in effective operation a new realm of meaning. The systematic exigence moves one from the realm of common sense to the realm of theory; the critical exigence moves one from the realm of theory to the realm of interiority; and the methodical exigence moves one from the realm of interiority to the realm of praxis. A final exigence, the transcendental, sublates all of these; it will be briefly discussed below and considered in greater depth in Chapter 4.

The following paragraphs will trace the subject's self-objectification and self-appropriation through the various realms.

Everyday life is the realm of common sense. Common sense is interested in getting things done; it is not concerned with theories or systems or introspective ponderings, unless the task in question cannot be accomplished in any other way.[59] Yet common sense, as the primordial mode of the existential subject, is also embedded within the dramatic pattern of experience, which is ordered by the narrative mode.[60] As discussed above, the narrative mode already includes a primal manifestation of the systematic exigence, namely, the demand that experience fit into a coherent and intelligible story line. It is when the narrative mode is unable to provide adequate coherence and

---

[58]Ibid.

[59]Lonergan, *Insight*, pp. 178-79.

[60]Ibid., pp. 187f.

intelligibility that the systematic exigence pushes onward to a new realm, the realm of theory.

The speciality of the theoretic realm is explanation. As mentioned above, Lonergan distinguished description (an account of things in their relation to us) from explanation (an account of things in their relations to one another).[61] Description, even when it strives for objectivity, remains embedded in the common sense and narrative perspective of the observer. Explanation, on the other hand, transcends that perspectival level of coherence in favor of an insight into the coherence and intelligibility of the thing in itself, apart from its relation to the observer's common sense concerns and narrative context. The typical example of the difference is Eddington's two tables: the described table is brown, heavy, a place to write; the explained table is a lot of empty space laced with a pattern of moving atomic particles.

Just as the systematic exigence had a preliminary manifestation in the realm of common sense (in the coherence of the story line), so the critical exigence has a preliminary manifestation in the realm of theory: namely, the concern to develop an epistemological theory. Epistemology is an explanatory theory of human knowing. It encounters a major difficulty, however, in trying to explain what seem to be two different and contradictory forms of knowing, namely, common sense and theory. Which is "real" knowing?[62] It is when epistemology fails to be able to provide such an explanatory theory that the critical exigence pushes onward to the realm of interiority.

Interiority, in the words of Matthew Lamb, is "an experience of consciousness as a state which is its own act of awareness"; it is "the defining characteristic constitutive of the subject-as-subject."[63] Grounding human knowing through a move from the realm of theory to the realm of interiority was Lonergan's first major innovation. He was

---

[61]Ibid., pp. 191-92.

[62]Cf. Lonergan, *Insight*, pp. 294-99; idem, *Method in Theology*, p. 83.

[63]Lamb, *History, Method, and Theology*, pp. 290-91.

not the first pioneer in this approach; Dilthey before him had argued that a move to interiority was required to ground the human sciences. Lonergan, however, saw that this move is necessary to ground any and all human knowing.[64]

The explication of this move is the main import of Lonergan's major philosophical work, *Insight*. It is chapter 11 of that book, "Self-Affirmation of the Knower," that establishes the grounds for this move; and Robert Doran, among others, has called this chapter "epochal . . . a breakthrough to a new differentiation and specialization of consciousness, the beginning of a new series of ranges of schemes of recurrence in cognitional and ultimately in existential praxis."[65]

In his later work Lonergan came to call the theoretical appropriation of this move to interiority "intellectual conversion," and he regarded it as essential for any serious intellectual work in the modern age. Of conversion, Lonergan wrote:

> Conversion is a change of direction and, indeed, a change for the better. One frees oneself from the inauthentic. One grows in authenticity. Harmful, dangerous, misleading satisfactions are dropped. Fears of discomfort, pain, privation have less power to deflect one from one's course. Values are apprehended where before they were overlooked. Scales of preference shift. Errors, rationalizations, ideologies fall and shatter to leave one open to things as they are and to man as he should be.[66]

Intellectual conversion occurs when the realm of interiority is explicitly distinguished from the realms of common sense and theory, and is recognized as their ground. Lonergan wrote, "Differentiated consciousness appears when the critical exigence turns attention upon interiority, when self-appropriation is achieved, when the subject relates

---

[64]See Lamb, *History, Method and Theology*, pp. 156f.

[65]Doran, *Psychic Conversion*, p. xii.

[66]Lonergan, *Method in Theology*, p. 52.

his different procedures to the several realms, relates the several realms to one another, and consciously shifts from one realm to another by consciously changing his procedures."[67] Without such intellectual conversion, many scientific and theological controversies are irresolvable; for different mixes of common sense and theory, and different theoretical perspectives, can find no common language and procedure for dialogue until "through the realm of interiority . . . differentiated consciousness [can] understand itself and so explain the nature and the complementary purposes of different patterns of cognitional activity."[68]

In calling this a "conversion," Lonergan asserts that this move to interiority is far more than the discovery of new information, or even of a new way to organize information. It does involve these aspects, but if it were limited to these it would remain fundamentally on the levels of experience and understanding, respectively. The move to interiority is, rather, fundamentally an epochal shift at the level of judgment.

This shift is explicated in chapter 11 of *Insight*. The judgment in question responds to the question: Am I a knower? If I am not a knower, or if I don't know whether I am a knower or not, no claim of knowledge on my part has any foundation whatsoever. Yet the common sense answer ("Obviously, I'm a knower") has long since been deconstructed by Kant; and Kant's own attempt at a theoretical answer ("I am a knower of phenomena as organized by the transcendental precepts") has likewise been deconstructed by the deconstructionists.

The fault in these responses, according to Lonergan, is that both approaches begin from a position *after* the distinction of subject and object.[69] The common sense approach simply assumes that distinction without question and without seeing it as problematic; the Kantian theoretical approach recognizes that the distinction exists and that it is

---

[67]Ibid., p. 84.

[68]Ibid., p. 115.

[69]See above, p. 56.

a problem; neither offers any viable way to overcome it. Lonergan gives the question a different starting point:

> How does the knower get beyond himself to a known? The question is, we suggest, misleading. It supposes the knower to know himself and asks how he can know anything else. . . . we contend that, while the knower may experience himself or think about himself without judging, still he cannot know himself until he makes the correct affirmation, I am.[70]

In other words: the knower does not automatically "know" even him or herself. To assume such knowledge as foundational is to assume that the foundation is a subject aware of self as distinct from objects. That the subject does have a fundamental self-experience has been discussed in the subsection on "The Subject-as-Subject." This becomes self-knowledge, however, only when it has been processed according to the norms of any knowing: namely, experience, understanding, and judgment. The judgment, "I am a knower," can only be made by one who has painstakingly attended to the process of his or her own knowing; has diligently sought to understand its patterns; and has arrived at the foundational judgment that, indeed, this process--as experienced and understood--is a fact.

The self-affirmation of the knower, then, occurs when the knower (after a thorough process of attention and understanding) judges that, in fact, he or she knows something. Lonergan emphasizes that this is not a judgment that one is *necessarily* a knower, but simply a judgment that one *is* a knower. "I might not be yet, if I am, I am. I might be other than I am, yet, in fact, I am what I am."[71] He concludes his argument by showing how, indeed, this self-affirmation provides the only coherent basis for any claim of knowledge whatsoever.

---

[70]Lonergan, *Insight*, p. 377.

[71]Ibid., p. 329.

> Am I a knower? The answer, Yes, is coherent, for if I am a knower, I can know that fact. But the answer, No, is incoherent, for if I am not a knower, how could the question be raised and answered by me? . . . Am I a knower? If I am not, then I know nothing. My only course is silence.[72]

This process of appropriating the realm of interiority is extraordinarily difficult because it requires deploying the cognitional operations differently from the way they are normally employed in common sense, theoretical, or introspective inquiries.[73] Cognitive inquiry usually operates on the data of sense. Even introspection treats the subject as object, that is, as a phenomenon that can be known though intentional consciousness in the same way as other objects experienced through the data of sense.

Interiority, however, requires relying primarily on the data of consciousness. It involves, as Lonergan put it, a "going back and forth between experience which has been given form by understanding and conception[,] and experience in the strict sense."[74] "Experience in the strict sense" cannot be found by introspecting (making consciousness an object), but only by heightening one's presence to oneself by raising the level of one's activity.[75] The fruit of such heightening of self-presence is the possibility of objective knowledge of self; one is promoted "from consciousness of self to knowledge of self."[76]

Appropriation of interiority, then, is the completion of the critical exigence, which seeks the ground that underlies any knowledge at all. Yet just as in the subsection on self-transcendence judgment was called only the "apogee" of the microstructure of cognitive self-transcendence,

---

[72]Ibid.

[73]Cf. Matustik, *Mediation of Decontruction*, p. 161.

[74]Lonergan, *On the Ontological and Psychological Constitution of Christ*, p. 131.

[75]Lonergan, "Cognitional Structure," pp. 226-27.

[76]Lonergan, *Method in Theology*, p. 259; cf. also p. 262.

so interiority is likewise only the apogee of the macrostructure of existential self-transcendence. Lonergan wrote:

> The withdrawal into interiority is not an end in itself. From it one returns to the realms of common sense and theory with the ability to meet the methodical exigence. For self-appropriation of itself is a grasp of transcendental method, and that grasp provides one with the tools not only for an analysis of common sense procedures but also for the differentiation of the sciences and the construction of their methods.[77]

The methodical exigence pushes one from the realm of interiority, which primarily involves the full appropriation of judgment through self-affirmation, to the realm of praxis, which involves the full appropriation of decision. As Robert Doran summarized:

> The integrative moment in the retrieval of oneself in transcendental method occurs not when one affirms the reality of one's experienced and understood experiencing, understanding, judging, and deciding, but when one decides to operate in accord with the norms immanent in the spontaneous relatedness of one's experienced, understood, affirmed experiencing, understanding, judging, and deciding.[78]

Existential authenticityZ is a matter of choosing to operate according to the authentic (that is, immanent) norms of attentiveness, intelligence, rationality, and responsibility. It is this which constitutes the "founding act"[79] that is fully adequate as a foundation for both inquiry and action in today's world.

This existential authenticity is already well-founded in any individual who has undergone what Lonergan calls "moral conversion," that is, a change in "the criterion of one's decisions and choices from

[77]Lonergan, *Method in Theology*, p. 83.

[78]Doran, *Psychic Conversion*, p. 46. Cf. also Lonergan, *Method in Theology*, p. 15.

[79]On the "founding act," see the corresponding subsection in Chapter 2.

satisfactions to values."[80] Such an individual has made an existential, self-constituting choice to operate according to the norms inherent in the human good as he or she apprehends it in a grounding judgment of value. Yet, in Lonergan's view, authenticity is complete only when it is fully differentiated through intellectual conversion.

The one who is morally converted, says Lonergan, "still needs truth, for he must apprehend reality and real potentiality before he can deliberately respond to value. The truth he needs is still the truth attained in accord with the exigences of rational consciousness."[81] The methodical exigence--the demand for a conscious, deliberate choice of operating according to immanent norms--can only be fulfilled when the content of those immanent norms is known; and the content of the immanent norms can only be known by unswervingly following the systematic and critical exigences to their own proper fulfillment in explanatory self-knowledge based in the appropriation of interiority.

F. The Subject in Love: Transcendence and Religion

There is, however, yet another exigence--one which radically sublates all the others. The transcendent exigence has to do with the ultimate teleology of self-transcendence. Every act of self-transcendence, whether intellectual, rational, or moral, exhibits directionality--that is, the subject experiences it as opening out onto a broader horizon of intelligibility, truth and value. Sooner or later, however, the subject is bound to ask whether in the last analysis that directionality is nothing more than meaningless wandering.

The question of whether or not there is any ultimate ground of intelligibility, truth and value toward which self-transcendence stretches

---

[80]Lonergan, *Method in Theology*, p. 240.

[81]Ibid., p. 242.

is actually implied in every human question.[82] Before and after any specific, conceptualized answer to this question, there is the unrelenting, ever-present dynamism of the question itself: the longing, in every dimension of one's being, for an ultimate and total experience of coherence and goodness. As Lonergan put it, the question of God

> rises out of our conscious intentionality, out of the *a priori* structured drive that promotes us from experiencing to the effort to understand, from understanding to the effort to judge rightly, from judging to the effort to choose rightly. . . . The question of God, then lies within man's horizon. Man's transcendental subjectivity is mutilated or abolished, unless he is stretching forth towards the intelligible, the unconditioned, the good of value. The reach, not of his attainment, but of his intending is unrestricted.[83]

The transcendent exigence operates alongside the systematic, critical and methodical exigences to demand that their inquiries always remain unrestricted. No theoretical system, no level of knowledge of self, is "the final answer"--unless the transcendent exigence, which continually raises more profound questions, is deliberately quashed.

At the same time the transcendent exigence, if allowed to operate on its own terms, does not interfere with the previous exigences.[84] The attempt to reduce the question of God to a question answerable at the level of the systematic, critical, or methodical exigences short-circuits the total dynamism of self-transcendence and results in unsatisfactory answers not only to the question of God, but to the questions proper to the other exigences as well. As Lamb summarizes, "Lonergan . . . investigates the autonomous operations of the systematic, critical, and

---

[82]See Lonergan, *Insight*, pp. 634-39; *Method in Theology*, pp. 83-85.

[83]Lonergan, *Method in Theology*, p. 103.

[84]See Lamb, *History, Method and Theology*, pp. 191-95.

methodical exigences, and only in the context of their critical appropriation does the God-question become a *real* question."[85]

The transcendent exigence, then, is more than just a dynamism within the search for knowledge. If that were its entire nature, it would mainly serve to drive human beings into exhaustion as they spiralled higher and higher on a rigorous--and disturbingly elitist--quest for more total visions.[86] Fundamentally, the transcendent exigence is the quest for love: to be loved, to be in love, to love, with the totality of one's being.[87] As such, it sublates all other manifestations of self-transcendence--that is, it integrates them within a "higher system" (in this case, an ultimate "system" which is the totality of being) while respecting the integrity of the lower systems on their own level.[88]

Lonergan summarized:

> The transcendental notions, that is, our questions for intelligence, for reflection, and for deliberation, constitute our capacity for self-transcendence. That capacity becomes an actuality when one falls in love. Then one's being becomes being-in-love. . . . As the question of God is implicit in all our questioning, so being in love with God is the basic fulfilment of our conscious intentionality.[89]

The transcendent exigence, then, begins to be fulfilled every time a human being falls in love. It is completely fulfilled when the loving and being loved have the character of ultimacy; that is, when one falls in

---

[85]Ibid., p. 192.

[86]See Ibid., pp. 186-91.

[87]See Lonergan, *Philosophy of God*, pp. 52-55.

[88]See Lonergan's comment in *Method in Theology*, p. 241, on sublation: "What sublates goes beyond what is sublated, introduces something new and distinct, puts everything on a new basis, yet so far from interfering with the sublated or destroying it, on the contrary needs it, includes it, preserves all its proper features and properties, and carries them forward to a fuller realization within a richer context." See also *Insight*, p. 256.

[89]Lonergan, *Method in Theology*, p. 105.

love with God and experiences the gift of God's love. This surrender, which Lonergan says is not an act, but "a dynamic state that is prior to and principle of subsequent acts,"[90] is religious conversion. As Lonergan put it, "Religious conversion is [conversion] to a total being-in-love as the efficacious ground of all self-transcendence, whether in the pursuit of truth, or in the realization of human values, or in the orientation man adopts to the universe, its ground and its goal."[91]

This dynamic state of being in love with God, says Lonergan, occurs on the level that has previously been called "experience in the strict sense"; that is, it is a modification of the infrastructure of consciousness, prior (in the formal, not temporal, sense) to the activation of the suprastructure of operations leading to knowledge.[92] In fact, it may remain unknown--a "weak, low voice" in the polyphony of consciousness,[93] or a "vector, an undertow, a fateful call to a dreaded holiness."[94]

Once the experience of God's love begins to be objectified, however, it becomes a demand upon the existential subject: "Will I love him in return, or will I refuse? Will I live out the gift of his love, or will I hold back, turn away, withdraw?"[95] This is the core of the call to choose to live according to the immanent norms of the universe, that is, moral conversion. At a yet further stage of objectification comes the call to intellectual conversion, in which one seeks grounds for the clarification of doctrinal and theological questions in the light of the basic experience of God's love.

---

[90]Ibid., p. 240.

[91]Ibid., p. 241.

[92]See Lonergan, "Religious Experience," p. 125; idem, *Philosophy of God*, pp. 17, 38, 50-51; idem, *Method in Theology*, pp. 106, 122.

[93]Lonergan, "Religious Experience," p. 125.

[94]Lonergan, *Method in Theology*, p. 113.

[95]Ibid., p. 116.

Lonergan asserts, then, that from a causal point of view religious conversion is "prior" to moral conversion, and moral conversion is "prior" to intellectual conversion.[96] As fully objectified and appropriated, any one of the conversions can be "first" temporally; but as "undertow," the transcendent exigence is the fundamental, pervasive directionality that underlies all conversion. The methodical exigence--the insistent call to praxis according to the immanent norms of existence--likewise sublates the critical and systematic exigences. Thus, a statistical analysis would find that the appropriation of religious conversion has proceeded further in more people than has the appropriation of moral conversion, while the appropriation of moral conversion, in turn, has proceeded further in more people than has the appropriation of intellectual conversion.

Much more will be said about religious conversion in a later chapter, for the subject matter of this inquiry is the perspective on religious conversion herein termed "mystical transformation." First, however, we must step back from this exposition of basic terms and relations to a more abstract consideration of the theory that undergirds them.

---

[96]Ibid., p. 243.

CHAPTER 4

INTERSUBJECTIVITY AND MEDIATION

The preceding chapter has laid out the basic network of terms and relations derived from Lonergan's phenomenology of the human subject. Yet Lonergan claims that this is much more than just a descriptive phenomenology; it is also both an explanatory account, with profound consequences for theory in all fields, and a praxis of self-appropriation, with profound consequences for the existential subject. This chapter explores some of these further implications.

A. The Notion of Mediation

Mediation and Dynamic Structure

Lonergan's notion of mediation provides the theoretical infrastructure for the transition from descriptive phenomenology to explanation. The notion of mediation is not another basic term or relation derived from basic operations, but more on the order of a theorem--a "set of coordinates" that shows how the basic terms and relations must be ordered.[1] It arises from "operations on operations" that grasp deep

[1]On the definitions of "theorem," "terms and relations," etc. see "The Structure of Theory" in Chapter 1.

structural relations and isomorphisms that are not accessible at the level of direct insight into phenomena. In the present inquiry, a grasp of the notion of mediation will enable a much more adequate insight into human intersubjectivity. It will enable the nuanced differentiation and integration of various aspects of the life of the existential subject, i.e., the subject's participation in intellectual, interpersonal, social, and mystical fields.

This is Lonergan's general definition of mediation:

> [A]ny factor, quality, property, feature, aspect, that has a source, origin, ground, basis, and consequences, effects, derivatives, a field of influence, radiation, expansion, an expression, manifestation, revelation, outcome, may be said to be *immediate* in the source, origin, ground, basis, and *mediated* in its consequences, effects, derivatives, outcome, in its field of influence, radiation, expansion, in its expression, manifestation, revelation.[2]

Lonergan acknowledges that this notion of mediation is extremely general--"even more general than the notion of causality."[3] The value of the notion is that it is simple, yet ramifies to explain great complexity. It is something like the general form of a mathematical function which, once mastered, can be employed in the analysis of an infinite variety of phenomena. Some analyses will be very simple, while others may be very complex and involve multiple, mutually regulating instantiations of the procedure; yet the basic function remains the same.

The key to understanding mediation is understanding the concept of structure, because the notion of mediation provides an "axiom of general patterns of structures"[4]--that is, it gives an explanatory, completely generalized view of the relations between wholes and their

---

[2]Lonergan, "The Mediation of Christ in Prayer," *Method: Journal of Lonergan Studies* 2 (1984), p. 2.

[3]Ibid.

[4]Matustik, *Mediation of Deconstruction*, p. 6.

parts. It will be helpful to quote again, and at greater length, Lonergan's definition of structure:

> Not every whole is a structure. When one thinks of a whole, there may come to mind some conventional quantity or arbitrary collection whose parts are determined by an equally conventional or arbitrary division. In such a case, for example a gallon of milk, the closed set of relations between the whole and parts will be a no less arbitrary jumble of arithemetic ratios. But it may also happen that the whole one thinks of is some highly organized product of nature or art. Then the set of internal relations is of the greatest significance. Each part is what it is in virtue of its functional relations to other parts; there is no part that is not determined by the exigences of other parts; and the whole possesses a certain inevitability in its unity, so that the removal of any part would destroy the whole, and the addition of any further part would be ludicrous. Such a whole is a structure.[5]

The notion of mediation, then, offers a functional understanding of the structural relations between being (the absolute whole) and any existent ("parts" of the structure of being), as well as of the relations between any whole existent and its structurally coherent parts. This notion underlies Lonergan's central concepts of "isomorphism" and "the integral heuristic structure of being." Both of these concepts derive from the basic affirmation that there is a relation of "whole" and "structurally-coherent parts" between being and self-transcending consciousness, such that appropriation of the structure of self-transcending consciousness converges upon knowledge of being.

The development of the notion of mediation begins from attention to the phenomenological data presented in the preceding chapter. Within this, says Lonergan, one discovers the dynamic structure of human knowing as intending being.[6] The subject-as-subject is intrinsically self-transcending toward knowing being; it has an intrinsic orientation toward

---

[5]Lonergan, "Cognitional Structure," p. 222.

[6]Ibid., p. 228.

objectivity. This objectivity, however, cannot be properly understood without a grasp of the idea of dynamic structure.[7]

The subject-as-subject is a whole which is mediated in its dynamic, structured activity of knowing. Human knowing is a formally dynamic structure: "It is self-assembling, self-constituting. It puts itself together, one part summoning forth the next, till the whole is reached."[8] The various operations of knowing arise immanently, calling one another forth until an objective judgment of what exists (the "virtually unconditioned") is reached.

This structural unity of the subject-as-subject and the subject-as-objective-knower is, as Matthew Lamb calls it, a "unity of identity and non-identity";[9] for the subject-as-subject does not exist apart from its dynamic, self-transcending activity (hence, identity) and yet neither can it be reduced to any or all of these activities or their fruits (hence, non-identity). More abstractly: a structured whole does not exist apart from its being mediated in its parts, yet the whole is something distinct from the sum of its parts.

The real key to Lonergan's position is insight into how the link between these two (identity and non-identity, being and human knowledge) is the dynamic, structured activity of consciousness. That insight, articulated in theory, is the notion of mediation. The same insight, when it is an insight into one's own actual activities of knowing, is the basis of methodical self-appropriation. The objective grasp of the structure of one's knowing is a grasp of the "arc of self-transcendence" that constitutes the relation of knower and being. The grasp of one's own being as an unrestricted intention of being is, concretely, a grasp of the dynamic structure of one's own being as a mediation of being.

---

[7]Ibid., p. 231.

[8]Ibid., p. 223.

[9]Lamb, *History, Method, and Theology*. This phrase and its many implications are the theme of Lamb's entire treatise. Though Lamb does not expressly emphasize the terminology of mediation, his theme is closely related to the one being presented here.

When one makes an objective judgment concerning the structures of consciousness, "the subject-as-subject mediates the subject-as-object."[10] Self-appropriation, or knowledge of the subject-as-object, is the apogee of the self-mediation of the subject-as-subject. Yet there must always be a caution. It is all too easy to reify that self-knowledge into a conceptual system, and become an idealist who does not make the crucial distinction between explaining the concrete and articulating "the general structures in which any explanation would occur."[11]

To summarize: Lonergan's notion of mediation, as "an axiom of the general patterns of structures," states that being is mediated in intelligible structure. Real existents, therefore, exhibit structure. Whatever is structured has an intelligibility that can be expressed in a set of terms and relations; and insight is a grasp of that structure. Insight can subsequently be articulated in a nest of terms and relations (an "intellectual conjugate") that prescinds from all factors irrelevant to the actual structure of the existent (i.e., the "empirical residue").[12] As Matustik puts it, the notion of mediation provides "a means of classifying the functional relationships (1) between basic and derived terms and (2) in development, between the basic group of operations and higher, differentiated stages of mediate operations."[13]

---

[10]Lamb, *History, Method, and Theology*, p. 382.

[11]Ibid., p. 388.

[12]On Lonergan's definition of "conjugates," see *Insight*, pp. 78-82; for discussion of different types of conjugates, see also ibid., pp. 254-67, 434-42; on the human capacity for intellectual conjugates, ibid., pp. 266-67, 514-20. See also Lamb, *History, Method, and Theology*, pp. 415-22.

[13]Matustik, *Mediation of Deconstruction*, p. 3. For additional background on the notion of mediation, see Appendix A, "Background to the Notion of Mediation."

Developments of the Notion of Mediation

The most important complexifications of the notion that Lonergan develops are the concepts of mutual mediation, self-mediation, and mutual self-mediation. Mutual mediation is exhibited in any functional whole that consists of a variety of functioning parts. Each part carries out its proper function immediately while mediately receiving the benefits of the functions of all the other parts. As a functional whole a mammal, for example, consists of the function of obtaining oxygen, which is immediate in the respiratory system and mediated in the entire body; the function of digesting food, which is immediate in the digestive system and mediated in the entire body; etc. The mammal as a whole can function properly only if all the parts are mediating one another properly.[14]

Self-mediation is "a whole that has consequences that change the whole."[15] An example is the development of a living organism. That development is immediate in the organism as a whole and mediated in all the stages, parts, etc. Organic self-mediation exhibits what Lonergan calls "displacement upwards" in that the functioning and development of all the parts and stages only have coherence when viewed from the perspective of the whole organism.[16]

On another level of self-mediation one finds the intentional self-mediation of animal consciousness. Consciousness (the whole) is mediated to itself in its acts of intending objects (the parts). This is a "displacement inwards" in that a correct grasp of the coherence of any or all of the intentional acts depends on a grasp of their relation of mediacy to the immediate inner center, consciousness.[17]

---

[14]Lonergan, "Mediation of Christ in Prayer," pp. 4-6.

[15]Ibid., p. 6.

[16]Ibid., p. 7.

[17]Ibid., pp. 8-9.

At the third level of self-mediation is the existential self-mediation of human self-consciousness. The self-conscious subject (the whole) is mediated to itself in its acts of existential commitment (the parts). This is a "deliberate shift of center" in that the subject freely and deliberately affirms that he or she will henceforth be mediated within a specific, concrete set of relationships.[18]

Finally Lonergan discusses mutual self-mediation. The primary example here is human relationships. In a relationship there is self-mediation, in that the concrete nature of the self-conscious subject is mediated in every dimension of the relationship--words and gestures, patterns of behavior, acts of committment, etc. There is also mutual mediation, in that the relationship itself constitutes a functional whole within which all the acts of each party are mediated to the whole and so constitute a substantively changed set of circumstances within which all the other parties mediate themselves. The greater the degree of existential commitment within a relationship, the greater the degree to which this mutuality exercises a constitutive effect upon the individual's self-mediation.[19]

The notion of mediation, and especially its development into the notion of mutual self-mediation, provides the infrastructure for a more adequate understanding of human intersubjectivity.

B. Intersubjectivity, Meaning, and Mediation

Meaning and Intersubjectivity

In Chapter 2, it was stated as an hypothesis that the ground of consciousness is best understood as a "full" state of intersubjectivity which is mediated in the various forms of interhuman intersubjectivity. The discussion of mediation in section I of this chapter gives a context

---

[18]Ibid., pp. 9-12.

[19]Ibid., pp. 12-14.

to this statement. The ground of consciousness is the "whole" of which mediated intersubjectivity is the structured articulation. While no particular instance of mediated intersubjectivity can express the entirety or "fullness" of the whole, each particular instance nevertheless *is* an articulation of the ground. It is this which makes it possible for us to approach a knowledge of the ground state through objectification and appropriation of the structured mediations.

At this point it may be helpful to clarify the distinctions among three forms of intersubjectivity. The first is vital or primordial intersubjectivity, which is a fusion in the "world of immediacy" that "precedes the distinction of subjects and survives its oblivion."[20] The second is intersubjectivity as shared meaning, which involves myriad forms of mediated communication among autonomous, self-mediating subjects. The third is mystical intersubjectivity, which is a "mediated return to immediacy"--that is, a conscious appropriation of the ground of consciousness.

Detailed discussion of mystical intersubjectivity will be the topic of Chapter 5. Our concern in the the following pages will be with the other two forms of intersubjectivity, and in particular with the second--that is, intersubjectivity as shared meaning. The reason for this focus should be evident from the preceding discussions of mediation and of Lonergan's foundational methodology. Lonergan's claim is that we can affirm and appropriate the ground of consciousness only by objectifying and appropriating its mediations. Hence, the next step in our movement toward verification of the hypothesis that the ground of consciousness is a state of intersubjectivity is a study of mediated intersubjectivity--that is, meaning.

Lonergan defined meaning as follows:

> [M]eaning is an act that does not merely repeat but goes beyond experiencing. For what is meant, is what is intended in questioning

[20]Lonergan, *Method in Theology*, p. 57. See also the section on "The Subject as Intersubjective" in Chapter 3.

> and is determined not only by experience but also by understanding and, commonly, by judgment as well. This addition of understanding and judgment is what makes possible the world mediated by meaning, what gives it its structure and unity, what arranges it in an orderly whole of almost endless differences partly known and familiar, partly in a surrounding penumbra of things we know about but have never examined or explored, partly an unmeasured region of what we do not know at all.[21]

Perhaps in earliest infancy, or in occasional physically and emotionally intense adult experiences (panic, orgasm, ecstasy), the subject exists in a "world of immediacy" in which immediate experience undergoes relatively little processing through understanding, judging or deliberation.[22] The human world, however, is primarily a "world mediated by meaning." The processing of understanding, judging and deliberation occurs continuously, and gradually builds up increasingly complex habitual patterns through which experiences are interpreted.

The subject-as-subject is the center of immediacy which mediates itself in its meaning-making operations. The dynamism of the subject is such that the flow of experience is always and everywhere on the move toward meaning. The subject, by operating, makes meaning; meaning is a structuring, that is, a mediation, of one's presence in the world. To learn to operate in the world is to learn how to structure one's interaction with the world meaningfully.

Primordial intersubjectivity--the "'we' that precedes the distinction of subjects"--is the psychological ground of all mediated meaning. Without that primordial sense of belonging to and with other human beings, there would be no urge toward communication and no taste for

---

[21]Lonergan, *Method in Theology*, p. 77.

[22]Research on infants indicates that there is no period of "absolute immediacy" in human experience; see Daniel N. Stern, *The Interpersonal World of the Infant* (New York: Basic, 1984). For Lonergan, both immediacy (self-presence) and mediation (intentional presence to objects) are present in every moment of experience. The term "world of immediacy," therefore, refers to a state of relative undifferentiation in which one has little or no ability to distinguish self-presence from presence to objects.

the painful struggle involved in its refinement. The telelogy of that struggle is toward common meaning--that is, an intersubjectivity that is mediated not only in experience, but in free and conscious understanding, judgment and decision.

Between these two poles--primordial intersubjectivity and the fulfillment of mediated intersubjectivity in "the achievement of common meaning"--lies a long, arduous, and frequently abortive journey of the differentiation of consciousness. Despite the complexifications, frustrations, and detours inherent in the journey, all human acts of meaning can be located somewhere along this path.

Humans are capable of mediating themselves through an immense variety of carriers of meaning; Lonergan names empirical presence, art, symbols, language, and the total person.[23] They are also capable of an even greater variety of differentiations of meaning, structuring it according to the myriads of languages, cultures, professions, interests, etc. Yet underlying all these complexifications is the basic structure of the subject's self-mediation.

One's acts of meaning constitute the structure of one's personal horizon. One's horizon is the range of things one knows or potentially knows--that is, can inquire about.[24] The most fundamental limit on this range is the groups of operations one has mastered.[25] The more the human person grows in the mastery of operations that enable him or her to structure interaction with the world meaningfully, the more the world becomes "mediated by meaning." For the adult, "the world of immediacy shrinks into an inconspicuous and not too important corner

---

[23]Lonergan, *Method in Theology*, pp. 57-73. Note that in this section Lonergan uses the term "intersubjectivity" to refer primarily to empirical presence.

[24]Ibid., pp. 235-37.

[25]Bernard Lonergan, *Lectures on Education* (unpublished lectures delivered at Xavier College, Cincinnati, OH, 1959; available from The Lonergan Center, Boston College, Chestnut Hill, MA 02167), p. 191; cf. also idem., *Method in Theology*, pp. 27-30.

of the real world, which is a world we know only through the mediation of meaning."[26]

The following quote summarizes Lonergan's perspective on meaning:

> What are historical facts? For the empiricist they are what was out there and was capable of being looked at. For the idealist they are mental constructions carefully based on data recorded in documents. For the critical realist they are events in the world mediated by true acts of meaning.[27]

Lonergan's theory of meaning, then, is a realist constructivism. It is constructivist because the subject's world is structured primarily by his or her own acts of meaning;[28] it is realist because the acts of meaning take place, not in pristine solitude, but in presence to physical and human "others." The distinction between "experience" and "knowledge" is key: knowing is never simply "taking a look," but before one can know one must have an experience. The act of meaningful structuring is one's own, but it is also always a response to, and an appropriation of, something that has its own structure. It is, therefore, immediately a hermeneusis of one's own experience, but mediately a hermeneusis of the structure of an existent distinct from oneself.

Against the Counterpositions

This discussion of Lonergan's theory of meaning provides a basis for further clarification of what is meant by speaking of the human subject as "intersubjective." Three counterpositions must be rejected.

---

[26]Lonergan, "Dimensions of Meaning," p. 255.

[27]Lonergan, *Method in Theology*, p. 239.

[28]See Lonergan, *Lectures on Education, p. 193*, for a repudiation of the idea that constructivism (such as that of Piaget) is necessarily idealist or subjectivist. Lonergan wrote: "Piaget has to be completed by adding a fuller appreciation of the subject, of what has meaning to the subject."

Lonergan's theory of meaning, as explicated here, affirms the fundamental reality of both the subject-as-subject and the subject as intersubjective. It also clarifies, however, that neither the subject-as-subject nor the subject as intersubjective is an "entity" that can be properly known by direct apprehension. Both are known (in the explanatory sense) only by a transcendental analysis of the operations of consciousness, that is, of the acts of meaning-making that constitute the arc of self-transcendence. To claim otherwise tends to reduce the subject either to a mere structure of relations (the subject as constituted *only* by intersubjectivity) or to a solipcistic monad (the subject-as-subject as an "entity").

The first counterposition, then, reduces the human person to an entity constituted by its intramundane relations. Lonergan vigorously argued against this. In an early work, he made the traditional scholastic argument:

> I grant that every person is caught up in a web of interpersonal relations. Infinite persons are constituted by such relations; finite persons have such relations as properties consequent on their being. That such relations, however, are constitutive of finite persons, I deny. . . . Relations which are interpersonal and finite cannot subsist because they follow on operations and these operations are of necessity accidental.[29]

A subject who is both primordially and mediately intersubjective is not the same as a subject who is constituted by relations. To be constituted by relations would be to exist first as an object, a thing-among-things whose identity is derived solely from its relations with other things. To be primordially and mediately intersubjective is to be a subject whose self-mediation begins from presence-with other subjects and extends from there into knowing and loving them. Identity is derived from the

[29]Lonergan, *On the Ontological and Psychological Constitution of Christ*, p. 30.

function of self-mediation, in which "The terms fix the relations, the relations fix the terms, and the function fixes both."[30]

The second counterposition would be the denial of fundamental intersubjectivity. An article by Paul Kidder[31] addresses the question of how Lonergan's system escapes the charge of solipcism--a charge which is commonly leveled at those who make an analysis of subjectivity the foundation of their system of thought. Husserl, for example, built his system on the notion of a "transcendental ego" that stands "*above* the whole manifold but synthetically unified flow in which the world has and forever attains anew its content of meaning and its ontic validity."[32] Husserl never provided a convincing response to the charge that such a transcendental ego can have no real knowledge of, let alone a constitutive relationship with, other subjects.

For Lonergan, on the other hand, says Kidder, the subject is not "transcendent" to its own worldly horizon; rather,it is capable of an act of "transcending" by which it appropriates the horizon *as* horizon. That "transcending" moment is what Lonergan calls "insight." "Hence instead of thinking in terms of Husserl's extramundane entity, the transcendental ego, Lonergan identifies an extramundane, transcendental moment in the dynamic process of knowing, a moment that is distinct, but not separate from the process as a whole."[33] Lonergan's response to the charge of solipcism, then, would be that the functional interrelationship between the intersubjectively-constituted horizon and the knowing subject is such that neither is an "ultimately autonomous, ultimately prior term. . . . A

---

[30]Matustik, *Mediation of Deconstruction*, p. 18.

[31]Paul Kidder, "Lonergan and the Husserlian Problem of Transcendental Intersubjectivity," *Method: Journal of Lonergan Studies* 4 (1986): 29-54.

[32]Edmund Husserl, *The Crisis of European Sciences and Transcendental Phenomenology*, trans. David Carr (Evanston, IL: Northwestern University Press, 1970), p. 150.

[33]Kidder, "Transcendental Intersubjectivity," p. 48.

person is attracted to belief in the utter priority of one over the other only by ignoring details of that functional interrelationship."[34]

The third counterposition, finally, would reduce the human person to an entity that is intersubjective at the vital or primordial level. Lonergan caustically criticized the then-popular "personalism" for this, faulting it for its overemphasis on:

> an 'I' and 'Thou' that add up to the single personal total of 'Us' talking about 'Ourselves' and what 'We' have done and shall do. . . . the whole stress falls on the interpersonal situation, the psychic interchange of mutual presence, the beginnings of what may prove to be a lifelong union.[35]

The problem with this, he asserted, is that a position that reduces persons back to the level of merely vital intersubjectivity contradicts its own personalist values. It fails to recognize that the self-transcending dynamism of the human person experiences no fulfillment--in interpersonal relations or anywhere else--without the full operation of intelligence, rationality, and responsibility.

Indeed, the fact that primordial intersubjectivity is the ground of meaning does not mean that a naive, unmediated return to that state is necessarily either possible or good. The desire for such a naive immediacy, in fact, is little more than animal; it must be "displaced upward" through conversion until one can, perhaps, effect a "mediated return to immediacy" in adult loving, in mystical prayer, or in methodical self-appropriation.[36]

In sum, Lonergan argues that it is only in "collective responsibility for common or complementary action," undertaken by intelligent and free subjects, that we can properly speak of "the collective subject

---

[34]Ibid., p. 50.

[35]Lonergan, "Cognitional Structure," p. 237.

[36]See Lonergan, *Method in Theology*, pp. 76-77; also Matustik, *Mediation of Deconstruction*, p. 37.

referred to by 'We,' 'Us,' 'Ourselves,' 'Ours.'"[37] While intersubjectivity has its ground in the primordial "'we' that precedes the distinction of subjects," it is fully mediated only in the community of existential subjects who freely and responsibly strive toward common meanings. Our next section will consider this process in greater detail.

Meaning and the Formation of Community

The meanings which mediate the world of the adult human, according to Lonergan, have four major functions: cognitive, effective, constitutive, and communicative.[38] The specification of the four functions distinguishes four ways in which meaning mediates the human world. Exercise of the cognitive function is a sort of "knowledge for its own sake": one seeks to know what is real, but without any necessity of acting upon it or of committing oneself to it. Exercise of the effective function gives technical knowledge. It secures the "transformation of [the] environment . . . through the intentional acts that envisage ends, select means, secure collaborators, direct operations."[39] Exercise of the constitutive function leads to fully human meaning. This is the kind of meaning that establishes and structures "the family and mores, the state and religion, the economy and technology, the law and education."[40] It is in the field of constitutive meaning, Lonergan wrote,

> that man's freedom reaches its high point. There too his responsibility is greatest. There there occurs the emergence of the

---

[37]Lonergan, "Cognitional Structure," p. 237.

[38]Lonergan, *Method in Theology*, pp. 76-81; also idem, "*Existenz* and *Aggiornamento*" and "Dimensions of Meaning."

[39]Lonergan, "Dimensions of Meaning," p. 255.

[40]Lonergan, "*Existenz* and *Aggiornamento*," p. 244.

> existential subject, finding out for himself that he has to decide for himself what he is to make of himself.[41]

Exercise of the communicative function, finally, yields common or shared meaning. "The genesis of common meaning," Lonergan wrote, "is an ongoing process of communication, of people coming to share the same cognitive, constitutive, and effective meanings."[42] The teleology of the communicative function is towards community, "an achievement of common meaning" in which not only experiences, but understandings, judgments and decisions are shared.[43] Lonergan wrote, "Through communication there is constituted community and, conversely, community constitutes and perfects itself through communication."[44]

The telelogy of communicative meaning toward community can only be fulfilled by the full activation and differentiation of the other functions as well. The constitutive and communicative functions, in particular, have a relationship of mutual mediation in the constitution of community.

First of all, the common meaning that makes communities is also necessarily constitutive meaning, for it "is realized by decisions and choices, especially by permanent dedication, in the love that makes families, in the loyalty that makes states, in the faith that makes religions."[45] And, conversely,

> As it is only within communities that men are conceived and born and reared, so too it is only with respect to the available common meanings that the individual grows in experience, understanding, judgment, and so comes to find out for himself that he has to decide for himself what to make of himself. This process for the

---

41Lonergan, "Dimensions of Meaning," p. 255.

42Lonergan, *Method in Theology*, p. 357.

43Ibid., p. 79.

44Ibid., p. 363.

45Ibid., p. 79.

> schoolmaster is education, for the sociologist is socialization, for the cultural anthropologist is acculturation. But for the individual in the process it is his coming to be a man, his existing as a man in the fuller sense of the name.[46]

The world mediated by meaning, then, is an intersubjective world. The trajectory of human meaning finds its fulfilment in the community of existential subjects. Indeed, the relationship between the community and the existential subject can best be characterized as one of mutual self-mediation. First of all, the self-mediation of the subject is mediated in the formation of community; the subject's self-transcending dynamism is the ground that finds its proper manifestation in acts that form community. When Lonergan wrote that "the world constituted by meaning, the properly human world, the world of community is the product of freely self-constituting subjects,"[47] he indicated how the existential subject mediates itself in constitutive meaning shared within a community.

But, likewise, the community's self-mediation is mediated in the formation of the subject's act of meaning. A community, said Lonergan, mediates itself by its history: "The history that is written about is the mediation, the revelation, of the common sense of the community; the history that is written is the fully reflective product of that self-manifestation."[48] The community's dynamism toward the historical achievement of common meaning is the ground that finds its proper manifestation in the fully responsible, traditioned-yet-creative, community-making act of meaning on the part of an existential subject.

Thus, it is only by the constitutive meaning-acts of existential subjects that community can be formed; but these acts themselves are a mediation of communally structured meaning. Just as in general the act of meaning is immediately act of the subject but mediately response to

---

[46]Ibid.

[47]Lonergan, "*Existenz* and *Aggiornamento*," p. 244.

[48]Lonergan, "Mediation of Christ in Prayer," p. 11.

external event, so the constitutive act of meaning is immediately existential (i.e., the preserve of the individual subject) but mediately communitarian: constitutive meanings are a creative personal appropriation (affirmation and transformation) of the communally-structured meanings of a tradition.

It is important to note that constitutive acts of meaning are not some rare form reserved to exceptional individuals. Every use of a shared human language, every participation in a cultural institution, involves an at least rudimentary constitutive act of meaning. While the fullest instantiation of a constitutive act of meaning would be a creative, courageous, deeply kenotic act of self-mediation for the sake of community-building, even the baby's first communicative gesture manifests the same structure.

The notion of mutual self-mediation between existential subject and community is able to account for a double, mutually mediating priority: the priority of the existential subject's (authentic or unauthentic) act of constitutive meaning, and the priority of the community's (authentic or unauthentic) historical tradition of meaning.

The center of the task of the critical interpretation of mediated meaning, then, is the discernment of authenticity. This applies both to interpretation of the subject's self-mediating activity and to interpretation of the community's historical tradition. Authenticity fundamentally consists in obedience to the transcendental precepts, and it may exist even where self-appropriation remains inarticulate and unsystematic. As noted in Chapter 3, deliberate, consciously chosen authenticity requires objective knowledge of the transcendental precepts; and this reaches its full form in explanatory self-appropriation. This fullness of authenticity is closely related to what Lonergan calls the "methodical control of meaning."

Method, Praxis, and Authenticity

Since the human world is a world mediated by meaning, and since that meaning has a dynamism toward common meaning, the human world is always and everywhere a cultural world: a world in which every aspect of life is shaped by meanings developed by, and shared among, a delimited cultural group. In order to maintain and develop their common meanings, cultures develop "controls of meaning." Control of meaning begins with reflection on meaning;[49] with reflection, criteria are developed for resolving cases of disputed meaning.

In the earliest, least differentiated cultures, control of meaning (insofar as it exists) is largely mythic. Mythic control resolves disputes on the basis of symbolic and narrative harmony. The story line or symbolic expression may develop a new twist--it may even incorporate radically new meanings--but above all it must remain recognizably "our story."[50]

Mythic control is limited because it is characteristic of cultures in which the four functions of meaning have not yet begun to be differentiated. Mythical and magical meanings arise when the constitutive function is inextricably blended with the cognitive and effective functions.[51] It was a great step forward when the Greeks began to differentiate the cognitive function as a distinct function with its own proper methods and criteria.[52] This gave rise to classical culture, with its capacity for the theoretical control of meaning.

The theoretical control of meaning clearly distinguishes between common sense meanings, which are embedded in limited personal and cultural horizons, and theoretical meanings, which are universal, explanatory definitions. Control of meaning, in classical culture,

---

[49]Lonergan, "Dimensions of Meaning," p. 255.

[50]Lonergan, *Method in Theology*, pp. 306-7.

[51]Ibid., pp. 87, 306.

[52]Lonergan, *Method in Theology*, pp. 90f.; idem, "Dimensions of Meaning," pp. 258f.

involved discovering a "universal fixed for all time";[53] to control meaning was to be able to get behind shifting appearances and contingencies to the unchanging truth.

Classical control of meaning fulfills the demands of the systematic exigence. Modern culture is characterized by response to the demands of the critical exigence. No longer is it sufficient to differentiate the two worlds of common sense and theory; one must also differentiate the world of interiority. No longer does the cutting edge of the search for control of meaning reside in the search for universal, necessary, explanatory definitions; now the cutting edge is in the search for understanding of the structures of subjectivity itself. The critical control of meaning recognizes that the controls themselves are "involved in an ongoing process"[54]; hence even science, in the modern world, "is not true; it is only on the way towards truth."[55]

Critical control of meaning, unhindered by the classical expectation of limited, standardized, never-changing truths, gives the modern seeker an awesome degree of openness to new realms and forms of knowledge. Yet in the end the critical control of meaning breaks down in the face of the discovery that inauthenticity, manifested in a foundational incoherence, appears to pervade the very roots of human subjectivity. The age of innocence, "the age that assumed that human authenticity could be taken for granted," is over.[56] Explicitly formulated in nihilism and deconstructionism, the modern crisis of meaning is a radical questioning of the very possibility of any authentic human meaning.

Lonergan's assertion, then, is that post-modern culture is in desperate need of the development of a new control of meaning, which

---

[53]Lonergan, *Method in Theology*, p. 29. See also idem, "Dimensions of Meaning," pp. 256-62.

[54]Lonergan, *Method in Theology*, p. 29.

[55]Lonergan, "Dimensions of Meaning," p. 259.

[56]Lonergan, "Ongoing Genesis," p. 156.

he terms "methodical." It is important to clarify immediately what Lonergan does and does not intend by the use of the term "method" in this context. Gadamer, for example, rejects the primacy of method because for him the term connotes an assumption that "logical clarity, coherence, and rigor" are the criteria of intelligence and reasonableness.[57] This understanding of method is, in fact, typical of many modern schools of thought which operate primarily within the systematic exigence and regard physics, mathematics, or logic as the best approaches to the systematic coordination of knowledge.

For Lonergan, however, method "takes command when one assigns logic its subsidiary role."[58] The coherence and intelligibility that he claims are foundational are not based in any logic, system, or technical proficiency. They are based, rather, in the self-mediating subject who is aware of his or her own operations and can, on the basis of that awareness, appropriate them knowledgeably. It is an *ad hominem* argument;[59] the basis of the claim is an appeal to examine one's own performance and to find therein the purported coherence and intelligibility. The critical control of meaning broke down because it made the subject its object and then found that this object was fundamentally unknowable; Lonergan's solution is to let the subject be subject again.

As Lonergan acknowledged, "The argument does not prove that in the subject as subject we shall find the evidence, norms, invariants, and principles for a critique of horizons; it proves that unless we find it there, we shall not find it at all."[60] Lonergan has gone all the way

---

[57]Fred Lawrence, "Gadamer and Lonergan: A Dialectical Comparison," *International Philosophical Quarterly* 20 (1980), p. 35.

[58]Lawrence, "Gadamer and Lonergan," p. 35. Lawrence takes this quote from Lonergan, "Method: Trend and Variations," an unpublished lecture given at Austin College, Sherman, TX, in 1974 (available from The Lonergan Center, Boston College, Chestnut Hill, MA 02167).

[59]Matustik, *Mediation of Deconstruction*, pp. 176-78.

[60]Lonergan, "Notes on Existentialism," p. 28.

with Gödel and with the deconstructionists, agreeing that so long as we are restricted to the level of logic and system and objectifiable meanings, the human condition can only be affirmed as fundamentally incoherent and unintelligible. He then goes one step further, however, and asserts that the activity of meaning-making, which precedes and produces all logics, systems, and objectified meanings, has a coherence and intelligibiity which can be experienced, understood, affirmed, and appropriated.

Method, then, "emerges within the shift from merely logical considerations to a hermeneutics of conscious intentionality as not merely cognitive but existential."[61] Methodical control of meaning is not simply a sophisticated differentiation of the cognitive function of meaning; it is primarily an existential skill in experiencing, understanding, judging and putting into action *all* the functions of meaning. The objectified, explanatory, cognitive component of this existential skill is what Lonergan terms knowledge of "generalized empirical method."[62]

Lonergan makes an essential point when he notes that generalized empirical method is not found by attending to "the individual subjectivity that is correlative to the world of immediacy," but by appropriating "the individual subjectivity that is correlative to the world mediated by meaning and motivated by value."[63] This distinction is crucial because it explains why methodical self-appropriation is not a merely private concern, but has everything to do with the historical processes of the achievement of common meaning.

Occurrences in the world of immediacy may be private, but the meaning one appropriates in the world mediated by meaning is always a mediation of common meaning. Even though the foundation of Lonergan's appeal is *ad hominem*--that is, it is an appeal to the subject-

---

[61]Ibid.

[62]For discussion, see above, Chapter 3.

[63]Lonergan, "Ongoing Genesis," p. 151.

as-subject--its articulation in generalized empirical method is equally rooted in the public realm where meanings are arrived at and verified in intersubjective discourse.

Generalized empirical method is an explanatory articulation of the structure of authenticity, both in individual meaning-making and in the historical process of a community's meaning-making. If methodical self-appropriation remained only at the level of explanatory articulation, however, it would not actually address the existential problem of authenticity--the problem which lies at the very heart of the modern crisis. That problem demands an existential response; that is, it demands *praxis*.

Praxis, Lonergan wrote, "raises the final issue, What are you to do about it?"[64] Praxis goes beyond simply knowing to taking a personal stand. Methodical self-appropriation is, finally, more adequately defined as a form of praxis than as a form of knowledge. Method as praxis, Lonergan said, "discerns a radically distorted situation; it retreats from spontaneous to critical intelligence; it begins from above on the level of evaluations and decisions; and it moves from concord and cooperation towards the development of mutual understanding and more effective communication."[65]

As noted earlier, Lonergan believed that the most profound social and cultural changes--the changes that mark off one historical epoch from another--are, at root, changes in the control of meaning.[66] The differentiation of the methodical control of meaning offers the contemporary world a solution to its present social and cultural disarray.

Method, Matustik wrote, "is the final liberation of the initial theorem of mediation."[67] He concluded:

---

[64]Lonergan, "Ongoing Genesis," p. 159.

[65]Lonergan, "Ongoing Genesis," p. 163.

[66]Lonergan, "Dimensions of Meaning," pp. 255-56.

[67]Matustik, *Mediation of Deconstruction*, p. 145.

> Lonergan thematizes the emergence of the *existential* subject as the highest form of self-mediation. This emergence of self-constituting *human autonomy* is to operational development what the differential equation is to solving the mathematical function. The subject on the level of responsible self-presence becomes the source of possible novel development, i.e., the source of its own diversifications functioning differently under variable conditions.[68]

The methodically self-appropriated subject is a post-modern variant of the fully free human being, for he or she is able to fully and freely mediate self in the world. Such a person is able skillfully to differentiate and employ not only the operations appropriate to experiencing, understanding, judging and deciding about meaning as it is mediated from the past, but also the operations appropriate to committing to, determining, articulating and communicating meaning as it is mediated into the future.[69]

The Teleology of Human Intersubjectivity

These affirmations of "autonomy" and "freedom," however, need to be placed in the context of the foregoing discussion of the mutual self-mediation of individual and community. As Lonergan put it:

> The autonomy of the individual is not the whole story. From the community he has his existence, his concrete possibilities, the constraints that hem him in, the opportunities he can seize and make the most of, the psychological, social, historical achievements and aberrations that constitute his situation. Destiny is perhaps the working out of individual autonomy within community, and so the summation of destinies in a community is the history of the community.[70]

---

[68]Ibid., pp. 129-30.

[69]Ibid. See also Lonergan, *Method in Theology*, p. 144, on method and the mediation of past and future.

[70]Lonergan, "Mediation of Christ in Prayer," p. 12.

Full human development is as much a matter of matured intersubjectivity as of matured individuality. In technical terms, fully-developed intersubjectivity could be defined as "the achievement of appropriated mutual self-mediation at the level of existential commitment." This "packed" definition indicates that fully-developed intersubjectivity involves at least three essential elements:

1. a relation with an other or others in which both parties are deeply implicated in the other's self-mediation;
2. a high degree of existential commitment within this relationship;
3. a high degree of appropriation of one's self-mediation.

The position taken here is that the full development of intersubjectivity, as thus defined, is identical with the full development of the self-mediating subject. In other words: for human beings, full self-mediation *necessarily* involves deep mutuality, existential commitment, and self-appropriation, all functioning in an integrated manner within a life of concrete relatedness. Furthermore, as is evident from the section above on the mutual self-mediation of existential subject and community, the individual with fully developed intersubjectivity is also a person who necessarily lives in community[71] and who enables the further development of true community.

It is to be noted again that the self-appropriation that is essential for fully-developed intersubjectivity does not necessarily have to include explicit, theoretical differentiation and naming of all the operations of intelligence. In other contexts the requisite self-appropriation goes under such names as "self-knowledge," "discernment," "wisdom," "virtue," etc. All these are names for aspects of the skillfulness in the praxis of

---

[71]Obviously, "lives" here is not synonomous with "resides." Rather, it refers to a dimension of vital daily interchange that might be lived out through involvement in family, neighborhood, civic affairs, church, the contemplative prayer of the hermit, or innumerable other forms.

intelligent living that is the core of the "methodical control of meaning." While full methodical control does require the theoretical differentiation along with this skillfulness, the foundation of method is praxis--not theory.

Having articulated the "end" toward which human intersubjectivity develops, our next task is to examine the structures within which this development takes place. First, however, another theoretical interlude will be required in order to indicate how the theory of mediation presented in section I of this chapter correlates with an explanatory view of concrete developmental processes.

C. Science and the Study of Developing Intersubjectivity

"Below Upward" and "Above Downward" Operations

In Lonergan's later writings one occasionally encounters references to the distinction between development from "below upward" and from "above downward."

> On this view of human development advance ordinarily is from below upwards. It is from experiencing through inquiry to understanding; from intelligent formulations through reflection to judgment; from apprehended reality through deliberation to evaluation, decision, action.
>
> Still the ordinary process is not the exclusive process. Man's insertion in community and history includes an invitation for him to accept the transformation of falling in love: the transformation of domestic love between husband and wife; the transformation of human love for one's neighbor; the transformation of divine love that comes when God's love floods our inmost heart through the Holy Spirit he has given us (Rom 5:5).

> . . . in the measure that this transformation is effective, development comes not merely from below upwards but more fundamentally from above downwards.[72]

This distinction, then, is crucial for Lonergan's understanding of what we are here calling "fulfilled intersubjectivity." As this text indicates, when we think of "development" we usually think first of the "below upward" movement--that is, the step-by-step movement of gradual self-transcendence which was discussed in Chapter 3. What is more, it is this dimension of development that is acknowledged and studied by the empirical sciences such as psychology, sociology, and anthropology. Yet Lonergan notes that, in order to account for the possibility of wholehearted and responsible participation in history, in human community, and in divine life, we must also postulate another set of dynamics in human development--an "above downward" movement of what has traditionally been called "grace."[73]

The immediate difficulty with this language of "below upward/above downward" is that it tends to raise the specter of outdated "supernaturalist"[74] interpretations of God's activity in the world and in the human soul. This is, of course, far from Lonergan's meaning. An understanding of how this metaphorical language fits into the sophisticated theoretical framework of Lonergan's foundational methodology is necessary in order to overcome the tendency to interpret "above downward" dynamics as an extrinsicist "divine intervention."

---

[72]Lonergan, "Christology Today: Methodological Reflections," in *Third Collection*, pp. 76-77.

[73]On these dynamics and the theology of grace, see Maurice Schepers, "Human Development: From Below Upward and From Above Downward," *Method: A Journal of Lonergan Studies* 7 (1989): 141-44.

[74]As David Tracy notes, in modern religious studies "the concept 'supernatural' . . . is roughly equivalent to 'fundamentalism.'" This is how the term is being used in this sentence. Tracy also notes that in *Grace and Freedom* Lonergan developed a "more restricted use of the *theorem* of the supernatural." For Tracy's comments, see *Blessed Rage for Order*, pp. 8, 19. For discussion of Lonergan's "theorem," see the section in Chapter 5 entitled "The Specificity of Mystical Experience."

Only then will it be possible fully to coordinate Lonergan's insights on development with those of the empirical sciences.

Perhaps the best-known discussion of the implications of Lonergan's use of the "below/above" metaphor occurs in Fred Crowe's lectures on education,[75] where he compares the "below upward" movement to the student's gradual, effortful movement from the accumulation of experience, to insights into the experience, to reasoned judgments, to the ability to make prudent and practical decisions. He then suggests that the "above downward" movement corresponds to the role of tradition and teacher, who present already-formed methods, judgments, and understandings to the student and expect him or her to conform to them until the appropriate time comes to strike out independently.[76] Crowe's interpretation offers an appealing way of applying the metaphor of "below" and "above" to the relationship of individual and community, but it is not terribly helpful in understanding its full theoretical context.

In order fully to understand Lonergan's language of "below/above," the first step is to accept that it is *metaphorical* language. As metaphor, it has great power to foster the flash of insight into a certain isomorphism between the physical experiences of "movement upward/movement downward" and the structures of development to which Lonergan is referring. The attempt to maintain the metaphorical language when one moves into the realm of theory, however, leads to the "supernaturalist" problem discussed above. Instead, we must search for the theoretical context--the structurally-related set of terms and relations--for which the metaphor is "shorthand."

In my view, Lonergan's language of "below upward/above downward" is best understood as an imagistic expression of the relation

---

[75]Frederick E. Crowe, *Old Things and New: A Strategy for Education* (Atlanta, GA: Scholar's Press, 1985).

[76]Crowe took this approach from Lonergan's comments in "Natural Right and Historical Mindedness," in *Third Collection*, pp. 180-81.

between two quite sophisticated sets of terms and relations, namely, the "theorem of emergence" and "the theorem of mediation." The theorem of mediation was presented in section A above. We must now examine the theorem of emergence, which is especially crucial for the coordination of Lonergan's thought with that of empirical science.

"Emergence" in Lonergan's System of Thought

The general meaning of the notion of emergence is that within a given system, a higher level of organization has emerged out of a lower level of organization and the higher level is found to exhibit properties that could not necessarily have been inferred even from the most complete knowledge of the lower level.[77] Lonergan offered the key to his view of emergence in *Insight*.

> The prototype of emergence is the insight that arises with respect to an appropriate image; without the insight, the image is a coincidental manifold; by the insight the elements of the image become intelligibly united and related; moreover, accumulations of insights unify and relate ever greater and more diversified ranges of images, and what remains merely coincidental from a lower viewpoint becomes systematic from the accumulation of insights in a higher viewpoint.[78]

Lonergan's most extensive development of the notion of emergence is in his theory of "emergent probability" in *Insight*. There, he strove to show how a world-order characterized by the continual emergence of higher levels of organization is compatible with the randomness and non-determinism that empirical studies find in the natural universe. His concern was to show that, since there is always some (even if small) probability of the occurrence of a higher level of organization, sooner or later it *will* occur. Higher levels are likely to involve more and more

---

[77]See Stephen Pepper, "Emergence," *Journal of Philosophy* 23 (1926): 241-45.

[78]Lonergan, *Insight*, p. 481.

complex "schemes of recurrence," which assure some degree of stability. Thus, over long periods of time and high numbers of events, higher and higher levels of organization will continually emerge, gain stability, and include within their schemata more and more of the available resources.[79]

The process of emergence from lower to higher can metaphorically be called a "below upward" process, while the effect of the higher level of organization upon the lower level can be called an "above downward" process. As the text quoted above indicates, development "from below" is isomorphic with the process that leads from experience to insight and beyond. An accumulation of data falls into seemingly coincidental patterns (images), until suddenly the insight emerges. Once the insight has emerged, however, one can--in fact, must--speak of development "from above": the new whole is the organizing structure of its lower manifolds.[80]

In *Insight*, Lonergan explicitly discussed the relations among various levels of reality in terms of emergence and "higher systems." He wrote:

> The conjugate forms of the atom constitute the higher system of the atom's own subatomic elements. The conjugate forms of the organism constitute the higher system of the organism's own chemical processes. The conjugate forms of the psyche constitute the higher system of the animal's own organic processes. In like manner, the conjugate forms of human intellectual activity constitute the higher system of man's sensitive living. In each case an otherwise coincidental manifold of lower conjugate acts is rendered systematic by conjugate forms on a higher level.[81]

---

[79]See Lonergan, *Insight*, pp. 115-28.

[80]For discussion of the relations of sequential lower manifolds and higher integrations, see Lonergan, *Insight*, pp. 254-67.

[81]Lonergan, *Insight*, p. 515. On emergence, see also ibid., pp. 451-58.

The higher the phenomenon, the more its development "from below" can only be understood in terms of the structure "from above" of which it is a mediation.[82] Lonergan gave as an example the difference between structure in chemical compounds and in multicellular organisms:

> [W]hile the chemical elements appear as dominated by the manifolds that they systematize, a multicellular structure is dominated by an idea that unfolds in the process of growth . . . . While chemical compounds and unicellular entities systematize aggregates that, at least initially, are put together non-systematically, multicellular formations systematize aggregates that they themselves assemble in systematic fashion.[83]

When one moves to yet higher levels of integration in conscious animals and, finally, in self-conscious human beings, the decisiveness of the "from above" component continues to increase exponentially.[84] In humans, intelligence (for Lonergan, the "spiritual" dimension) is the decisive dimension integrating all material substrates as it mediates itself in knowing.[85]

It is important to note that Lonergan did not explicitly employ the below/above metaphor in *Insight*. At that stage in his thinking his main concern was to find a way to correlate contemporary scientific insights with theological reflection. It was only later, when his concern shifted from the strictly intellectual aspect of judgment to its existential or praxis dimension, that he began to employ the metaphor and

---

[82]See, in addition to references below from Lonergan's *Insight*, Lamb, *History, Method, and Theology*, p. 416.

[83]Lonergan, *Insight*, p. 264.

[84]See Lonergan, "Mediation of Christ in Prayer," pp. 8-12.

[85]Lonergan, *Insight*, pp. 514-20, 266-67. See also below, "The Structure of Developing Intersubjectivity."

to emphasize the importance of the "above downward" dynamism in that context.[86]

Mediation, Emergence, and Science

The above discussion indicates how the metaphor of "below upward/above downward" can be understood in terms of the theorem of emergence. As stated above, my contention is that this metaphor has a yet more profound resonance as an imagistic expression of the relationship between the theorem of emergence and the theorem of mediation. In this section we will make explicit the relation between these two theorems and discuss its importance for the coordination of Lonergan's thought with that of the empirical sciences.

The theorem of mediation states that a whole is mediated in its parts in such a way that the parts can only be adequately explained in terms of the whole, while an explanation of each of the parts, no matter how comprehensive, cannot adequately explain the whole. The theorem of emergence states first that there is a fundamental dynamism in creation toward the emergence of new, more comprehensive wholes; secondly, that once a new whole has emerged--whether in insight, or in the evolution of concrete phenomena--one adequately understands it only by grasping the whole as operating "from above," as well as the component parts that articulate the structure "from below."

The two theorems, in other words, offer different but easily convertible explanatory views of the same set of relations. We might say that the theorem of mediation takes the "above downward" direction of operation as the norm and explains "below upward" operation (i.e., the space-and-time articulation of parts) in terms of a more fundamental dimension of which the structured articulation is a mediation. The theorem of emergence, on the other hand, takes the "below upward"

[86]See, for example, Bernard Lonergan, "Healing and Creating in History," in *Third Collection*, p. 106.

direction of operation as the norm and explains "above downward" operation (i.e., the influence of higher levels of organization) in terms of a quantum leap beyond what could be expected from the original level of organization alone. Both theorems are ways to explain functionally both the proper autonomy of lower levels of organization within their own sphere, and their integral and constitutive relations with higher or more comprehensive levels of organization.

The approach taken here presumes that the theorem of mediation is the more fully explanatory of the two. The theorem of emergence, however, is more directly in tune with an empirical approach which begins from "below upward"--that is, by seeking the patterns manifested at a lower level and only subsequently discovering that these patterns are best explained by hypothesizing a higher, sublating level of organization.

Indeed, it was the philosophy of science that was the original context within which the language of emergence--and specifically the metaphor of "below upward/above downward"--was developed. Some philosophers, past and present, have employed this theorem to articulate the relationship between different levels of a natural hierarchy--for example, the relationships between the physics of a cell and its chemistry, or between its chemistry and its biology.[87] In fact, the argument over to what degree this terminology of "above and below" is simply evocative at a common-sense level, and to what degree it actually conveys explanatory insight, is very much alive in that forum.

Until recently mainstream science has been strongly committed to micro-deterministic theories, which affirm only "below upward" dynamism as explanatory. These theories argue that apparent "above downward" influence can ultimately be explained through thorough

---

[87]Philosophies of emergence were first developed, and enjoyed a brief heyday, in the 1920s. See S. Pepper, "Emergence"; C.L. Morgan, *Emergent Evolution* (London: Williams and Norgate, 1923); W.E. Ritter, *The Unity of the Organism* (Boston: The Gorham Press, 1919); R.W. Sellars, *Evolutionary Naturalism* (Chicago: Open Court, 1922); J.C. Smuts, *Holism and Evolution* (New York: Macmillan, 1926). The notion of emergence is presently being re-examined by some philosophers of science; see references in subsequent footnotes.

knowledge of the lower system. Recently some macro-deterministic theories, which also affirm an independent "above downward" dynamism, have begun to achieve respectability, thus breaking the former absolute hegemony of micro-deterministic theory in scientific explanation.[88]

Writing of the new "mentalist" paradigm which accepts "subjective phenomena, including mental images, feelings, thoughts, memories and other cognitive contents of inner experience" as legitimate explanatory constructs,[89] Roger W. Sperry observes:

> According to the new mentalist view . . . things are controlled not only from below upward by atomic and molecular action but also from above downward by mental, social, political and other macro properties. Primacy is given to the higher level controls rather than to the lowest. The higher, emergent, molar or macro phenomena and their properties throughout nature supersede the less evolved controls of the components.[90]

Disciples of Lonergan often lament the fact that Lonergan's work on emergent probability has never really been taken seriously by mainstream scientists or philosophers of science.[91] This lack of attention needs to be seen in light of the fact that the period during which Lonergan wrote and presented his views (the 1940s-60s) was the

---

[88]For contrasting views of the controversy, see: Robert L. Klee, "Micro-Determinism and Concepts of Emergence," *Philosophy of Science* 51 (1984): 44-63; and Roger W. Sperry, "Discussion: Macro- Versus Micro-Determinism," *Philosophy of Science* 53 (1986): 265-270.

[89]Roger W. Sperry, "Structure and Significance of the Consciousness Revolution," *Revision* 11, no. 1 (1988), p. 39.

[90]Sperry, "Structure and Significance," p. 44.

[91]For an example of such a lament, see Kenneth R. Melchin, *History, Ethics and Emergent Probability: Ethics, Society and History in the Work of Bernard Lonergan* (Lanham, MD: University Press of America, 1987), p. 59. For a list of works which discuss Lonergan's theory in light of issues in science, mathematics, and the philosophy of science, see ibid., pp. 88-89.

era of least respectability for philosophies stressing emergence, especially those with macro-deterministic overtones. Also, Lonergan's main field of both intellectual and sociological insertion was theology, making it less likely that those in fields that rarely interact with theology would even be aware of his work or, if they were, would feel compelled to take the time to fathom it.

Whether scientists will ever take Lonergan seriously is for them to decide, but the more significant fact may well be that by including the notion of emergence in a significant way within his system of thought, Lonergan prepared the way *within* theology for a correlation between theological and scientific insights. This correlation is essential for the development of a truly contemporary foundational theology.

The convergence between Lonergan's system of thought and the newer scientific theories that employ emergence and/or some version of macro-determinism as a paradigm may provide the opportune moment for the development of a foundational theology that is rooted both in the deepest traditions of classical Christian mysticism and in contemporary empirical studies of consciousness and its transformation.

D. The Structure of Developing Intersubjectivity

As we have seen, development can be understood either from the perspective of emergence (higher levels of organization emerging out of lower levels) or from the perspective of mediation (an underlying structure of the "whole" being mediated in the time-and-space articulation of parts). In human development, each of these perspectives contributes to insight into the structures of development toward fulfilled intersubjectivity.

Basic Structure: Body, Psyche, Spirit

As has been noted, we can discern three basic forms of intersubjectivity in human life: the primordial intersubjectivity that precedes the distinction of subjects, the mediated intersubjectivity of shared meaning, and the mystical intersubjectivity of a "mediated return to immediacy." We can now relate these to the concrete structures of human personhood.

In human beings the most significant levels of organization are the organic, the psychic, and the spiritual. Each of these has a certain autonomy on its own level; that is, there are laws and "schemes of recurrence" proper to each dimension, and these are not eliminated or overridden by their unification within the single "thing" that is a human being.[92] At the same time, however, there is an intricate interaction among the levels. The lower levels provide the indispensable materials for the higher levels, while the higher levels further differentiate and bring coherence to the lower levels.

The psyche, says Lonergan, gives representation and integration to neural (that is, organic) patterns and processes.[93] The multileveled flow of unconscious, neurally-based patterns is continual and uncontrolled. Out of this chaotic richness emerges the new, psychic level of organization. At this level the plethora of imagistic representations is sifted, and the "selected" images gain a loose narrative framework within which they can enter the subconscious as dreams and subliminal fantasies.

Even though the psyche operates as "higher system" to the organic level, the psyche still remains, in Lonergan's view, a basically material dimension of reality. Lonergan distinguishes the spiritual dimension from the material by defining the spiritual as "intelligibility that is intelligent,"[94] thus equating it with the operations of intelligence as

---

[92]On Lonergan's definition of a "thing," see *Insight*, pp. 245-70.

[93]See Lonergan, *Insight*, pp. 189-99, 467-69.

[94]Ibid., p. 516.

presented in Chapter 3. In humans, intelligence is entirely freed from being intrinsically constituted or conditioned by its material substrate;[95] for it is not neural structure (a strictly material dimension), but psychic contents (which are already structured by intelligence) that conscious intelligence integrates as it mediates itself in knowing.

Here we see the spiritual level of organization emerging out of the psychic. The operations of intelligence bring about a level of psychic coherence and organization that could not be achieved by the psychological level operating on its own. The exotic richness and confusion of night-dreams exemplify how the psyche operates when the constraint of conscious understandings, judgments, and commitments is reduced.[96] If an individual operated from this level in daily life, he or she would be diagnosed as psychotic--that is, severely deficient in normal and necessary psychic structure. For human beings, the spiritual level of organization is normative.

On a practical level, being "spiritual" in Lonergan's definition means first of all that normally the individual's conscious understandings, judgments and commitments sublate the raw material of psychic imagery and affects. This does not mean that the operations of intelligence can supercede or tyrannically restructure the psyche's autonomous activity according to its own laws, but it does mean that new "above downward" factors of organization are introduced into that activity. This "disciplining" of the psyche by conscious intelligence makes it possible for the psyche to produce such works as a Shakespeare play, a Beethoven symphony, or the countless lesser but still remarkable cultural products that make up human life.

Lonergan summarized:

> . . . inasmuch as we are material, we are constituted by otherwise coincidental manifolds of conjugate acts that unconsciously and spontaneously are reduced to system by higher conjugate forms. But

---

[95]Ibid., pp. 514-20.

[96]For Lonergan's comments on dreams, see *Insight*, pp. 194-98.

> inasmuch as we are spiritual, we are orientated toward the universe of being, know ourselves as parts within that universe, and guide our living by that knowledge.[97]

Ultimately, spirit is "consciousness-as-conscious"; its primary mediation is intentional consciousness and its operations. Lonergan makes the case that spirit is the "central form" of the human being. It cannot be any material dimension, including psyche, because while intelligibility that is not intelligent cannot ground and structure intelligibility that is intelligent, the latter *can* ground and structure the former.[98]

This is another way of saying that psyche, as it is structured in human beings, is a mediation of spirit. It is spirit that is the "alpha and omega," so to speak, of the material (organic and psychic) structures that it sublates; spirit is the "whole" of which material structures are mediations. Mediation, rather than emergence, is the proper explanatory context for understanding the structure of the human person. As discussed above, this does not mean that spirit is independent of, or tyrannically dominant over, its lower manifolds. On the contrary, the relation of mediation means that spirit has no existence apart from its activity of integrating the materials of psyche and expessing itself in them.

It is of the utmost importance to note that in this schema psyche and spirit are not two "things" or two "locations." There is only one "thing"--a human being--and one "location"--the electrochemical processes of a living body. Spirit is not an entity, but the capacity for a set of recurrent activities--the "operations of intelligence." Spirit is distinct from psyche neither in location nor in the materials that it organizes, but in the entirely new level of organization that it brings to the materials of psyche.

---

[97]Ibid., p. 516.

[98]Ibid., p. 520.

Psyche, Spirit, and Community

Essential to this new level of organization that spirit brings to psyche is what we are calling "fulfilled intersubjectivity." The psyche in itself is the home of primordial intersubjectivity, which Lonergan termed "the 'we' that precedes the distinction of subjects and survives its oblivion."[99] The distinction of subjects is an act of conscious intelligence--that is, of spirit--on the journey of differentiation. That journey culminates when mediated intersubjectivity is fulfilled in community, "the achievement of common meaning." Common meaning is not primarily a matter of shared experiences or of shared psychic manifolds, but of shared understandings, judgments, and--above all--commitments.[100]

Community, then, is fundamentally a product of spiritual activity. Community cannot be formed solely by operating on the psychic level. A group formed by the influence of very powerful psyhic commonalities but with a minimum of conscious understanding, judgment, and commitment may be a mob or a mass, but not a community. We can state as a principle that the less conscious intelligence is operative in the formation of a group, the less possibility that the group is a true community.

Yet, lest conscious intelligence appear to be cut free of its moorings, another principle must be stated. As our discussion of the relation of mediation between psyche and spirit has indicated, spiritual activities--the operations of intelligence--do not occur except as the higher integration of psychic materials. The common meaning that defines community has to emerge from an underlying psychic manifold; and that psychic manifold presumably must include an adult form of primordial intersubjectivity that is conducive to the conscious insights,

---

[99]Lonergan, *Method in Theology*, p. 57. See also, in Chapter 3, "The Subject as Intersubjective."

[100]Lonergan, *Method in Theology*, p. 79. See also above, "Meaning and the Formation of Community."

judgments and commitments of community.

The basic insight is that the relation of mediation between psyche and spirit is played out in the forum of the "primordial intersubjectivity" of the psyche and the "mediated intersubjectivity" of the spirit. As indicated above, a "conducive" form of psychic intersubjectivity does not *produce* community, but it does serve as a necessary, if not sufficient, condition. On the other hand, the emergence of community institutes an "above downward" influence upon psychic structures that further shapes psychic intersubjectivity in the direction of "conducive" forms.

This means that the question of healthy versus immature or pathological forms of "primordial intersubjectivity" is extraordinarily interrelated with the question of "fulfilled intersubjectivity." In our concern with the latter, we must first situate it as essentially a work of spirit, rather than of psyche. Equally important, however, will be situating this work of spirit in relation to the participating work of psyche. Part II of this inquiry carries out this double agenda, within the context of the project's particular interest in mystical transformation, intersubjectivity, and theological foundations.

CHAPTER 5

A THEORY OF MYSTICAL EXPERIENCE AND TRANSFORMATION

Chapters 2, 3, and 4 of Part I have concentrated on developing the general categories--that is, the nest of terms and relations that articulate the structure of the human subject. A particular concern has been to clarify the structures of the subject's intersubjectivity. In this chapter our goal will be to link these general categories to the special categories involved in a theological understanding of mystical experience and transformation.

A. The Specificity of Mystical Experience

The position taken here is that the essence of mysticism cannot be understood without a correct estimation of its unique relation to the realm of transcendence. The realm of transcendence can be understood either as the "ground" of all phenomena or as an "absolute whole" that sublates all phenomena. The theory that will be developed in this chapter explains mystical experience as an opening to this dimension which grounds and sublates all other dimensions of reality. The mystical quest strives for a radical return to the immediacy of the originating source of all self-transcendence; its focus is "otherworldly" in that sense.[1]

Another way of saying this is to affirm that in mystical experience an "above downward" dynamic is at work such that explanations from "below upward" will always finally have to acknowledge their own basic inadequacy.[2] Mystical experience is not fully reducible to any dimension less than the "absolute whole," even though it has effects and ramifications throughout all aspects of the human person and his or her life.[3]

To begin to explain mysticism by asserting its relation to the realm of transcendence may be regarded by some as beginning with a (rather grandiose) conclusion instead of with verifiable evidence. The claim here, however, is that it is not inappropriate to begin with a hypothesis that draws not only on modern insights but also on classical theological understandings of mysticism, which firmly asserted that true mysticism is rooted in the realm of transcendence. The hypothesis will attain the status of a conclusion only if evidence is marshalled that is acceptable and convincing (or at least potentially so) to modern and post-modern thinkers.

In a community of contemplative practitioners, it might be possible to share "evidence" of the realm of transcendence directly through shared mystical experience. In a community of scholars, however, evidence must be shared within the framework of names (terms and relations) for such experiences derived from the differentiation of interiority. An inquiry such as this one, then, must

---

[1]For Lonergan's use of the term "otherworldly," see *Method in Theology*, p. 242, where he wrote: "Religious loving is without conditions, qualifications, reservations . . . This lack of limitations, though it corresponds to the unrestricted character of human questioning, does not pertain to this world. Holiness abounds in truth and moral goodness, but it has a distinct dimension of its own. It is other-worldly fulfilment, joy, peace, bliss."

[2]The Lonerganian context of these terms, "below upward" and "above downward," is provided in Chapter 4.

[3]Cf. Lonergan, *Method in Theology*, pp. 105, 242, 342.

draw its evidence primarily from the realm of interiority. This chapter will explore this evidence and seek to place it within an explanatory theoretical framework.

To differentiate interiority means to heighten one's self-presence and, on that basis, to recognize clearly the distinctions among experience, understanding, judgment, and decision. It then becomes possible to know which realm of meaning (common sense, theory, interiority, praxis, or transcendence) one is operating in. Many misunderstandings of mysticism result from the failure adequately to carry through this process. Before entering into the detailed discussion of mystical experience from the point of view of interiority, we first need a perspective on the relationships among the various realms of meaning. An adequate understanding of mystical experience will require a coordination of insights related to several realms of meaning.

As noted, the key to an understanding of mystical experience is a correct assessment of its relation to the realm of transcendence. For Lonergan, the primary evidence of the realm of transcendence is the transcendental exigence.[4] The transcendental exigence is the drive toward ultimacy--ultimate intelligibility, ultimate value, ultimate love, ultimate wholeness, etc. It operates within every other exigence (systematic, critical, methodical) and every other natural human drive or force, instigating the restlessness that is never totally satisfied with less than the ultimate. Although the name "transcendental exigence" is obviously a theoretical term, it is based in the concrete experience of that ceaseless longing for "more" that is so well expressed in Augustine's well-known phrase, "Our hearts are restless, Oh God, until they rest in Thee."[5]

---

[4]For a more complete discussion, see the section in Chapter 3 entitled "The Subject in Love: Transcendence and Religion."

[5]*The Confessions of St. Augustine* I,1 (1), trans. John K. Ryan (Garden City, NY: Image Books, 1960). See also Lamb, *History, Method and Theology*, pp. 186, 486f.

Religious conversion is the concrete appropriation of the transcendental exigence within a human life. The particular character of mystical experience is that it is, in a unique way, a fulfillment of the transcendental exigence. Mystical experience is not so much an experience "of" something as a revelation of what grounds all experience; that is, it is not so much an experience within intentional consciousness as an opening up to the transcendent ground of consciousness. Experienced as an "interconnection of consciousnesses"[6] with the divine at the very foundation of one's being, mystical experience has a character of ultimacy that is not approached within any other realm of experience.

As noted above, misunderstandings of mystical experience often result from a combination of an inadequate differentiation of interiority and an incorrect assessment of the meaning of "transcendence." For example, if an experience of ultimacy is only understood within the realm of common sense, it is likely to be interpreted as the activity of some particular "part" of the human being, such as an "inner sense," "spiritual intuition," or "soul." In this case the realm of transcendence is given a specific location within the structure of the world.

A temptation for those more intellectually inclined is to attempt to understand the experience of ultimacy primarily within the realm of theory. One who has assimilated the theoretical stucture of Lonergan's basic phenomenology of the subject might interpret the experience of ultimacy as pure "experience" in the sense of the first operation of intentional consciousness.[7] Like the common sense interpretation, this way of speaking may have some validity in a limited context--in this case, the theoretical discussion of the operations of intentional

---

[6]James R. Price III, "Lonergan and the Foundation of a Contemporary Mystical Theology," *Lonergan Workshop* 5 (1985), pp. 187-88. See detailed discussion in the following subsection.

[7]For discussion of this meaning of "experience," see "The Subject-as-Subject" in Chapter 3.

consciousness. It cannot, however, provide an adequate account of mystical experience, which transcends intentional consciousness.

A more subtle misunderstanding may occur when differentiation reaches the point of recognizing the realm of interiority. In interiority, one begins to appropriate one's non-objectifiable self-presence. In doing this one is getting in touch with what might be called "natural transcendence" or the "relative ground of consciousness"--that is, consciousness-as-conscious as the ground of all one's intentional activity. The realm of transcendence, however, is the absolute ground of this relative ground. If this distinction is not made, it is likely that the experience of ultimacy will be relegated to the realm of the "noumenal."

As experienced in the realm of interiority and as critically understood on that basis, the realm of transcendence is indeed "noumenal" if that term is taken to mean that transcendence cannot become an object of intentional consciousness. From the perspective of intentional consciousness, the apophatic "not this, not that" or "nada, nada" is the most adequate articulation of mystical experience. Yet the noumenal quality of mystical experience need not be seen only as an absence or lack of intelligible evidence; it can also be construed as evidence in itself for the transcendent nature of the experience.

Such a perspective only arises, however, from a correct theoretical understanding of "transcendence." In order to understand mystical experience adequately, one needs both the data of interiority and a theory that correctly construes that data. The core of such a theory derives from an "inverse insight"[8] facilitated by the notion of mediation: transcendence, unlike everything else that exists, cannot ever be understood as one among many parts. As a critical category, transcendence does not mean "pure" transcendence existing in some "place" beyond the concrete and seeking a way into the concrete; rather, it refers to the whole, the ultimate, the totality, as transcending, including and being mediated in all the parts. Thus, the "realm of

---

[8]On "inverse insight," see Lonergan, *Insight*, pp. 21-23. The term is also defined in Chapter 3 above, under "The Subject as Self-Transcending."

transcendence" is the immediacy of the ground of being which is being mediated in all that exists.

A fully explanatory perspective requires terming the realm of transcendence a "highest level" or an "absolute whole," because--as discussed above--no thing, system, etc. can be independent of or "over against" transcendence. While from a perspective within a lower system--for example, the system of human consciousness--transcendence may well appear to operate as a distinct "system," in itself it is the whole of which all systems at all levels are mediations.

The "transcendental exigence" which Lonergan adduces as evidence of the realm of transcendence is really the dynamism of the whole as a whole. It is the self-mediating activity of the total "system" of being, which is "higher level" to all the systems in creation. Thus, even as it operates alongside of and within every other exigence, the transcendental exigence in itself is truly transcendental: that is, it does not substitute itself in the place of the autonomous operation of other exigences or natural forces operative at any other level of human life.[9]

Strictly speaking, then, it is not possible to "locate" transcendence within the data of intentional experience. When interiority is differentiated, however, the data of intentional experience can provide evidence for a *theorem* of transcendence. A theorem does not claim to point out or provide access to new data; rather, it is an insight into how to organize the given data in a way that accounts for all the observed phenomena. As Lonergan said in another context, a theorem is

> something known by understanding the data already apprehended and not something known by adding a new datum to the apprehension . . . . something like the discovery of gravitation and not something like the discovery of America.[10]

---

[9]See Lamb, *History, Method, and Theology*, pp. 191-92.

[10]Lonergan, *Grace and Freedom*, p. 143; cf. also ibid., p. 16.

The theorem of transcendence states that there is a transcendent ground of all experience which is the "whole" underlying the coherence of and among all possible intentional experiences. Our preliminary position is that mystical experience can only be understood by affirming such a theorem. The evidence for the validity of this position is, first of all, the inadequacy of any explanatory construct that accounts only for those expressions of mystical experience which can be apprehended at an intentional level. More positive evidence will be developed in the following section, in which we will do a more detailed analysis of mystical experience from the point of view of interiority.

B. Differentiating Religious Conversion

The preceding section has provided a theoretical perspective on the relationship between mystical experience and the realm of transcendence. In *Method in Theology*, Lonergan spoke of the possibility of a conscious differentiation of this realm.

> Quite distinct from [the] objectifications of the gift of God's love in the realms of common sense and of theory and from the realm of interiority, is the emergence of the gift as itself a differentiated realm. It is this emergence that is cultivated by a life of prayer and self-denial and, when it occurs, it has the twofold effect, first, of withdrawing the subject from the realm of common sense, theory, and other interiority into a "cloud of unknowing" and then of intensifying, purifying, clarifying, the objectifications referring to the transcendent whether in the realm of common sense, or of theory, or of other interiority.[11]

Even though the realm of transcendence is strictly "noumenal" in relation to intentional consciousness, Lonergan indicates here that it is nevertheless possible for consciousness to become reorganized around an "experience" of this realm. The present section seeks to develop a

[11]Lonergan, *Method in Theology*, p. 266.

set of terms and relations which can better articulate the type of experience to which Lonergan refers in this text.

The Mystical Dimension of Religious Conversion

Lonergan's standard term for the reorganization of consciousness around an experience of the transcendent is "religious conversion." In *Method,* Lonergan defined religious conversion as conversion "to a total being-in-love as the efficacious ground of all self-transcendence."[12] James R. Price III has noted, however, that Lonergan did not consistently transpose his discussion of religious conversion into the categories of interiority.[13] It is only when we make this transposition that it becomes possible to clarify the distinction between garden-variety religious conversion and the extraordinary transformation experienced by the "mystics."

Often Lonergan referred to religious experience in a combination of common sense and doctrinal language, i.e., "God's love flooding our hearts."[14] Price suggests that consistent transposition into the language of interiority begin by noting the crucial difference between two of the most common phrases Lonergan used to speak about religious conversion. The two are "God's love flooding our hearts"--a phrase that suggests an experience in which the activity is all on the side of God--and "being in love with God"--a phrase suggesting an experience in which all human faculties are aroused and active at the deepest levels. Lonergan himself did not make a consistent distinction between these, but Price finds in the two phrases a basis for differentiating Lonergan's notion of religious experience into two distinct kinds of experiences, namely, "religious consciousness" and "mystical consciousness."

---

[12]Lonergan, *Method in Theology*, p. 241; cf. also Chapter 3 under "The Subject in Love."

[13]Price, "Foundation," p. 167.

[14]See, for example, Lonergan, *Method in Theology*, p. 105.

Religious consciousness, says Price, corresponds to "being-in-love." It is a form of intentional consciousness that is characterized particularly by judgments of value in which the value apprehended is ultimate--that is, God. He quotes Lonergan, who wrote that "being in love with God" is "the type of consciousness that deliberates, makes judgments of value, decides, acts responsibly and freely."[15] Religious consciousness, then, is the full activation of intentional consciousness in explicit existential response to God's love. It is "a type of consciousness on the level of responsibility. As such, it is an intentional response to the apprehension of the transcendent grounding of one's own intentionality."[16]

Mystical consciousness, on the other hand, corresponds to "God's love flooding our hearts." It is a "resting" in God analogous to the primordial intersubjectivity discussed in Chapter 3, in which there is a "we" that precedes the distinction of one subject from another. It is

> not the intentional awareness of an object, but an interconnection of consciousnesses . . . an experience of vital union with a consciousness the nature of which radically transcends the human. . . . the vital union of an individual's consciousness-as-conscious with its conscious ground.[17]

Price's distinction corresponds to the hypothesis being developed in this project: the ground of the subject, prior to the differentiation of subject and object, is a state of primordial intersubjectivity that is open to a state of "mystical intersubjectivity" with its own transcendent ground. Mystical experience, then, involves a conscious but non-intentional awareness of the transcendent ground of consciousness. What Lonergan

---

[15]Lonergan, *Method in Theology*, p. 107; Price, "Foundation," p. 169.

[16]Price, "Foundation," p. 183.

[17]Ibid., pp. 187-88. In later work Price has added additional nuances to his definition of "mystical consciousness"; see the following subsection.

called "differentiation of the realm of transcendence" is the reorganization of intentional consciousness by such an experience.

Price's distinction of two dimensions of consciousness within what Lonergan calls "religious conversion" is central for this inquiry. Further distinctions, based on further analysis on the level of interiority, will be made in the following subsection. First, however, we return briefly to the realm of theory to grasp the significance of this basic distinction in relation to our previous discussion of the theorem of mediation.

The applicability of the theorem of mediation to religious conversion is clearly suggested when Lonergan says of "being-in-love with God" that though it is "not the product of our knowing and choosing, it . . . manifests itself in acts of kindness, goodness, fidelity, gentleness, and self control."[18] Lonergan here describes religious conversion as having its source in the non-intentional immediacy of an "interconnection of consciousnesses" with divine love, but as being mediated in the intentional activity of a changed way of life. It is, in the traditional theoretical language of Christian theology, "operative grace" first, but secondarily effective in "cooperative grace"--i.e., "the gradual movement towards a full and complete transformation of the whole of one's living and feeling, one's thoughts, words and omissions."[19]

Religious conversion, then, involves two essential dimensions: a mystical dimension, which is the immediate ground and source of religious conversion, and an existential dimension, which is the mediation of religious conversion in human life. Because of the relationship of mediation, the two dimensions can be formally distinguished, but are not concretely separated, in any actual instance of religious conversion. Religious conversion is a transformation of the human being as a whole; when "the gift of God's love occupies the ground and root of the fourth and highest level of man's intentional

---

[18]Lonergan, *Method in Theology*, pp. 105-6.

[19]Ibid., p. 241.

consciousness,"[20] the "mystical" interconnection of consciousnesses is of a piece with its mediation in intentional operations. The rest of this chapter will be devoted to further explicating both the specificity of the mystical dimension and its integral participation in religious conversion as a whole.

The Range of "Mystics"

The approach taken here begins with a non-elitist application of the term "mystical." If a "mystical experience" is defined as "the vital union of an individual's consciousness-as-conscious with its conscious ground,"[21] such experiences are potentially available to anyone at any time--since both the individual's consciousness-as-conscious and the transcendent ground of consciousness are, by definition, "always there." This broad definition of mystical experience presumes that it occurs in at least a minimal degree in all persons who implicitly or explicitly open themselves to any degree of awareness of these depth dimensions of reality.

By this broad definition, "mystical experiences" can be explicit or implicit, known or unknown, as overwhelming as a bolt of lightening that knocks one off one's horse or as subtle as the background music to which one never alludes. Mystical experiences can and do happen to people who have no expectations of them, make no preparations for them, and do little or nothing in response to them. These experiences can nevertheless be "transforming" to the degree that they effect a conscious or unconscious shift in the individual's understandings, judgments and decisions.

Yet there are also individuals--"mystics" in a much narrower sense--for whom mystical experiences become the defining characteristic of their lives. These are individuals in whom what Lonergan called the "differentiation of the realm of transcendence" has progressed to its

---

[20]Ibid., p. 107.

[21]Price, "Foundation," p. 188.

culmination. Their consciousness and, indeed, their lives have been completely reorganized around--that is, transformed by--mystical experience. It will be important for our purposes to distinguish carefully between broad and narrow senses of the term "mystical transformation."

In its broad sense, as discussed above, mystical transformation is more or less synonomous with religious conversion; that is, it is simply the mediation of the mystical "gift of God's love" within the experience, understanding, judgment, and decisions of the existential subject. The narrow sense of mystical transformation, however, is that existential mediation as it occurs in one who is a "specialist" in mystical experience. The commonality and distinction between these two groups requires some delineation.

In a recent article, Price suggested that there are a variety of possible "spiritual mediations" of the transcendent ground of consciousness.[22] These include art, intellectual work, dreams, visions, and a variety of other forms. In popular use the term "mystical experience" is often used loosely to refer to many of these; almost any extraordinary religious phenomenon, especially if it happens in relation to someone already designated a "mystic," qualifies.

While under the broad definition of mysticism given above this has some validity, Price seeks to make some distinctions which will clarify who can properly be called a "mystic" in a narrower sense. All the religious mediations named in the preceding paragraph are experienced within the realm of intentional consciousness; the mystic in the narrow sense, however, must have an experience that transcends this realm. Price finds evidence in spiritual literature for two successive forms of such an experience, which he terms the "contemplative mediation" of the transcendent ground.

The first form of contemplative experience, which Price terms "bare consciousness," is "consciousness which is devoid of both operations and objects. . . . the subject is conscious, alert, aware, but

---

[22]James R. Price III, "Contemplation and Mediation: Mysticism, Philosophy, and Social Responsibility," *Journal of Religion* (forthcoming).

not conscious *of* anything."[23] This, however, is not yet mystical union, but only a state of "spiritual access" that must precede mystical experience *per se*. Price continues, describing the second, properly mystical form of contemplative experience:

> The defining characteristic of mystical consciousness is the explicit awareness of the transcendent emerging within or on the basis of bare consciousness. . . . The mystic's consciousness becomes conformed to, or mediated by, the operation of the transcendent ground itself.[24]

Mystical experience in the narrow sense, then, is a "reconfiguring" of the operations of consciousness so that they no longer mediate experience in the ordinary intentional manner, but instead are themselves direct mediations of the transcendent ground of consciousness. In mystical consciousness, as distinct from bare consciousness, the individual *does* have "experiences," "operations," "images," "knowledge," etc., but these are only analagously like their counterparts in intentional consciousness.[25] Mystical experience and knowledge literally cannot be "imagined," and yet within that state the transcendent will--in the words of Pseudo-Dionysius--"completely fill our sightless minds with treasures beyond all beauty."[26]

Thus, Price's discussion of the contemplative mediation provides a basis for clarifying the relation between the broad and narrow senses of "mystical transformation." The broad sense of mystical transformation occurs with any mediation of the transcendent ground

---

[23]James R. Price III, "Transcendence and Images: The Apophatic and Kataphatic Reconsidered," *Studies in Formative Spirituality* 11, no. 2 (May 1990), p. 198. See also Price, "Contemplation and Mediation."

[24]Price, "Transcendence and Images," pp. 198-99; see also idem, "Contemplation and Mediation."

[25]Price, "Transcendence and Images," pp. 198-200.

[26]*Pseudo-Dionysius: The Complete Works*, trans. Colm Luibhéid (New York: Paulist, 1987), p. 135.

within human experience; the narrow sense of mystical transformation is something that occurs only with the contemplative mediation.

The preliminary form of the contemplative mediation is "bare consciousness"--an experience of consciousness without operations or objects. True mysticism, however, goes beyond this to a "reconfigured" operation of consciousness which is a direct mediation of the transcendent ground. It is here that "mystical intersubjectivity"--the vital sense of one's own ground as in union with divine consciousness--becomes one's reality. As Price put it:

> [W]hen the contemplative state is fully developed and differentiated, the contemplative is aware of contemplation as a mutual mediation. . . . [in which] the contemplative's consciousness is mediated by the transcendent ground of consciousness.[27]

Mystical transformation in the narrow sense occurs when the individual has gone beyond the emptiness of "bare consciousness," in which all the usual forms of the mediation of consciousness are stilled, to the transformed fullness of "mystical intersubjectivity," in which the mutual mediation with the transcendent is consciously appropriated.

Consciousness and Transcendence

A controversy sometimes arises over whether contemplative experience, defined here as an opening to the transcendent ground, is "conscious" or not. One's answer to this question depends on whether one defines consciousness as necessarily being reflexive, that is, intentional. Indeed, pure "consciousness without an object" shares with unconsciousness the fact that it involves no "consciousness-of"--that is, intentional consciousness. It radically differs from unconsciousness, however, in that there is a form of awareness. This awareness is an opening to the

---

[27]Price, "Contemplation and Mediation."

"consciousness-as-conscious" that grounds all the reflexive activity of consciousness.

An understanding of these distinctions is helpful in clarifying the discussion about a possible "fifth level" of consciousness. Lonergan spent his whole life developing his theory of the differentiation of human consciousness on four basic levels: experience, understanding, judgment, and decision. Late in his life, in a somewhat offhand manner, he spoke of a "fifth level of consciousness" which would be the basis for the functional specialty of "spirituality."[28] This notion of the "fifth level" needs to be explored in the light of the preceding discussion.

For Lonergan, the differentiation of consciousness on the four basic levels is simply an increasing awareness, objectification, naming, and appropriation of what is happening in every act of intentional consciousness. The corresponding realms of meaning, therefore, emerge out of one another in a continous process. Common sense resolves into common sense and theory; common sense and theory resolve into interiority; and common sense, theory and interiority resolve into praxis.[29] To speak of a "fifth level," however, requires a shift into a new context.

It seems likely that what Lonergan meant by the "fifth level" was what in *Method* he had referred to as "transcendence as a differentiated realm." As discussed above, he called this an "emergence of the gift [of God's love] as itself a differentiated realm" that withdraws the subject

---

[28]Bernard Lonergan, response during question session, June 16, 1981, Lonergan Workshop, Boston College, Chestnut Hill, MA. Tape available, Lonergan Research Institute, Toronto. For further discussion, see Carla Mae Streeter, *Religious Love in Bernard Lonergan as Hermeneutical and Transcultural* (unpublished Th.D dissertation; Toronto: Regis College, 1986), pp. 158-174.

[29]For this use of the term "resolves," see Lonergan, *Method in Theology*, pp. 265-66. I have added here the realm of praxis, corresponding to decision. For discussion, see section entitled "The Subject as Objectified in Self-Appropriation" in Chapter 3.

from the realms of common sense, theory, and other interiority.[30] In the terms developed earlier in this inquiry, it is, fundamentally, a shift from intentional consciousness to consciousness-as-conscious. Its fruits may be an "intensifying, purifying, clarifying"[31] of intentional consciousness, but in itself it is of a different order.

As a common-sense label, "fifth level" makes sense because it points to the "beyondness" of the transcendent realm. It does not work, however, as an explanatory term. The position taken here is that calling this shift to consciousness-as-conscious a "fifth level" misrepresents its relation to the four basic levels. When one speaks of a "fifth" following four which have emerged as differentiations of a single order of experience (i.e., intentional experience), the tendency is to subsume the fifth to the same order of experience. The transcendent realm, then, becomes another "thing" within the purview of intentional consciousness.

Transcendence in itself, however, can never be an object of intentional consciousness; it is the ground of consciousness, the whole from which consciousness and all other "parts" of creation emerge, and it is never appropriate to regard it as one part among other parts. What has been termed the "fifth level of consciousness" would be better called conscious differentiation of the ground of the four levels of consciousness.

C. Developing a Model of Mystical Transformation

A model, Lonergan wrote, is an "interlocking set of terms and relations" that is developed as an hypothesis in foundations and is then further

[30]Lonergan, *Method in Theology*, p. 266. For a fuller quotation, see above, "Differentiating Religious Conversion."

[31]Lonergan, *Method in Theology*, p. 266.

developed and verified in interaction with concrete data.[32] This section will work towards such a model. The goal will be to clarify the structural relations among the various terms and relations introduced so far in our effort to develop an explanatory perspective on mystical experience and transformation.

Linking General and Special Categories

The first task of this section is to indicate how it is possible to move from the general categories articulating the structure of the human subject to the special categories needed for explicitly theological reflection. The question at hand is where the strictly "intraworldly" or "natural" structures of the human subject intersect with what is "transcendent" or "supernatural." The distinctions made so far help to indicate where we may find such a bridge.

Longergan, reflecting on the Christian life of prayer and growth in Christ, discussed that intersection in a mixture of doctrinal and philosophical language:

> Each of us is to himself something immediate. It is what is meant by *Existenz*, oneself as one is, as capable of a decision that disposes of oneself, and yet as incapable of an absolute disposition. . . . It is not one's thinking about all that but each of us in his or her immediacy to himself or herself. In that immediacy there are supernatural realities, realities that do not pertain to our nature, that result from the communication to us of Christ's life. . . . This supernatural reality is something in us that is immediate and it becomes mediated in the life of prayer.[33]

In this text the term "supernatural realities" corresponds to what we have earlier termed the "transcendent ground of consciousness." What Lonergan here calls one's own immediacy to oneself (i.e., the "subject-

[32]Ibid., pp. 292-93.

[33]Lonergan, "Mediation of Christ in Prayer," pp. 15-16.

as-subject") can be termed the "relative ground of consciousness," while the supernatural dimension is the transcendent ground of that relative ground. The clue that this text gives us is that the bridge between "natural" and "supernatural," and between general and special categories, is to be found in a correct assessment of the "relative ground of consciousness"--the immediacy of the subject in him/herself, within which a mediation of the transcendent ground of consciousness can take place.

Lonergan spoke of this when he called the immediacy of the subject an "openness"--an openness to self-mediation in the operations of intentional consciousness *and* an openness to a mutual self-mediation with the transcendent ground of consciousness. In the essay "Openness and Religious Experience," Lonergan called openness "the pure desire to know . . . the wonder that is the beginning of all science and philosophy . . . the natural desire to know God by his essence." He continued:

> . . . openness as fact is the inner self, the self as ground of all higher aspiration.
>
> Openness as achievement is the self in its self-appropriation and self-realization.
>
> Openness as gift is the self entering into personal relationship with God.[34]

Spelling this out in terms of the notion of mediation: the immediacy of the subject-as-subject is an openness to self-mediation in the self-transcending operations of intentional consciousness. The immediacy of the subject-as-subject, however, is also an openness to the mediation of the transcendent immediacy of the transcendent ground of consciousness.

From a theoretical perspective, then, the link between general and special categories is found in the immediacy or "openness" of the subject-as-subject. Our next task is to return to the perspective of

[34]Lonergan, "Openness and Religious Experience," in *Second Collection*, pp. 199, 201.

interiority to discover whether verification of this link can be found there. This task is complicated by the fact that, if there really is a "point of intersection" between two distinct mediations--the self-mediation of the created subject and the self-mediation of the transcendent ground *in* the created subject--the two will be inextricably intertwined in all mediated experience. This makes it extremely difficult to distinguish between what is a mediation of the "general" structures of the subject (self-mediation) and what is a "special" mediation of the transcendent. For this reason our analysis focuses on the case of the mystic in the narrow sense. In the mystic, who has experientially differentiated the "special" mediation to its fullest degree, there must be a clear experiential marker indicating where one crosses the line between "general" and "special."

Karl Rahner's comments on the relation between the ordinary "graced" person (i.e., one in whom mediation of the transcendent occurs but is not consciously differentiated) and the extraordinary mystic indicate how this is so. Rahner points out that the "specific difference" in the experience of the extraordinary mystic cannot be the fact of transcendence being mediated at the root of the individual's being, for this is equally a factor in the lives of all who are open to grace. In this, Rahner affirms a view similar to our "broad" definition of mystical experience.[35] The unique factor in the extraordinary mystic (that is: mysticism in the narrow sense), then, must be a specific psychological differentiation, which Rahner speaks of as the "natural phenomena of suspension of the faculties."[36]

The suspension of the faculties, in Price's terminology, is "bare consciousness"--consciousness without operations or objects. By calling it a "natural phenomenon" and an "extraordinary psychological differentiation," Rahner asserts that this state of consciousness does not

---

[35]See above, p. 125.

[36]Karl Rahner, "Mystical Experience and Mystical Theology," *Theological Investigations* 17 (1973), especially pp. 95-99.

necessarily require an explanation in terms of any "supernatural" activity. That is: to explain "bare consciousness" one need not necessarily postulate an "above downward"[37] mediation from the realm of transcendence; one can speak instead of an asymptotic approach of human consciousness to its own ground. Employing the notion of emergence,[38] bare consciousness would then appear as a leap to a new level (indeed, a "relatively transcendent" level) within the natural, "below upward" process of self-appropriation.

Insofar as bare consciousness is a psychological differentiation, it is at least partly able to be "acquired" through practices of meditation and concentration. It is, in this sense, a "mediated return to immediacy"[39] in that the contemplative employs the mediating knowledge of a contemplative tradition both in learning how to stabilize him or herself in the immediacy of consciousness-as-conscious, and in interpreting this experience within other realms. Insofar as this differentiation of consciousness merely empties out the operations of intentional consciousness--without essentially reconfiguring the way consciousness operates--it is in continuity with the basic structures of the subject as presented in Chapters 2-4, and hence with the basic structure of the "general categories."

At the same time, however, bare consciousness is the necessary (but not sufficient) condition for the extraordinary mediation of the transcendent experienced by the mystic (in the narrow sense). This "mystical consciousness" is not in any sense acquirable; it is not accessible to the subject from within the subject's own structures. To access it in this way is as impossible as "lifting oneself by one's own bootstraps"; structures cannot fully encompass their own ground.

---

[37]On the meaning of "above downward" and "below upward" in Lonergan's thought, see Chapter 4.

[38]See the discussion of "emergence" in Chapter 4.

[39]Lonergan, *Method in Theology*, pp. 29, 77.

Hence, bare consciousness is--from the point of view of interiority--the "bridge" between the general categories and the special theological categories required to explain mysticism. It corresponds to what Lonergan called "openness" or the immediacy of the subject-as-subject. Both Rahner and Price spell this out, indicating how this "bridge" is such that it not only reveals how it is possible for the "natural" human subject to be open to the transcendent in extraordinary cases (i.e., mystical experience in the narrow sense), but also how the transcendent is operative in human life even when it is completely unrecognized. Rahner states that his own view is that

> man's transcendental nature was always and everywhere and from the very beginning finalised and given radical form by God's self-communication in grace . . . [so that] . . . Every natural act of suspension of the faculties and so forth, would . . . always and everywhere be elevated by grace.[40]

Price expresses a similar view: The natural substratum and "specific difference" of the contemplative state is an experience of consciousness-as-conscious without objects or operations, but this state itself is--whether recognized as such or not--a mediation of the transcendent ground of consciousness and so a "mutual mediation" with the divine. In mystical experience in the narrow sense, this mutual mediation is explicitly and consciously appropriated.

Correlation with Christian Doctrine

Doctrines, says Lonergan, express judgments of fact and judgments of value.[41] Doctrines express these judgments in terms of the special theological categories that have been developed through work in the functional specialty of foundations. At this point we can briefly consider

---

[40]Rahner, "Mystical Experience and Mystical Theology," p. 97.

[41]Lonergan, *Method in Theology*, p. 132.

how the categories developed so far in this inquiry might reconfigure the expression of some Christian doctrines.

A traditional Christian theological anthropology, expressed in biblical language, affirms that humans are created in the "image and likeness" of God (Gen 1:26-27) and, in addition, are cabable of being gifted with the Spirit who alone "knows what lies at the depths of God" (1 Cor 2:11). Expressed in the terminology of the present inquiry, these doctrinal statements state as a judgment of fact that the transcendent divinity is mediated in the human being, and, additionally, that humans have a potential openness to the very immediacy of God.

Part of the hypothesis being explored here is that the "openness" that constitutes the immediacy of the subject-as-subject is itself the primordial expression or mediation of divine being in humanity. Correlated with the biblical language of theological anthropology: the "image and likeness" of God in humanity is "consciousness-as-conscious," which is a mediation of the transcendent ground of consciousness and, as such, an openness to all of being.[42] When it has been appropriated as "bare consciousness," this immediacy of the human subject can be transformed into a direct and conscious mediation of the transcendent ground--that is, of the "Spirit of God."

Such an interpretation would appear to gain support from another text where Lonergan spoke of God as "mediated" in the world:

> To conceive God as originating value and the world as terminal value implies that God too is self-transcending and that the world is the fruit of his self-transcendence, the expression and manifestation of his benevolence and beneficence, his glory.[43]

Thus, Lonergan affirms that God is "self-mediating" in the sense that there is an immediate ground and its integral mediations or expressions.

---

[42]Cf. Lonergan's statement that "the correlative to the pure desire [i.e., openness] is being, *omnia*." Lonergan, "Openness," p. 200.

[43]Lonergan, *Method in Theology*, p. 116.

In the case of God, the immediate ground is the "supernatural" ground of all creation, and in some form or other all creation is included in the mediations of this ground. God's self-mediation reaches some kind of fulfillment in being fully received and enhanced within human beings,[44] and human self-mediation reaches a radical fulfillment in fully appropriating its own groundedness in God.

In speaking of God's "self-mediation," it is essential to keep in mind that this term does not necessarily imply the existence of a delimited divine "self." As an explanatory term, "self-mediation" means that the reality in question is a whole that carries within itself its dynamism toward mediation in structure. The essential affirmation here is that God *is* mediated, and that that mediation arises from a dynamism innate to God (not, that is, from any external source).

It would require far more space than it is possible to give here to work out all the implications of applying this notion of "self-mediation" to God. As always when speaking of God, use of this terminology must be acknowledged to be to some degree "analogical." That is: the terminology is not fully adequate to the reality of God, but it does accurately articulate a dimension of that reality as reflected in other, more humanly accessible realities. Obviously, it would require a lengthy treatise to work out a full theology of God and the world, with due respect for such concerns of orthodoxy as the radical distinction between the two, the fact that some mediations are more immediate to God than others, etc. Our concern here is simply to confirm whether the terminology of a "mutual self-mediation" between God and the human being has the potential to be correlated with more traditional statements of Christian doctrine.

Within the Christian tradition the doctrine of the incarnation, which states that the transcendent has in fact been mediated historically

---

[44]This does not necessarily imply that God "needs" human beings in order to fulfill self-mediation, or that there may not be other dimensions of creation in which God's self-mediation is more complete. What is being affirmed is that, if humans are in any sense a mediation of God, that mediation can have degrees of fulfillment depending on the cooperation of the individual with it.

as a human being and that human beings have access to God through that mediation, gives the notion of mutual self-mediation between human and divine a very concrete expression. As Lonergan put it:

> Christianity involves not only the inward gift of being in love with God but also the outward expression of God's love in Christ Jesus dying and rising again. In the paschal mystery the love that is given inwardly is focused and inflamed, and that focusing unites Christians not only with Christ but also with one another. . . . There is an intersubjective element to love that is present in Christianity, inasmuch as God is expessing his love in Christ as well as giving you the grace in your heart, and this element is missing when the Incarnate Lord is missing.[45]

In other words, Christian doctrine affirms that the transcendent divinity is mediated in Christ's life, death, and resurrection, as well as in everything that has flowed from that within the intersubjective structures of this world--specifically, the Church both as institution and as mystical communion. This affirmation grounds the concrete application of the notion of mutual self-mediation within the Christian life of prayer.

> The notions we have developed of self-mediation and mutual self-mediation can be applied to our own subjectivity, to what is immediate within us. . . . Their ontological immediacy is promoted to an intentional immediacy through the life of prayer. Christ is mediator in the life of prayer insofar as that life itself is a transition from the immediacy of spontaneity through the objectification of ourselves in acts. The acts of living and the acts within praying are referred to Christ. By that process we perfect ourselves, by a self-mediation that is related to another person.[46]

Christian prayer, then, is an appropriation within one's own self-mediation of the mediation of the transcendent in Christ. It is a "mutual self-mediation" in that in this activity both the self-mediation of the

---

[45]Lonergan, *Philosophy of God*, pp. 10, 20; cf. also 67.

[46]Lonergan, "Mediation of Christ in Prayer," p. 19.

created subject and the self-mediation of the transcendent reach a fulfillment which neither can reach without the other.

While the transcendent ground of consciousness need not be mediated in a historical person for it to be mediated, Christian doctrine affirms that this has in fact occurred in Jesus Christ. For this reason Christians express their experience of mutual self-mediation with the transcendent in terms of a personal intersubjectivity with Christ, who is both an individual human being and the unique mediation of the divine. The present inquiry is a study of a Christian mystical text; the researcher is Christian and is working within a Christian theological context. In this context, the doctrinally-based language of personal intersubjectivity is normative. Nevertheless, it is important to emphasize that this language is here being placed within a larger explanatory context, namely, the notions of mediation of the transcendent ground of consciousness and of mutual self-mediation between divine and human.

A Schematic Review of the Proposed Model

This section will summarize as schematically as possible the terms and relations that have been proposed so far in our effort to develop an explanatory theory of mystical transformation. Although this will involve some repetition of what has been said above, it is hoped that it will provide the reader with easier access to the proposed model.

The human being is a self-mediating subject. The immediate ground of this self-mediation is the "subject-as-subject" or "implicit consciousness." Even in its most primitive forms, the self-mediating subject is intersubjective; a "primordial intersubjectivity" precedes and underlies any differentiation of subject and object. The *telos* of human self-mediation is also intersubjective; fulfilled "mediated intersubjectivity" is the existential subject in community.

The immediate ground of consciousness is also an openness to the transcendent ground of consciousness. In fact, the immediate ground of consciousness is, in itself, a mediation of the transcendent ground of consciousness. In religious experience the individual becomes aware of this mediation within intentional consciousness. This is "mystical experience in the broad sense." When this awareness is appropriated within the individual's existential self-mediation, we can speak of religious conversion or of "mystical transformation in the broad sense."

"Mystical experience in the narrow sense" occurs when the individual becomes conscious of the mediation of the transcendent ground of consciousness *at* the level of his or her immediate ground of consciousness. A prerequisite of this is passing beyond intentional consciousness to a state of "bare consciousness"--that is, consciousness without objects or operations. In this state the operations of consciousness can be mystically reconfigured to become a more direct mediation of the transcendent ground of consciousness. This is "mystical transformation in the narrow sense."

Mystical experience in the narrow sense is not an experience of God as an "object," nor of oneself as a sheer "subject," but of a state of "mystical intersubjectivity." It is a non-objectifiable presence of the divine at the level of one's own self-presence. It can be called a "mutual mediation with the divine" in that it is a modification of the self-mediation both of the individual human subject and of the divine within creation.

Mystical transformation in either the broad or the narrow sense is mediated within the normal structure of the subject's self-mediation. Because it involves an increasing awareness and appropriation of the subject's own ground, genuine mystical transformation is also an increasing fulfillment of the subject's self-mediation as an existential subject in community. In plainer language: mystical transformation increases both autonomy (capacity for existential self-determination and commitment) and communality (capacity to give oneself for the sake of structures of shared meaning, shared goods, etc.).

D. Mystical Transformation and the Structures of the Subject

Part II of this inquiry explores whether the model developed above can be verified and expanded in interaction with the data of a concrete instance of mystical transformation. This will involve two analyses of the data. The first will be an interiority analysis, which will check the validity of the basic structure of terms and relations that has been set up in this chapter to clarify the specificity of mystical experience and transformation. The second will be a psychoanalytical analysis, which will test the claim that this transformation, which is specifically mystical and thus not reducible to the terms of the general structures of human intersubjectivity, is nevertheless mediated within them. This concluding section of this chapter, by schematically exploring how mystical transformation is related to the general structures of the human subject, prepares the way for that second step.

The Psychological Mediation of Mystical Transformation

Human subjects as we know them are always embodied. The body, as a physical reality, is in a complex relation of mutual mediation with the entire physical universe as a totality. The consciousness of the embodied subject is necessarily mediated within the experience of that body with its myriad explicit and implicit relationships to other realities. The subject's ongoing integration of that complex experience makes up the psychological stream of consciousness.

The "psychological realm," then, is the concrete horizon of the human subject. As such, it is the mediation in the world of the consciousness which is immediate in the subject-as-subject. The concrete manifestation of everything that has been discussed so far occurs within the psychological realm. This is equally true of infantile immediacy, mediated intersubjectivity, bare consciousness, mystical experience, or anything else that might be given a name within our framework of terms.

Empirical psychology usually regards its domain as the study of the mutual mediation of intentional consciousness and the world. It generally prescinds from any affirmations about the immediacy of the subject-as-subject, regarding the philosophical and ethical issues involved as outside its domain. Yet this does not mean that mystical transformation, which as defined here involves a mediated return to the immediacy of consciousness-as-conscious, cannot be studied from a psychological perspective.

Concretely, any actual experience of the immediacy of consciousness-as-conscious is a psychologically mediated experience. Even "bare consciousness," which is unmediated by any image, thought, affect, etc., is "mediated" in that it is a mediation of consciousness within the psyche and body of a human person. According to this position, if "bare consciousness" is experienced by a human being it is psychological in that it is a manifestation of consciousness within the world.

One could, of course, hypothetically postulate a state of consciousness that has no connection whatsover with any other reality experienced or known by human beings. Yet as soon as such a condition is in any way imaged, named, or claimed to have any other ramifications within a human embodied life, it is being given a psychological status. Thus, any state which can in any way be talked about involves a psychological dimension. Furthermore, the more claims one makes for the value or transformative impact of such a state, the more one must acknowledge that the role of the psychological dimension is constitutive.

Some might wish to define the psychological realm more strictly (i.e., in terms of time-and-space bound, intentional phenomena) and then debate whether the strictly contemplative dimension, which transcends intentional consciousness, is "psychological." Even by such a restricted definition, however, what has here been called "mystical transformation," which involves the full operation of the existential component of religious conversion (i.e., self-mediation) in conjunction with the mystical component (i.e. mutual self-mediation with divine transcendence), is psychologically manifested.

The view taken here also gives an explanatory perspective on why mystical experience cannot be reduced to its psychological concomitants. The psychological component of the experience is its mediation within the world; the immediate ground of the experience, however, is "otherworldly." The transcendent ground of consciousness is truly expressed within human consciousness, but cannot be reduced to it.

Mystical Transformation and Intersubjectivity

In Chapter 4 it was stated that fully developed human intersubjectivity[47] involves at least these three essential elements:

1. a relation with an other or others in which both parties are deeply implicated in the other's self-mediation--in other words, an intensive relationship of mutual self-mediation;
2. a high degree of existential commitment within this relationship;
3. a high degree of appropriation of one's self-mediation.

Part of the hypothesis being developed here is that genuine mystical experience enhances the development of intersubjectivity by contributing to the enhancement of all three of these elements. From what has been said above, it is not at all difficult to make a case for the latter two--that is, for the enhancement in the mystic of the degree of self-appropriation and of the capacity for existential commitment. These are basically corollaries of the hypothesis that opening to the transcendent ground of consciousness maximizes the operations of consciousness, and even raises them to levels beyond their power to achieve on their own.

---

[47]That is, "mediated intersubjectivity," or the intersubjectivity of the self-mediating existential subject. See sections in Chapter 4 on "Intersubjectivity, Meaning, and Mediation" and "Psyche, Spirit, and Community."

The statement that the mystic has an enhanced capacity for relations with an other or others in which both parties are deeply implicated in the other's self-mediation, however, requires a somewhat more involved discussion. In the popular mind "mystics" are commonly thought to be primarily focused on the individual spiritual journey, with relatively little attention given to the interpersonal, social or political dimensions of life.

While solitude is a strong component of most contemplative disciplines, and followers of such disciplines do focus strongly on their own and others' growth as individuals, this does not necessarily mean that they are "individualists." As Rahner put it:

> . . . the true law of things is not: The more special and distinct in character, the more separated, isolated and discontinuous from everything else, but the reverse: The more really special a thing is, the more abundance of being it has in itself, the more intimate unity and mutual participation there will be between it and what is other than itself.[48]

In this study, the principle articulated by Rahner has already been discussed in the section on the mutual self-mediation of subject and community, where it was pointed out that the full self-mediation of the existential subject necessarily creates community and the full self-mediation of a community necessarily fosters the free, community-making praxis of existential subjects.[49] Hence, if mystical experience is really enhancing the full self-mediation of the existential subject, it is also enhancing the creation of some form of community.

Rahner offers some clues as to why the intrinsic link between the mystic and community is often missed. A major reason, he suggests, is that we often fail to distinguish between three levels of individuality and

---

[48]Karl Rahner, "On the Significance in Redemptive History of the Individual Member of the Church," in *The Christian Commitment* (New York: Sheed and Ward, 1963), pp. 77-78.

[49]See "Meaning and the Formation of Community" in Chapter 4.

collectivity. Material or biological individuality corresponds to the collectivity of the society or group; spiritual or personal individuality corresponds to the collectivity of the community; theological individuality corresponds to the collectivity of union in Christ.[50] Many errors in understanding the relationships between individuals and collectivities result from trying to match one level of individuality to a different level of collectivity.

In the terminology employed in this inquiry, material individuality and group collectivity correspond to the "primordial intersubjectivity" which is native to the psyche.[51] Spiritual individuality and community collectivity correspond to the "mediated intersubjectivity" of which the spirit is capable. Theological individuality and the collectivity of union in Christ correspond to the "mystical intersubjectivity" of the mystic.

The third, then, is the defining form, the *sine qua non*, of the mystic's individuality and collectivity; it results from openness to the transcendent ground, in which all things find their true being. Since it is an error to try to correlate one level of individuality with a different level of collectivity, it is not quite correct to say that mystical transformation necessarily creates community; the link is not that direct. Drawing upon the terms and relations developed here, we say instead: mystical transformation is necessarily *mediated in* the formation of community.

Indeed, we can go further and suggest that the deeper the experience of mystical individuality and collectivity, the more it will be mediated in community and even in what Rahner calls "societies or groups"--that is, in social, political, institutional collectivities. In this way Rahner explains the foundation of the Church itself out of Christ's

---

[50]Karl Rahner, "The Individual in the Church," in *Nature and Grace* (New York: Sheed and Ward, 1964), p. 16.

[51]For a review of the terminology of "psyche" and "spirit," see "Basic Structure: Body, Psyche, Spirit" in Chapter 4. On the three levels of intersubjectivity, see "Meaning and Intersubjectivity" in the same Chapter.

mystical experience.[52] On a smaller scale, the same pattern is manifested in the activities of the numerous mystics who have founded religious communities and spiritual traditions, many of which have persisted in institutional form over long periods of time and under remarkably diverse conditions.

Community, then, is properly the fruit of the activity of existential subjects as personal, spiritual beings. Nevertheless, it is possible that it may also be a mediation as from "above downward" of experiences of mystical individuality and collectivity. At the same time, community is necessarily mediated or expressed on the psychic and societal levels as well. In the present study, we will explore a mystic's psychological manifestation of intersubjectivity to see whether we find therein evidence of a striking transformation toward the potential for community.

Mystical Transformation and Praxis

The above subsection offers a perspective on how mystical transformation is mediated in community, as from "above downward." A major question remains, however, about how this process works when viewed from "below upward"--that is, from the perspective of the activity of the human spirit. Praxis--free, existential, concrete commitment that is acted upon--is the full mediation and highest activity of the human spirit. It is in the praxis of self-mediating existential subjects that community is actually formed. How does openness to the transcendent ground make a difference in praxis, without annihilating the freedom which is the essence of the human spirit?

Here the insights of St. Ignatius Loyola and his modern interpreters offer an approach to answering that question. Ignatius' *Spiritual Exercises*[53] are a systematic approach to making an "election"

---

[52]See Rahner, "On the Significance," p. 91.

[53]*The Spiritual Exercises of St. Ignatius: A Literal Translation and A Contemporary Reading*, trans. and ed. by David L. Fleming (St. Louis: Institute of

that is consciously open to the will of God. In the terminology used here, we could say: Ignatius provides a methodical approach to the "below upward" process of entering upon praxis that is consciously open to the transcendent ground.

Karl Rahner clarifies the relationship between transcendence and the Ignatian election in terms of a modern philosophy of consciousness. Rahner describes the "consolation without cause," which for Ignatius is the chief factor in the discernment of God's will, as an experience where "there is no longer 'any object' but the drawing of the whole person, with the very ground of his being, into love, beyond any defined circumscribable object, into the infinity of God as God himself."[54]

This experience has been discussed earlier in this chapter as the "contemplative mediation" of the transcendent; it is an experience, first, of consciousness-as-conscious or "bare consciousness," and, on that basis, of the mystical mediation of the transcendent ground of consciousness.[55] Rahner expresses a similar explanation when he says that the "lowest level" of such an experience must be

> a synthesis of the intrinsic transcendent ordination of the mind to being in general, and of grace which supervenes to mould this natural unlimited receptivity and make of it a dynamic orientation toward participation in the life of God himself.[56]

Such an experience, says Rahner, does not directly reveal God's will for an individual. In order for it to do so, the experience would have to include as a constitutive part a "circumscribable object"--namely, the designation of the concrete path which this individual is to take. If this

---

Jesuit Sources, 1978).

[54]Karl Rahner, "The Logic of Concrete Individual Knowledge in Ignatius Loyola," in *The Dynamic Element in the Church* (New York: Herder & Herder, 1964), p. 135.

[55]See above, "Linking General to Special Categories."

[56]Rahner, "Logic," pp. 144-45.

were the case the experience would no longer be an example of the "contemplative mediation," which has been defined as a passage beyond intentional consciousness to consciousness-as-conscious.

The experience is the key to discernment of God's will, however, because it is by repeated juxtaposition of the "consolation without cause" and the potential object of choice that the individual can discover whether

> the two phenomena are in harmony, mutually cohere, whether the will to the object of Election under scrutiny leaves intact that pure openness to God in the supernatural experience of transcendence and even supports and augments it or weakens and obscures it.[57]

In Rahner's interpretation, then, the relationship between the realm of transcendence and praxis is that transcendence never dictates praxis, but it does concretely offer the human spirit the possibility of freely entering into praxis that is wholly in harmony with transcendence. Without the active mediation of transcendence that Christians designate "grace," this degree of harmony with transcendence would be impossible for the human spirit to discover, let alone to act upon.

Articulated in terms of emergence, the transcendent ground is the "higher level" (in this case, an absolute "highest level") which operates from "above downward" on all the "systems" (spiritual, psychological, physiological, etc.) of the human person. As discussed above in relation to psyche and spirit,[58] such an "above downward" influence does not distort, supercede, or extrinsically dominate the properly autonomous operation of the lower systems; rather, it sublates them and integrates them into levels of organization beyond their own capacity to achieve. Speaking of sublation, Lonergan wrote:

---

[57]Rahner, "Logic," p. 158.

[58]See "The Structure of Developing Intersubjectivity" in Chapter 4. Also note the discussion in the subsection on "'Below Upward' and 'Above Downward' Operations" of the problematic aspects of this "hierarchical" language.

> [W]hat sublates goes beyond what is sublated, introduces something new and distinct, puts everything on a new basis, yet so far from interfering with the sublated or destroying it, on the contrary needs it, includes it, preserves all its proper features and properties, and carries them forward to a fuller realization within a richer context.[59]

Spirit, then, is in an integral relation of mediation with its transcendent ground. The activities of spirit are not directly shaped by experiences of openness to the transcendent ground, but may be sublated into a larger context as from "above downward." Opening up to awareness of the transcendent ground of consciousness potentially can result in an increase in the coherence and fulfillment experienced in all the sublated systems, even when they are viewed strictly on their own terms. The operations of the spirit, culminating in praxis, can attain new levels of power and coherence in their own proper activities (experiencing, understanding, judging, committing) when the transcendental "above downward" factor is activated.

Conclusion

The way of understanding mystical experience that has been developed in this chapter is what Lonergan would call a "theorem": that is, it does not involve the discovery of new data, but rather brings to bear upon existing data a new set of mental coordinates that make it possible to make sense of the relationships within the data.[60] This theory of mystical experience and transformation has been developed out of Lonergan's general categories, and the data thus far alluded to have been primarily the "general" data of consciousness. It remains, therefore, to test, modify, and refine the theory through interaction with specific data provided by historical mystics.

---

[59]Lonergan, *Method in Theology*, p. 241.

[60]See Lonergan, *Grace and Freedom*, especially p. 16.

The goal of Part I has been to elaborate the theory--that is, to set up the "upper blade" of heuristic method. The goal of the remaining chapters will be to work with the lower blade; that is, to marshall the data and discover whether the new set of coordinates does, in fact, facilitate valuable insight into it.

PART II

TOWARD VERIFICATION

INTRODUCTION

Clarification of Subject Matter and Data

At this point it will be helpful to briefly review once again the basic hypothesis of this inquiry. Stated succinctly, it is that the transcendent ground of consciousness, which is the "foundation of foundations," is 1) best understood according to the analogy of a "state of intersubjectivity," and 2) most fully appropriated in the transformation consequent upon mystical experience. This "mystical transformation" will manifest as a positive transformation discernible in, but not reducible to, the world of mediated intersubjectivity.

If this view is accepted, one of the implications is that a prime source for theology becomes interpretation of mystics' written texts and/or other mediations of their experience within the world of intersubjective meaning. Such interpretation must be able to find evidence of the ultimately transcendent nature of mystical experience, while at the same time fully respecting the limitations inherent in its mediation within the intersubjective world.

Part II of this study is an experiment in this kind of interpretation of a text written by a recognized "mystic in the narrow sense."[1] The text chosen is the *Interior Castle*[2] of St. Teresa of Avila. Teresa is

[1]For the distinction between "narrow" and "broad" senses of mysticism, see "The Range of 'Mystics'" in Chapter 5,

[2]The Spanish title is *Moradas del Castillo Interior*, which would translate literally as "Dwelling Places of the Interior Castle." The traditional shortened English title is used here, except where specific reference is made to the Spanish text. The Spanish edition used for all Teresa's writings is *Santa Teresa de Jesús: Obras Completas*, 3 vols., ed. by Efrén de la Madre de Dios (Madrid: Biblioteca de Autores Cristianos, 1951-59). The English edition used is *The Collected Works of St. Teresa of Avila*, 3 vols., trans. and ed. by Kieran Kavanaugh and Otilio

widely acknowledged as an advanced Christian mystic, and she has been officially endorsed as a "Doctor of the Church," that is, a gifted and orthodox teacher of the truths of faith. The *Interior Castle* is her last and most thorough presentation of what she learned about mystical transformation over a lifetime of experience, study and reflection. It has been chosen for analysis here primarily because its subject matter, like that of this inquiry, is the nature of mystical experience and transformation. This chapter will provide biographical, historical, and literary background on the text, as well as a brief introduction to its imagery and teaching.

It is important to clarify some of the types of analysis of this text that the present inquiry does *not* claim to be undertaking. One of these is psychobiography. While it will not be possible to understand what the text says about the subject of mystical experience and transformation without knowledge about the time and place in which it was written, the life of the person who wrote it, the literary genre and sources, etc., none of these is the primary focus of *this* investigation.

Another investigation, still with the same subject matter, could take a more fully psychobiographical approach. In that case the relevant data would be everything that can be known from any source about the life of the mystic as it manifested mystical transformation. The present investigation, on the other hand, will employ psychobiography only as an adjunct to the study of what Teresa has to say about mystical transformation in the *Interior Castle*.

Just as this inquiry is not *per se* a study of the mystic's life, it is also not *per se* a strict textual study. A strict textual study would limit its analysis to discovering the sense of the text. The text itself, in other words, would be the subject matter of the inquiry. This study, on the other hand, takes the text as an ally in the inquiry into a common subject matter. The concern, then, is the *reference* of the text. Textual

---

Rodriguez (Washington, DC: ICS Publications, 1976-85). The *Interior Castle* is found in vol. 2 (1954) of *Obras Completas* and vol. 2 (1980) of *Collected Works*.

analysis, like psychobiography, is employed as an adjunct to the method being developed for the study of mystical experience and transformation.

Review of Method

As stated above, our project requires development of a method of interpreting the selected text that can both verify the specifically transcendental nature of mystical experience and respect the intraworldly nature of the forms in which it is mediated. The method developed here involves two distinct analyses and a concluding discussion of the implications of their correlation.

In the first half of Part II the text will be introduced and then analyzed from the point of view of interiority. Interiority, or awareness of consciousness and its operations, is a focus on the activity of spirit.[3] The basic claim is that the essence of mystical experience is a mediation in human consciousness of the transcendent ground of consciousness; we cannot study the transcendent ground of consciousness directly, but we can study the operations of consciousness (spirit) within which the transcendent ground is mediated. Through an intentionality analysis of changes in the mystic's operations of consciousness, we can establish what is specifically meant by the term "*mystical* transformation."

Another step, however, is required. Spirit is mediated in psyche; or, put another way, the operations of consciousness (spirit) are activities integrating and expressing themselves in the material content of consciousness (psyche). Mediated intersubjectivity is manifested in psychic formations that express and promote the sharing of life at the deepest levels. Hence, we can study changes in interhuman intersubjectivity through a study of changes in these psychic formations in relation to changes in the activity of spirit.

---

[3]For the meaning of the term "spirit" as used in this inquiry, see "Basic Structure: Body, Psyche, Spirit" in Chapter 4.

In the second half of Part II, the specifications of a psychological theory capable of mediating between the "primordial intersubjectivity" of the psyche and the "mediated intersubjectivity" of the spirit will be introduced and then applied in the analysis of the text. The psychological investigation will focus primarily on questions related to changes in the psychological construction of intersubjectivity during the course of the spiritual journey.

What evidence is there for changes in the way Teresa psychologically constructed her interpersonal and social relationships? Do these changes move in the direction of more positive, coherent, inclusive relationships? Do they suggest a move toward increasing freedom and maturity, psychologically defined? What insight does the psychological level offer in regard to the extraordinary spiritual and social impact of Teresa's life, her writings, and her work as a foundress? These are among the questions that the psychological analysis will consider.

The first step in our methodical analysis (the interiority analysis) studies the spiritual subject as operating. This step is a methodical "mediated return to immediacy" in that it establishes the primacy of the immediate subject-as-subject by knowledge and appropriation of its operations. As a study of mystical experience, however, it goes beyond this to examine how this immediacy of the subject-as-subject can become the locus of a mediation of the transcendent ground of consciousness, and how this is best understood analogically as a "state of intersubjectivity."

The second step (the psychological analysis) studies the psychological subject as concretely and constitutively related to objects, with "objects" primordially meaning, "other subjects."[4] This step is concerned with the concrete shape of the subject's intending of objects,

[4]Although it is somewhat disconcerting to the uninitiated, this use of the term "objects" to mean other personal subjects is traditional in psychoanalytic literature. A justification for this is the fact that the earliest and most foundational differentiation of "subject and object" in human life is, indeed, a differentiation of subject from subject--that is, of self from primary caretaker.

that is, how the subject's relations with objects (other existents) are in fact structured within consciousness. Despite the concern with objects, this remains a study of the *subject* (not of objects per se, nor of the subject as object-among-objects) because the perspective from which this relatedness is studied is strictly confined to that of the subject.[5]

Stated in terms of mediation, we could say that the first step focuses on the activity *of* mediation, while the second step focuses on the mediated consciousness of the mystic at its culmination "in the world." The first step, then, studies consciousness as mediating; the second, consciousness as mediated. My claim is that this double analysis provides evidence that mystical transformation and psychological intersubjectivity are intrinsically linked, yet also operate on different levels and so cannot be reduced to one another. A proper method for studying mysticism and its effects must take full cognizance of the difference of levels in order to avoid the reduction of phenomena on one level to that of another.

The concluding chapter will consider the degree to which the evidence of these textual analyses verifies the explanatory model which was set forth in Part I. On this basis, it will summarize the potential implications of this study for foundational theology, the psychology of religion, and spirituality.

---

[5]This important distinction will be more thoroughly examined in the subsection entitled "The Concept of the Selfobject" in Chapter 8.

CHAPTER 6

THE TEXT: TERESA'S *INTERIOR CASTLE*

A. The Life and Times of Teresa of Jesus

A Brief Biography

Teresa de Ahumada, whose religious name was Teresa de Jesús and who is commonly known today as St. Teresa of Avila, was born in 1515 in the Castilian town of Avila. Teresa was the third child born to Beatriz de Ahumada, who was the second wife of cloth merchant Alonso de Cepeda. There were two additional older children from Alonso de Cepeda's first marriage, and after Teresa would come seven younger ones. Of these twelve[1] siblings, the only girls were the oldest (María, b. 1506), the youngest (Juana, b. 1528), and Teresa (b. 1515). Teresa grew up in a world of boys; her closest companions were Rodrigo (b. 1513) and Lorenzo (b. 1519). Beatriz de Ahumada died shortly after Juana's birth in 1528, when Teresa was 13. Alonso de Cepeda, to whom Teresa was deeply attached, lived until 1543.

With great sorrow at leaving her family, Teresa entered the Carmelite convent of the Incarnation in Avila in 1535, at age 20. Shortly after her profession in 1537 she became very ill; in 1539 she

[1]Teresa herself says there were twelve (*Life* 1,3), but the names and biographies of only eleven are known.

nearly died, and subsequently was partially paralyzed for three years. While many commentators have assumed this to be an hysterical paralysis, a recent analysis by a pathologist concludes that Teresa suffered from an aggravated form of brucellosis (an infection and inflammation of the nervous and glandular systems caused by a bacteria transmitted by domestic animals).[2] The consequences of this illness plagued Teresa throughout her life, playing an important role in her frequent episodes of vomiting, headaches, and general ill health.

Although she experienced occasional glimpses of the higher states of prayer early in her religious life, during most of her first nineteen years as a religious Teresa seems to have been neither extraordinarily gifted nor extraordinarily devoted in regard to prayer. She suffered from much conflict over her own laxness and tepidity, and even gave up prayer for two years (1542-1544) out of "humility." In 1554, however, she had an intense conversion experience while praying before a graphic image of thc wounded Christ. From that time (age 39) until her death in 1582 (age 67), she developed rapidly in the highest mystical gifts. The "spiritual betrothal" came in 1556; intellectual visions began in 1559; imaginative visions and the wounding of the heart were given in 1560; and she received the grace of "spiritual marriage" in 1572.

Along with these mystical graces came a call to found a new monastery where the laxness and tepidity that characterized life at the Incarnation (and a great many other religious houses of the time) would not be the norm. Despite numerous obstacles, this dream was realized in 1562 when Teresa founded the monastery of San José (St. Joseph's) in Avila.

In the same year she was asked by her confessors and advisors to write an account of her life and prayer experiences. *The Book of Her*

---

[2]Avelino Senra Varela, "La Enfermedad de Santa Teresa de Jesús," *Revista de Espiritualidad* 41 (1982): 601-12.

Life[3] was written then and revised a few years later, in 1565. This book was held by her confessor, Domingo Báñez, OP, who would not permit the other nuns of St. Joseph's to read it. He did agree, however, that she could compose a second book just for the nuns. This was *The Way of Perfection*,[4] written in two versions during 1566. Teresa's first two major works, then, were written many years before she experienced the spiritual marriage and at a time when her vision of herself as a foundress was limited to the single community of San José de Avila.

During the following sixteen years she presided over the founding of fifteen more monasteries for nuns and two for friars. These communities became known as the "Discalced Carmelite reform." Her third major text, *The Book of Her Foundations*,[5] recounts the story of these foundings; it was begun in 1573 and completed shortly before her death in 1582.

Right in the midst of this whirlwind of travel and business affairs, she was in 1571 elected prioress of the still-unreformed Incarnation (her original monastery). Making the best of a difficult charge, she called John of the Cross to be the nuns' confessor and set out to gently set things in order in this massive and chaotic religious house. The following year (1572), while directed by John of the Cross, she received the culminating mystical grace, the spiritual marriage.

The book with which we are primarily concerned, *Moradas del Castillo Interior*, was written in 1577 during an imposed lull in her travels as foundress. Before discussing the specific events that

---

[3]The Spanish title is *Libro de su Vida*. This work will be referred to here as *Life*. It is found in vol. 1 (1951) of *Obras Completas* and vol. 1 (1976) of *Collected Works*.

[4]The Spanish title is *Camino de Perfección*. This work will be referred to here as *Way*. It is found in vol. 2 (1954) of *Obras Completas* and vol. 2 (1980) of *Collected Works*.

[5]The Spanish title is *Libro de las Fundaciones*. This work will be referred to here as *Foundations*. It is found in vol. 2 (1954) of *Obras Completas* and vol. 3 (1985) of *Collected Works*.

surrounded its composition, we must briefly review some relevant factors in the cultural and political milieu of the times.

Teresa's Milieu

The cultural and political reality of the time in which Teresa lived was much more complex than is conveyed by the simple term "the Golden Age." The reign of the Catholic monarchs, Ferdinand and Isabella, had at least superficially consolidated Spain religiously. Then in 1517 came Carlos I, under whom Castile became the center of a multiterritorial empire. Toward the end of his reign, however, Carlos began a process of nationalistic withdrawal and isolationism that accelerated under his successor Felipe II, who acceded to the throne in 1556. Meanwhile, Spain's enormous expansion overseas, especially in the Americas, fueled an intense crusading spirit in which Teresa fervently participated, though *a lo divino* (that is, in a spiritual, not secular, mode). Teófanes Egido summarizes his brief review of historical scholarship on this period by saying that for Castile, the years between 1560 and 1580--Teresa's peak years of activity--were "the best in its history."[6]

Yet there were dark sides to the glory of the Golden Age, and these influenced Teresa at least as much as did the cultural, intellectual and spiritual vibrancy of the era. Recent research has revealed that Teresa's father was a *converso*--a member of a family of Jews forcibly converted to Christianity during the Toledo persecution of 1485.[7] Like many of the *conversos*, Alonso de Cepeda was a member of the merchant class who was eager to enter the lower ranks of the nobility. In order to do so, the family had to make a concerted effort to obscure all traces of Jewish lineage.

---

[6]Teófanes Egido, "The Historical Setting of St. Teresa's Life," trans. Steven Payne and Michael Dodd, *Carmelite Studies* 1 (1980), p. 127.

[7]See the discussion and bibliography in Egido, "Historical Setting," pp. 122-82. For detailed discussion, see Homero Seris, "Nueva genealogía de Santa Teresa," *Nueva Revista de Filologia Hispanica* 10 (1956): 365-84.

This effort was motivated by both economic and cultural necessity, for throughout the sixteenth century "purity of blood" (that is, no Jewish or Moorish ancestry) was demanded of all who aspired to any degree of social acceptance, political or ecclesiastical power, or economic privilege. Subsequent to the Catholic monarchs' "cleansing" of Spain by the expulsion and/or forced conversion of all Jews and Moors, which culminated in 1492, purity of blood had become one of the two main components of Spanish culture's conception of "honor"; and without honor, a person lived in disgrace.

The other component of "honor," applying only to women, was sexual purity.[8] As a young teenager Teresa apparently endangered herself and her family in the latter regard through some brief--perhaps quite innocent--dalliance with a cousin (*Life* 2). This, added to the all-pervading family concern with hiding its "impure blood," made Teresa extraordinarily sensitive to the obsessive quality of the concern with "honor."

Teresa's family was on the whole very successful in hiding its lineage. The possibility of discovery was an ever-present threat, however, that influenced every decision made by the family or by its individual members. Though in all that she wrote she took great care never overtly to reveal the family secret, close analysis of Teresa's writings reveals that one of her most consistent themes is the rejection of this cultural obsession.[9]

One of Teresa's closest confidants, Jerónimo Gracián--who did not know the truth about her heritage--wrote that she had told him that "it grieved her more to have committed a venial sin than if she had been descended from the vilest and lowest peasants and Jewish converts in the whole world."[10] She herself stated as a principle that "I have always

---

[8]Egido, "Historical Setting," p. 150.

[9]Ibid., pp. 154-58.

[10]Jerónimo Gracián de la Madre de Dios, *Espíritu y revelaciones y maner de proceder de la Madre Ana de San Bartolomé, examinado por el P., su confesor*, ed.

esteemed virtue more than lineage."[11] Téofanes Egido calls this "a revolutionary basic axiom ahead of its time, virtually subversive, which is difficult to appreciate today."[12] Teresa's response to her own potential marginality was to become a sort of closet social protester, firmly rejecting the validity of one of the most basic tenets of her culture's organization of meaning.

The expansive cultural and intellectual trends of the time also had a dark side. Carlos I, who was soon to become the emperor Charles V of Hapsburg, was installed as king in 1517, just two years after Teresa's birth. During the years of his reign Castile opened up to Europe and to the possibility of a pluralistic society. Erasmus, who was challenging the hegemony of the scholastic intellectual worldview with his new historical and humanist philosophy, was widely read and acclaimed during the first fifteen years of Carlos' reign. After that, however, political and theological counterattacks led to increasing isolationism. This hardened into a rigid policy with the ascent of Felipe II to the throne in 1556.

During the years of Teresa's maturity when she was involved in all the politics of her Reform, Spain's political isolationism went hand-in-hand with a concerted theological and ecclesiastical reaction against humanist and other anti-scholastic influences. As Ciriaco Morón-Arroyo summarizes, "The Scholastics reacted with all theoretical and political means in their power in order to sustain what were, in their opinion, the unchangeable pillars of the Church. Thus a struggle ensued which in Spain is the cornerstone of intellectual life throughout the sixteenth century."[13] The Inquisition, which since 1478 had been hard at work

---

Silverio de Santa Teresa, *Biblioteca Mistica Carmelitana* 17 (Burgos, 1933): 259, as cited by Egido, "Historical Setting," p. 134.

[11]*Foundations* 15,15.

[12]Egido, "Historical Setting," p. 165.

[13]Ciriaco Morón-Arroyo, "'I Will Give You a Living Book': Spiritual Currents at Work at the Time of St. Teresa of Jesus," *Carmelite Studies* 3 (1984), p. 100.

uprooting secret practitioners of Judaism and Islam, took aim with a vengeance against humanists, protestants, and illuminists. It was the 1559 index of the inquisitor Valdés that deprived Teresa of most reading matter on spiritual topics in the vernacular;[14] allowing "idiots" (those who did not know Latin) to read these was regarded as too dangerous.

Two aspects of the spiritual ferment in sixteenth century Castile which are particularly relevant to the work of St. Teresa are the general movement for the reform of religious institutions and the illuminist movement. Both of these were widespread and extremely influential in the Church of that time and place.

While the general reform movement of the era had many manifestations, including, among others, the foundation of the Jesuits by Ignatius of Loyola, its most immediate impact on Teresa came through the influence in Avila of the reforming crusade of Juan de Avila.[15] Juan de Avila, known as "Maestro Avila," was actually from La Mancha, but he corresponded regularly with a group of religious reformers in Avila who strove to implement his ideas. Francisco de Salcedo, the "saintly gentleman" whom Teresa consulted about her prayer life in 1554 (*Life* 23,6) and who became one of her closest friends, belonged to the group and introduced her to Gaspar Daza, who was its head. Daza, a prebendary of Avila's Cathedral Chapter, would later preside at the opening ceremony for Teresa's first reformed convent, St. Joseph's of Avila. Julian de Avila, one of Teresa's most faithful collaborators in her founding labors and later her biographer, also was a member of this group.

Juan de Avila and his followers focused much of their reforming effort on the cultivation of fervent and well-trained secular clergy. In that era ordination to the priesthood was often tied to wealth and class. The reformers, countering this, sought a priesthood of those with

---

[14]See *Life* 26,5.

[15]For discussion, see Jodi Blinkoff, "St. Teresa of Avila and the Avila of St. Teresa," *Carmelite Studies* 3 (1984): 53-68.

apostolic fervor, regardless of economic and social background. Teresa adapted these concerns within her own reform. She viewed her reformed monasteries as fortresses of prayer in support of apostolic endeavor[16] (active participation in which was for the most part closed to women); and she repeatedly insisted that the main criteria for acceptance of a sister must be her spiritual suitability, not her dowry.[17]

More important, perhaps, than the specific programs of this and other reforming groups of the time is simply the fact that Teresa lived in a milieu where the most fervent Christians were busy advocating and implementing concrete reform, and many of these reformers were among her most active supporters in her own reforming efforts.

Teresa's reform also drew upon elements associated with the illuminist movement. *Alumbrados*, or illuminists, first appeared on the Spanish scene early in the sixteenth century, and throughout the period of Teresa's writings their ideas were a force to be contended with--at times in reality, at times simply as "straw men" set up by others to be knocked down. The illuminists were, somewhat remotely, heirs of the fourteenth century *devotio moderna* movement which had countered the intellectual, systematizing approach of scholastic theology with an affective, experiential, practical spirituality. Many illuminists were Franciscans or associated with that order, which traditionally has stressed affectivity, simplicity and concreteness.

Spanish illuminism was even more directly linked with Rhineland mysticism than with the *devotio moderna*. The *alumbrados* advocated profound interior prayer leading to experiential union with God. One school taught that what was mainly required was total abandonment to God; the seeker need not fight against any temptations or exercise effort in the ascent to union. These *dejados* or "abandoned" mystics were soon condemned. The reknowned Franciscan spiritual writer Francisco de Osuna, whom many of the *dejados* claimed to be following, then

[16]See, for example, *Way* 3,1-2.

[17]See, for example, *Foundations* 27,12.

clarified his position to what soon became known as that of the *recogidos* or "recollected" mystics.

The *recogidos* advocated effortful recollection, which consists in "renouncing the objects of the senses, the images of fantasy, and the ideas of the intellect in order to rest in the pure love of the divinity."[18] This would culminate in a "prayer of quiet" in which the soul is in a state of complete passivity and emptiness awaiting God's activity. The *recogido* method as taught by Osuna was not in conflict with scholasticism; in fact it drew upon it. It also drew upon the Franciscan and *devotio moderna* traditions of affective prayer, simplicity, and openness to practice by people in all walks of life.

Osuna's synthesis made the *recogidos* at least potentially respectable, and it had a profound effect upon Teresa's own development. Her uncle Pedro de Cepeda gave her Osuna's main mystical text, the *Third Spiritual Alphabet*,[19] in 1538 when she was resting at his house during the first of her illnesses during the early years of her religious life. This book would be one of those placed on the Index in 1559; but in the meantime, Teresa says, she was "very happy with this book and resolved to follow that path with all my strength" (*Life* 4:7).

Victor García de la Concha has argued that in many ways Teresa was a member of the *recogido* movement. Her reading list over the years included all the authors most admired by that movement: Osuna, Bernardino de Laredo, Pedro de Alcantará, Juan de Avila, Luis de Granada, Alonso de Madrid, Francisco de Evia, Bernabé de Palma. From the *recogidos*, says García de la Concha, Teresa de Jesús acquired a method of contemplation more affective than intellectual, a direct and colloquial style of presentation with a heavy sprinkling of images from daily life, a focus on description of personal experience, and a

---

[18]Moron-Arroyo, "Spiritual Currents," p. 101.

[19]Francisco de Osuna, *Tercera parte de libro llamada Abecedario spiritual* (Madrid: Escritores misticos espanoles, 1911).

willingness to experiment and to correct oneself as one learns more from experience.[20]

Yet on one key point she would, in her maturity, severely critique the leading *recogido*, Osuna. He asserted that recollection demanded that one be denuded of everything sensual without exception, including the humanity of Christ. Teresa's own synthesis--so much more lively and experience-based than Osuna's rather wooden presentation--returned the humanity of Christ to the center of all prayer. By passing beyond active recollection and the prayer of quiet to union, rapture and spiritual marriage, she grasped the essence of Christian mysticism as fundamentally a living relationship with God in Christ that does not exclude--even though it surpasses--the body and its sensual experiences.

Teresa's accomplishments, both as a spiritual teacher and as a reformer and foundress, appear even more remarkable when one is aware of the highly conflicted territory upon which she trod. As Egido summarizes,

> The reigning climate of suspicion identified Lutheranism, illuminism, recollection, and mysticism without any great effort to distinguish them from one another. Moreover, given the combination of 'orantes' [pray-ers], women, and Jewish ancestry, we can understand the real battle which Madre Teresa--with these three counts against her--had to wage so that her 'spiritual' orientation not be denounced by the zealous watchdogs of the faith, and so that she might transmit a reform made up of communities of pray-ers ['orantes'].[21]

Events Surrounding the Writing of the Interior Castle

A study of the events that occurred in Teresa's life during the time she was writing the *Interior Castle* leaves the reader astonished that, in the midst of an agonizing barrage of ill health, worldly demands and

---

[20]Victor García de la Concha, *El Arte Literario de Santa Teresa* (Barcelona: Editorial Ariel, 1978), pp. 65-68.

[21]Egido, "Historical Setting," p. 130.

outright persecution, she was able to write anything--let alone a sublime spiritual treatise.

Once she responded to the call to become a foundress Teresa's life was never without innumerable tribulations and annoying business affairs; yet 1577, the year during which she wrote the *Interior Castle*, encompassed some of the most distressing and potentially disasterous days of her reform effort. Teresa composed the *Interior Castle* in two parts during that year. Between June 2 and mid-July, in Toledo, she wrote the chapters up to V:2, with V:3 completed shortly after her mid-July move to Avila. The remainder was written in Avila during November; it was finished on November 29.

During the months prior to writing the *Interior Castle*, Teresa was biding her time in Toledo (rather than being on the road making foundations, as she had been most of the time for the preceding ten years) because a savage controversy over her reform was raging at the highest levels of church and state.[22] At bottom, the controversy had to do with the Carmelite leaders' fear that they were losing control of the monasteries of the Discalced reform. This was not only a question of power, though it certainly was that; it was also a question of scandal--for reports were being circulated that accused members of the reform, and in particular Madre Teresa and her dear friend Fray Jerónimo Gracián, of behavior of the most outrageous sort. The controversy was greatly aggravated by the fact that the Discalced friars and, later, Teresa herself were disobeying direct orders given by the Carmelite General (Rubeo) that they not make foundations outside Castile, in Andalusia.

Teresa's excuse for permitting this disobedience, and for finally actually participating in it, was that it had been ordered by the Apostolic Visitator, Vargas--who, as a representative of the Pope, she took to be

---

[22]For a relatively succinct but complete review of this controversy, see Efrén de la Madre de Dios and Otger Steggink, *Tiempo y Vida de Santa Teresa* (Madrid: Autores Cristianos, 1968), pp. 577-605. For a shorter discussion in English, see Kieran Kavanaugh and Otilio Rodriguez, "The Book of Her Foundations: Introduction," in *The Collected Works of St. Teresa of Avila*, vol. 3 (Washington, DC: Institute of Carmelite Studies), pp. 58-73.

of higher authority than the General of the order. She blithely ignored the fact that the Pope himself actually favored the General's position. She even claimed that, when she made the first Andalusian foundation of nuns at Beas in February, 1575, she did not know it was in Andalusia.[23] By the time she began making the foundation at Seville in May, however, she knew very well what she was doing. At this point she also made a personal vow of obedience to Gracián, who by then was the new Apostolic Visitator and--even more significantly--a man to whom she was intensely attracted. Gracián ordered her to make the foundation, and she made it.

Meanwhile, the King of Spain, Felipe II, miffed by the Pope's failure to get his approval before issuing orders concerning Spanish monasteries, began issuing various counterorders. The plot becomes extremely complex at this point, what with the King, the Pope, the General, and various apostolic visitators, apostolic commissaries, nuncios, provincials, inquisitors, benefactors and confessors all locking horns in a most unedifying spectacle. Before it was over, John of the Cross would spend nine months in prison and Teresa would spend her darkest hours believing that perhaps the reform would after all be destroyed.

Even as she was setting out for Seville in May of 1575, the Carmelite Order, to which the reformed monasteries were still subject, was holding a chapter at Piacenza in Italy. The chapter decreed that all Discalced houses in Andalusia were to be immediately disbanded, and that the Discalced were not to distinguish themselves in name, clothing or custom from other Carmelites. An order was also promulgated that Madre Teresa must retire to a monastery of her choice in Castile, and from thence make no new foundations. When she learned of the order Teresa listened first to Gracián, who ordered her not to obey it immediately. She took her time, remaining in Seville until it was well established and then, in June of 1576, traveling to Córdoba and Malagón

[23]Beas was in the ecclesiastical province of Andulusia, although according to civil jurisdiction it was in the province of Castile. See *Foundations* 24,4.

before arriving in Toledo. There she stayed for a year, departing for Avila in July of 1577 to carry out the transfer of her first foundation from the jurisdiction of the bishop to that of the order. It was during that interlude in Toledo that she began the *Interior Castle*.

Even apart from the order to stay put, by the time Teresa arrived in Toledo she was really in no condition to continue her travels. She was 62 years old and her health, always tenuous, was reaching a new low. The foundation in Seville had involved an extraordinary amount of stress, culminating when one of the novices there denounced Teresa to the Inquisition and she had to undergo a formal investigation. Despite her love for Gracián, disobeying the General was extremely costly to her; she wrote, "he [the General] was induced into becoming displeased with me, which was the greatest trial I suffered in the work of these foundations, even though I have suffered many. . . . going against the will of my superior was like a death to me."[24] To complete her distress, Gracián did not prove to be nearly as supportive as she had hoped; worried about the accusations that were circulating, he kept his visits with her to a minimum.

Meanwhile, the business affairs and worries endemic to being a foundress did not let up. Teresa had to break off writing the *Interior Castle* in mid-July for her trip to Avila to negotiate the transfer of the monastery there, as she felt the Lord asked her to do. Her letters from the period reveal her still deeply involved in her other foundations' affairs, including difficult financial problems, questions of which postulants to accept, and new threats of scandal. Then in October, before she could get back to the *Interior Castle*, the nuns of the Incarnation (her original community prior to her foundation of reformed convents) re-elected her prioress. This precipitated a great brouhaha during which the nuns who voted for Teresa were violently calumniated and excommunicated, and another prioress was forcibly imposed.

---

[24]*Foundations* 28,2.

Even before she began to write the *Interior Castle*, Teresa was in such weak physical condition that she repeatedly stated her inability to write anything without the help of a secretary. Her statement in in the Prologue to the *Interior Castle* that "I have been experiencing now for three months such great noise and weakness in my head that I've found it a hardship even to write concerning business matters" was echoed many times over in her letters.[25] Why, then, did she set out to compose a lengthy manuscript? It was certainly not by her own choice. Once again it was Gracián's order that set her on her way. When she told him that her teachings on many spiritual matters (in the *Life* and the *Way*) were unavailable because held by the Inquisition, he ordered her to write another book in which she would "put down the doctrine in a general way without naming the one to whom the things you mentioned there happened."[26]

She resisted, protesting--with much justification, as we have seen--that her health was atrocious and, moreover, that she was overwhelmed with business affairs. She relented, however, and by the time she wrote IV:1,10, where she describes her physical problem in the most picturesque terms, she affirmed that these counterindications had not hindered her spiritual insight:

> It seems as if there are in my head many rushing rivers and that these waters are hurtling downward, and many little birds and whistling sounds, not in the ears but in the upper part of the head where, they say, the higher part of the soul is. . . . I wouldn't be surprised if the Lord gave me this headache so that I could understand these things

---

[25]See, for example, her letters written during this period: #175 (Feb. 27), #176 (Feb. 28), #177 (March 2), #180 (April 17), #185 (June 28), #186 (July 2), #193 (August), #198 (October); in *The Letters of Saint Teresa*, 2 volumes, translated and annotated by the Benedictines of Stanbrook (London: Thomas Baker, 1926).

[26]Antonio De San Joaquin, "Anotaciones al P. Ribera," *Año Teresiano*, 12 vols. (Madrid, 1733-1769, 8:149-150; cited by Kavanaugh and Rodriguez, "The Interior Castle: Introduction," *Collected Works* 2, p. 263.

> better. For all this turmoil in my head doesn't hinder prayer or what I am saying, but the soul is completely taken up in its quiet, love, desires and clear knowledge.

Some of the sisters who lived with Teresa during the months when she composed the *Interior Castle* later testified that extraordinary phenomena accompanied her writing. One of the more restrained testimonies is that of María del Nacimiento:

> . . . this witness saw that it was after Communion that she wrote this book, and when she wrote she did so very rapidly and with such great beauty in her countenance that this witness was in admiration, and she was so absorbed in what she was writing that even if some noise was made there, it did not hinder her; wherefore this witness understood that in all that which she wrote and during the time she was writing she was in prayer.[27]

Other witnesses spoke of raptures, intense light, writing that appeared on the pages without being inscribed.[28] While some or all of these reports may embroider the facts, the *Interior Castle* is unquestionably an inspired account of mystical transformation.[29] At this point it will be valuable to briefly review the imagery and teaching of the book.

---

[27]*Biblioteca Mistica Carmelitana*, ed. Silverio de Santa Teresa, vol. 18 (Burgos: El Monte Carmelo, 1934), p. 315; quoted in Kavanaugh, "The Interior Castle: Introduction," *Collected Works* 2, p. 267.

[28]For a review, see Efrén and Steggink, "Introducción a las Moradas," *Obras Completas* 2, pp. 311-13.

[29]For additional background on literary and experiential sources which scholars believe influenced the imagery and ideas of the *Interior Castle*, see Appendix B, "The *Interior Castle*: Literary Sources and Influences."

B. Overview of the Text

Introduction

The full Spanish title of the text, *Moradas del Castillo Interior*, translates literally as "Dwelling Places of the Interior Castle." This title aptly indicates both the essential content and the basic structure of the book. The book is about the spiritual journey, depicted as a series of different styles of dwelling with God interiorly. The allegory of the human soul as a castle, at the center of which God dwells in glory, provides the stable framework within which a great diversity of images and insights are synthesized into an integrated narrative.

An even deeper organizing principle of the work is autobiography. Gracián had ordered her to write "in a general way," mainly to avoid trouble with the inquisition, so she could not make the autobiographical dimension explicit; yet her primary source clearly was her own experience. Both style and content were certainly influenced by many persons, books and cultural assumptions; nevertheless, Teresa's genius as a spiritual writer is most manifest in her unswerving fidelity to description of her own experience.

Her relative lack of formal education turned out, in its own way, to be an advantage; for her focus was not on expressing her insights with technical coherence within a pre-given terminology, but on understanding her experience and expressing that with whatever images and terms came to hand. Her tendency to use even technical terms loosely has been extremely annoying to those who wish to systematize her thought and to coordinate it with that of other spiritual writers. In the present inquiry, many difficult questions are avoided by taking as our norm the terminology and teaching as expressed in Teresa's most mature work, the *Interior Castle*, rather than trying to work out a coordination of the terms and teachings from all of her writings. Even with this limitation, however, one must be aware of the pitfall of attempting rigorous systematization where what is actually given is astute description.

Basic Images

As she begins the *Interior Castle*, Teresa invites us to "consider our soul to be like a castle made entirely out of a diamond or of very clear crystal, in which there are many rooms, just as in heaven there are many dwelling places" (I:1,1).[30] After elaborating on the many and various dwelling places in the castle, she continues: "in the center and middle is the main dwelling place where the very secret exchanges between God and the soul take place" (I:1,3).[31] Since this castle is the soul, she says, we are already "in" it; but we may be in it in many different ways, ranging from being in the outer courtyard with the guards and vermin to being at the very center with God. The door for entering the castle is prayer and reflection; without these, we will always remain outside and as if paralyzed.

This basic image gives Teresa the scope she needs to articulate a "theological anthropology" much more engaging than that of the scholastics, although to some degree she coordinates her allegorical imagery with their technical vocabulary. The senses and faculties are compared to people who live in the castle as vassals of the soul and, ultimately, of the Lord at its center. The higher faculties are the higher-level servants who guard the castle and direct the lower-level servants. In the rooms farther from the center there is constant danger and annoyance from worldly cares, distractions and temptations, which are compared to poisonous creatures or little lizards which can worm their way in as far as the fourth dwelling places. The Lord in the center is like a brilliant sun or a crystal-clear fount which is always there, but which can be completely darkened and sullied by mortal sin.

These basic allegorical correspondences recur throughout the entire book, although often with playful variations. In general, the

---

[30]"considerar nuestra alma como un castillo todo de un diamante u muy claro cristal, adonde hay muchos aposentos, ansí como en el cielo hay muchas moradas."

[31]"en el centro y mitad de todas éstas tiene la más principal, que es adonde pasan las cosas de mucho secreto entre Dios y el alma."

allegory of the castle is much more prominent in the discussion of the first four dwelling places; it then recedes, only to be brought to the fore again as Teresa wraps up her narrative in the discussion of the Seventh Dwelling Place.

In the Fifth Dwelling Places, just at the point where the castle allegory recedes (without, however, disappearing), Teresa introduces two other major allegorical images which she will carry through to the end of the book. The first is that of the silkworm who builds a cocoon and then emerges as a beautiful white butterfly. This image dramatizes the transition from prayer as our own activity to prayer as God's activity in us; for the worm must work to build the cocoon, but transformation is the work of God (V:2,5-7). The shift from the dwelling and castle imagery to that of the cocoon and butterfly is an iconic representation of a leap into the vibrancy, freedom, and mobility of a living being. Once the soul is thus freed to fly, the images of "butterfly" and "dove" become more or less interchangeable. The flying creature settles down again and joyfully dies, however, in the seventh dwelling place.

The second additional allegory, also introduced in the Fifth Dwelling Place, is that of courtship and marriage. This set of images expresses the intimate personal and relational nature of the union with God. It is an iconic representation of the fact that mystical transformation has to do most with that which is most uniquely human--the capacity for wholehearted love and commitment.

As in the traditional pattern of arranged marriages in sixteenth century Castile, Teresa depicts several stages that precede the marriage: first a series of visits for the couple to come to know one another and to fall in love; then a "joining of hands" in which they make an agreement to marry; then a public betrothal ceremony through which they enter the state of betrothal; and finally the sacrament of marriage by which they enter the state of matrimony. Teresa compares the visits, falling in love, and "joining of hands" to the Fifth Dwelling Places, while the Sixth corresponds to the state of betrothal and the Seventh to the state of matrimony.

In addition to these, Teresa also uses a very large number[32] of other images to express her experience of the spiritual journey. Some of these are connected to the structuring allegories; others are not. Among those that function as background themes, recurring fairly often, are those related to water (i.e. fount, well, stream, river, rain); those related to fire (i.e. flame, brazier, spark); those related to travel (i.e. journey, path, road); and those related to war (i.e. soldiers, weapons, enemy, victory). These, however, do not structure the "action" of the narrative in the way the three discussed above do.

The Terminology of Factulty Psychology

Despite the previous caution against over-zealous attempts to find systematic exposition in Teresa's writings, we must nevertheless recall that Teresa did know and use some parts of the technical vocabulary common in her milieu to describe and explain spiritual experiences. To understand what she was trying to say, as well as to discern when she used these technical terms inaccurately or loosely, one must be aware of what those terms meant in that milieu.

The set of technical terms most relevant to this inquiry is that having to do with the faculty psychology of the time, which was basically Thomist.[33] This psychology considers the soul, *el alma*, to be the body's governing principle. The soul consists of two strata. The lower strata is the animal soul (*la parte inferior* or *la parte sensitiva*) in which inhere the senses. The senses, *los sentidos*, include both exterior senses (sight, hearing, smell, taste, touch) and interior senses (imagination and "phantasy," *la imaginación* and *la fantasía*). The higher stratum (*la parte superior*) is the seat of the rational faculties of

---

[32]Based on the index of figures of speech provided in the back of Kavanaugh and Rodriguez, *Collected Works*, vol. 2, I would estimate the number in the *Interior Castle* at about 200.

[33]For an overview of faculty psychology in that era, see E.W. Trueman Dicken, *The Crucible of Love* (London: Darton, Longman & Todd, 1963), pp. 327-35.

will, understanding and memory (*la voluntad, el entendimiento, la memoría*). This higher stratum is also called *el espíritu*, the spirit. The term "faculties," *las potencias*, could be applied either to the corporal faculties (the senses) or to the spiritual faculties (will, understanding, memory).

Teresa never made a systematic effort to explain the different spiritual states using this terminology; indeed, as she herself frequently averred and later commentators affirmed, "her theoretical ignorance of psychology was profound."[34] Nevertheless the language of faculty psychology does appear at certain points as she struggles to make important distinctions.[35] She distinguishes, for example, between *las potencias* (here meaning the spiritual faculties, especially *la voluntad*) and *la imaginación* (V:3,10), as well as between *el entendimiento*, the spiritual faculty, and *el pensamiento*, the chatter of thinking (which she equates with *imaginación*; IV:1,8).

In both of these examples she introduces the terminological distinction in the effort to explain the experience of being much distracted or even upset and at the same time being able to be recollected in one's spiritual faculties. The experience comes first; the terminology is there not for its own sake, but because the experience demands it. As Hoornaert summarizes, "Though she sometimes gets involved in her terminology, she never confounds realities, of which words are but the

---

[34]Rodolphe Hoornaert, *Saint Teresa in Her Writings*, trans. Joseph Leonard (NY: Benziger Bros., 1931), p. 314. This translation does not contain all the material of the original edition, *Sainte Thérèse écrivain, son milieu, ses facultés, son oeuvre* (Paris: Desclée de Brouwer, 1922).

[35]On Teresa's use of this terminology, see Hoornaert, *Saint Teresa in Her Writings*, pp. 314-17; Gaston Etchegoyen, *L'Amour divin: Essai sur les sources de Sainte Thérèse* (Bordeaux-Paris: Féret et Fils, 1923), pp. 125-28; and Joseph Chorpenning, "The Theological Method of St. Teresa of Avila's *Interior Castle* (unpublished STL dissertation, Washington, DC: Catholic University, 1981), pp. 25-28.

envelopes. . . . We understand her thoughts not so much by the exact denomination of the faculties as by a description of their action."[36]

These terms have been briefly introduced here in order to facilitate presentation of the overview of the text. They will be discussed in greater detail in subsequent chapters.

The Seven Dwelling Places

A first important question is whether Teresa actually teaches that there are seven "stages" in spiritual growth, or whether the seven-fold structure she depicts is intended more as a rhetorical device than as a descriptive or explanatory claim. The answer to this must be somewhat equivocal.

On the one hand she makes it clear that there are not merely seven, but "many dwelling places: some up above, others down below, others to the sides" (I:1,3). The plural title of each of the sections, i.e. *Moradas Primeras*, *Moradas Segundas*, etc., all the way up to *Septimas Moradas*, indicates that this is no simple vision of a seven-story soul or of a lockstep seven-stage progression. As she puts it, "You mustn't think of these dwelling places in such a way that each would follow in file after the other . . . . The things of the soul must always be considered as plentiful, spacious, and large; to do so is not an exaggeration" (I:2,8). The argument that the division into seven is somewhat arbitrary is reinforced by the fact that (as would-be systematizers constantly bemoan) Teresa's descriptions of the various states often overlap. Those who believe that there should be clear boundaries between stages frequently accuse her of being poor at making these distinctions.

The problem, most likely, is simply her descriptive honesty. From a descriptive or "common sense" perspective, different states very often do appear to overlap, blur into one another, succeed one another

[36]Hoornaert, *St. Teresa in Her Writings*, p. 316.

in irregular and confusing ways, etc. Within this welter of potentially confusing experiences, however, Teresa still manages to discern definite transitions. My analysis suggests that for the Fourth, Fifth, Sixth, and Seventh Dwelling Places, she describes a single definite experience or type of experience that initiates the soul into a new level or dimension of spiritual experience. She does not claim, however, that these initiating experiences are magical transformations that eliminate the multiplicity and ambiguity of the ongoing stream of experience.

In the *Interior Castle* Teresa does not spend a great deal of time describing the early stages of the spiritual life, which she covered in much more detail in the *Life* and especially in the *Way*. The First Dwelling Places are the condition of those who have only made the very first movement toward attentiveness to God; they have "entered the castle," but they are still largely deaf to God and their lives remain massively disordered. Already, however, God is at work in their lives (I:2,5-7). In the Second Dwelling Places the individual is able to hear God speaking through sermons, books, trials, etc., and responds by struggling to overcome the disorder that pervades the exercise of the faculties.

By the time people reach the Third Dwelling Places, they have their lives largely in order. A great danger arises, however, in that they may imagine that they have already achieved all that is necessary in regard to the spiritual realm. At the same time they are likely to experience dryness and boredom in prayer. The double temptation of this stage is either to become self-satisfied and self-righteous in a condition of comfortable piety, or to become bored and to abandon prayer and religion entirely.

Of the Fourth Dwelling Places Teresa writes, "Supernatural experiences begin here" (IV:1,1). For the first time, the soul hears the call of the Lord himself. This stage is often designated as the "prayer of recollection" (*recogimiento*) or the "prayer of quiet" (*quietud*), as the soul begins to enter into a state of concentration and tranquility beyond its own powers to construct. The term "recollection" is used to emphasize the remaining active elements, while "quiet" stresses the more passive component. The initiating experience is described thus:

> Like a good shepherd, with a whistle so gentle that [the sense and faculties] themselves almost fail to hear it, He makes them recognize His voice and stops them from going so far astray so that they will return to their dwelling place. . . . Don't think that this recollection is acquired by the intellect striving to think about God within itself, or by the imagination imagining Him within itself. . . . I don't know in what way or how they heard the shepherd's whistle. It wasn't through the ears, because nothing is heard. But one noticeably senses a gentle drawing inward, as anyone who goes through this will observe . . . . (IV:3,2-3)

This prayer of recollection or quiet, then, is the transition between active meditation and infused contemplation. Characteristic of this stage is the prayer of spiritual delight (*el gusto*). Spiritual delight differs radically from consolation (*contentos*) in that the latter is gained by our own efforts reaching out for God, while *el gusto* begins in God and only subsequently overflows into the faculties and body (IV:2,1-6).

Teresa writes, "I don't think the experience [of spiritual delight] is something, as I say, that rises from the heart, but from another part still more interior, as from something deep. I think this must be the center of the soul . . . " (IV:2,5). Like all Teresa's terms, *el centro del alma* has a primarily experiential reference; yet its connotation, as in the more philosphically sophisticated writings of John of the Cross, includes the metaphysical and theological notion of God as constituting the inmost center of the human soul.[37] Already in the Fourth Dwelling Places, God's activity in the soul is beginning to bring about a radically new type of activity and knowledge in the soul itself.

---

[37]See John of the Cross, *The Living Flame of Love* I:9-13, in *The Collected Works of St. John of the Cross*, trans. Kieran Kavanaugh and Otilio Rodriguez (Washington, DC: Institute of Carmelite Studies, 1973). For summary and commentary, see Dicken, *Crucible*, pp. 366-67.

This change takes a quantum leap forward with the entrance into the Fifth Dwelling Places. The remaining dwelling places are all degrees of union (*unión*). In union, says Teresa, it is as if God can "enter the center of the soul without going through any door" (V:1,12) Here is her description of the initial experiences of union:

> There is no need here to use any technique to suspend the mind since all the faculties are asleep in this state--and truly asleep--to the things of the world and to ourselves. . . . . In sum, it is like one who in every respect has died to the world so as to live more completely in God. (V:1,4)

In the Fifth Dwelling Places the experience of union is so far beyond the normal capabilities of the faculties that they are as if "asleep" or "dead"; "during the time of this union [the soul] neither sees, nor hears, nor understands" (V:1,9). Yet this is by no means a mere "dreamy state" (V:1,4-5), for "when [the soul] returns to itself it can in no way doubt that it was in God and God was in it." The sign of true union is this "certitude . . . that only God can place there" (V:1,9-10).

Teresa adds, "I would say that whoever does not receive this certitude does not experience union of the whole soul with God, but union of some faculty, or that he experiences one of the many other kinds of favors that God grants souls" (V:1,11). "Union" as a term specific to the fifth and subsequent dwelling places, then, refers to "union of the whole soul" or to God's full entrance into the "center of the soul," as distinct from the absorption, recollection, or stilling of one or more faculties. The latter phenomena do in fact occur as concomitants of union, especially in the beginning, but they are not part of its essential nature.

The worm who builds a cocoon, "dies" and is transformed into a butterfly is an image of the work, death and transformation that characterize the transition into union. Teresa writes, "we will not have finished doing all we can in this work when, to the little we can do, which is nothing, God will unite Himself, with His greatness, and give it such high value that the Lord Himself will become the reward of this work" (V:2,5). The soul comes forth from union able to "fly" like the butterfly or the dove. Penances, sufferings, and good deeds that formerly seemed impossible or very distressing now seem easy (V:2,8).

In the Fifth Dwelling Places the soul is like a woman who has met the man she will marry and has fallen deeply in love, but there is as yet no betrothal contract (V:4,4). Entrance into the state of betrothal is what characterizes the Sixth Dwelling Places. In discussing the Fifth Dwelling Places, Teresa commented that "although what is in this [Fifth] dwelling place and the next [the Sixth] are almost identical, the force of the effects is very different" (V:2,7). She wanted to emphasize both the sameness and the difference between the fifth and subsequent dwelling places. The nuptial imagery captures this: the sameness is that all are developments of the initial "falling in love" which is *unión*; at the same time the differences are as significant as those between the stages of the sixteenth-century marriage process.

In that era, the state of betrothal constituted a quite distinct social condition, with privileges, customs and responsibilities carefully distinguished from those of the prior state of being single and the subsequent state of being married. Thus Teresa's nuptial allegory images definite and specific changes of state within the continuity of a developing relationship of "union."

Over one third of the *Interior Castle* is concerned with the Sixth Dwelling Places, and the variety of experiences discussed within these pages is formidable. Yet all these varieties of experiences are categorized as belonging to the Sixth Dwelling Places because they have a common essence. The word Teresa most frequently uses to summarize these experiences is *arrobamiento*, "rapture." She directly relates rapture to betrothal when she states, "thus you will see what His Majesty does to conclude this betrothal, which I understand comes about when He gives the soul raptures that draw it out of its senses" (VI:4,2).[38]

[38]"Y ansí veréis lo que hace Su Majestad para concluir este desposorio, que entiendo yo deve ser cuando da arrobamientos, que la saca de sus sentidos."

What characterizes rapture, it seems, is that the faculties are totally unable to operate in their normal manner and yet they are neither "absorbed" as they were in the Fourth Dwelling Places (cf. VI:2,2-5) nor "asleep" as they often were in the Fifth Dwelling Places. Rather, "the soul was never so awake to the things of God nor did it have such deep enlightenment and knowledge of His Majesty" (VI:4,4). This supernatural learning about the things of God in the most interior part of the soul is of the essence of rapture. Indeed, Teresa writes:

> I hold that if at times in its raptures the soul doesn't understand these secrets, its raptures are not given by God but caused by some natural weakness. . . . In a rapture, believe me, God carries off for Himself the entire soul, and, as to someone who is His own and His spouse, He begins showing it some little part of the kingdom that it has gained by being espoused to Him. (VI:4,9)

It seems to the soul that it "was entirely in another region different from this in which we live, where there is shown another light so different from earth's light that if he were to spend his whole life trying to imagine that light, along with the other things, he would be unable to do so" (VI:5,7). The experience is so extraordinary that one does not know whether it has taken place in the body or out of the body (VI:5,8).

Teresa frequently speaks of this experience as extraordinarily delightful (*sabroso*), but she equally frequently speaks of it as one of extraordinary pain (*pena*). This pain reaches an excruciating peak of intensity at the point of transition to the Seventh Dwelling Places, when the soul is wounded in its "very deep and intimate part" (VI:11,2) and left "like a person hanging, who cannot support himself on any earthly thing; neither can it ascend to heaven" (VI:11,5). What is happening here, says Teresa, is that God is bringing the soul "into His own dwelling place." Now the soul is being "called to enter its center," whereas in earlier stages of union (Fifth and Sixth dwelling places) it was only "called to the superior part" (VII:1,5).

The difference between this state and earlier ones, says Teresa, is that now the union is permanent. Before, God and the soul were like two wax candles whose flames could unite but could also separate. Now the soul is like rain that has fallen into a river, so that "there is no means of separating the two" (VII:2,4). Joined with God in its own center, the soul is completely at peace; just as the "empyreal heaven where the Lord is does not move as do the other heavens," so "in the soul that enters here there are none of those movements that usually take place in the faculties and the imagination . . ." (VII:2,9). This peace and quietude at the center is permanent, even though the "faculties, senses and passions" continue to be involved in prodigious activity and trials (VII:2,10-12).

This total union and peace at the "center" is the essential characteristic of the Seventh Dwelling Places. As for the faculties, they "have nothing to do with what goes on in this dwelling place" (VII:3,10), and yet they are not "lost" (i.e., enraptured or suspended)[39]. As Teresa summarizes:

> [I]n this temple of God, in this His dwelling place, He alone and the soul rejoice together in the deepest silence. There is no reason for the intellect to stir or seek anything, for the Lord who created it wishes to give it repose here and that through a small crevice it might observe what is taking place (VII:3,11).

In the Seventh Dwelling Place, then, the faculties seem to operate in a somewhat more "normal" manner. Raptures are very rare and not nearly so overwhelming (VII:3,12). Whereas before the soul remained in many ways "blind and deaf," now "our good God desires to remove the scales from the soul's eyes and let it see and understand, although in a strange way, something of the favor He grants it" (VII:1,5-6). Visions in the "very interior center" (VII:2,3) are a part of this new "seeing." Yet the "seeing" seems to have a very down-to-earth

---

[39]See Kavanaugh and Rodriguez, *Collected Works*, vol. 2, p. 498 n. 12: "In Teresa's terminology 'not lost' is the equivalent of not being enraptured. In this dwelling place the faculties remain in amazement but not ecstatically suspended."

component as well, for Teresa repeatedly emphasizes that in this dwelling place one's energy, desire and capability for practical service on behalf of others reach new peaks.

CHAPTER 7

TERESA'S MYSTICAL TRANSFORMATION: AN INTERIORITY ANALYSIS

A. Introduction

This chapter engages in an interiority analysis of our chosen text, the *Interior Castle*. It is important to note that in doing this, we are asking the text questions that are structured more by our contemporary needs and concerns than by the explicit intentions of the text's original author. Teresa's consciousness was not fully differentiated in Lonergan's sense; that is, she did not have an explicit and systematic ability to recognize, name, and methodically move among different realms of meaning (common sense, theory, interiority, praxis, transcendence). She had not "appropriated interiority" in the full technical sense. Her writings give evidence, nonetheless, that the depth of her contemplative praxis was such that she had a remarkably "objective" awareness of the patterns of conscious activity.

"Objective" is placed in quotation marks here because her awareness was certainly not systematically explanatory. On the contrary, Teresa is best known (and loved) for her pungent images and her breathlessly dynamic writing style. Yet through these images, jumbled as they often are from a "systematic" perspective, shine the insights of a genius in the architectonics of human consciousness.

Teresa's writings demonstrate how the interiority of a true contemplative far surpasses that of a mere methodologist.

As discussed in Chapter 3, Matthew Lamb has defined interiority as "an experience of consciousness as a state which is its own act of awareness."[1] Strictly speaking, interiority as a form of awareness can only occur within one's own consciousness. It is not possible directly to be aware of or to affirm another's consciousness-as-conscious; nor is it even possible directly to communicate one's own such awareness.[2] Since Teresa's consciousness is not directly available for consultation, our analysis has to rely on her written communication about her experience. Such communication, of course, is already an objectification and interpretation of the operations of consciousness. The "interiority analysis" that is to be done in this chapter, then, cannot involve interiority in the strict sense. It is, rather, an attempt to trace the changing patterns of conscious activity from the perspective afforded by interiority: that is, the perspective of consciousness-as-conscious as the ground of its own mediation in intentional operations.

In the following discussion, "contemplative interiority" refers to the simplification and "centering" of awareness that occurs as a result of regular practice of the contemplative disciplines of prayer and meditation. The difference between this and what might be called "methodical interiority" is that the latter tends to occur in the context of explicitly philosophical concerns, and its interest is more strongly focused toward the objectification and refinement of the intentional operations of consciousness.

Ultimately, these are not two different interiorities; the difference is in the context and goal of practice. Their relationship to one another can best be understood by reviewing the notion of the "integral relation

---

[1]Lamb, *History, Method and Theology*, pp. 290-91. For discussion, see "The Subject as Objectified in Self-Appropriation" in Chapter 3.

[2]Or, if such awareness and/or communication *is* possible--i.e., in some parapsychological or mystical form--it involves modes of experience and expression that are not germane to the present genre.

of mediation" as presented in Chapter 4.[3] The non-objectifiable awareness of the subject-as-subject is intrinsically self-transcending, thus generating the intentional operations of consciousness. These culminate in objective knowledge and increased self-appropriation. The notion of mediation affirms that source (the subject-as-subject) and mediations (the articulated structure of consciousness) are integral to one another.

The practical implication of this is that contemplative interiority, which focuses more rigorously on appropriating the source or center of awareness, nevertheless results in clarification and refinement of the intentional operations of consciousness. Methodical interiority, on the other hand, while giving more energy to appropriating the articulated structure of consciousness, can do so only on the basis of heightened awareness of the source.

Interiority analysis, of course, is an activity deriving from the practice of methodical interiority. It strives for an objective and theoretically differentiated understanding of the operations of consciousness. Contemplatives, however, often present their insights in common sense, metaphoric expressions. One who is attempting a systematic interiority analysis must be aware of the differences between these two genres.

In the *Interior Castle*, Teresa's root metaphor has a spatial quality: the soul is a castle within which God dwells as Lord, and toward the center of which the soul orients its spiritual longings. Spatial imagery, if interpreted literally, tends easily to reification, since our experience of things that exist in space is of solidity and continuity over time. Yet Teresa's metaphor of the interior castle, as interpreted here, is an expression of the opposite of reification--namely, the dynamism of the flow of life and love in the heart of existence where human beings truly "dwell." This tension between the tendency of the spatial imagery to reification and its intended reference to a non-objectifiable dynamism is another expression of the paradoxical relationship, noted above, between

---

[3]See "Mediation and Dynamic Structure" in Chapter 4. Cf. also "The Subject as Self-Transcending" in Chapter 3.

the non-objectifiable dimension of the praxis of interiority and the abstract quality of its objectified fruits. Teresa's brilliant common-sense articulation of the architectonics of human consciousness expresses in its root metaphor the basic tension of consciousness itself.

B. An Interiority Analysis of the *Interior Castle*

Our procedure in this analysis will be to begin with a brief descriptive interpretation of what Teresa's text implies about a given stage in the process of mystical transformation, then to interpret her insights more systematically in the context of the model developed in Chapter 5. Included in the title preceding the discussion of each stage is a phrase summarizing the aspect of the model in which relevant correlations have particularly been found.

Prologue and First Dwelling Places: The Transcendent Ground

From the very first pages of the *Interior Castle*, Teresa emphasizes repeatedly that her story is entirely about the power flowing from the "center of the soul," where God dwells. The main point of her brief Prologue is that the content and value of the book derive entirely from its rootedness in the indwelling God. She observes that she is like a parrot who speaks only what it has been taught (Prologue 2), and that anything of value in the text has its foundation in the Lord, not herself (Prologue 4). Both structure and content of the book flow from the simple affirmation which she will state explicitly in one of its concluding chapters: "the Sun of Justice . . . dwells within [the human soul] giving it being" (VII:1,3).[4]

---

[4]To avoid multiple footnotes, all references to the *Interior Castle* will be included in the text. The number of the Dwelling Place will be written in roman numerals, followed by a colon. Chapter and paragraph number, both in arabic numerals, will be separated by a comma. The paragraph numbering follows that in

In the chapters of the First Dwelling Places this affirmation is expressed, not conceptually, but in the foundational image of the soul as a "castle made entirely out of a diamond or very clear crystal." The castle's reason for being and the organizing principle of all its structures and activities is the Lord who dwells at its center. Indeed, it is only from the center that one can see that the whole edifice is transparent crystal, so all the surrounding rooms are illuminated at once in the single flash of Light from the center.

This foundational image is profoundly non-linear; by imaging the soul as a structure entirely transparent to the "Sun" which is both its center and its source of being, Teresa is able to place before our minds the essential unifying dimension that lies behind all the "parts" and "stages" of the journey of spiritual transformation. It cannot be stressed too many times that only by keeping this inaugural image of the "diamond castle" constantly at the foundation of our thoughts can we traverse the rest of her presentation with the proper perspective.[5]

The beginner, whose awareness of the center is still quite abstract and tenuous, may be tempted to imagine the many dwelling places as arranged in a "file [one] after the other" (I:2,8). This tends to lock the seeker into very limited possibilities of movement. In fact, says Teresa, the dwelling places are all arranged around the center like leaves around the heart of a palmetto. Thus even at the descriptive level, it is inaccurate to construe Teresa's story as an account of a linear, step-by-step journey from one place to another, i.e., from "world" to "God." It is more like an account of a series of finer and finer refractions of one's awareness of the light from a single divine "place" that

---

the Kavanaugh-Rodriguez translation. All quotations are also from that edition.

[5]As we shall see, this vision which Teresa presents as the beginning and the foundation was actually, for her, the end of the journey; for this vision of God as "all in all" is the signal characteristic of the spiritual marriage. See below, pp. ; also Mary Coelho, "St. Teresa of Avila's Transformation of the Symbol of the Interior Castle," *Ephemerides Carmeliticae* 38 (1987): 109-25.

encompasses the whole world. Those who pray discover this glorious "royal chamber" within themselves.

> The things of the soul must always be considered as plentiful, spacious, and large; to do so is not an exaggeration. The soul is capable of much more than we can imagine, and the sun that is in this royal chamber shines in all parts. It is very important for any soul that practices prayer, whether little or much, not to hold itself back and stay in one corner. Let it walk through these dwelling places which are up above, down below, and to the sides, since God has given it such great dignity. (I:2,8)

Teresa's image of the diamond castle with its center in God is primarily addressed, not to the theologian or the philosophical analyst, but to the spiritual seeker. From the very start, the sincere seeker must strive to take the perspective of the center. "Taking the perspective of the center" could be a definition of prayer, which Teresa asserts is "the door of entry to this castle" (I:1,7). Maintaining one's focus on the real center (the "sun" of God dwelling at the center and permeating all) is the key to becoming free to move all about the castle. At the same time, Teresa stresses that it is not only our activities, but God's, that constitute prayer as authentic. She complains that too often "only what we ourselves can do in prayer is explained to us; little is explained about what the Lord does in a soul, I mean about the supernatural" (I:2,7).

The activity of prayer is both our own and God's; the diamond castle is both God's dwelling place and our own center. Although we are already within it, we may be totally or partially unaware of its existence and beauty (I:1,2; I:2,14; VII:1,3; VII:2,4; etc). The goal of the spiritual journey is full awareness of what already is one's own. Without that awareness, one is like a paralyzed person who cannot control his or her own limbs (I:1,6; VII:1,3-4). It is only when one gains full awareness that one will experience oneself as an edifice of crystal permeated by the glorious light of God. Deliberate refusal of that awareness is like covering the crystal with a black cloth so that no light can come through (I:2,2-3).

Within the structure of terms and relations developed in this inquiry, we can say that in the Prologue and First Dwelling Places of the *Interior Castle* Teresa moves immediately to situate her presentation in relation to the realm of transcendence.[6] That is: she first of all wants to make it absolutely clear that *all* human experiences are explicitly sublated by the transcendent ground of consciousness, which is their ultimate source. For Teresa, this is true whether one is aware of it or not; the spiritual journey is the increasing awareness and appropriation of that fact.

Teresa expresses this insight in the spatial imagery of the "Sun" that permeates the diamond castle from its place at the castle's center and source. As noted in the introduction to this chapter, this spatial imagery must be carefully interpreted. Our first temptation, present from these earliest chapters, will be to envision the realm of transcendence as a "place" with a "location" within intrawordly structures. As stated in Chapter 5, transcendence can never be one among many parts; it is "the whole, the ultimate, the totality, as transcending, including and being mediated in all the parts." Correctly interpreted, Teresa's image of the Light at the center and source of the soul conveys this truth as well as is possible within the limitations of spatial imagery.

Teresa's second concern in these early chapters is to point out that the realm of meaning within which this relation of sublation between transcendence and the activities of consciousness can be clarified and enhanced is that of a contemplative interiority--that is, deep self-knowledge (I:2,8-11).[7] She frequently related self-knowledge to "humility," which is a basic honesty about who one is and is not. It

---

[6]On the realm of transcendence, see "The Specificity of Mystical Experience" in Chapter 5.

[7]For discussion of the relation between methodical interiority and "contemplative interiority," see above, "Introduction."

entails an unrelenting willingness to let everything about oneself, even what is most painful or shameful, come into the light of awareness.

Perhaps her foremost concern, however, is to emphasize that full self-knowledge is only possible when one sees oneself explicitly in the light of God. She says,

> In my opinion we shall never completely know ourselves if we don't strive to know God. . . . our intellects and wills, dealing in turn now with self now with God, become nobler and better prepared for every good. . . . There we shall learn true humility, the intellect will be enhanced . . . and self-knowledge will not make one base and cowardly. (I:2,9-11)

Openness to the transcendent ground of consciousness is the *sine qua non* of comprehensive awareness of the mediated structures of conscious activity. Without that openness to the ground, intensive pursuit of self-knowledge tends to get sidetracked into frightened scrupulosity or self-righteous pedantry.

Second and Third Dwelling Places: Religious Conversion

Throughout her discussion of the Second and Third Dwelling Places, which complete the introductory portion of the text, Teresa continues to emphasize that everything depends on attention and openness to the divine center. She speaks in very practical ways about how that center will be experienced in these early stages of the life of prayer. It is not yet a direct experience--that will come only in the Fourth Dwelling Places. Rather, the seeker is gradually more and more aware of God speaking through "words spoken by other good people, or through sermons, or through what is read in good books, or through the many things that are heard and by which God calls, or through illnesses and trials . . ." (II:1,3).

The task of those in this stage is to take charge of their lives from a place closer to the center than they have previously even known was possible. Teresa stresses that without God's active participation nothing of value can be achieved (II:1,6). Nevertheless, every form of human effort must also be expended. All the virtues and faculties--for example, reason, faith, memory, imagination, will, intellect (II:1,4)--must be exercised in the service of overcoming obstacles to greater God-centeredness.

By the time these preparatory stages are completed, one's life will be an exemplar of well-ordered and virtuous behavior. Teresa spends little time, however, discussing what that behavior should be or even how one is to achieve it at a practical level. Her whole focus is on the inner dimension. What matters most of all, she asserts, is love. If love is genuine, it will manifest itself in "the determination of our wills," which is the main "work" that God needs from us. If our determination to join our will with that of the Lord is firm, the external works will certainly follow (III:1,7; cf. also II:1,6-8).

Teresa's description conforms very closely to Lonergan's explanation of religious conversion. First comes "God's love flooding our hearts"--the grace of God's love experienced at the very center of one's being. The first fruit of this is an existential commitment to a new set of values. From that commitment flow new ways of perceiving, thinking, and behaving. It is an "above downward" process in that the transcendent ground ("God's love") has a transformative influence on spirit (the natural human capacity for knowing, loving and choosing), which in turn has a transformative influence on psyche and body (concrete ways of perceiving, thinking, behaving, etc.).

In her discussion of the first three Dwelling Places, then, Teresa has established all the basic principles of religious conversion. The single principle governing all others is the centrality of the divine center. This divine center, which is also our own center, is to be approached by increasing awareness (self-knowledge). Ultimately religious conversion is a gift--that is, it is the divine center (in the terms developed here: the transcendent ground of consciousness) whose activity is most decisive. The human contribution is primarily an act of existential self-commitment. External works of love and virtue will necessarily follow as the mediations of these acts of the divine center and of the human spirit.

These basic principles of religious conversion are the foundation upon which Teresa's discussion of full mystical transformation is built. Mystical transformation is not something different from religious conversion, but its fulfillment. These principles, therefore, are never superceded; the higher dwelling places simply deepen and elaborate upon them.

Fourth Dwelling Places: Contemplative Interiority

Even though their lives are finally in good order, individuals in the Third Dwelling Places become increasingly dissatisfied because the door to the center where God dwells remains closed (III:1,6). That door begins to open in the Fourth Dwelling Places, where "supernatural experiences begin" (IV:1,1). Supernatural experiences, for Teresa, are conscious experiences of God's presence and activity at the center of one's soul. In the terminology developed in previous chapters, they are "mystical experiences."

A mystical experience, it will be recalled, is (in the words of James R. Price) "the vital union of an individual's consciousness-as-conscious with its conscious ground."[8] It is distinguished from what Price termed "religious consciousness" in that the latter remains within the realm of intentional consciousness; as discussed in Chapter 5, however, the mystical dimension is implicit in all genuine religious experience. In Teresa's presentation the Fourth Dwelling Places are a transitional realm between religious experience in which the mystical dimension is only implicit, and religious experience in which the

---

[8]Price, "Foundation," pp. 187-88.

mystical dimension will become explicitly conscious. Those at this stage have not yet definitively crossed the border to being "mystics in the narrow sense," but they stand poised at the crossing-point.

In her discussion of the Fourth Dwelling Places, Teresa faces the difficult task of talking about a whole series of gradations of experience that lie between the two extremes of ordinary intentional activity and contemplative "rest," while at the same time maintaining clarity about the basic distinction. The three chapters of the Fourth Dwelling Places describe a range of experiences that occur at this border between "active recollection" and "infused contemplation." The term "contemplative interiority" is chosen to summarize this stage because it is here that the individual experiences the simplification of attention and centering that are the first harbingers of the explicitly contemplative mediation of transcendence.[9]

Despite the fact that Teresa's order of presentation and use of terminology are often rather jumbled, the gist of her meaning is usually remarkably clear. She describes how the first inkling of a form of mystical experience begins with a "gentle drawing inward . . . [like] a hedgehog curling up or a turtle drawing into its shell" (IV:3,3). This "prayer of recollection" (*recogimiento*) is already mystical in that the "drawing inward" is accomplished by the Lord himself:

> Like a good shepherd, with a whistle so gentle that even [the faculties] themselves almost fail to hear it, He makes them recognize His voice and stops them from going too far astray so that they will return to their dwelling place. And this shepherd's whistle has such power that they abandon the exterior things in which they were estranged from Him and enter the castle. (IV:3,2)

Yet in this early stage of recollection, the intentional activity of the individual is also essential. As the quotation above suggests, the acts of

---

[9]On the contemplative mediation and its relationship to "mystical experience in the narrow sense," see "The Range of 'Mystics'" in Chapter 5. On contemplative interiority, see "Introduction" in this Chapter.

"returning," "abandoning," and "entering" are intentional acts of the soul--even though they are done under the influence of divine power. What is more, at this point "meditation, or the work of the intellect, must not be set aside" (IV:3,8).

As the divine influence intensifies, however, one will move into the far more intense "prayer of spiritual delight" (*gustos*). In spiritual delight the activity is almost entirely God's. Teresa compares spiritual delight to a fountain that wells up of its own accord from an inner spring. "Consolation" (*contentos*), by contrast, is like a fountain created by the heavy labor of building intricate aqueducts to bring water from a distant place (IV:2,2-4). Here Teresa makes explicit her basic distinction between the activity of intentional consciousness and the "resting" that characterizes contemplative and mystical experience.

In her valiant struggle to express both subtle gradations and clear distinctions, Teresa makes use of the terminology of faculty psychology. When, for example, she distinguishes between intellect (*el entendimiento*) and mind or imagination (*el pensamiento* or *la imaginación*) (IV:1,8), she employs the classical faculty psychology distinction between the higher and lower faculties to clarify her experience of a deep inner recollection coinciding with noise and activity on a more surface mental level. This basic distinction between an inner dimension that is recollected in God and an outer dimension that may continue in activity--a distinction which is a leitmotif of the entire discussion of the Fourth Dwelling Places--appears in more than one mode. In IV:1,8 the inner recollected dimension is the intellect, while the mind or imagination "flies about" or is "distracted." In IV:3,7-8 the inner dimension that is at rest is the will, while the intellect "clamors."

Assuming that Teresa is not simply confused in her use of terminology here, she appears to be talking about two different levels of recollection in these texts. IV:1 evidently refers to an "active recollection" in which one actively concentrates at a deep (but still intentional) level while paying no attention to surface mental activity, while IV:3 refers to a "passive recollection" in which one experiences one's center beginning to be drawn beyond intentional consciousness while elements of intentional activity continue on their own. These two, in fact, define the perimeters of the Fourth Dwelling Places. The various experiences that Teresa discusses as typical of this stage lie somewhere between the active meditation and concentration of the earlier stages, and the "union" with suspension of the faculties that will define the Fifth Dwelling Places.

A term that Teresa selects to characterize this transitional stage is "absorption" (*absorción*). In spiritual delight, she says, "the faculties are not united but absorbed and looking in wonder at what they see" (IV:2,6). Here, "absorption" seems to be something like fascination; that is, it is a semi-involuntary concentration and simplification of intentional consciousness. Union, on the other hand, will pass beyond intentional consciousness. Absorption, even when it is intense, is not necessarily a sign of union, and it is the latter that is the true goal of the spiritual life (cf. V:3,12).

In her discussion of these experiences of absorption and suspension, the basic faculty psychology distinction between "intellect" and "will" becomes very important for Teresa. For the most part, Teresa seems to regard absorption as something that happens to the intellect--a sort of "stopping" that occasionally goes so far as to be a "suspension" (see IV:3,4; 3,6; 3,7). When God gives absorption it may be good, but when cultivated it can become an illusory "languishing" or "dreamy state" that leads one astray (IV:3,11-13; cf. also V:1,4). More essential to the spiritual life, for Teresa, is something that happens to the will: a gift of "recollection" (IV:3,7) and a response of active love (IV:2,8; cf. also V:3,11-12).

Even as the will enters into this recollection and rest the intellect (*entendimiento*) may continue to "clamor," but one should "leave the intellect go and surrender oneself into the arms of love" (IV:3,8). Although it may be appropriate to gently "strive to cut down the rambling of the intellect," one should never try to shut it down or suspend it by one's efforts. Teresa asserts that

> When His Majesty desires the intellect to stop, He occupies it in another way and gives it a light so far above what we can attain that it remains absorbed. Then, without knowing how, the intellect is much better instructed than it was through all the soul's efforts not to make use of it. Since God gave us our faculties that we might work with them and in this work they find their reward, there is no reason to charm them; we should let them perform their task until God appoints them to another greater one. (IV:3,6)

In this text, an important nuance is lost in the translation. The Spanish original of the first two lines is:

> Cuando Su Majestad quiere que el entendimiento cese ocúpale por otra manera y da una luz en el conocimiento tan sobre la que podemos alcanzar, que le hace quedar absorto, y entonces, sin saber cómo, queda muy mejor enseñada, que no con todas nuestras diligencias para echarle más a perder.

The English translation assimilates *el conocimiento* into *el entendimiento*, "intellect." In this context the most relevant translation of *el conocimiento*, however, is "consciousness." Although it is important not to overinterpret Teresa's admittedly loose terminology, this is an important subtle distinction. The intellect will be suspended from its normal, intentional activity when--and only when--a transcendent light is given in *el conocimiento*, "consciousness."

Faculty psychology has helped Teresa to express many of these nuances. The problematic dimension of the use of faculty psychology terminology in these distinctions, however, is the way it tends to create a certain disjunction between "will" and "intellect." Over the centuries much ink has been spilled over whether the primary "location" of mystical experience is in the will (as love) or in the intellect (as light). Individual quotations from the Fourth Dwelling Places could be used to support either case. For example, IV:3,7-8 states that recollection is "given to the will," so that the will can be at rest in the love of God while the intellect clamors; IV:3,6 speaks of an even more powerful experience as a "light given in consciousness" that can suspend the intellect.

The framework of terminology developed in this work makes it possible to interpret these texts in a way that clarifies the unity of the activities of "intellect" and "will" in a single dynamism of consciousness. The basic mystical experience begins as an implicit sense of "vital union" (Price's term) at the ground of consciousness--in Lonergan's term, "God's love flooding our hearts." As discussed in the sections on the basic structure of religious conversion, the first fruit of this is a radical existential commitment to a new set of values. This is what Teresa speaks of throughout the first four sets of Dwelling Places as the "determination" of the will which enfleshes love.

At its first dawning such an experience of the mystical dimension may be like background music that is barely attended to; still later, like a uniquely charming voice amid the polyphony of voices that make up intentional consciousness.[10] This is the trajectory of experiences delineated in the first four sets of Dwelling Places. In the Fourth Dwelling Places, a threshold is approached; soon the mystical dimension will assert itself as not just one voice amid the polyphony, but the very source of all the music. One is on the verge of passing from "religious consciousness" to "mystical consciousness"--an explicit awareness of the vital union at the level of consciousness-as-conscious.

The more one opens to the ground of consciousness, the more it pervades the entirety of one's being. Actually, the language of "revelation" would be more exact: the more the realm of transcendence reveals itself, the more one discovers that this is the "one thing necessary" in oneself. This explicit opening up of the realm of transcendence--the ground of consciousness--is what Teresa refers to as a "light" at the level of consciousness, first "absorbing" and later "suspending" all intentional activity.

---

[10]The musical analogy is from Lonergan, "Religious Experience," p. 125.

Perhaps the real question at the basis of the controversy over whether mystical experience is primarily of the will or of the intellect is how to define "intellect." If intellect means the intentional, cognitional activities of understanding and judgment, it cannot directly attain to "consciousness-as-conscious." In my reading, this is Teresa's general use of the term. For her, "will" comes closer to expressing the experience of the deepest stratum of human existence as primordially intersubjective and existential.

Those who would make intellect primary, however, seem to mean by it something more like "consciousness." In this case it encompasses the ground of consciousness as well as its mediations, which are all the intentional activities of consciousness. "Intellect" then becomes an umbrella term for every possible form of "knowing," from implicit consciousness and primordial intersubjectivity to cognitive activity and existential commitment. This is closer to Lonergan's model, which is based on an analysis of consciousness.

A criticism of Lonergan's model may arise from the assumption that it is based on the narrower definition of intellect and hence marginalizes much that has traditionally been expressed by the term "will" (i.e., intersubjectivity, affectivity, existential commitment). Chapters 2-4 of this study have shown how this is far from the case. The criticism may arise from the critics' failure to complete the move from faculty psychology to interiority analysis. The real issue is not the definition of intellect, but attention to the integrated activity of human consciousness.

Within the limitations of the terminology available to her, Teresa herself struggled to clarify the difference between a disjointed and an integrated perspective. In line with her foundational image, she focuses her understanding of the unifying dimension of conscious experience on its source in the "center of the soul." She then discusses why it is important to distinguish this true center from another supposed center, the "heart."

True spiritual delight, she asserts, arises from the "center of the soul" (IV:1,5 and 2,5), while consolations are received at the level of the heart only. Consolation restrains the heart by keeping it within its natural activities of emotion and passion, while spiritual delight expands the heart and the whole being to previously unknown depths of grandeur, sweetness, and freedom (IV:3,9). It is clear that, in Teresa's view, the "heart" is sublated by the "center of the soul"; the heart is one among many parts, while the center of the soul is the ground of all.

"Center of the soul" is for Teresa the umbrella term for the unmediated ground of which all operations and experiences are mediations. The various "locations"--heart, mind, intellect, will--name some of the various modes in which the light is refracted or mediated from its source at the center. On a common sense descriptive level, naming various refractions of the light as distinct faculties or regions of experience has some validity; on an explanatory level, however, it is important to clarify their integration as modes of activity within a single consciousness. Teresa's term "center of the soul," which expresses this in spatial imagery, is parallel to Lonergan's theoretical terms "consciousness-as-conscious" or "implicit consciousness."

It is noteworthy that it is exactly when she begins to discuss the emergence of explicit awareness of this "center" that Teresa's struggle to find the appropriate terminology to distinguish different dimensions of experience intensifies. It is here, in the Fourth Dwelling Places, that the spiritual seeker appropriates the contemplative interiority in which deepened awareness of both the ground and the mediated structure of conscious activity becomes possible. Teresa's struggle with language reflects the struggle involved in this contemplative differentiation of consciousness.

To summarize: so far, our interiority analysis has discovered evidence in the *Interior Castle* to confirm and expand our model of human consciousness and religious experience. Teresa's presentation of the spiritual journey through the first four Dwelling Places first firmly asserts the primacy of the transcendent ground of consciousness as the source of all human experience. It then indicates how conscious experience of this transcendent ground is mediated first in moral and religious conversion and then, at more subtle levels, in a profound shift in the focus of intentional consciousness toward "absorption" and, later, "suspension." As this shift progresses, the individual enters upon contemplative interiority--that is, a conscious awareness of, and ability to differentiate between, the ground and the various operations and modes of consciousness. The passage from mere "absorption" to full "union" is the passage from disciplined contemplative practice, through contemplative interiority, to the fullness of mystical experience.

The contemplative interiority of the Fourth Dwelling Places, then, is still only the transition-point between "mystical experience in the broad sense" and "mystical experience in the narrow sense." So far, our interiority analysis has provided new insight into the dynamics of mystical experience in the broad sense, as well as the characteristics of this transitional stage. Our next task will be to discover whether interiority analysis will be able to shed additional light on the specificity of mystical experience in the narrow sense.

Fifth Dwelling Places: Bare Consciousness and Mystical Transformation

While the Fourth Dwelling Places were a transitional phase, the Fifth Dwelling Places mark the decisive entrance into the state Teresa calls "union." Teresa describes what this experience is like:

> There is no need here to use any technique to suspend the mind since all the faculties are asleep in this state--and truly asleep--to the things of this world and to ourselves. As a matter of fact, during the time the union lasts the soul is left as though without its senses, for it has no power to think even if it wants to. In loving, if it does love, it doesn't understand how or what it is it loves or what it would want. In sum, it is like one who in every respect has died to the world so as to live more completely in God. Thus the death is a delightful one, an uprooting from the soul of all the operations it can have while being in the body. (V:1,4)

Union, says Teresa, is "above all earthly joys, above all delights, above all consolations, and still more than that" (V:1,6). In this way she clarifies the fact that union is a definitive step beyond even the "spiritual delights" experienced in the Fourth Dwelling Places. The difference, she says, is "like that between feeling something on the rough outer covering of the body or in the marrow of the bones" (V:1,6).

The inability of the soul at this stage to experience, understand, or judge in the normal, step-by-step manner is expressed by Teresa in terms of a "sleep" or "suspension" of the faculties. During the short time that this dimension of union lasts, senses, imagination, memory, and intellect are inoperative (V:1,4; 1,9; 1,12). It seems that in union intentional consciousness has been completely transcended. This corresponds to what James R. Price has designated the contemplative mediation, which begins with "bare consciousness"--an experience of consciousness without operations or objects--and is fulfilled in mystical consciousness.[11] No object or operation of consciousness is suitable to serve as a "door" to union; rather, the divine Lord who enters the center of the soul must come in "without going through any door" (V:1,12). The divine cannot "enter" human consciousness from without, as an object of intentional consciousness; it can only well up at the ground of consciousness itself.

From the point of view of ordinary intentional consciousness, "bare consciousness" or "consciousness without an object" is very difficult to distinguish from unconsciousness. It may, in fact, be experienced as a greater or lesser degree of "loss of consciousness"; yet the individual is not unconscious in the same sense as would be someone asleep, or in a "dreamy state" (V:1,4-5), or in a coma. Teresa acknowledges that it is crucial to have criteria by which to discern the difference between true "union" and mere sleepiness or dreaminess. In her discussion of this question, she clarifies how union is more than simply "bare consciousness."

---

[11]See "The Range of 'Mystics'" in Chapter 5.

The main criterion for discerning true union, she says, is an absolute certitude that remains after the experience; for "God so places Himself in the interior of the soul that when it returns to itself it can in no way doubt that it was in God and God was in it" (V:1,9-10). Thus, Teresa's desciption of what is experienced subsequent to an episode of "bare consciousness" correlates quite closely with our previous definition of mystical experience as a conscious awareness and appropriation of a "mutual mediation with the divine" at the level of consciousness-as-conscious.

What Teresa calls "a certitude remaining in the soul that only God can place there" (V:1,10), then, is the primary form of "mystical transformation"--that is, the mediation of mystical intersubjectivity within intentional consciousness. Teresa speaks of this state in terms of God being "joined and united with the essence of the soul" (V:1,5). In our terms, we would say that the first evidence in intentional consciousness of the mediation of the divine at the level of consciousness-as-conscious is a transformation at the level of judgment. The transformation is so radical that "even though years go by without God's granting that favor again, the soul can neither forget nor doubt that it was in God and God was in it" (V:1,9).

Stated in terms of the theory of emergence,[12] what is happening here is that a more comprehensive level of organization--that is, the "absolute system" of the divine, in relation to which human consciousness is a sublated system--is operating from "above downward" on its sublated system and transforming it as a whole. Instead of true judgment arising through a laborious process of sifting experience, having insights, comparing various conceptualizations, etc., the fulfillment of the process (certitude) is "given" even though experience and understanding seem to be completely blank (V:1,10).

To say that union and mystical transformation come from "above downward" is to affirm, with Teresa, that the essence of union is grace--

---

[12]See "Science and the Study of Developing Intersubjectivity" in Chapter 4.

that is, it is not acquirable by human effort. Yet this does not mean there is nothing one can do to prepare oneself for it. The will has no direct role in bringing about union (V:1,12), but it does prepare for union by acts involving steadfast determination to seek only God. Prior to the explicit mystical experience of union, there must be repeated implicit mystical experiences of "God's love flooding our hearts" followed by a response of existential self-gift in love.

Chapter 2 of the Fifth Dwelling Places compares this preparatory work to the silkworm's building of its cocoon, within which it will "die" and be transformed. One weaves the cocoon by "getting rid of our self-love and self-will, our attachment to any earthly thing, and by performing deeds of penance, prayer, mortification, obedience, and of all the other things you know" (V:2,6). By the time the gift of union is given, the will "has been entirely surrendered to [God]" and so has no "part to play" in the final entrance of God into the center of the soul (V:1,12).

While chapter 1 of the Fifth Dwelling Places was taken up with presenting the core experience of mystical union and chapter 2 emphasized its preparation and its transforming effects, chapter 3 takes a step back to recall the grounding of explicit mystical union in the general structure of religious conversion. The true essence of union, Teresa says, is not the experiential "delightful union" that she described in V:1. Rather, what is fundamental is union with God's will; the "delightful union" proceeds from that, not vice-versa (V:3,3).

Hence, whether a person has extraordinary experiences of mystical union or not, she may be truly in union with God. As before, Teresa stresses that the essential thing is a true determination of the will to do God's will (V:3,3; 3,5).[13] If this determination is genuine, one cannot be led astray by internal or external temptations (V:3,12). The primary

---

[13]See also *Spiritual Testimony* 25:3, in Kavanaugh and Rodriguez, *Collected Works*, vol. 1. There Teresa wrote: "Getting back to union, I understood that it consists in the spirit being pure and raised above all earthly things so that there is nothing in the soul that wants to turn aside from God's will. . . . we can say of a soul that invariably has determination like this that it is always in union."

criterion for discernment of whether this union of will is genuine is love of neighbor. Teresa wrote, "if we practice love of neighbor with great perfection, we will have done everything" (V:3,9). What is more, "When you see yourselves lacking in this love, even though . . . you experience some little suspension in the prayer of quiet . . . believe me you have not reached union" (V:3,12).

Once again, Teresa is emphasizing that what is happening in the Fifth Dwelling Places continues to enact the basic structure of religious conversion. Mystical transformation is not something different from religious conversion, but a particularly intense fulfillment of it. Religious conversion consists of "God's love flooding our hearts" and transforming our beings at their roots, beginning with our way of valuing and loving. The true sign of conversion is existential transformation. If the contemplative or mystical dimensions (that is, the conscious "resting" in God, or the "suspension of the faculties") become disjointed from the total structure of religious conversion, they are of little use and may even be dangerous. Teresa, the great mystic, will return repeatedly to this theme: it is not having experiences that counts, but being truly converted--and showing it in action.

Teresa expresses the radical nature of the conversion that "union" involves by comparing it explicitly to death. In the union of wills the death required is an overcoming of anything that distracts one from total determination to serve God. In the "delightful union" there is such a total stilling of all inner and outer activity that it even physically resembles death (V:1,4). In either case, receiving the gift of union is impossible unless one dies (V:3,5). Like the silkworm who must enter the cocoon and lose all in order to become a butterfly, the soul must leave behind all things and be prepared to lose even its very structure in order to be transformed.

Like the worm who becomes a beautiful flying creature, the soul transformed by union has an entirely new structure and new capacities. The new structure is a new likeness to God. Teresa compares this to the way soft wax is restructured when it is impressed with a seal (V:2,12).

First the wax must be softened so as to break down old structures and resistances and dispose it to receive a new imprint. This is comparable to withdrawal from intentional consciousness and entrance into the state of "bare consciousness." The new imprint comes from the welling up of divine consciousness at the center of that pristine state. This is the beginning of mystical transformation in the "narrow sense."

This new mediation of divine life in human consciousness is characterized by Teresa as a matter of the soul having "charity [put] in order within her" (V:2,12). Whereas before the soul's loves were driven by a variety of motivations, now its love is directly moved by divine lovc. The result is not only an entirely new level of joy (V:1,6), but also an entirely new level of pain. This pain is a grief felt in "the intimate depths of our being" (V:2,11). It arises from an intense sense of compassion with God, whose infinite love is constantly being rejected and trampled upon (V:2,10-14).

This transformation of affect is one of the strongest evidences of the divine life mediated in the center of the soul. As the union with the divine mediated at the level of consciousness-as-conscious is further mediated in every dimension of human experience, the individual discovers capacities for feeling and loving at a depth never before imagined. Once one has tasted this divine depth of love, no lesser love can fully satisfy one (V:2,8). As discussed above, Teresa stresses that this love is not a matter only of inner feeling, but of greatly increased care to live wholeheartedly for God and to put oneself out for others. The one who is faithful to this gift will bear much fruit, bringing many others to the service of God (V:4,6).

While a transformation of affect and of active caring is remarkable, Teresa suggests that the transformation union effects has a yet more remarkable quality. She writes, "I hold that it is God's desire that a favor so great not be given in vain; if a person doesn't herself benefit, the favor will benefit others" (V:3,1). Even if the individual to whom the momentary gift of union has been given is careless and returns to an unspiritual life, the transforming power of that moment of union is so great that it will continue to bear its fruit even after the individual no longer is actively concerned to do so.

Evidently what happens in union so transcends the individual that, to a certain degree, it can "carry on" without the individual's active participation. Stated in terms of emergence, "union" is the emergence in individual consciousness of awareness of participation in a level of organization that is higher and more comprehensive than that of the individual consciousness. Once this breakthrough of "mystical intersubjectivity" has occurred, that higher level exerts a greatly enhanced "above downward" influence upon the individual consciousness. That means that the deliberate, intentional activities of the individual are sublated within a more comprehensive "plan" which may not be accessible to the individual at the intentional level of consciousness.

In a certain sense the "union" that characterizes the Fifth Dwelling Places is the end of the journey. The emptying out of intentional consciousness reaches a limit in "bare consciousness," and explicit mystical transformation in the narrow sense--the mediation of divine consciousness in human consciousness--has already begun. Teresa acknowledges this when she says, "what is in this dwelling place and the next are almost identical" (V:2,7). Her sentence continues, however, by stating that "the force of the effects [in the Sixth] is very different." The Sixth and Seventh Dwelling Places will not bring a radically new state, for they are degrees of mystical union. In them, however, this union will be stabilized, and its mediation within all dimensions of human life will be brought to completion.

Sixth Dwelling Places: Mystical Knowledge

At first glance, the Sixth Dwelling Places seem the most difficult to summarize in a brief treatment. Teresa herself required nearly 70 pages (out of a total of 170)[14] to discuss them, and within those pages she covered a stunning variety of experiences that one may encounter at this stage of the journey. The limits of the present inquiry preclude detailed consideration of all these experiences. Instead, our goal will be to summarize and interpret the basic transforming process that is going on here.

The Sixth Dwelling Places are another "between" or transitional stage, but in a less radical sense than was the case for the Fourth Dwelling Places. Whereas the Fourth Dwelling Places marked the transition into "union," the Sixth Dwelling Places mark the transition from momentary to permanent union. From an explanatory perspective the significance of the Sixth Dwelling Places is rightly downplayed, because what really count are the breakthrough to union (Fifth Dwelling Places) and its ultimate establishment as a permanent condition (Seventh Dwelling Places).

From a descriptive perspective, however, the passage between these two is likely to be lengthy and extraordinarily demanding. In Teresa's own case it took most of her life; for while she received her first experiences of union early in her religious life (about age 21) and began to have such experiences regularly in midlife, she did not arrive at the "spiritual marriage" (Seventh Dwelling Places) until the age of 57. For this reason she felt it necessary and valuable to give a protracted account of some of what happens during that transition.

Teresa had portrayed the experience uniquely characteristic of the Fifth Dwelling Places as a "union" usually accompanied by such a profound suspension of the faculties that only by the effects following afterward (especially the "certitude" of God's presence) can one clearly

---

[14]In the English translation of Rodriguez and Kavanaugh.

distinguish it from unconsciousness. In the Sixth Dwelling Places, however, the experience of union appears in much more varied guises.

Sometimes it involves an even more extreme suspension, one which Teresa designates "ecstasy" (*éxtasis*; VI:4,13) or "rapture" (*arrobamiento*; VI:4,9).[15] In this case breath may be suspended and all the "doors of the dwelling places" (the senses, faculties, etc.) are closed. Afterward a high degree of absorption of the will and withdrawal of the intellect may continue for days (VI:4,14). This differs from the suspensions experienced in the Fifth Dwelling Places primarily in degree; the duration and depth of the suspension is greater, and the effects following afterward are more pronounced and longlasting.

The raptures or ecstasies of the Sixth Dwelling Places, however, also differ from what is experienced in the Fifth in that suspension of the ordinary activities of the faculties may at times coexist with an extraordinary form of "knowing." Teresa says that sometimes "When the soul is in this suspension, the Lord likes to show it some secrets, things about heaven, and imaginative visions" (VI:4,5). Even though one may be very inarticulate about these experiences afterward, the knowledge is real. Teresa compares it to being ushered into a room full of awe-inspiring treasures where one may be so overwhelmed by the abundance of beauty that afterwards one cannot describe any of the treasures specifically, but one knows that one has been there and has seen many wonders (VI:4,8).

"Rapture" (*arrobamiento*) is the experience uniquely characteristic of the Sixth Dwelling Places,[16] and Teresa is quite clear in stating that this new form of knowing is of the essence of true rapture. She asserts:

> I hold that if at times in its raptures the soul doesn't understand these secrets, its raptures are not given by God but caused by some natural

---

[15]Teresa states that the two are essentially the same (heading of VI:4).

[16]Teresa uses a great many words to talk about the experiences of the Sixth Dwelling Places. Here we are using "rapture" to refer to the overall category of experiences, while other terms refer to subcategories.

> weakness. It can happen to persons with a weak constitution . . . that any spiritual force will overcome the natural powers, and the soul will be absorbed as I believe I mentioned in reference to the prayer of quiet. These experiences have nothing to do with rapture. In a rapture, believe me, God carries off for Himself the entire soul, and, as to someone who is His own and His spouse, He begins showing it some little part of the kingdom that it has gained by being espoused to Him. (VI:4,9)

As in the Fourth Dwelling Places, Teresa wishes to distinguish between "absorption" and the deeper spiritual states. Again, "absorption" seems to refer to a state of intentional consciousness in which attention is totally riveted at a deep, prelinguistic level by pleasurable inner feelings. "Union," on the other hand, wells up from beyond intentional consciousness. Those who cultivate absorption, perhaps even thinking that because it takes them beyond ordinary discursive or imagistic consciousness it is a form of union, are making a costly and dangerous mistake (VI:7,13-15).

The presence of the concentration, pleasure, and imagelessness that characterize absorption, then, is not a sure sign of union. Sometimes union may be accompanied by such absorption, but it need not be. In chapter 2 of the Sixth Dwelling Places Teresa described such an experience of union without absorption:

> . . . this activity comes from the place where the Lord who is unchanging dwells. The activity is not like that found in other feelings of devotion, where the great absorption in delight can make us doubtful. Here all the senses and faculties remain free of any absorption, wondering what this could be . . . . (VI:2,5)

Here Teresa states that the essential quality of union is that it "comes from the place where the Lord who is unchanging dwells." She notes that this favor "proceeds from the interior part of the soul" (VI:2,7) and cannot be confused with any experience proceeding from the imagination or other faculties. Speaking of the "very interior part" where "the Lord dwells" is Teresa's way of describing the mediation of the divine at the level of consciousness-as-conscious. In the "bare consciousness" experiences of the Fifth Dwelling Places this mediation at the ground of consciousness overwhelmed and "blanked out" the ordinary, intentional activity of consciousness; here in the Sixth Dwelling Places, the transformation of the ground is more and more fully mediated within a transformed form of intentional activity that can properly be called "mystical knowledge."

This knowledge, says Teresa, is "inscribed in the very interior part of the soul" so that it can never be doubted or forgotten (VI:4,6). Once again, Teresa is emphasizing that the first mediation of the ground within intentional consciousness occurs in the certitude instilled at the level of judgment (cf. also VI:9,10). In addition, however, this extraordinary experience of "knowing" may be mediated at the level of understanding and/or images in the form of "visions."

Visions may be intellectual or imaginative. In an intellectual vision, the soul "will feel Jesus Christ, our Lord, beside it. Yet, it does not see Him, either with the eyes of the body or with those of the soul" (VI:8,2). Here there is not only the certitude of presence, but also a clear understanding of who it is who is present and of his personal response at each moment (VI:8,3). Blessed with such a continuous lively awareness of God's presence, the soul "goes about almost continually with actual love for the One who it sees and understands is at its side" (VI:8,4). Such visions can last for "many days and sometimes even more than a year" (VI:8,3).

Imaginative visions, on the other hand, may come and go as quickly as a "streak of lightning" (VI:9,3), and in any case it is impossible for them to last long (VI:9,4; cf. also 9,8). Here, says Teresa, the Lord gives the soul a glimpse of a glorious image of his sacred humanity (VI:9,3). She continues:

> Although I say "image" let it be understood that, in the opinion of the one who sees it, it is not a painting but truly alive, and sometimes the Lord is speaking to the soul and even revealing great secrets. But you must understand that even though the soul is detained by this vision for some while, it can no more fix its gaze on the vision than

> it can on the sun. Hence the vision always passes very quickly, but not because its brilliance is painful, like the sun's, to the inner eye. . . . The brilliance of this inner vision is like that of an infused light coming from a sun covered by something as transparent as a properly-cut diamond. (VI:9,4)

The characteristic of the imaginative vision is this "light" that seems to come from such an entirely different region than the one in which we live that "if [one] were to spend his whole life trying to imagine that light . . . he would be unable to do so." Its effect, she observes, is that

> within an instant so many things together are taught [one] that if he were to work for many years with his imagination and mind in order to systematize them he wouldn't be able to do so, not with even one thousandth part of them. (VI:5,7)

This "light" is by no means impersonal; Teresa takes great care to emphasize that in the imaginative vision it is a consoling, awe-inspiring--and sometimes terrifying--glimpse of the Lord himself (VI:9,3-7; 9,14). When it is authentic, it leaves behind the fruit of increased humility, fortitude, and virtue (VI:9,11; 9,17). These, rather than the power of the experience itself, are the sure signs for discerning whether it is truly from God.

These descriptions of both intellectual and imaginative visions graphically illustrate how divine life and knowledge can be mediated in human consciousness. Yet Teresa is very insistent that such visions, and the extraordinary knowledge that accompanies them, are not essential for the union with God that is the goal of human life. She states that "there are many holy persons who have never received one of these favors; and others who receive them but are not holy" (VI:9,16; cf. also 8,10). Visions and other extraordinary experiences should never be desired or requested, for with such lack of humility one would quickly discover that "by the very way you think you will gain, you will lose" (VI:9,15).

In these statements Teresa indicates that despite the large number of pages she devotes to the extraordinary knowledge that may come in the Sixth Dwelling Places, she remains clear on its place within the basic structure of religious conversion. She asserts, "One should consider the virtues, and who it is who serves our Lord with greater mortification, humility, and purity of conscience; this is the one who will be the holiest" (VI:8,10). Extraordinary experiences are not union itself, but one of its possible mediations. Their main value is that they inflame love and are a help toward possessing the virtues (VI:9,17-18).

In terms of our explanatory framework, Teresa's statements are best understood by clarifying why these experiences are valuable and yet are not of the essence of "union." The key insight is that if union is the mediation of the divine at the level of consciousness-as-conscious, it can never be an "experience" in the sense of something encountered within the realm of intentional consciousness. Neither the transcendent realm nor consciousness-as-conscious can ever be an object of intentional consciousness.[17] That is why the "bare consciousness" of the Fifth Dwelling Places appears as more like unconsciousness than like anything else in experience; and it is also why Teresa can assert that people who are not aware of having any special spiritual experiences at all can be in union.

All "experiences of union"--beginning with the "certitude" that follows bare consciousness in the Fifth Dwelling Places, and continuing with the visions and other extraordinary experiences of the Sixth Dwelling Places--are mediations of union within some level of intentional consciousness. Union mediates itself by restructuring and expanding intentional consciousness in definite ways. Properly discerned, these are not only signs of the authentic breaking through of union; they also contribute to its gradual stabilization into a permanent state.

The mediations of union that Teresa concentrates on fall into three major categories: 1) increased active love of God and neighbor; 2) certitude of God's presence; and 3) extraordinary understanding of God

---

[17]On the transcendent realm, see "The Specificity of Mystical Experience" in Chapter 5. On consciousness-as-conscious, see "The Subject-as-Subject" in Chapter 3.

and God's ways. Normally all three will be present at least to some degree. If they are ranked, however, the first appears as the most essential sign of union, the second is the next most noteworthy, and the third is least essential. This order of mediation is exactly in accord with the essential structure of religious conversion as understood by Lonergan.

God's love transforming the heart comes first, and is followed closely by existential determination (active love) and conviction (certitude). This love and conviction from "above downward" are in themselves the most essential forms of religious knowledge. In Teresa's case, the "above downward" dynamic--the opening up of divine presence at the ground of consciousness--was so extraordinarily powerful that it was also mediated in experiences of supernatural light, living images, a feeling of the personal presence of Jesus and various saints, and insight into many divine "secrets." Yet the center of all these, insofar as they are authentic, must be the same as in more garden-variety experiences of religious conversion: namely, God's love calling for a response of love and existential determination. As Teresa works her way through the eleven chapters of the Sixth Dwelling Places, she returns again and again to her basic principle of discernment: what is born of God's love will bear fruit in love of God and neighbor, manifested in determination and active self-giving. Without that as their center, Teresa's cornucopia of experiences would be nothing more than a wild ride through the outer (or inner) reaches of the psyche.

It so happens that in Teresa's own case mystical union was also mediated in both extraordinary understanding and extraordinary conceptual knowledge. Her experiences, fed from "above downward," formed the basis of gradually increasing conceptual knowledge from "below upward" as she gained broadened experience, clearer understanding, and more educated judgment in regard to spiritual realities. Thus the conjunction of mystical gift and natural intellectual labor enabled her to become a "doctor of the Church,"[18] teaching millions about the ways of God. It is important to remember, however, that she herself taught that neither extraordinary understanding nor extraordinary conceptual knowledge is essential to union.

Teresa also emphasized that no matter how gifted one is with extraordinary "above downward" experiences, one must still work from "below upward" as well. She wrote:

> To be always withdrawn from corporeal things and enkindled in love is the trait of angelic spirits not of those who live in mortal bodies . . . . when the fire in the will . . . is not enkindled and God's presence is not felt, it is necessary that we seek this presence. (VI:7,6 . . . 9)

In this part of her presentation Teresa consistently refers to the central experience of "God's love flooding the heart" in terms of the enkindling of the will with love. Since this condition is not yet permanent, one often must "blow on the fire" by working with the intellect (VI:7,8). For those in whom union has already broken through, this work with the intellect is not discursive reflection but "representing truths to the intellect by means of the memory" (VI:7,10-12). It is a "dwelling on the mysteries" in an imagistic mode.

With this distinction between engaging in discursive or conceptual thought and dwelling on images, Teresa shows her wisdom as a "methodologist." Concepts are a reified end product of cognitive activity; it is difficult and slow work to go from there either backward (to lively images) or forward (to existential determination). Images, on the other hand, have much more potential for being fertile "sparks" for a knowledge-process that need not linger with concepts but can easily leap onward to judgments and determination.

In addition, the images to which Teresa refers here are not impersonal mental pictures, but rather are "the mysteries"--patterns of

---

[18]Teresa was officially named a "Doctor of the Church" in 1970. She was one of the first two women ever to be so designated.

engagement between the personal Lord and his people. Since intersubjective engagement is the original ground of human existence,[19] by meditating on such an image one enters the reflection process with such intersubjectively-oriented capacities as affect, desire, and love already engaged. Teresa's faculty psychology required her to speak of this activity simply as that of the memory (that is, picture-making faculty) and intellect. An interiority analysis can take a more holistic perspective, viewing it as a total activity of consciousness that engages the deepest levels of memory, affect and desire in a thrust forward toward loving knowledge and commitment.

Even though Teresa is clear that in the strict sense "union" goes beyond all concepts, beyond all images, and even beyond all "experiences," she is also clear that as long as one is a mortal human being this transcendence is integrally related to its mediations within human moral, affective, intellectual, and corporeal existence. This integral relation of mediation[20] can be "read out" starting either from the side of the ground or from the side of the mediations. As a principle for discerning whether or not an individual is in union, the integral relation means that one can be certain of the presence of union only when one sees its characteristic mediations (love, certitude, wisdom, etc.).

As a principle for entering into contemplative prayer, the integral relation means that one disposes oneself for union by actively setting up processes that engage one's whole being at its deepest level. Union itself is sheer gift, only available as a breakthrough from "above downward"; for this reason any attempt to grasp it directly by stilling or vacating all operations of intentional consciousness is misguided. The appropriate procedure, rather, is to engage intentional consciousness

---

[19]See "The Subject as Intersubjective" in Chapter 3. See also John McDargh, *Psychoanalytic Object Relations Theory and the Study of Religion* (Lanham, MD: University Press of America, 1983).

[20]For discussion of the term "integral relation of mediation," see "The Notion of Mediation" in Chapter 4.

with known mediations of the divine. Anthropologically, this means love, faith, ethical behavior, true doctrine. Theologically--for the Christian--it means Christ. These two come together in Teresa's prescription for prayer: gentle and loving "dwelling" on the mysteries of Christ's life.

Addressing the concern that such active meditation might be inappropriate for the advanced or might even impede union, Teresa wrote:

> . . . I know that [dwelling on the mysteries] will not impede the most sublime prayer. I don't think it's good to fail to dwell often on these mysteries. If as a result the Lord suspends the intellect, well and good; for even though the soul may not so desire He will make it abandon what it was dwelling on. And I am very certain that this procedure is not a hindrance but a very great help toward every good . . . . (VI:7,12)

Teresa acknowledges that "anyone whom the Lord places in the seventh dwelling place rarely, or hardly ever, needs to make this effort" (VI:7,9). Those in the Sixth Dwelling Places, however, are not yet in that condition of permanent companionship with the Lord. They are still involved in the arduous process of the radical restructuring of spirit and psyche that precedes permanent union. This restructuring is extraordinarily painful--so much so that Teresa says more than once that the individual "longs to die" (VI:6,1; 7,3; 11,1) or even is in "danger of death" (VI:11,4; 11,11).

From the very beginning of her presentation of the Sixth Dwelling Places Teresa stresses that this part of the spiritual journey will involve a great many interior and exterior trials. Even the much enhanced joy of these Dwelling Places comes inextricably mixed with a paradoxical pain that "reaches to the soul's very depths" (VI:2,4). This pain is "great, although delightful and sweet," and "the soul . . . would never want to be deprived of this pain" (VI:2,2). This pain, Teresa suggests, is the intensity of the unsatisfied desire for God; it is like the spark of a fire that smolders but never quite lights (VI:2,4; cf. also 4,3). The ever-intensifying desire for God that characterizes these Dwelling Places is a terrible affliction, and yet at the same time it is distinguishable from the pain given by "the devil" because it is accompanied by a kind of peace (VI:6,6; cf. also 11,6).

At times, however, there is pain without this mitigating joy and peace. The advanced state of these souls means that they have more, not less, awareness of their sinfulness and weakness. One may be convinced that one is utterly without love or grace (VI:1,11), and that one's sins are so great that one is in imminent danger of permanently losing God (VI:7,2-3). Convinced that one is rejected by God, one may even suffer "an interior oppression so keen and unbearable that I don't know what to compare this experience to if not to the oppression of those who suffer in hell" (VI:1,9).

In addition, the total loss of control over oneself that occurs with sudden raptures can be terrifying--like being impetuously snatched up by a "great and powerful Giant" (VI:5,2-3). The final transition into permanent union takes all these forms of suffering to their ultimate limits. Teresa writes of how the soul suddenly experiences a "blow" that comes from "elsewhere (the soul doesn't understand from where or how)." She continues:

> . . . in my opinion, it isn't felt where earthly sufferings are felt, but in the very deep and intimate part of the soul, where this sudden flash of lightning reduces to dust everything it finds in this earthly nature of ours; for while this experience lasts nothing can be remembered about our being. In an instant the experience so binds the faculties that they have no freedom for anything except those things that will make this pain increase. (VI:11,3)

This blow causes such radical pain that "though [one] is a person who has suffered and is used to suffering severe pains," one cannot avoid crying out (VI:11,3). The essential source of the pain is total awareness of distance from God (VI:11,3; 11,5). This is not merely a conceptual or emotional awareness, for it literally brings a person very near to death and "leaves the body very disjointed" (VI:11,4). One has absolutely no control over the experience; the soul can no more resist it than "it can, if thrown into a fire, stop flames from having heat and burning it" (VI:11,8).

This final experience of radical pain in the "very deep and intimate part of the soul" seems to be a sort of "last stand" of intentional consciousness experienced as separate from its own ground. The fact of separateness--expressed here as "distance from God"--becomes the all-involving focus of intentional consciousness at this point; desire for oneness totally consumes it, and yet it can do nothing to achieve what it desires. Teresa wrote:

> As for now, the reasoning faculty is in such a condition that the soul is not master of it, nor can the soul think of anything else than of why it is grieving, of how it is absent from its Good, and of why it should want to live. It feels a strange solitude because no creature in all the earth provides it company, nor do I believe would any heavenly creature, not being the One whom it loves; rather, everything torments it. But the soul sees that it is like a person hanging, who cannot support himself on any earthly thing; nor can it ascend to heaven. (VI:11,5)

The "double bind" in this experience is that the very nature of intentional consciousness is to desire, that is, to intentionally move toward the good; and yet it is totally incapable of overcoming its sense of separateness from that which is the ultimate goal of all its desiring--i.e., the divine which is mediated at the ground of consciousness. Intentionality, by definition, involves a subject intending an object; it requires a "standing over against" on the part of the subject who objectifies some portion of total experience in order to know it and to act deliberately upon it. Intentionality cannot overcome the subject-object distinction any more than a person can literally lift herself by her own bootstraps. The resolution to this radical double bind can only come from beyond intentional consciousness.

Seventh Dwelling Places: Mystical Intersubjectivity

Although the Seventh Dwelling Places are for Teresa the culmination of the spiritual journey, it is noteworthy that her account of the most sublime mystical gifts is interwoven with straightforward realism. In very down-to-earth language she notes the human person's continuing potential for imperfection, instability, and sin (VII:2,9; 3,14; 4,1-3). As long as one remains in this earthly life, a grain of relativity remains in the "permanent" peace, stability and perfect love that come in the Seventh Dwelling Places (cf. VII:2,1).

The Seventh Dwelling Places are, nevertheless, a profoundly new order of experience. The shattering pain at the end of the Sixth Dwelling Places does indeed mark a breakthrough of the "center dwelling place" to more complete pre-eminence. The divine Spouse, says Teresa, brings the soul "into His dwelling place which is this seventh" (VII:1,3). This is something more than either the "union" of the Fifth Dwelling Places or the "rapture" of the Sixth Dwelling Places, even though in both of these God was truly united with the soul. To explain the crucial difference, Teresa states that in the earlier unions and raptures the soul seemed to be called to its "superior part," whereas here the soul fully and definitively enters its "center" (VII:1,5).

Teresa's lack of an adequate explanatory framework within which to place her experiences shows through as she struggles to describe what she means by this key distinction. At one point she remarks in frustration, "This center of our soul, or this spirit, is something so difficult to explain, and even believe in, that I think, Sisters, I'll not give you the temptation to disbelieve what I say, for I do not know how to explain this center" (VII:2,10). This quotation, in which Teresa appears to equate "center of the soul" and "spirit," exemplifies the difficulties in analyzing her use of terminology; for elsewhere there is evidence that "spirit" is essentially equivalent to "superior part"--which (as noted above) she carefully distinguishes from the "center."

The essential distinction between "superior part" and "center" appears to be that even though the center is "the center of the soul itself" (VII:2,9), it is more essentially "the room where [God] dwells alone" (VII:1,3). The "center" actually belongs to God even more intrinsically than it belongs to the soul. Ultimately, the center is the absolute ground of consciousness; that divine center is mediated in the "openness" or "relative ground of consciousness" that is the ground of a human being.[21] The "superior part," on the other hand, is a mediation that belongs essentially to the soul and so must go out of itself to enter into God.

In terms of our explanatory schema, the "center" has already been correlated with consciousness-as-conscious or the ground of consciousness, where the transcendent can be mediated "without going through any door" (VII:2,3). As for the "superior part," in her *Spiritual Testimonies* Teresa speaks of the "spirit" as "the higher part of the will."[22] If the assumption that "superior part" is equivalent to "spirit" is correct, "superior part" would then correlate with the highest intentional operations of which the human person is capable; namely, acts of existential valuing, decision, and self-transcendence.[23]

The experiential distinction between the "superior part" and the "center" is well illustrated by the way Teresa describes the "flights of the spirit" and "raptures" of the Sixth Dwelling Places contrasted with the peaceful dwelling of the Seventh. In the flight of the spirit, Teresa wrote, "sometimes suddenly a movement of the soul is felt so swift that it seems the spirit is carried off, and at a fearful speed especially in the beginning" (VI:5,1). The image is of a loss of control, experienced as a destabilizing--though temporary--surrender of one's power of

---

[21]On these distinctions, see "Linking General and Special Categories" in Chapter 5. See also the reference to the works of John of the Cross in Chapter 6, footnote 36.

[22]*Spiritual Testimonies* 25.

[23]Cf. Lonergan's comments on religious experience in *Method in Theology*, pp. 105-7.

existential self-determination. In the Seventh Dwelling Places these "flights" are never experienced, and other forms of rapture are rare as well (VII:3,12).

Instead, Teresa writes, "in this temple of God, in this His dwelling place, He alone and the soul rejoice together in the deepest silence" (VII:3,11). In another place she describes this stillness more fully:

> The Lord puts the soul in this dwelling place of His, which is the center of the soul itself. They say the empyreal heaven where the Lord is does not move as do the other heavens; similarly, it seems, in the soul that enters here there are none of those movements that usually take place in the faculties and the imagination and do harm to the soul, nor do these stirrings take away its peace. (VII:2,9)

These texts indicate that with entrance into the Seventh Dwelling Places there has been a definitive shift in the soul's "center of gravity." Instead of being snatched out of itself and thrown completely off balance by a powerful breakthrough of the transcendent ground, the soul is at home and in perfect peace there. No longer is union experienced as "proceeding" from the soul's center (cf. VI:2,5-7), for now the soul is permanently *at* the center. Once this state has been established, it is essentially stable. Even though there is not always the same level of intense awareness (VII:1,9) and there may even be severe challenges (VII:4,2), Teresa states that in her experience "the essential part of the soul never moved from that room" (VII:1,10). This stability is largely a result of the fact that achieving the state is an act of God, not of the soul. Teresa notes:

> . . . the faculties and senses have nothing to do with what goes on in this dwelling place. . . . Nor does the Lord in all the favors He grants the soul here . . .receive any assistance from the soul itself, except what it has already done in surrendering itself totally to God. (VII:3,10)

The stabilization of this state of mystical union in the Seventh Dwelling Places reaches a point where it permeates normal everyday activities, instead of being an experience that overwhelms or draws one away from those activities (cf. VII:1,8). Teresa asserts that the assurance of this union is so complete that its peace is not disturbed by "times of war, trial and fatigue" that may continue to cause tumult and trouble in the other dwelling places--that is, in the "faculties, senses and passions" (VII:2,10-11; cf. also 4,10).

The first intimations of this capacity to sustain the experience of mystical union at the same time as some form of intentional consciousness occurred in some of the raptures and visions of the Sixth Dwelling Place. There, however, the objects upon which intentional consciousness could focus during the time of union were almost entirely of an extraordinary kind--i.e., the "secrets" of God. In rapture, Teresa described the faculties as largely "suspended," even though some extraordinary form of understanding was nevertheless able to occur (VI:4,5). In the Seventh Dwelling Place, however, the faculties are ordinarily not suspended at all.

On this point Teresa states, "In my opinion, the faculties are not lost here; they do not work, but remain as though in amazement"; even as God and the soul "rejoice together in deepest silence," the intellect is permitted to observe what is taking place at the center as if "through a small crevice" (VII:3,11). Elsewhere, she clarified the distinction between earlier states and this one:

> [In union or rapture] . . . the Lord joins the soul to Himself. But he does so by making it blind and deaf . . . . when He joins it to Himself, it doesn't understand anything; for all the faculties are lost.
>
> In this seventh dwelling place the union comes about in a different way: our good God now desires to remove the scales from the soul's eyes and let it see and understand, although in a strange way, something of the favor He grants it. (VII:1,5-6)

In the Seventh Dwelling Places, then, the experienced relationship between the "center" and the activity of the faculties exhibits a certain paradox of oneness and separateness. This can be explained in terms of our previous discussion of the integral relation between the immediate ground of consciousness and its mediation in operations.

In ordinary intentional consciousness there is no awareness of the immediate ground of consciousness. When that awareness first breaks through, it eclipses intentional consciousness; and in any case, intentional consciousness can never grasp the immediate ground in its focus. As awareness of the immediate ground becomes habitual, however, the fact that it is the ground *of* the operations comes into awareness. Whereas from the side of intentional consciousness, separateness is necessarily the reality, from the side of the ground, oneness is the yet deeper reality. The paradox of this state of consciousness is that, indeed, there both *is* and *is not* a radical distinction between the immediate ground and its mediations in the operations of consciousness: all is one, and yet the ground is infinitely more than its mediations.

This paradox of oneness and separateness--with oneness being the more foundational truth--is expressed thus by Teresa:

> In the spiritual marriage the union is like what we have when rain falls from the sky into a river or fount; all is water, for the rain that fell from heaven cannot be divided or separated from the water of the river. Or it is like what we have when a little stream enters the sea, there is no means of separating the two. Or, like the bright light entering a room through two different windows; although the streams of light are separate when entering the room, they become one. (VII:2,4)

The oneness of God and the soul is such that it is as if the soul had died, and only Christ lives (VII:2,5; 3,2). The "water," "milk," or "Sun" which belong to the Lord at the center overflow to all the faculties and to the whole corporeal being (VII:2,6; cf. also 3,8). Here we see the true origin of Teresa's foundational vision of the "diamond castle" (I:1,1): it was her own experience of the spiritual marriage in which the light at the center of the soul truly does permeate the totality of the being.[24]

In this culminating stage, then, unitive consciousness, which first broke through in the Fifth Dwelling Places and was joined with a form of extraordinary intentional consciousness in the Sixth, is now joined as well with the state of ordinary intentional consciousness. This makes it possible to be consciously in union and busy about the world's business at the same time. Even though to some degree this may lead to a sense of "division" in the soul--as if one part (like the biblical Mary) rests in the enjoyment of union while the other (like Martha) is engaged in business affairs (VII:1,10)--at the same time the two are in complete harmony and recognize each other as equally essential to the work of service that is to be done (VII:3,10-12).

It is here, in the discussion of the culmination of mystical union, that the full context of Teresa's consistent emphasis on the priority of concrete, active love comes into focus. When she insists that spiritual growth is not only a matter of prayer and contemplation, but of virtue (VII:4,9), service (VII:1,8), and unremitting struggle on all levels (VII:4,10), she speaks from the perspective of one who knows that the mystical dimension permeates all as surely as a light placed at the center permeates a room.

Teresa notes that the effect of spiritual marriage on the soul is that it is "fortified, enlarged, and made capable" (VII:3,12). This enhancement of capacities wells up from its center in the love of God and reconfigures every dimension of the individual's activity. The soul becomes capable--even desirous--of great suffering for the sake of love (VII:3,4-7). Teresa assures those who are gifted with the most sublime mystical union that they can expect to have less exterior peace and quiet than ever, since mystical gifts are given not so that one can enjoy rest at the center, but for the sake of serving the needs of all (VII:4,5-15). "This is the reason for prayer, my daughters, the purpose of this

[24]See Coelho, "Transformation of the Symbol of the Interior Castle."

spiritual marriage: the birth always of good works, good works," she admonishes (VII:4,6).

The astute reader may note that visions, which are a prominent dimension of Teresa's presentation of the Seventh Dwelling Places, have not yet been discussed. The reason for this delay is that, in my view, the nature and import of visions can only be correctly assessed in the context of the preceding discussion of cognitive, existential, and behavioral structures of the culminating mystical union.

Teresa states that the first breakthrough of the Seventh Dwelling Places is marked by visions that appear in "the very interior center of the soul" (VII:2,3; cf. also 1,5-7; 2,2). She emphasizes that "You must understand that there is the greatest difference between all the previous visions and those of this dwelling place" (VII:2,2). The first such vision is "an imaginative vision of His most sacred humanity so that the soul will understand and not be ignorant of this sovereign gift" (VII:2,1). Later there are intellectual visions of the greatest delicacy and grandeur, including one of the Most Blessed Trinity (VII:1,6; 2,3). Teresa wrote:

> What God communicates here to the soul in an instant is a secret so great and a favor so sublime--and the delight the soul experiences is so extreme--that I don't know what to compare it to. I can say only that the Lord wishes to reveal for that moment, in a more sublime manner than through any spiritual vision or taste, the glory of heaven. One can say no more--insofar as can be understood--than that the soul, I mean the spirit, is made one with God. . . . For He has desired to be so joined with the creature that, just as those who are married cannot be separated, He doesn't want to be separated from the soul. (VII:2,3)

The import of these visions is the communication of the most profound level of intersubjectivity with God. It is here, in the culminating "spiritual marriage," that we see the strongest evidence for our original hypothesis that the prime analogue for the transcendent ground of consciousness is "a state of intersubjectivity." Teresa can find no better terminology for the fulfillment of mystical union than the language of romantic love and marital union. While some might argue that this language should be understood as merely evocative or descriptive, not explanatory, a case can be made that it is, indeed, explanatory.

The preceding analysis of this culminating state in terms of the "immediate ground of consciousness" and its "mediation in operations" concluded that in the spiritual marriage there is a "paradox of oneness and separateness" because awareness of the "one" ground permeates the "separate" mediations and yet is not swallowed up by, or reduced to, any of them. This impersonal terminology has been helpful in clarifying these structures and relationships; yet it fails to convey adequately the most central fact about the reality under discussion. The "ground of consciousness" is not an object, but a "subject-as-subject" whose self-presence precedes and underlies its presence-with other realities. In fact, a subject-as-subject is more fully itself in its presence-with other subjects than in its presence-with objects. Hence, the language of personal, loving relationship--despite the difficulties presented by its anthropomorphic and metaphorical qualities--conveys an essential and even "explanatory" dimension of mystical union.

What seems to happen in the fulfillment of mystical union is that the self-presence of the human subject and its presence-with the transcendent ground of consciousness become one. This state is neither a solipcistic consciousness (sheer, solitary self-presence) nor an annihilated consciousness (a total takeover of individual consciousness by an "other" consciousness); it is, rather, a grounding state of intersubjectivity. The divine, mediated at the ground of one's consciousness, is no longer experienced as in any way an "object"; it is present as infinite love, paradoxically both "other than" and "at one with" one's very self.

It is in this state that the unique type of vision characteristic of the Seventh Dwelling Places occurs. The contents of the two such visions that Teresa mentions are the sacred humanity of Jesus (VII:2,1) and the Most Blessed Trinity (VII:1,6; 2,3). It would require more space than it is possible to give here to analyze these in detail. Our claim, however, is that only by understanding these in terms of a grounding state of "mystical intersubjectivity" is it possible to assess correctly both their nature (i.e., that they are neither "objective" in a physical sense nor "subjective" in a hallucinatory sense) and their uniqueness (in comparison to all other experiences and "visions").

C. Concluding Discussion

This interiority analysis of the *Interior Castle* has produced a reading significantly different from those in most classical discussions of the process of mystical transformation. Jordan Aumann's recent presentation of a classical view, for example, summarizes the process in the following terms:

> The prayer of union is that grade of mystical prayer in which all the internal faculties are gradually captivated and occupied with God. In the prayer of quiet only the will was captivated; in the sleep of the faculties the intellect was also captivated, although the memory and the imagination remained free. In the prayer of union [i.e., Fifth Dwelling Places] *all* the interior faculties, including the memory and the imagination, are captivated. . . . in the prayer of conforming union [i.e., Sixth Dwelling Places] God captivates even the external senses, with the result that the soul is totally divinized, so to speak, and prepared by God to move to the full and final commitment of the transforming union [i.e., Seventh Dwelling Places].[25]

It is obvious, first of all, that Aumann accepts as his basic theoretical framework a faculty psychology that, though compatible in basic terminology with Teresa's, is considerably more abstract and systematized. Our critique of Teresa's faculty psychology (i.e., that it tends to break up the integrity of the activity of consciousness into

---

[25]Jordan Aumann, *Spiritual Theology* (Huntington, IN: Our Sunday Visitor, 1980), pp. 340 and 344.

various disjointed "locations")[26] could be applied with even greater force to that of Aumann.

Even more important, however, is the fact that Aumann's schema is unable to account for what I would regard as two of the most essential aspects of Teresa's presentation. One of these is the holism of her view of the spiritual life: for her, all spiritual and/or mystical transformation is constitutively related to the whole of life--specifically, one's existential determination and one's concrete activities of love. The other is the truly radical nature of the transition that takes place in the Fourth and Fifth Dwelling Places, when the individual moves into "union."

Aumann's schema places the entire process of mystical transformation on a single continuum of withdrawal and interiorization. Although neither he nor other classical interpreters fail to emphasize the contextualization of mystical transformation within a life of virtue and service, they do not provide an explanatory perspective on why this is not just a pious admonition, but constitutive of the *nature* of mystical transformation. The result is that those who use such a schema as the basis for developing a concrete praxis of spiritual life tend to emphasize a discipline of prayerful withdrawal along with a rather stilted practice of pious "good deeds," rather than a deep engagement in the work and controversy of all aspects--emotional, intellectual, interpersonal, political, etc.--of human life.

Besides not accounting for the constitutive relation between mystical transformation and the holistic transformation of one's humanity, Aumann's schema does not even really account for the specificity of mystical transformation. Although he states that God gradually "captivates" deeper and deeper dimensions of the human person, he again provides no explanatory view of how this occurs or of why the stages that occur after the onset of mystical "union" have a fundamentally different quality than what occurs before.

---

[26]See above under "Fourth Dwelling Places."

A full study and critique of Aumann's and other commentators' presentations of mystical transformation is beyond the scope of the present study. The reason for this brief discussion, however, is to point up how the model developed here is able to respond to key modern and post-modern concerns far more adequately than traditional approaches have been able to do.

Our interiority analysis of the *Interior Castle* has confirmed that the model developed in Part I is a plausible explanatory schema, giving insight into both the specificity of mystical transformation and its constitutive relation with holistic human transformation. Specifically, our interiority analysis has confirmed the plausibility of both the "prime analogue," in which mystical experience is understood as a breakthrough of the transcendent ground of consciousness in a "state of intersubjectivity," and of the basic isomorphism of mystical transformation with the general structure of religious conversion.

To complete the project of this inquiry, however, another major task remains. The first analysis of the text confirms the *plausibility* of the original hypothesis and the developed model; the second analysis will work toward *verification* within a strictly intraworldly forum. Our original hypothesis stated that because mystical transformation involves the breakthrough of a grounding (i.e., specifically mystical) intersubjective state, it will be mediated in a transformation of interhuman intersubjectivity. By studying this level on its own terms, we may be able to discover additional evidence confirming the hypothesis.

In saying that the following study of the psychological mediation of mystical transformation may help to verify our hypothesis and model, we do not claim that this very limited study can achieve complete and adequate verification. Much less do we claim to be able to "prove" our hypothesis. Rather, the most significant implications of including as a constitutive part of this study an example of an effort toward verification within a non-theological framework are methodological. In brief: this approach is, methodologically, a statement that such non-theological frameworks both have their own validity as analyses of dimensions of intraworldly reality with a certain proper autonomy, *and* have something essential to contribute to a specifically theological analysis that acknowledges a "supraworldly," transcendent dimension.

In practice, such non-theological frameworks are legion: they may be psychological, sociological, anthropological, biological, etc., and within each field there are many schools of thought and many potential methods. In choosing one field (psychology) and one school of thought within that field (self-psychological psychoanalysis), I can hardly claim to be exhausting the possibilities for verification (or dis-verification) of my hypothesis and model. I do claim, however, that this kind of analysis is particularly apt for this project, and that employing it will be helpful in informing our concluding judgment of the adequacy or inadequacy of the model presented in Part I.

CHAPTER 8

INTRODUCTION TO RELEVANT ASPECTS OF SELF PSYCHOLOGY

The task of this chapter will be to correlate the terms and relations thus far explicated with some terms and relations from psychological theory.

A. A Central Term: "The Self"

The psychological theory chosen for the purposes of this inquiry is "self psychology." Self psychology, a branch of psychoanalytic thought, has its main roots in the work of Heinz Kohut (1913-1981). It takes its name from Kohut's most groundbreaking theoretical innovation, namely, the redefinition of the self as "the center of the psychological universe."[1]

Kohut set self psychology apart as a distinctive psychoanalytic theory by asserting that, both phenomenologically and theoretically, "self" is the central term around which other terms and relations are arranged. As will be discussed below, Kohut's notion of "self" is in some ways a psychological analogue to Lonergan's "subject-as-subject."

---

[1]Heinz Kohut, *The Restoration of the Self* (Madison, CT: International Universities Press, 1977), p. xv.

While the differences between the empirical and theoretical contexts of Kohut's and Lonergan's concepts must be respected, it is important to note from the start that, more clearly than most other psychoanalytical theorists, Kohut offers a point of entry for the philosophical and theological notion of the "subject" as a unified center of initiative.

A correlation with Lonergan's phenomenology and theory will be facilitated by the following chart, delineating a series of possible meanings of the term "self."

MEANINGS OF THE TERM "SELF"

A. The Self as Experienced and Described:

1. Conscious self-representations; "identity."
2. The unconscious, depth-psychological structure of dynamic self- and other-representations.
3. A personal agent: one who acts, knows, chooses, loves, etc.
4. The implicit, non-objectifiable conscious center presupposed by personal agency.

B. The Self as Explained:

1. An "agency" in the psychoanalytic sense; a set of functions of the psychic apparatus.
2. A set of dynamic patterns of relationship to the absolute whole (the transcendent ground of consciousness) and to all things within the world.

Lonergan began his phenomenological investigations by attending to a limited component of A(3), namely, the self as knower. From this starting point he inferred A(4), the subject-as-subject, and related the two with B(2), an explanatory theory of the self-transcending subject. Subsequently he developed a more fully adequate understanding of A(3) by attending to other aspects of personal agency--i.e., the self as doer, chooser, lover, etc. He also made occasional stabs at relating A(1) and A(2) to the explanatory system,[2] but he never made this a thoroughgoing focus of his attention.

Kohut, on the other hand, began his investigations as a psychoanalytically-trained clinician focusing on A(2), the depth-psychological structure of self- and other-representations. In his early work he maintained allegiance to the mainstream psychoanalytical tradition, carefully distinguishing the appropriate psychoanalytical meaning of the term "self" from that intended by either A(1), identity, or B(1), impersonal psychic agency. For that mainstream tradition it went without saying that notions of A(3), personal agency, and A(4), consciousness as such, were outside the realm of the empirical psychoanalyst's expertise.

Kohut's subsequent bold innovation was to assert that A(2), depth-psychological structure, could not be adequately understood without an at least implicit postulation of something like A(3), the personal agent, and A(4), the non-objectifiable conscious center of personal agency. Without overstepping the bounds of his field of expertise to make philosophical or theological judgments about personal agency or consciousness as such, he simply affirmed that an accurate description of actual psychological configurations must include the qualities generally associated with those dimensions--i.e., the experiences of centeredness, duration through time and cohesion in space, initiative, aliveness, etc. Thus, while Kohut's main focus throughout his life continued to be on A(2), that is, the depth-psychological study of the structures of self- and other-representations, he placed this study on a profoundly different footing.

---

[2]See especially Chapter 6 of *Insight*.

In Lonergan's terms, we might say that his breakthrough was to find within psychology itself the grounds for the distinction between "psyche" and "spirit." Psyche, for Lonergan, is the "higher system" that gives a higher level of organization to all the sensitive and organic processes by which an animal or human being is in mutual mediation with the totality of the physical world. Spirit, on the other hand, is the higher system to psyche; it is the conscious intelligence that can abstract from, and make choices in regard to, the configurations presented to it by psyche.[3] Spirit, then, is the moving force that transforms the mutual mediation of psyche and world into true "self-mediation."

Despite the presence of the term "self" in "self-mediation," it is important to remember that Kohut's notion of "self" has its roots in a different universe of discourse than does Lonergan's. My contention is that Kohut's notion of "self" is an insight into how psyche itself attests to the existence of a "higher system" that sublates the "lower system" of the structured psyche, giving it new levels of coherence and yet not interfering with its own proper autonomy. This interpretation, while essential for the purposes of this inquiry, certainly goes beyond what Kohut himself would have affirmed. The remainder of this chapter, and the following one, will attempt to present Kohut's ideas largely in his own terms.

B. Foundations of Self Psychology

The Specificity of Self Psychology

The following paragraphs briefly summarize the most important ways in which Kohut's "self psychology" differs from classical, Freudian psychoanalysis.

1) Self psychology de-emphasizes "drives" (libido, aggression) as prime movers in the human psyche. It focuses instead on a core self

[3]See Lonergan, *Insight*, pp. 514-20.

innately seeking coherence, self-expression, and fulfillment. In this view, drive-expressions isolated from the whole self, such as perverse lust or violent anger, are indications of a breakdown of the self; they are not "normal" at any stage.

2) Instead of regarding the oedipal period as crucial for all future psychological structure, self psychology focuses on the basic structures of the core self which develop throughout infancy and early childhood. Self psychology contends that if these structures are strong and healthy, the oedipal period need not be a "crisis," nor need it lead to a "complex."

3) The Freudian id, ego and superego are mechanistic psychic systems whose built-in dynamics of development only secondarily draw upon environmental and interpersonal experiences. The "self" in self psychology, on the other hand, is defined as existing from the start in a world of intersubjective relations; these relations are constitutive for the self's development and structure-building.

Kohut's Notion of "The Self"

In his first major book, *The Analysis of the Self* (1971), Kohut defined "self" in terms similar to those of the reigning psychoanalytic orthodoxy of the time, namely, the ego psychology of Heinz Hartmann.[4] The self, he wrote, "emerges in the psychoanalytic situation and is conceptualized . . . as a content of the mental apparatus."[5] Yet only a few years later, with the publication of *The Restoration of the Self* (1977), Kohut noted that the definition of the self as a "content of the mental apparatus" fails

---

[4] For Hartmann's definition of the "self," see Heinz Hartmann, "Comments on the Psychoanalytic Theory of the Ego," in *Essays on Ego Psychology* (New York: International Universities Press, 1964), p. 127.

[5] Heinz Kohut, *The Analysis of the Self: A Systematic Approach to the Psychoanalytic Treatment of Narcissistic Personality Disorders*, Monograph Series of the Psychoanalytic Study of the Child, no. 4 (Madison, CT: International Universities Press, 1971), p. xv.

to account for the phenomena encountered in clinical work.[6] Commenting on the inadequacy of a psychology that envisions the psyche as a mental apparatus, Kohut wrote:

> But while it is true that many psychological activities and interactions lend themselves to being satisfactorily explained within this framework, it is equally true that there are some phenomena that require for their explanation the positing of a psychic configuration--the self--that, *whatever* the history of its formation, has become a center of initiative: a unit that tries to follow its own course.[7]

At this point he began to distinguish between "the self in the narrow sense," which is adequately defined in Hartmannian terms, and "the self in the broad sense," which is his concern in *Restoration* and subsequent works. He asserted that this broader definition of the self was, in fact, implicit even in *Analysis*, but that only in *Restoration* is he spelling out the implications of "the psychology of the self in the broad sense of the term, i.e., a psychology in whose theoretical framework the self occupies a central position."[8]

Theoretical exactness was not Kohut's interest; he viewed himself first as a clinician, second as an empirical scientist, and only thirdly as a theoretician. Rather than giving a definition of the term "self (in the broad sense)," he preferred to describe it phenomenologically.

> There are a number of things that define this experience. The self is the center of initiative. We experience ourselves as the center of initiative. We know we are influenced, we know we listen to other people's opinions, we consider choices. And yet somewhere there is a sense of comparative independence, of assertiveness, of initiative. That's one feature.
>
> Another feature is cohesion in space and continuity in time. There is also a sense of cohesion versus fragmentation; a sense of the

---

[6]Kohut, *Restoration of the Self*, p. xv.

[7]Kohut, *Restoration of the Self*, p. 245.

[8]Kohut, *Restoration of the Self*, p. 207.

> harmony of oneself versus the chaos of oneself; a sense of strength about the self versus a sense of weakness, lack of vitality; a sense of feeling alive. We must feel alive. Part of being less than a self (amusing as that sounds) is not to feel alive. . . . Now when you may say you have a fragmented self, you still say "self." But if it were totally fragmented, it wouldn't be a self.[9]

The self, then, "concerns a structure that dips into the deepest reaches of the psyche."[10] It is to be distinguished from "identity," which, he wrote, is "not a depth-psychological concept."[11] As he put it in a somewhat later article, a person's sense of identity

> pertains to his conscious and preconscious awareness of the manifestations of a psychological surface configuration--it concerns a self-representation that relates to the conscious and preconscious goals and purposes of his ego and to the conscious and preconscious idealized values of his superego.[12]

"Self," on the other hand, is a depth configuration, fundamentally unconscious although manifested in the conscious and preconscious structure of representations.

---

[9]Heinz Kohut, "On the Continuity of the Self and Cultural Selfobjects," in *Self Psychology and the Humanities*, pp. 234-35.

[10]Kohut, "Creativeness, Charisma, Group Psychology," p. 206 n. 21.

[11]Heinz Kohut, "Discussion of 'The Self: A Contribution to Its Place in Theory and Technique' by D.C. Levin," in *The Search for the Self*, ed. by Paul H. Ornstein (New York: International Universities Press, 1978), vol 2., p. 579. In the schema developed above, p.236, this is the distinction between A(1) and A(2).

[12]Heinz Kohut, "Creativeness, Charisma, Group Psychology: Reflections on the Self-Analysis of Freud," in *Self Psychology and the Humanities: Reflections on a New Psychoanalytic Approach*, ed. by Charles B. Strozier (New York: W.W. Norton, 1985), p. 206 n. 21.

Method: Introspection and Empathy

At the basis of Kohut's realignment of psychoanalytical theory was his redefinition of the field of psychology in terms of the specificity of its method. In a 1959 address Kohut set forth his conviction that the psychological field is distinguished from the physical field by the different operations we employ to know it. Thus, "We speak of physical phenomena when the essential ingredient of our observational methods includes our senses, we speak of psychological phenomena when the essential ingredient of our observation is introspection and empathy."[13]

As he clarified later, this does not mean that there are "separate biological and psychological universes," but simply that there are two sets of instruments for knowing reality.[14] Outer reality can be known by the instruments attuned to extrospection; inner reality can only be known by specific kind of introspection that constitutes empathy.

Empathy is not a magical immediate perception of another's experience, but a "vicarious introspection"[15] in which one recognizes and shares in the meaning of what the other experiences inwardly. To be empathic is to have the natural or acquired capacity to "think and feel oneself into the inner life of another person."[16] Without empathy, psychology becomes only the measurement of physical events and the understanding of cause and effect sequences. Kohut gives the example of a stone dropped by man A onto man B, killing him. Without empathy, we can describe the physical sequence of events--including, perhaps, subtle biochemical events of the arousal of aggression in man

---

[13]Heinz Kohut, "Introspection, Empathy, and Psychoanalysis: An Examination of the Relationship Between Mode of Observation and Theory" (1959), in *Search for the Self*, vol. 1, p. 206.

[14]Heinz Kohut, *How Does Analysis Cure?*, ed. by Arnold Goldberg with the collaboration of Paul E. Stepansky (Chicago, IL: University of Chicago, 1984), p. 32.

[15]Kohut, "Introspection, Empathy, and Psychoanalysis" (1959), pp. 207ff.

[16]Kohut, *How Does Analysis Cure?*, p. 82.

A--but we will be unable to grasp the psychological meaning of the occurrence.[17]

In the 1982 paper Kohut explained more thoroughly why he felt this methododological clarification was so essential. Concepts derivable only from an extrospective framework--for example, "drive" (from biology) and "adaptation" (a term from social psychology adopted by Hartmann)--subtly lead psychoanalysts to think of their task in terms of externally influencing or educating the analysand. In Kohut's view, this is a betrayal of psychoanalysis both as a science and as a healing art.

This betrayal results from the failure to recognize the absolute centrality of the self. It is the vicissitudes and destiny of the self that psychoanalysis as science seeks to understand and as healing art seeks to liberate from pathology. Yet the self is never reducible to an object that can be fully known or made accessible for manipulation. The self can only be known by introspection and empathy; and the method of introspection reaches its limit when it encounters "What we experience as freedom of choice, as decision, and the like . . . the I-experience and a core of activities emanating from it [that] cannot at present be divided into further components by the introspective method."[18]

Images, Representations, and Structures

Self psychology has been chosen for this inquiry because it offers an approach to the understanding of the structure and transformation of the subject's representational world (i.e., way of constructing images of self and others) that is particularly apt for the study of a text such as the *Interior Castle*, which recounts the story of an interior journey of transformation.

Kohut's writings were based largely on clinical work and were oriented to clinicians. The potential for application of his ideas in a

---

[17]Kohut, "Introspection, Empathy, and Psychoanalysis" (1959), pp. 207-8.

[18]Ibid., pp. 231-32.

non-clinical theoretical inquiry will be facilitated by making explicit a model of psychic structure which can mediate between concrete examples and theoretical claims. One such model is that of the "representational world" which was first set forth by Sandler and Rosenblatt in 1962.[19]

Out of the multitude and flux of impressions, the young child gradually constructs "representations" of self and of a variety of other persons, situations, things, etc. Only with such representations can the child have meaningful perceptions of persons and interactions; without the inner representation, every encounter would have to be constructed "from scratch." The most important representations, around which others are organized, are those of the self and of the most significant "objects" (normally, loved and loving persons) in the child's world.

A representation is distinguished from an image in that "A representation can be considered to have a more or less enduring existence as an organization or schema which is constructed out of a multitude of impressions."[20] An image is much more transitory and subject to variation. Many images (with a repertoire of variations) are summarized in the formation of a single representation. Thus, summarized in one's "Mother representation" can be images of Mother hugging, Mother slapping, Mother ignoring, Mother apologizing, etc. Once precipitated, the representation can govern a similar repertoire of transitory fantasy and thought images.

The various representations are interlinked to form a sort of internal drama or fantasy in which the stock of characters respond in expectable ways to the situations presented to them.[21] As Sandler and Rosenblatt summarized:

---

[19]See J. Sandler and B. Rosenblatt, "The Concept of the Representational World," *The Psychoanalytic Study of the Child* 18 (1962): 128-45.

[20]Sandler and Rosenblatt, "Representational World," p. 133.

[21]For an engaging account of the formation and playing out of this internalized drama, see Ernest Becker, *The Birth and Death of Meaning*, 2nd ed. (New York: Free Press, 1971), esp. chaps. 3-9.

> The representational world might be compared to a stage set within a theater. The characters on the stage represent the child's various objects, as well as the child himself. Needless to say, the child is usually the hero of the piece. . . . Whereas the characters on this stage correspond, in this model, to self- and object *representations*, their particular form and expression at any one point in the play correspond to self- and object *images*.[22]

The value of this concept for psychobiographical research has been formulated by Robert Stolorow and George Atwood:

> [The representational world] is the structure of a person's subjective world as disclosed by an intensive investigation of the repetitive themes and leitmotifs which dominate his life. The representational world constitutes a kind of pre-reflective background into which the events of the person's life are continuously assimilated and on the dimensions of which his experiences continuously take form.
>
> In our . . . research, the first phase consists of a provisional descriptive characterization of the individual's representational world. This means discovering and formulating the unique dimensions on which his experiences are organized, the central concerns and dilemmas which are for him subjectively salient, and the recurrent thematic configurations of self- and object-representations (and associated affects) which pervade his world.[23]

When the "self" was discussed above, it was emphasized that for Kohut "the self in the broad sense" is not to be reduced to a content of the mind or psyche, that is, a self-representation. Thus, the "self in the broad sense" is not a character in the drama of the representational world. It would be more adequately compared to the drama's author, who creates all the characters and arranges all their interactions without ever appearing on stage. The relation between the "self in the broad sense" and its self-representations is best understood through the concept of "structure."

---

[22]Sandler and Rosenblatt, "Representational World," p. 134.

[23]Robert D. Stolorow and George E. Atwood, *Faces in a Cloud: Subjectivity in Personality Theory* (Northvale, NJ: Jason Aronson, 1979), p. 43.

The self, says Kohut, is dynamically oriented toward attaining structure. If there is absolutely no structure--a total lack of order, cohesion, centeredness--there really is no self.[24]

> The structure of the self, in other words, is the theoretical correlate of those attributes of the self which, in their sum total, define this central concept of self psychology. . . . its cohesion, its strength, or its harmony . . . a person's experience of being whole and continuous, of being fully alive and vigorous, or of being balanced and organized . . . . our abiding experience of being a center of initiative, of being a recipient of impressions, of having cohesion in space and time, and the like.[25]

Structures are not so much something with physical existence as the dynamic patterns of activity which result in the physical expressions of representations, behaviors, etc. Structure, then, mediates between the self in the broad sense and the self in the narrow sense. As Atwood and Stolorow clarify:

> These psychological structures are not to be viewed simply as "internalizations" or mental replicas of interpersonal events. Nor should they be regarded as having an objective existence in physical space or somewhere in a "mental apparatus." Instead, we conceptualize these structures as systems of ordering or organizing principles . . . [they are] cognitive affective schemata . . . through which a person's experiences of self and other assume their characteristic forms and meanings.[26]

Thus, structure is a dynamic activity--the self's unrelenting work to organize its experience and to maintain order and a sense of control in the midst of life's vicissitudes.

---

[24]Kohut, "On the Continuity of the Self," p. 235.

[25]Kohut, *How Does Analysis Cure?*, p. 99.

[26]George E. Atwood and Robert D. Stolorow, *Structures of Subjectivity: Explorations in Psychoanalytic Phenomenology* (Hillsdale, NJ: Analytic Press, 1984), p. 34.

This model of psychic structure clarifies the significance of the various phenomena we discover when we set out to use the method of introspection and empathy to explore a given psychological field. First we will encounter images. Gradually we will discern representations and their organization within the drama of the representational world. Only with continuing empathic immersion--and with the aid of appropriate theory--will we discover the shape of the underlying structures of the self.

C. Structuralization and Transformation in Self Psychology

The Concept of the Selfobject

The key to self psychology's unique contribution is the contention that structuralization of the self occurs only with the participation of other persons in the life of the self. If (from the perspective of the subject) other persons fail to participate in the life of the self, or if they participate in grossly faulty ways, self-structure will not develop or will enshrine severe distortions.

To describe the specific nature of the requisite participation, Kohut formulated the concept of the "selfobject." From a common sense perspective, the selfobject is a person, group, or fantasied being whose care and attention the individual experiences as absolutely essential to his or her well being. A more accurate theoretical definition, however, clarifies the fact that the selfobject is not, strictly speaking, an entity distinct from the self; it is, rather, a way in which the self constructs its experience of others. As some of Kohut's followers put it,

> It is often forgotten that the term *selfobject* does not refer to environmental entities or caregiving agents--that is, to people. Rather, it designates a class of psychological *functions* pertaining to the maintenance, restoration, and transformation of self-experience. The term *selfobject* refers to an object *experienced subjectively* as serving certain functions--that is, it refers to a *dimension* of

> experiencing an object . . ., in which a specific bond is required for maintaining, restoring, or consolidating the organization of self-experience.[27]

Despite Kohut's careful theoretical definition of the term "selfobject" as referring not to a person but to a dimension of the self's experience, he also defended using the term in a more "common sense" way in general exposition. He explains, for example, that while complete theoretical consistency would forbid the use of such phrases as "self-selfobject relationships," any discussion of clinical material or even of many theoretical points would become hopelessly convoluted if one insisted on such terminological purity. He opts instead for "trusting the mind of the reader to make whatever conceptual adjustments are necessary."[28] This same policy is followed in this study as well.

In the same discussion Kohut also clarifies that the term selfobject has both a general and a specific meaning. The general meaning refers to an aspect of self-experience that is continuous throughout life, namely, "that dimension of our experience of another person that relates to that person's functions in shoring up our self." The specific meaning refers to the archaic experience--i.e., the selfobjects in their function of participating in the formation of the self in early childhood. The relation between these two forms the basis of Kohut's clinical theory. He summarizes this basis as "the hypothesis that the self-object transferences during analysis are in essence a new edition of the relation between the self and its self-objects in early life."[29]

In terms of psychoanalytic tradition, what Kohut did by developing the concept of the selfobject was to profoundly reorient the

---

[27]Robert D. Stolorow, Bernard Brandchaft, and George E. Atwood, *Psychoanalytic Treatment: An Intersubjective Approach* (Hillsdale, NJ: Analytic Press, 1987), pp. 16-17. See also Kohut, *How Does Analysis Cure?*, p. 49.

[28]For discussion, see Kohut, *Restoration of the Self*, pp. 49-52; this quote, p. 50.

[29]Kohut, *Restoration of the Self*, p. 173 n.2. (Note that in *Restoration of the Self* Kohut still spelled this term "self-object." His spelling in *How Does Analysis Cure?*, "selfobject," has become the accepted norm.)

understanding of narcissism. The classic Freudian doctrine of narcissism was that it is the "libidinal cathexis of the ego." An element of "primary narcissism" is normal and necessary, but if the libido fails to be invested in objects or if too much of it is withdrawn from objects onto the ego, pathology results. Maturity and health, then, mean a movement away from narcissistic investment to investment in objects.[30]

Kohut, however, contended that there is a normal and healthy trajectory of narcissistic investment throughout life, and that it is only by understanding the dynamics of that trajectory in its healthy form that we can understand and remedy "derailments." Instead of defining narcissism in terms of the investment of libido in the ego, he defined it in terms of the development and firming of structures in the self. Narcissism is healthy and mature, he wrote, when

> [one has] been able to establish one sector within the realm of the self through which an uninterrupted flow of the narcissistic strivings can proceed toward creative expression . . . . Such a sector includes always a central pattern of exhibitionism and grandiose ambitions, a set of firmly internalized ideals of perfection, and a correlated system of talents and skills . . . .[31]

In his view, the pathology that results from failures in the structuralization of narcissism is, in general, more severe and more pervasive than the pathology resulting from failures in object investment (i.e., oedipal difficulties) which are the focus of classical psychoanalytic work. While Kohut, unlike some of his followers, always maintained that classical theory has value within its own field of competence--that is, in the treatment of the structural-conflict neuroses--he asserted that

---

[30]See Sigmund Freud, "On Narcissism: An Introduction," in *The Standard Edition of the Complete Psychological Works of Sigmund Freud*, trans. and ed. by James Strachey (London: Hogarth Press and the Institute of Psychoanalysis) 14:73-102.

[31]Kohut, *Restoration of the Self*, p. 54.

even these are more deeply understood when the narcissistic deficiencies which predispose the individual to the oedipal conflict are grasped.[32]

The Nuclear Self and the Selfobject Transferences

In Kohut's view, the self gains a characteristic pattern or "nuclear self" during the first three to five years of life, and the basic structure of this pattern will not subsequently change. In regard to this, he distinguishes clearly between the essentially unchanging shape and content of the self--"the distinctive individuality which distinguishes it from other selves with their respective shapes and contents"--and a more labile component, the self's "firmness and freedom to carry out its intrinsic program of action."[33]

The basic premise of self-psychological psychoanalysis is that when the latter is lacking and the self is "composed of structures that are riddled with defects and lacunae, and/or seriously enfeebled, and/or disharmonious," it is indeed possible to remedy this so that the self can experience itself as strong, competent, harmonious, cohesive, continuous, etc.[34] Analysis cannot, however, create a nuclear self *de novo* once the critical period has been missed. Psychosis, in which the nuclear self is missing, involves a "persisting hollowness in the center of the patient's self," so that a state of "prepsychological chaos" is surrounded by purely defensive structures.[35]

In normal development, the nuclear self is formed by the infant and young child's experience of itself as held within an empathic selfobject milieu. The selfobjects selectively respond to the emerging potentialities of the child, so that "some archaic mental contents that had

---

[32]See Kohut, *How Does Analysis Cure?*, especially pp. 4-7, 13-33.

[33]Ibid., p. 42.

[34]Ibid., p. 99.

[35]Ibid., pp. 8-9.

been experienced as belonging to the self become obliterated or are assigned to the area of the nonself while others are retained within the self or are added to it."[36] If the selfobjects are at least moderately empathic with the child's real feelings, needs, and efforts to express itself, an adequate nuclear self will be established by this process.

It is generally not possible to determine the exact timing of the emergence of the nuclear self. Kohut believed that this central self-structure does not emerge gradually through the integration of various fragmentary "self nuclei" (as suggested by E. Glover), but rather arises from a rudimentary sense of "cohesive self" that is present from the beginning.[37] Yet there is a moment, says Kohut, when "something clicks and we have a degree of autonomy: this degree of autonomy we call the self. It becomes a center of independent initiative that points to a future and has a destiny."[38]

In Kohut's earlier work, he hypothesized that the nuclear self is fundamentally shaped by two basic types of selfobject experiences.[39] The first is "mirroring," in which the child experiences him/herself as being admired, enjoyed, appreciated. This builds up what Kohut called the "grandiose-exhibitionistic self"--a component of self structure through which the self has a bedrock conviction of its own goodness, beauty, invincibility, competence, etc. Mirroring is particularly crucial for the formation of the nuclear self during the second to fourth years of life (ages 1-3).[40] The result of healthy development in this sector of the self will be the establishment of strong "nuclear ambitions."

---

[36]Kohut, *Restoration of the Self*, p. 177.

[37]Heinz Kohut, "Remarks About the Formation of the Self: Letter to a Student Regarding Some Principles of Psychoanalytic Research," in *Search for the Self* 2:737-70, especially pp. 747-49.

[38]Heinz Kohut, "The Psychoanalyst and the Historian," in Strozier, *Self Psychology and the Humanities*, p. 218.

[39]In his last major book he added a third basic type; see below, pp. 253.

[40]Kohut, *Restoration of the Self*, p. 179.

The second basic type of selfobject experience is "idealizing." In this case the child experiences the selfobject as perfect, beautiful, caring, protective, etc. This builds up the self structure of the "idealized parent imago"--a bedrock conviction that the world is a safe, orderly, and wonderful place, that "somebody out there cares about me," and that there is something (somebody) worth working for. Kohut places the critical period for the development of the idealizing component of the nuclear self in the fourth to sixth years (ages 3-5). The result of healthy development in this sector will be the establishment of strong "nuclear idealized goals."

Kohut's original theory of the self envisioned these two as the basic polar components, with each individual establishing both a unique shape and content for each component and a characteristic relationship or "tension arc" between them. Of the latter, Kohut wrote:

> Just as there is a *gradient* of tension between two differently charged (+, -) electrical *poles* that are spatially separated, inviting the formation of an electrical *arc* in which the electricity may be said to flow from the higher to the lower level, so also with the self. . . . With the term "tension arc," . . . I am referring to the abiding flow of actual psychological activity that establishes itself between the two poles of the self, i.e. a person's basic pursuits toward which he is "driven" by his ambitions and "led" by his ideals.[41]

Insight into the bipolar nature of the self, then, undergirded Kohut's insight into the clinical phenomena of transference. In *The Analysis of the Self* he delineated two basic types of narcissistic transference, the merger or mirroring transference (in which the self desperately seeks mirroring to make up for lacks in early structuralization of the grandiose-exhibitionistic self) and the idealizing transference (in which the self desperately seeks someone to idealize to make up for lacks in the structuralization of the idealized parent imago). He also described

---

[41]Kohut, *Restoration of the Self*, p. 180. See also idem, "Forms and Transformations of Narcissism," in Strozier, *Self Psychology and the Humanities*, pp. 107-9.

the possibilities for fluctuation between these two types of transferences, according to the dynamics of the bipolar self.

This original perspective counted the alter ego or twinship transference, in which the self seeks another person "exactly like" itself, as a subclass of the mirroring variety. As time went on Kohut distinguished, between the poles of the self, "an intermediate area--the executive functions (talents, skills) needed for the realization of the patterns of the basic ambitions and basic ideals that were laid down in the two polar areas."[42] In his final book Kohut revised his theory to name this as a third basic component of the self, with its critical period in later childhood (latency) and its characteristic shape as a "need to experience the presence of essential alikeness."[43]

Despite having designated certain age periods as most critical for each of the three components of the nuclear self, Kohut emphasizes that all are developing from birth and that all continue to be active throughout life. If development is incomplete or faulty in childhood, the self's inherent dynamism demands a continual struggle throughout life to complete what is unfinished. This is why the narcissistic transferences occur, both inside and outside of clinical settings: the self is always seeking its opportunity to gain its coherence, firmness, etc.

Kohut observes that for the formation of a nuclear self it is not so much the "conscious encouragement and praise [or] conscious discouragement and rebuke" that is decisive, but "the deeply anchored responsiveness of the self-objects, which, in the last analysis, is a function of the self-objects' own nuclear selves."[44] When even a modicum of this responsiveness is available--even in combination with considerable "emotionally deleterious and self development-stifling" behavior--the individual may be able to maintain a remnant of the

---

[42]Kohut, *Restoration of the Self*, p. 49.

[43]Kohut, *How Does Analysis Cure?*, p. 194.

[44]Kohut, *Restoration of the Self*, p. 100.

nuclear self in hope of a future time when the availability of more empathic selfobjects will permit a renewal of structure-building.[45]

From this it is evident that formation of a nuclear self does not require a totally empathic, trauma-free environment (which, of course, never exists). If, however, the individual is blessed with a maximum of empathy and a minimum of narcissistic trauma, the nuclear self that is formed may be one of "primary structures"--that is, structures formed with relative ease by the gradual internalization of the functions performed by the original selfobjects. Kohut thought that this would usually mean that the mirroring component would primarily involve the mother as selfobject; the idealizing component would also involve the father; and the alter ego component would primarily involve the same-sex parent.[46] In such "ideal" circumstances, the greater dominance of one component or another would be determined by the child's innate endowment and, perhaps, subtle differences in the strength of the selfobjects' responsiveness to that endowment.

Many other patterns are possible, however. Kohut asserts that a functioning self can be formed if at least two of the components find adequate sustenance; the third component can be weak and can still be "carried along" by the adequately structured components. Only if two of the self's main constitutents are "functionally destroyed" will there be a "manifest illness of the self."[47]

If one or both parents is not a good selfobject, the self will seek out alternatives. A viable nuclear self can also be formed with "compensatory structures"--that is, structures formed after it has become necessary to withdraw an original investment from certain traumatizing (i.e., profoundly unempathic) features of the selfobject milieu and to

---

[45]Kohut, *How Does Analysis Cure?*, pp. 131-2.

[46]Kohut, *Restoration of the Self*, pp. 179, 185-86.

[47]Heinz Kohut, "Self Psychology and the Sciences of Man," in Strozier, *Self Psychology and the Humanities*, p. 85.

reinvest in other, more responsive aspects.[48] For example, if the mother fails to mirror the child, the child will attempt to gain mirroring from the father (or whoever else is present in the environment); if the child succeeds, a basis for this component of the nuclear self is formed despite original traumatic disappointment. In such cases the greater dominance of one component over another may be influenced less by the child's innate endowment and more by the availability of healthy selfobject relations in one area and their unavailability in another.[49]

Kohut even suggests that the most creative, dynamic people may be those whose nuclear selves are built on compensatory structures; for these individuals, through some combination of innate vigor and a creative response to trauma, have been able to find a new route to an originally thwarted inner completeness.[50]

The Transformation of the Self

For Kohut, it is both theoretically and clinically inaccurate to speak of a "stage of narcissism" (i.e., libidinal investment in the self) followed by a "stage of object relations" (i.e., libidinal investment in others). He believed that forms of both narcissism and object relations are present from the very beginning of human life and continue into even the most highly developed maturity. His work, therefore, focused on the "forms and transformations of narcissism"[51]--that is, the forms and transformations of the self.

For Kohut, the foundation of the nuclear self must be laid down in early life. During later crisis periods, the foundational pattern can

---

[48]For discussion, see Kohut, *How Does Analysis Cure?*, pp. 42-44. 131-133.

[49]For discussion of an example, see Kohut, *Restoration of the Self*, pp. 214-16.

[50]Kohut, *How Does Analysis Cure?*, p. 44.

[51]This is the title of Kohut's groundbreaking 1966 essay. It is reprinted in Charles B. Strozier, ed., *Self Psychology and the Humanities* (New York: W.W. Norton, 1985), pp. 97-123.

mutate into more mature forms[52]--or crumble into pathology under the stress of demands beyond its ability to integrate. The most severe crises are those that revive the problematic dimensions of the period of the early formation of the self. The possible outcomes of such crises are either a replay of traumatic failure, or the discovery of a new solution that permits development to take up again where it left off. Self-psychological clinical theory focuses on how healthy self-development can be facilitated, both normally in early life and remedially in adulthood.

The form of narcissism in early life is an archaic, all-encompassing need for sustenance through contact with mirroring, idealizable, and alter-ego selfobjects. Very early, the infant forms global representations of self and others along these lines. Though by adult standards these representations are quite unrealistic, especially in the total attention and perfect empathy which they expect of the selfobjects, they are "phase appropriate" in that the infant self really does require an intense, in-depth participation in the life of at least one other person if it is to thrive and grow strong. With its own psychic structure only in the most rudimentary state, the infant must "borrow" by participation the psychic structure of the selfobjects in order to gain (and, upon disruption, regain) a semblance of calm, cohesiveness, safety, etc.[53]

Under "good enough" conditions this need is sufficiently met so that the inevitable frustrations that occur do not lead to a traumatic shattering of the fantasy of the perfect selfobjects, but instead lead to a gradual modification of the representations. This occurs by what Kohut calls "optimal frustration" and "transmuting internalization."

Optimal frustration is disappointment in one aspect or instance of what is expected of the selfobject. Since the disappointment is not total,

---

[52]See Heinz Kohut, "On Courage," in Strozier, *Self Psychology and the Humanities*, p. 11.

[53]See Kohut, *Restoration of the Self*, pp. 86-87.

the self-selfobject bond is only momentarily disturbed and reconciliation is soon achieved. Some of the expectation which had been included in the selfobject representation, however, is now "broken off" from that representation, depersonalized, and taken on as a function the self can at least temporarily perform for itself. Thus, the minor traumas of "optimal frustration" are the catalysts of self-structure.[54]

The process of incorporating these components of self-function is called "transmuting internalization" because it does not involve a wholesale identification with the selfobject, but rather the detaching of some aspect of its character which can then be built into the self's own structure according to the self's innate predispositions.

In a therapeutic relationship, transmuting internalization occurs when the functions that the therapist performs for the patient gradually are shifted into the patient's own internal world. When the therapist has consistently provided these functions for some time, the patient builds up a representation of someone performing that function for him or her. Then when on a particular occasion the therapist "fails" to fulfill that function, the patient is able to draw upon that representation to perform the function for him/herself. When this process occurs over and over again in very small and subtle forms, it eventually can lead to a point where a decisive difference in the strength and integration of the self is evident.[55]

Kohut compares this process to the way "foreign proteins" are ingested, broken down into parts, and reassembled according to an organism's own genetically determined specifications. In the case of the psyche the specifications are partially inborn, but once the process has begun and a rudimentary nuclear self structure has been laid down, it is this core structure that largely directs the ongoing structuring process.[56]

---

[54]See Kohut, *Analysis of the Self*, pp. 49-50.

[55]Ibid., pp. 38-41.

[56]See Kohut, *How Does Analysis Cure?*, p. 160; also idem, "On the Continuity of the Self," p. 238.

When optimal frustration and transmuting internalization are repeated in hundreds of micro-instances,[57] two favorable results occur: one, the self's representation of itself (its repertoire of habitual functions) gains cohesiveness, continuity, competence, etc; and two, the self's representations of selfobjects (its repertoire of functions it expects others to perform for it) grow more empathically attuned to what is realistically expectable. Thus, the self has gained "structure." As Kohut put it, there has occurred

> a gradual shift from the self relying for its nutriment on archaic modes of contact in the narcissistic sphere (in particular on mergers with the mirroring selfobject, mergers with the idealized selfobject, and twinship mergers . . .) to its ability to be sustained most of the time by the empathic resonance that emanates from the selfobjects of adult life.[58]

When this process has not gone well, however, an illness of the self may occur. One form of this involves what Kohut calls "disavowal." Disavowal is different from "repression." Repression occurs when unconscious material begins to rise into consciousness and is pushed back. Disavowal, on the other hand, occurs when a whole sector of the unconscious *and* its conscious manifestations are rejected from association with the central self, although they continue to exist on a "parallel track." Disavowal, in Kohut's view, involves a more serious psychic split than does repression.[59]

On the basis of his clinical experience Kohut reformulated the classical theory of the "Oedipus complex." A basically firm self, he wrote, is a prerequisite for even beginning to experience the Oedipal dynamics; and the result of a normal Oedipal phase is the further

---

[57]See Kohut, *Restoration of the Self*, pp. 31-33.

[58]Kohut, *How Does Analysis Cure?*, p. 70.

[59]For discussion, see Kohut, *Analysis of the Self*, pp. 176-99.

firming of the self.[60] He suggested that the "complex" with all its negative connotations of intense frustration, guilt, repression, harsh superego, murdurous urges, etc., actually is an abnormal development that only occurs because the child enters the Oedipal period (ages 4-6) with pre-existing self deficits.

While acknowledging that in a mild form the Oedipus complex may be as ubiquitous as dental caries, Kohut asserted that in the normal, "good enough" case the Oedipal phase is actually a joyful, vitalizing experience for the child. Having matured to a point where she or he can participate in the excitement of such activities of non-genital sexual interplay as affection, intimacy, seductiveness, possessiveness, assertiveness, competition, etc., the normal child "plays" with these capacities. The normal parent, says Kohut, responds with modulated sexuality and aggression, but even more importantly with pride, affirmation and shared joy in the child's new abilities. The result is the firming and vitalization of the child's self. Only if the child has a weak self to begin with, or if the parents or others react inappropriately, does this period result in pathology.

During psychoanalysis narcissism can be transformed into a more mature form, and the psychoanalyst looks for primary and secondary manifestations of this. The primary manifestations are changes in the narcissistic sector itself. In the area of the idealized parent imago, increased self-structure leads to strengthening of internalized values and standards and increased ability to regulate and channel drives. In the area of the grandiose self, increased self-structure leads to the integration of ambitions and purposes into the total personality, along with strengthened self-confidence and self-esteem.[61]

The secondary manifestations of transformed narcissism include increased ability to love. In Kohut's view this is not due to the

---

[60]Kohut, *Restoration of the Self*, pp. 227, 238-9; idem, *How Does Analysis Cure?*, p. 22.

[61]For review of these primary manifestations, see Kohut, *Analysis of the Self*, pp. 298-300.

transformation of narcissistic energy into object love (as in classical Freudian theory), but rather due to the freeing of hidden object love as the wall of regressive narcissistic fixation breaks down. It is also facilitated by the transformation of the idealizing selfobject transference into a healthy capacity to admire other persons, as well as by the general increase in self-confidence and self-esteem that permits one to take the risk of loving.[62]

Of particular interest for this inquiry is that Kohut went beyond his strictly clinical discussion to formulate a theory of the human and culture-building qualities of transformed narcissism. He envisaged five important human attributes as characteristic of transformed narcissism: creativity, empathy, the capacity to contemplate one's own impermanence, a sense of humor, and wisdom.[63] Empathy has already been given preliminary consideration in the section above on method in self psychology. Its implications for cultural and political life will be considered in Appendix C, "Self Psychology and the Psychology of Groups." Creativity will also be discussed there, while the other three attributes will be considered in the section of Chapter 9 on "Self Psychology and Religion."

D. The Self: A Reprise

In the final pages of *Restoration*, referring to the fact that he had never provided a comprehensive theoretical definition of the term "self," Kohut wrote:

> My investigation contains hundreds of pages dealing with the psychology of the self--yet it never assigns an inflexible meaning to the term self, it never explains how the essence of the self should be

---

[62]For discussion of these secondary changes, see Kohut, *Analysis of the Self*, pp. 296-98.

[63]Kohut, "Forms and Transformations," pp. 111f.

> defined. But I admit this fact without contrition or shame. The self . . . is, like all reality--physical reality (the data about the world perceived by our senses) or psychological reality (the data about the world perceived via introspection and empathy)--not knowable in its essence. We cannot, by introspection and empathy, penetrate to the self per se; only its introspectively or empathically perceived psychological manifestations are open to us. Demands for an exact definition of the nature of the self disregard the fact that "the self" is not a concept of an abstract science, but a generalization derived from empirical data.[64]

This quotation indicates both Kohut's clear recognition of the limits of psychological science, and his insight that the empirical data of psychology itself demands a concept such as "the self" even though the reality to which this concept refers can never be pinned down as an object-among-objects. In terms of the schema of possible meanings of the term "self,"[65] I have interpreted Kohut's "self in the broad sense" as like that of A(2), that is, descriptive at the depth-psychological level, with the added claim that adequate description requires an implicit affirmation of A(3), personal agency, and A(4), consciousness as such. I call this affirmation implicit, not explicit, because Kohut claims only that the empirical data on the level of A(2) is distorted unless notions such as "personal agency" and "center of consciousness" are included in one's description.

Kohut's own language is not always clear about these distinctions; some read him as going beyond his competency as a psychoanalyst by making even implicit affirmations about personal agency and consciousness. Atwood and Stolorow attempt to clarify these issues when they write:

> We have found it important to distinguish sharply between the concept of the self as a psychological structure and the concept of the *person* as an experiencing subject and agent who initiates action. Whereas

---

[64]Kohut, *Restoration of the Self*, pp. 310-11.

[65]See beginning of this Chapter.

> the self-as-structure falls squarely within the domain of psychoanalytic investigation, the ontology of the person-as-agent, in our view, lies beyond the scope of psychoanalytic inquiry. Psychoanalysis can only illuminate the *experience* of personal agency or its absence in specific contexts of meaning.[66]

Kohut, as noted above, did not want to pin down his definition of the self so clearly as this. He wanted to have it both ways: to work as a psychoanalyst with the self-as-structure, and at the same time to open psychoanalysis to yet deeper dimensions of the human person. The need felt by Atwood and Stolorow to clarify terminology and to denotate the limitations of psychoanalytic competence is legitimate. It may well be true that it is not possible to "have it both ways" and still remain within the field of competence of psychoanalysis as traditionally defined.

Yet what Kohut was trying to do is extremely valuable for inquiries such as the present one, which aim to develop a theoretical framework within which the distinct dynamics of psychological and mystical experience can be respected and at the same time be seen as integrally related to one another. The term "self," for Kohut, seems to refer to the liminal realm that links the unknowable mystery of the human person with the concrete psychological structures by which that person is manifested in the world. Using the terminology developed in Part I, we could say that his notion of the self acknowledges both the immediate, essentially unknowable ground of the self (the "subject-as-subject") and the manifestations of the self as mediated in the world.

While Kohut did not use the language of mediation, the notion of mediation as developed by Lonergan seems well suited to clarifying some of the ambiguity in Kohut's term "self." In terms of the discussion of "structures,"[67] he acknowledges the self-as-structure as the mediation-into-parts of the whole which, in itself, is something more

---

[66]Atwood and Stolorow, *Structures of Subjectivity*, p. 34.

[67]See above, "Images, Representations, and Structures."

than the sum of its parts.[68] The notion of mediation permits a conceptualization of an integral link between the self as ontological mystery and the self as phenomenological structure.[69]

With this conceptualization it is possible to treat either aspect on its own level, while recognizing the other aspect as equally real and constitutive. In these terms, we can clarify Kohut's work as dealing strictly with the mediated, phenomenological structures of the self, yet with acknowledgment of the deeper ground from which they emerge. Using Kohut's insights, we can explore the mediated, phenomenological structures of the mystically-transformed self from a strictly psychological viewpoint, without fear that this involves a reduction of the self to this dimension alone.

A note on how this differs from a Jungian view of "the Self" may also be helpful at this point, since Jung's ideas appear very frequently in discussions of the psychological dimension of mysticism. Juan Rof Carballo once made an analogy between the shift from the general psychoanalytical notion of the "self" to the Jungian notion of "Self" and the transformation of an ordinary house into a temple. In this transformation, says Rof Carballo, all the ordinary rooms of the house (kitchen, living room, bedrooms, etc.) have to be torn down or drastically remodeled.[70] Thus, for Jung the mystic who experiences the Self shifts into a set of psychic structures totally different from those of everyday life.

This metaphor of transformation has some validity in describing certain effects of the inbreaking of the mystical dimension. Our approach here, however, is to focus on the ordinary house and how it

---

[68]See, for example, Kohut, *Restoration of the Self*, p. 97: "it is possible to discern a self which . . . . has become a supraordinated configuration whose significance transcends that of the sum of its parts."

[69]On the notion of mediation, see "Mediation and Dynamic Structure" in Chapter 4.

[70]Juan Rof Carballo, "La Estructura del Alma Humana Según Santa Teresa," *Revista de Espiritualidad* 22 (1963), p. 421.

is transformed into a more orderly, well-functioning, hospitable home. Without denying that at another time or from another perspective the home may indeed be a "temple," we focus on the transformation of the ordinary, "marketplace" self instead of on a shift to an entirely new dimension.

In my view Jung's approach does not make a clear distinction between the mediational dynamics of the human psyche in its own terms and those related to the breaking-in of the transcendent ground. The similarity between Jungian analysis and the approach used here is that both focus on images and their transformation. With the notion of "archetypes," however, Jungians tend to detach the most significant of these images from their embeddedness in the concrete, intersubjective world. The result is a lack of attentiveness both to the genetic origins of the images within the individual's concrete network of intersubjective relations, and to their potential ramifications within that same network.

Kohut's theory, on the other hand, focuses rigorously on the development and transformation of psychic representations within the intersubjective fields of early life and of later self-selfobject relations. This makes it most appropriate as a framework of psychological terms and relations for the study of the relationship between mystical transformation and intersubjectivity.

CHAPTER 9

SELF PSYCHOLOGY AND THE INTERPRETATION OF A MYSTIC'S TEXT

The goal of this chapter will be to amplify certain aspects of Kohut's thought that have particular relevance to this inquiry. While the in-depth application of the self-psychological framework to the *Interior Castle* will not take place until Chapters 10 and 11, some preliminary discussion of background issues will take place in this chapter.

A. A Theory of the Text as Mediation of the Self

Mediation and the Self

The validity of the next phase of this inquiry is premised upon the notion that a written text is a mediation of the self of its author. Two caveats are immediately necessary. First, this does not mean that the meaning and value of the text are reducible to the psychological context of its production. Second, it also does not mean that any given text provides a complete--or even necessarily a representative--view of its author's psyche. Both of these misinterpretations of the original statement derive from a misunderstanding of the meaning of the notion of the mediation of the self.

The notion of a relationship between an immediate source and a mediated expression is extremely general. The same source can be mediated in many different expressions, depending on the historical moment, the resources available, etc. While all are mediations of the source, none is a total expression of the source and some may be quite pale or diluted expressions of the source. Human beings have extraordinarily rich capabilities for self-mediation in a wide variety of mediums. Each expression--whether in the psychic media of dream or fantasy, in the behavioral media of action, in the linguistic media of culture, or whatever--expresses the self in the given medium and yet is not a total manifestation of the self.

The two misinterpretations mentioned above result from reducing the process of mediation in one direction or another. The first reduces the process in the direction of the self, suggesting that mediation is *only* an expression of the self. This fails to give proper regard to the context and media of the expression itself. The second reduces the process in the direction of the expression, suggesting that mediation gives a *total* expression of the self. This fails to give proper regard to the reality of the self which is always more than the sum of its parts or expressions.

Concretization and Mediation

Atwood and Stolorow develop a self-psychological theory of human expressions that is very helpful in understanding how a text can be a mediation of the self. They propose the notion of "concretization" as a general term for human self-expression. The self "concretizes" when it gives its structures a shape within the spatio-temporal world.

The supraordinate human motive, Atwood and Stolorow assert, is the need to maintain the organization of experience.[1] This is equivalent

[1]Atwood and Stolorow, *Structures of Subjectivity*, p. 35.

to saying that the nature of the self is to mediate itself in coherent structure; any threat to the dynamic directionality of the self toward coherent structure will engender concerted efforts to counter that threat. The self, whether under conditions of normality or threat, expresses itself in "the encapsulation of structures of experience by concrete, sensorimotor symbols," which Atwood and Stolorow term "concretization."[2]

The form that concretization takes depends on what pathways are available for the mediation of the self. Examples of concretizations include behavioral patterns, symbolic objects, neurotic symptoms, and dreams. Each concretization gives expression--whether behavioral, linguistic, or imagistic--to that individual's basic structures of experience, that is, "the distinctive configurations of self and object that shape and organize a person's subjective world."[3]

Obviously, the self produces many different forms of concretization. Although every concretization is an expression of the self's structures, not all are equally expressive of the core or nuclear structures. The degree to which a given concretization is expressive of nuclear structures can only be ascertained within the context of broader knowledge of the person in question.

A written text is a form of concretization. Even in texts that are primarily factual or technical, elements of the author's self-structure can be found expressed in choice of genre, explicit or implicit metaphors, form of organization or lack thereof, etc. When the text is explicitly intended as an expression of the self--as is the case with any creative work, whether of fiction or non-fiction--this dimension becomes much more significant. Our hypothesis is that the *Interior Castle*, which is an imagistic presentation of the soul's journey from emptiness to fullness, is a text that expresses very significant dimensions of its author's nuclear self-structures.

---

[2]Ibid., p. 85.

[3]Ibid., p. 33.

Thus, the methods developed within psychoanalysis for the interpretation of certain types of concretizations (dreams, neurotic symptoms, etc.) can appropriately be employed in the interpretation of texts. Modifications are necessary, of course, in that a text, to a far greater degree than the concretizations typically dealt with in the clinical setting of psychoanalysis, has been released into the world of public intersubjectivity.

The Text Genre

A written text, as Paul Ricoeur notes, is separated from its author to a much greater degree than other forms of discourse. A text has a certain "semantic autonomy," such that it is no longer the case that its meaning is inextricably linked with the social, psychological, or intentional milieu of its origin. By being inscribed in writing, a text completes the trajectory of language from *bios* to *logos*--from being bound by its origins in the web of created things, to the free "re-writing" of the world with new possibilities.

Another way of speaking of this is in terms of transcendence and creativity. The text transcends its origins and creatively reconstructs a world. In fact, every concretization does this to some degree; the concretization is a creative attempt to "make the world over" according to the specifications of the self. The text genre, however, takes this process to its conclusion by drawing upon a wider range of public symbols and by separating itself more definitively from its producer. It "makes a world" that enters into the realm of public discourse and which, therefore, can have a powerful impact upon various "group selves."[4]

Despite its semantic autonomy, a text remains a work of human discourse and is never completely freed from the dialectic that engendered it. Ricoeur calls this "the dialectic between event and

---

[4]On the understanding of the "group self" in self psychology, see Appendix C.

meaning"--between an event of communication rooted in a specific time and place, and the meaning that strives to transcend its origins and re-write the world.[5] In discussing the value of psychoanalysis for text interpretation, Ricoeur said that the genius of psychoanalysis is its attention to the tension at the boundary where *bios* passes into *logos*--where life passes into discourse.[6] Texts, and especially symbolic texts, intensify the tension between the two dimensions and in doing so actually demand a method of interpretation that explicitly attends to both and to the dialectic between them.

Interpretation of texts must avoid both historicism and psychologism, which lean back toward *bios* and reduce the meaning of the text to its temporal origins, and logicism, which leans forward toward *logos* and reduces the text to an autonomous structure of impersonal meanings. Classical psychoanalysis, with its stress on instinct and on determinative orgins in early life, tended strongly to push back towards the *bios* dimension. Kohut's renovation of psychoanalysis, with its equal stress on the creative and future-oriented dynamism of the self as it moves into structures, realigns the tension.

A self-psychological approach to text interpretation does not view origins primarily in terms of history or instinct, but in terms of the self. Rather than having to search for the origins of textual expressions in early life experiences or in instinctual drives, the interpreter searches for the structures of the self. Structures, understood as psychological mediations of the self, are holograms containing the past, the present and the potential future. Hence, no matter what period of the individual's life the text derives from, the structures manifested in the text give insight into the whole.

---

[5]Paul Ricoeur, *Interpretation Theory: Discourse and the Surplus of Meaning* (Fort Worth, TX: Texas Christian University Press, 1976), pp. 11-12. On relation of author and text, see ibid., pp. 29-30; on *bios* and *logos*, pp. 57-63; on "re-writing," p. 42. See also idem, *Freud and Philosophy: An Essay on Interpretation*, trans. Denis Savage (New Haven, CT: Yale University Press, 1970).

[6]Ricoeur, *Interpretation Theory*, pp. 57-59.

The following section explores in greater detail the contribution of self psychology to the analysis of texts.

B. Self Psychology and Applied Psychoanalysis

Kohut and the Psychoanalysis of Creativity

"Applied psychoanalysis" is the term used in the psychoanalytic community for the application of psychoanalytic theories and methods outside the clinical setting--for example, in biographical, historical, or literary studies. In an early essay entitled "Beyond the Bounds of the Basic Rule," Kohut discussed three types of justifiable applied psychoanalysis. One is the use of established psychoanalytic knowledge as an adjunct to a study whose overall method and standards are determined by its primary purpose of understanding a significant figure, historical period, work of art, etc. Another is the converse: the use of biographical, historical or literary material to illustrate a clinical syndrome.

The third type of applied psychoanalysis was Kohut's favorite. He termed it "the psychoanalysis of creativity," and described it as "aimed at the elucidation of the contribution made by specific conflicts and other psychological constellations to the development, maintenance, and disturbance of normal or especially desirable ego functions."[7] It differs from the other two types in that the primary purpose of the study is neither outside the psychoanalytic realm (as in type one) nor completely "inside" psychoanalytic theory (as in type two's concern to illustrate a predetermined theoretical construct).

Kohut's approach to the psychoanalysis of creativity is to strive to understand the dynamic psychology of how people maintain a coherent sense of self and, in the struggle to do so, make special contributions to

---

[7]Heinz Kohut, "Beyond the Bounds of the Basic Rule: Some Recent Contributions to Applied Psychoanalyis," in *Search for the Self*, vol. 1, p. 301.

the concomitant struggles of various "group selves" in which they participate. It focuses, therefore, on the total existence and positive potential of the person and his or her products--not only on psychopathology or on the psyche as a realm detached from the whole person.

The present inquiry's psychoanalytic component is a study in the psychoanalysis of creativity. Its focus is on the formation and transformation of Teresa's self-structures in interplay with those of other persons (human and divine)[8] and groups. It is not a search for pathology, but rather an effort to understand the concrete pathways by which Teresa came to be able to make her extraordinary contribution to the human project.

While the concrete pathways of Teresa's journey may well be found to involve passage through elements of "pathology," this is no cause for alarm when it is studied in the context of a positive and holistic view of the person and her ultimate transformation. In fact, it may be cause for hope--hope that despite our own and others' psychological anomalies, any of us may be able to pursue the same journey of transformation as Teresa did.

Method in Applied Psychoanalysis

Although his approach is obviously not "theory-free," Kohut always strove to adhere to the principle that in psychoanalytic work one must do one's best to put theories and constructs in the back of one's mind and attend empathically to the particulars of the situation presenting itself. The various theories, concepts and models in the back of one's mind permit one to "play" with organizing the data in various ways until

---

[8]While divine "persons" obviously do not exist on the same physical plane as human persons, it is not necessary to affirm the existence of a "supernatural" plane in order to accord divine persons real existence in psychological life. Whatever their origin, divine figures operate in some individuals' psychic dramas with as much power and autonomy as do human figures.

a convincing configuration emerges. Only then is it appropriate to move from "experience near" understanding to "experience distant" explanation, in which theories play a major role.[9]

In applied psychoanalysis, then, the goal should not be to find data to fit into a preconceived theoretical framework, but to attend to the data on its own terms.[10] From a self-psychological point of view, a classical approach to applied psychoanalysis violates this because it always seeks a genetic explanation, with strong emphasis on the oedipal period. With historical figures the classical approach often means that available data has to be stretched or that presumptions have to be made without sufficient supporting data, since in most cases there is little reliable information about the early years.

Self psychology, on the other hand, focuses on the reliable data that *is* available, the great majority of which derives from the adult period of the individual's life. While data about formative early life experiences would be valuable, self psychology understands the pattern of the self as expressed in every sphere of involvement and in the overall course of the individual's life. The self-psychological view is that early experience shapes the nuclear self into a pattern oriented toward the living out of a particular future--a "destiny." The pattern can be recognized even if one does not know all the original factors that shaped it.

In studying the life course of an historical or literary figure, Heinz Kohut suggests, the self psychologist views it as "the struggles of a self to realize its basic pattern."[11] Historian Thomas Kohut (Heinz Kohut's son) expressed the value of this insight for applied psychoanalysis:

---

[9]For discussion of this methodology in the clinical setting, see Heinz Kohut, "The Curative Effect of Analysis: The Self Psychological Reassessment of the Therapeutic Process," in *How Does Analysis Cure?*, pp. 80-110.

[10]See the discussion by Heinz Kohut's son, a psychoanalytically-trained historian, in Thomas A. Kohut, "Psychohistory as History," *American Historical Review* 91, no. 2 (1986), pp. 336-54.

[11]Kohut, "Self Psychology and the Sciences," p. 82.

> . . . even if the historian is forced to do without this knowledge [of early life], he can more than compensate for it by studying the entire life-curve of his historical subject, which expresses both the experiences of childhood and the subsequent experiences of adult life. The course of an individual's life, in other words, tells us more about the essence of his personality than do the facts of his childhood.[12]

This approach is revolutionary for applied psychoanalysis because, as Charles Strozier notes, it "permits the observer to interpret what we actually see: a figure's goals and ambitions, his ideals, and all the complex interactions characterizing his work life."[13] Heinz Kohut concludes that a study of an historical or literary figure, undertaken from the perspective of a self-psychological search for the basic patterns of the self, may "furnish data that may be as significant and as reliable as those obtained during therapeutic analysis."[14]

A self-psychological approach is most appropriate for this study, since relatively little data about Teresa's early life is available and, in any case, the more significant--and better documented--parts of her life are the adult years. The approach here is to take a text, a single "mediation of the self," from her maturity and analyze it to discern the pattern of the self. As we will see, it turns out that the *Interior Castle* provides a view of the pattern of the self not only as it was manifested in one particular stage of life, but in its total trajectory through adulthood.

---

[12]Thomas Kohut, "Psychohistory as History," p. 342.

[13]Charles B. Strozier, "Heinz Kohut and the Historical Imagination," in Arnold Goldberg, ed., *Advances in Self Psychology* (New York: International Universities Press, 1980). See also idem, "Introduction," in Strozier, *Self Psychology and the Humanities*, especially pp. xxv-xxviii.

[14]Kohut, "Self Psychology and the Sciences," p. 82. For additional discussion of these issues, see John Demos's comments in "The Self in History," in Strozier, *Self Psychology and the Humanities*.

A Review in Light of Lonergan

It was noted above that Kohut distinguished three types of applied psychoanalysis, of which the third was his own real interest. A brief discussion of these, with help from the Lonerganian framework set up in Part I of this inquiry, will help to place what follows in the proper perspective.

The first type of applied psychoanalysis begins with a narrative (biographical, historical, or literary) and uses psychoanalytic methods and insights as one dimension of an attempt to clarify the structure and meaning of the narrative. The primary focus remains on the narrative--establishing its facts, clarifying its internal relationships, pointing out its significance within a given context. The present inquiry would be of this type if it were primarily a study of Teresa's life as a whole, an historical study of her teachings, or a textual study in the strict sense.

The second type of applied psychoanalysis begins with a psychoanalytic theory and seeks to show how it is corroborated in specific biographical, historical or literary examples. Here the primary focus is on the theory; the interest is in explicating the internal structure of the theory and showing how it gives valuable insight into concrete phenomena. The present inquiry would be of this type if it were primarily an attempt to illustrate the value of self psychological concepts by showing how they illuminate aspects of Teresa's life and writing.

In Lonergan's terms, we might say that the first type of study remains primarily in the realm of common sense (recalling, of course, that the "common sense" of the scholarly biographer, historian, or literary critic may be extraordinarily sophisticated), while the second type is concerned primarily with the realm of theory. In order to begin to deal with the realms of interiority and transcendence, we must turn to the third type of applied psychoanalysis.

The third type, which Kohut termed the "psychoanalysis of creativity," begins with an interest in human transcendence. It focuses on the question of how people transcend the chaos of life by finding creative ways to hold themselves together and, in the process, to make positive contributions to the upbuilding of groups in which they participate. The psychoanalysis of creativity is a work in the realm of interiority because it focuses explicitly on the inner structures that shape outward perception and behavior. In such an endeavor neither the narrative of events nor the theory is center focus; the focus, rather, is on the activity of construction that is manifested in the events and explained by the theory.

The subject matter of this inquiry is mystical transformation. It focuses on discerning the integral relationship between human transcendence in its ultimate form (mystical transformation) and the intersubjective structures of the self. While an account that focused on narrative could describe the co-occurrence of these dimensions in a specific case, and an account that focused on theory could give a coherent explanation of why they ought to co-occur, it requires an account focusing on interiority to both describe and explain the factual processes in which they coinhere.

In this inquiry, Chapters 7, 10, and 11 focus on two dimensions of interiority. Chapter 7 has provided an explicit interiority analysis, studying the operations by which the structures of the self have been constructed. Chapters 10 and 11, employing a psychoanalytic methodology, directly investigate the deep structures of the self as manifested in the text. Before proceeding to this second analysis, however, it will be helpful to fill in more of the background on Kohut's views on the phenomena of religious experience.

C. Self Psychology and Religion

A quiet but persistent theme in Kohut's writings is the affirmation of the positive potential of religion. He was well aware of the bad science, counterproductive moralizing, and outright pathology that can find shelter in human religion; yet he was also aware that religion often provides both individuals and cultures with psychological nourishment and support that is indispensable for their survival and creative growth. Whereas classical psychoanalytical theory is able to find only greater or lesser degrees of pathology in religious phenomena, self psychological theory is able to give a plausible account of both religion's positive potential and its characteristic distortions.

The Self in the Face of Finitude and Death

Kohut himself came from a non-practicing Jewish background, and it is fairly evident from the way he treated religious phenomena that he was not a believer or participant in religion in its orthodox or traditional forms. His own religious vision is perhaps best summarized in this section on how the self is able to face its own finitude. His most complete discussion of this topic was his 1959 essay "The Forms and Transformations of Narcissism." The third characteristic of transformed narcissism noted there was "acceptance of the fact that we ourselves are impermanent, that the self which is cathected with narcissistic libido is finite in time."[15]

Whereas classical psychoanalysis has tended to regard such acceptance as the (perhaps impossible) total abdication of narcissism through the final triumph of realism and reason, Kohut viewed it as a higher form of narcissism. He wrote:

> Just as the child's *primary* empathy with the mother is the precursor of the adult's ability to be empathic, so his *primary identity* with her must be considered as the precursor of an expansion of the self, late in life, when the finiteness of individual existence is acknowledged. . . . The achievement--as the certainty of eventual death is fully realized--of a shift of the narcissistic cathexes, from the self to a concept of participation in a supraindividual and timeless existence,

---

[15]Kohut, "Forms and Transformations," p. 118.

> must also be regarded as genetically predetermined by the child's primary identity with the mother.[16]

Thus, the narcissistic ability to participate in another's life, Kohut believed, has the potential to be transformed into a complete identification of self with the other. In primitive or regressive forms such complete identification would be an indication of a poorly structured self. In maturity, however, "the genuine shift of the cathexes toward a cosmic narcissism is the enduring, creative result of the steadfast activities of an autonomous ego, and only very few are able to attain it."[17] Mature "cosmic narcissism" is an identification of self with the cosmos, such that one's own demise is experienced as merely a passing over into the larger whole.

Humor and wisdom--the last two characteristics of transformed narcissism that Kohut noted--are also related to the ability to relativize the demands of the self, not by repressing or abdicating them but by transforming them. Like cosmic narcissism, humor is a way to overcome finiteness by opening to a "larger picture." As Kohut put it,

> Humor and cosmic narcisissm, . . . which permit us to face death without having to resort to denial, are metapsychologically based not on a decathexis of the self through a frantic hypercathexis of objects but on a decathexis of the narcissistic self through a rearrangement and transformation of the narcissistic libido; and, in contrast to states of extreme object cathexis, the span of the ego is here not narrowed but the ego remains active and deliberate.[18]

Wisdom, finally, summarizes all the other transformations of narcissism. In addition to having broad experience and knowledge, the wise person is creative, empathic, gently humorous, and able to accept finitude and

---

[16]Ibid., p. 119.

[17]Ibid., p. 120.

[18]Ibid., p. 121.

death. Wisdom represents the final integration of the cognitive function with narcissistic functioning. Of wisdom, Kohut wrote:

> The ultimate act of cognition, i.e., the acknowledgement of the limits and of the finiteness of the self, is not the result of an isolated intellectual process but is the victorious outcome of the lifework of the total personality in acquiring broadly based knowledge and in transforming archaic modes of narcissism into ideals, humor, and a sense of supraindividual participation in the world.[19]

In "On Courage," an essay from the early 1970s,[20] Kohut wrote of the most extreme cases of the courageous acceptance of death. This, he believed, becomes possible when the individual recognizes the life-threatening situation as a moment of supreme potential for the living out of the basic pattern of his or her nuclear self. That pattern may be primarily idealizing, in which case the individual peacefully, even joyfully, dies as a martyr rather than betray ideals and values; or it may be primarily "subject-bound grandiosity," in which case the individual experiences a surge of power and invincibility that fuels death-defying courage.[21] The idealizing pattern, Kohut believed, is most typical of those we call saints and martyrs. Such a person "will die without a trace of fear, die as a matter of fact proudly. He knows that he has supported his real self, which lives on."[22]

The Western literary tradition of tragedy, Kohut asserts, basically enshrines the story of the hero for whom "death coincides with the fulfillment of the deepest pattern of their nuclear selves, that is, . . . seeming defeat is actually a narcissistic triumph."[23] The tragic challenge--the call to be true to one's deepest self, even when it means

---

[19]Ibid., p. 122.

[20]Kohut, "On Courage."

[21]See Kohut, "On Courage," pp. 12-13, 19-20 n. 10.

[22]Kohut, "Conversations," p. 263.

[23]Kohut, "On Courage," p. 44.

destruction and death--is the essence of the human condition. The gospel story of Jesus, says Kohut, is the supreme rendition of this pattern of heroic tragedy.[24]

As noted above, Kohut's understanding of the self as it faces its ultimate challenge--acceptance of finitude and death--is the framework within which he understands religion. His view of the believer's relationship with God is derived from this framework.

Religious Experience: God as Selfobject

Kohut viewed the ordinary religious believer's relationship with God as an adult analogue of the archaic idealizing transference. As he put it, "the figure of the perfect and omnipotent God, with whom the powerless and humble believer wants to merge, corresponds to the ancient omnipotent self-object, the idealized parent imago."[25] Since selfobjects, for Kohut, are a lifelong need, this archaically-rooted God-experience is not classified *a priori* as regressive or pathological. Whether one's selfobjects are human or divine, mature selfobject experience always carries within itself the resonance of the archaic selfobject experiences:

> . . . the adult's experience of the selfobject is . . . an experience in depth: when the adult experiences the self-sustaining effects of a maturely chosen selfobject, the selfobject experiences of all the preceding stages of his life reverberate unconsciously.[26]

Like many selfobject experiences, the ordinary experience of God as selfobject functions most of the time as a background sense of vague but profound presence, care, support, goodness, etc. More intense God-experiences, according to Kohut, appear particularly in those individuals

---

[24]Kohut, "On Courage," p. 45.

[25]Kohut, *Analysis of the Self*, p. 106.

[26]Kohut, *How Does Analysis Cure?*, pp. 49-50.

whose nuclear selves are being organized around the idealizing sector--the "set of central values and ideals, the heir to the archaic idealized object."[27] When such an individual faces a crisis that carries within it the potential for physical and/or psychological annihilation, one of the resources upon which he or she may call is the archaic memory of an omnipotent idealized selfobject which supported the self when, in early childhood, it was chronically in danger of disintegration. Kohut observed that an intense sense of the presence of an external, benificent, omnipotent power often accompanies and enables some of the most remarkable acts of human courage.[28]

Kohut asserts that when this regression to the omnipotent idealized selfobject takes place in mature and courageous individuals, it differs from the related regressions that take place in narcissistic personality disorders and in psychosis. In the basically healthy individual the regression will be accompanied by other indications of mature transformation of the self, such as "a fine sense of humor," "subtle empathy," and "the suffusion of the personality with a profound sense of inner peace and serenity--a mental state akin to wisdom."[29]

Pathological Religious Experience

For Kohut, then, God-experience can be profoundly adaptive, even though in his view it partakes of illusion. The conviction of God's empathic presence often is an essential ingredient in a person's ability to negotiate the crises associated with fully living out the pattern of the nuclear self, particularly in the face of intense opposition. When the regression toward the omnipotent idealized selfobject is a dimension of pathology, however, the indications of maturity named above are not present. Instead, there may be

---

[27]Ibid., p. 19.

[28] Kohut, "On Courage."

[29]Ibid., pp. 15-16.

> . . . the fuzzy mysticism which characterizes certain regressive swings in narcissistic personality disturbances . . . [or] the anxious and bizarre mental state surrounding the delusional contacts with a bizarre god and with other distorted omnipotent figures which we encounter in the psychotic.[30]

In his first full-length exposition of self psychology, *The Analysis of the Self*, Kohut counted "disjointed mystical religious feelings; vague awe" as among the primary characteristics of the disintegrating self in those severe narcissistic personality disorders where the pathological regression is primarily in the idealizing realm. There may be "hypomanic fusion" with the archaic idealized parent imago, resulting in "a state of quasi-religious ecstasy." In serious cases there are persistent mystical and religious preoccupations that lack a focus upon a clearly-delimited figure. Such preoccupations are an indication of a chronic, disasterously failing search for a non-fragmenting idealizable selfobject.[31] Kohut also noted that religious symbolism can become involved in narcissistic disorders where regression is primarily in the realm of the grandiose self.[32]

What purports to be a "religious experience," then, may be in fact an indication of self pathology. Even in such cases, however, Kohut's approach gives an account of the positive function which religious preoccupations may be playing in the individual's life. The longing for or identification with divine figures, even when it is pathologically regressive, is an attempt to meet chronically unmet selfobject needs. Rather than attacking or disparaging these preoccupations, those concerned for such an individual's health need to recognize the survival function the religious concerns are serving.

---

[30]Kohut, "On Courage," p. 20.

[31]Kohut, *Analysis of the Self*, pp. 9, 85-86, 97.

[32]Kohut, *Restoration of the Self*, pp. 200-1.

The Value of Religion

In addition to these remarks on the role of religious concerns in individual psychology, Kohut made a number of comments on the broader issues of the role and value of religion in human life. He observed that much criticism of religion is directed at its attempts to give authoritative answers to questions that really belong to the domain of science. Religion, he said, is often "poor science," and insofar as this is true, Freud's accusation that it is "illusory" is justified. On the other hand, "as a supportive selfobject, religion is not poor by a long shot. . . . Religion constitutes a set of cultural values which [Freud] totally underestimated."[33]

While Kohut himself might have been somewhat taken aback by an effort, such as the present one, to employ his system of thought in a study that affirms the theological reality of mystical experience even as it tries to understand it psychologically, it is clear that for him the scientific pursuit of insight into human meaning-construction was part and parcel of the religious quest. My suspicion is that he would have recognized and affirmed this project as a part of that quest, even though his own theological position was far more reticent.

D. Conclusion

To review: In Chapter 6 above, it was stated that the goal of this portion of the inquiry would be "to come to an understanding of the concrete psychological structures by which the mystic mediates self within the existing world." In Chapter 8, the self-psychological notions of "self," "structure," "concretization," "representation," and "image" were

---

[33]Kohut, "Religion, Ethics, Values," in Strozier, *Self Psychology and the Humanities*, p. 261.

explicated. The present chapter has brought out additional self-psychological insight on applied psychoanalysis and religious experience.

It is now time to put all this together. The next tasks are 1) to gain insight into the structures of Teresa's self after her mystical transformation, and 2) to observe how those structures were formed by, and contributed to, intersubjective interplay. This can be done by a study of representations and images within a particular concretization of the self, the text of the *Interior Castle*.

The hypothesis is that these structures, which are the mediation in the psychological realm of the mystically transformed subject, will give evidence of a high degree of maturation and healing when judged by criteria of intersubjective harmony, effectiveness, participation, etc. At the same time the tensions and idiosyncracies that have resulted from the psyche's unique genetic trajectory will not be eliminated; rather, they will provide the content and "flavor" of the mystic's ongoing participation in intersubjective life at all levels.

Using the self psychological perspective, our interest is in studying how the self represents itself in its constitutive relations with selfobjects. The narrative of the *Interior Castle*, in fact, presents a linked series of such representations. My hypothesis is that these represent--from the point of view of Teresa's psyche at the time she produced the text--the psychological transformations through which she passed in the course of her spiritual journey.[34] In the following chapters this imagery will be examined from two different perspectives.

First, in Chapter 10 the imagery by which Teresa depicts the stages of transformation will be studied. We might say that this imagery presents a "synchronic view of a diachronic process": all the imagery emerges from Teresa's psyche at one point in her life, but it purports to depict all the stages and transformations that have led up to that point.

---

[34]As the introductory pages of Chapter 10 will spell out, the claim here is that this is a "psychically accurate" account; its "historical accuracy" is a distinct issue, which it is not possible to resolve without admitting extra-textual data and additional explanatory frameworks. An approach to these latter questions will be presented in Chapter 11.

Following this, in Chapter 11 the central representation of the *Interior Castle*, the castle/dwelling place, will be studied in its development through the course of Teresa's major writings. This second analysis, then, could be called a "diachronic view of a synchronic representation": the castle/dwelling place as it appears in the *Interior Castle* can be seen as a synchronic conjunction of all the elements that gradually accrued to it in a process of psychic transmutation over time.

CHAPTER 10

A SELF-PSYCHOLOGICAL ANALYSIS OF TERESA'S MYSTICAL TRANSFORMATION

A. A Psychoanalytic Approach to the Text

In the *Interior Castle* Teresa does not simply express the state of her self at the time of writing, but gives an account of a genetic series of previous states leading up to the present state. Yet she does not claim to be providing an historically accurate account of all the events that have made up her unique journey of psychological and spiritual transformation. Rather, she gives an interpretation of the entire journey from the perspective of the time of writing--that is, from her perspective as a 62-year-old woman who has been in the "spiritual marriage" for almost five years. Thus, when this account speaks of the earlier stages of the journey, we cannot presume that the imagery and relationships depicted are exactly as they would have been experienced and articulated by one passing through that stage. We must presume, instead, that as the self was transformed the memories of earlier experiences were reworked and rearticulated as well.

What the *Interior Castle* gives us, then, is a transformed self's account of its present condition, described in terms of a process of transformation toward that condition. While the images and relationships attributed to earlier stages can be presumed to be "truthful" in the sense that Teresa is sincerely striving to articulate her best insight into what happened, the meanings given to them and the way they are woven into the narrative as a whole are derived primarily from the condition of the self at the time of writing--that is, from the mystically transformed self.

In understanding this aspect of the *Interior Castle*, it may be helpful to compare it to a dream. In a dream, every image that is presented reverberates in several different dimensions. One of these dimensions is the "life review" or recapitulation of all the dreamer's previous life crises as they play into the present life crisis.[1] The focus of the dream is on resolving the immediate crisis, yet in order to do that the psyche must replay and reintegrate itself as a totality. For these purposes the presentation of the past in the dream need not be "historically accurate," but it will be "psychically accurate" in that all the aspects of past psychic experience that are relevant to the present crisis will be represented.

I find in the *Interior Castle* such a "life review" in the form of a linked series of representations that appear to express a series of transformations of the self-selfobject structure of Teresa's psyche. The first set of representations is centered around the great, glorious, all-powerful King, who is contrasted with the lowly, despicable worm who is the spiritual seeker. In the second set of representations the ugly worm builds a cocoon and comes forth as a beautiful, free butterfly. In the third set of representations the spiritual seeker has become the betrothed, romantically sought by and seeking the Spouse. In the fourth set of representations, the butterfly dies. The fifth set of representations, finally, involves the consummation of the spiritual marriage.

While each of these sets of representations dominates a particular phase of Teresa's account of her spiritual transformation, often there is an overlap or overflow from one phase to others. Thus, elements of some of these sets of representations can appear in a variety of places

---

[1]See Erik H. Erikson, "The Dream Specimen of Psychoanalysis," *Journal of the American Psychoanalytic Association* 2 (1954): 5-56, esp. pp. 35-37.

in the text and with a variety of connections to other images. As is always the case with psychic imagery, each individual image is "overdetermined" so that it is not possible to pin it down to a single location in the networks of meaning. The following exposition traces only one strand in Teresa's multilayered tapestry of meaning. This strand is, however, a most significant one.

This chapter divides the imagery of the text into three phases: a "phase of primary healing" during which a basic process of psychological integration takes place; a "transitional or 'working through'[2] phase" which is both a fulfillment of the phase of primary healing and an opening to an out-of-the-ordinary psychological development; and a "phase of reconfiguration" in which this extraordinary development is fulfilled.

B. The Phase of Primary Healing

The King and the Worm

I entitle the first set of representations "The King and the Worm," although it includes many images besides the specific ones of "King" and "worm."[3] Images of God as "Lord," "King," "His Majesty," "Emperor," and "Master" pervade the *Interior Castle* from beginning to end. On nearly every page one can find awe-filled statements about God's glory, grandeur, majesty, beauty, purity, perfection, beneficence, etc. The rubric of "King" is apt for summarizing this theme, since the

---

[2]"Working through" is a technical term in psychoanalysis. After a significant breakthrough, there is usually a lengthy period--often characterized by considerable resistance--during which the fruits of this breakthrough are slowly integrated into various sectors of the individual's functioning.

[3]As discussed in Chapter 8 under "Images, Representations, and Structures," a "representation" is a more comprehensive and enduring schema than an "image." Hence, more than one image can be summarized in a representation.

allegory that structures the narrative is that of a King who resides in the center of the soul, which is his castle or palace.

The self who is in relationship to this King is, first of all, the dwelling place of God. As such, the soul must be envisioned as "fit for a King"; for "What do you think that abode will be like where a King so powerful, so wise, so pure, so full of all good things takes His delight?" (I:1,1) The soul, created in God's image and likeness, is beautiful and of "marvelous capacity."

While Teresa often repeats this theme of the preciousness and grandeur of the soul,[4] it is strongly tempered by an emphasis on the soul's lowliness. This emphasis is especially prominent in the early dwelling places. The most extreme expression of this is in I:1,3, when the soul is imaged as a "foul-smelling worm" with whom the divine Lord can commune only because of God's immense goodness and mercy. The early dwelling places also contain repeated references to the "vermin" and "lizards" that pervade the soul, leading it astray and making it a disgusting companion.[5]

An even more pervasive way in which Teresa stresses the soul's lowliness is to speak of its total dependence on God for every good. Since God is the soul's own "center," its' "sun," and the "fount" of its life, being cut off from God means total disorganization, terrifying darkness, and utter fruitlessness (I:2,1-5). Teresa's habitual emphasis on humility also plays into this theme. For her the awareness of one's smallness, sinfulness and dependence in relation to God is of the essence. In VI:10,7, for example, she says that "God is supreme Truth; and to be humble is to walk in truth, for it is a very deep truth that of ourselves we have nothing good but only misery and nothingness." She

---

[4]See, for example, I:1,8; VII:1,1; Epilogue 3; etc.

[5]See, for example, I:1,6 and 8; I:2,12-18; II:1,1-8; III:1,8, where these disgusting and malevolent creatures pose a real threat to the soul's safety and salvation. References to "reptiles" or "poisonous creatures" in later dwelling places always emphasize that they are very rarely present or are under control; see IV:1,9; V:1,5; VII:2,11.

begins and ends her book by insisting that she will be able to say absolutely nothing of value unless God gives her the words; she compares herself to a parrot who speaks only what it has heard (Prologue 2). She even denigrates her own womanhood: "Let your grandeur appear in a creature so feminine and lowly, whatever the cost to her, so that the world may know that this grandeur is not hers and all may praise You" (VI:6,4).

The rubric of "worm," then, sums up all Teresa's expressions of lowliness, despicability, inadequacy, etc., in relation to God. In this first set of representations the relationship between God and self is characterized by benevolent omnipotence on the part of God and humble dependence on the part of the self. God is imaged as the perfect, omnipotent, wise, benevolent environment within which the self can function and find happiness; without God, the self is disorganized, miserable, barren, and ultimately annihilated. In the first three dwelling places especially, the image of the "King" as omnipotent, benevolent, but rather threatening dominates. The self, like a foolish and immature servant, has to be reminded frequently to enter the castle, to remain at her duties there, to avoid activities that would offend the King. Extreme dangers--paralysis, chaos, darkness--will assail the one who ignores these warnings.

It is important to emphasize that this approach is not claiming that the "humility" which Teresa advocates can be simplistically equated with self-hatred or "poor self image." In this type of analysis we must carefully distinguish between the (usually conflictual) "psychic subsoil" from which an image or theme emerges, and the "spiritual resolution" within which it may be transformed and integrated into a new level of functioning. In fact, we could argue that transition from conflict and fragmentation in a particular area of psychic life, to its resolution and integration at a higher level, is of the essence of mystical transformation (in both the broad and narrow senses). Discovery of a degree of conflict or pathology in a mystic's "psychic subsoil," then, need not be regarded as an indication that he or she is not a spiritually transformed person.

Indeed, some such deeply-felt lack of personal integration may be a necessary dimension of the mystic's motivation to undergo the rigors of a search for the ultimate spiritual level of integration.[6]

Basic Structure of Teresa's Self: A Preliminary Interpretation

1. The Idealizing Selfobject Transference

Using self-psychological concepts, the psychological structure depicted as characteristic of these earlier dwelling places can be interpreted as an idealizing selfobject transference that includes many archaic features.[7] An individual employing this structure at an archaic level typically has a deep sense of the self's fragility and a panicky fear of its imminent fragmentation; this is countered by linking the self at the deepest level with a benevolent, protective selfobject who embraces the self and holds it together.

In her presentation of the first three Dwelling Places, Teresa indicates how the individual employing this structure can make gradual improvements in ability to live everyday life in an orderly and responsible manner. In the First Dwelling Places, the soul lives on the brink of chaos, with "disturbed senses" and "bad management" of the faculties (I:2,4). In the Second Dwelling Places, the battle between the forces of chaos and those of godly order is in full swing. "What an uproar the devils instigate here!" remarks Teresa, explicitly comparing the "devils" to temptations to live according to materialistic and

---

[6]In "Psychoanalysis and the Interpretation of Literature: A Correspondence with Erich Heller," *Critical Inquiry* 4 (1978), p. 449, Kohut wrote that it is "the very incompleteness of man's self, O'Neill's 'Man is born broken'" which continually spurs the search for wholeness.

[7]For definition and discussion of the "idealizing selfobject transference," see Chapter 8 under "The Nuclear Self and the Selfobject Transferences." In psychoanalytical usage, "archaic" means infantile, regressive, unintegrated, etc. See the section entitled "The Transformation of the Self" in Chapter 8 for discussion.

ephemeral values instead of spiritual, lasting ones (II:1,3-5). While persons in the Second Dwelling Places often give in to these disintegrating forces, they also often turn away from them (II:1,2).

It is only in the Third Dwelling Places that individuals have "won these battles" (III:1,1). They have now achieved a way of life that is "upright and well-ordered . .. both in body and soul" (III:2,1). Teresa describes these persons thus:

> They long not to offend His Majesty, even guarding themselves against venial sins; they are fond of doing penance and setting aside periods of recollection; they spend their time well, practicing works of charity toward their neighbors; and are very balanced in their use of speech and dress and in the governing of their households . . . . (III:1,5)

This process of gradually increasing calmness and self-control can be compared to what occurs in a therapeutic relationship. According to the self-psychological view, improvements come about first of all because a selfobject (the therapist, or, in this case, God) temporarily takes over certain functions for the "patient," freeing him or her from the feelings of alienation and panic that flow from the gut-level fear that at any moment the self may fall apart or be annihilated. It is the attempt to counter this panic that leads to such immature "acting out" behavior as overindulgence in sensual gratification, imperious tantrums, frantic demands for power, etc. The presence of the selfobject enables the self to feel that it is safe and whole, so that it can begin to calm down and make more reasoned choices about its behavior.[8]

The strongest evidence for this interpretation of the first three Dwelling Places of the *Interior Castle* is the stress Teresa places on the presence and help of God as the *sine qua non* of any spiritual growth. This emphasis is especially pronounced in her discussion of the First

---

[8]For more detailed discussion of the self-psychological perspective on these topics, see Chapter 8.

Dwelling Places;[9] she thus places it as the foundation and context of all that follows. The intensive human effort to develop self-control, virtuous habits, and an orderly life, which is a large part of her counsel for those in the Second and Third Dwelling Places, is based in the presupposition that one has already discovered the center of all order and value in the love of the living God.[10] It is this discovery that is the essential moment in one's liberation from the chaos of disordered desire.

The hypothesis being developed here is that, at a psychological level, the "God" figure as depicted in these early Dwelling Places is functioning as an idealized selfobject for a somewhat archaically structured self.[11] It is important to recall that, in self-psychological theory, selfobjects are technically not "environmental entities" but rather are a way the self structures its experience in order to maintain its (the self's) sense of integrity, continuity, aliveness, etc.[12] Thus, to say that the God figure here is functioning as an idealized selfobject is not to say that this is an adequate account of the theological or spiritual reality of God's activity. Rather, it is to say that this is the "place" that a particular individual has been able to give God in her "representational world."[13]

---

[9]See, for example, I:1,5-9; I:2,1-8. The discussion in Chapter 7 of this Dwelling Place is also relevant. The same idea, though with less stress, occurs in the Second Dwelling Places; see II:1,2 and 6-11.

[10]See, for example I:2,1-2, where Teresa remarks that "works [that] do not proceed from that principle, which is God, who is the cause of our virtue being really virtue, and are separated from Him . . . cannot be pleasing in His sight. . . . Just as all the streams that flow from a crystal-clear fount are also clear, the works of a soul in grace, because they proceed from this fount of life, in which the soul is planted like a tree, are most pleasing in the eyes of both God and man. There would be no freshness, no fruit, if it were not for this fount sustaining the tree . .

[11]For a discussion of Kohut's understanding of similar phenomena, see "Religious Experience: God as Selfobject" in Chapter 9.

[12]See "The Concept of the Selfobject" in Chapter 8.

[13]On the "representational world," see "Images, Representations, and Structures" in Chapter 8.

This self-psychological account offers a way of understanding the healing and transforming effect of God's presence from a strictly psychological viewpoint. If, within the individual's psychological structure, God is functioning as a selfobject, God can be contributing to the increase of internalized self-structure (secure sense of oneself as vital, capable of initiative, coherent, continuous, etc.) on a psychological level. The question of the theological reality of God's activity as originating from beyond the psychological level is distinct; while within the larger focus of an inquiry such as this one it must be addressed, it need not (in fact, cannot) be dealt with on the level of the psychological analysis itself.

If the present, strictly psychological analysis were separated from the context of the total inquiry, a reader would be justified in calling it "reductionistic"--since here spiritual and mystical transformation is, indeed, being analyzed strictly in terms of the human psyche. In the context of the whole inquiry, however, this is not reductionism; it is, rather, respect for the proper autonomy of the psychological mediation and of the science of psychology.

2. The Traumatized Grandiose Self

As presented above, Teresa clearly depicts those in the Third Dwelling Places as having made much progress in comparison to their former state. Yet she also makes it very clear that their spiritual journey is far from over. She writes:

> After these years, when it seems they have become lords of the world, at least clearly disillusioned in its regard, His Majesty will try them in some minor matters, and they go about so disturbed and afflicted that it puzzles me and even makes me fearful. It's useless to give them advice, for since they have engaged so long in the practice of virtue they think they can teach others and that they are more than justified in feeling disturbed. (III:2,1)

The delicate sarcasm illustrated by this text plays throughout Teresa's presentation of the Third Dwelling Places. Persons in this stage imagine themselves "lords of the world" and masters of spirituality, but under the duress of criticism or temptation they often behave little better than spoiled children.

Teresa's mocks the illusory pride of these persons in order to encourage them to abandon themselves and press onward to the Dwelling Places where God's active presence can pervade the soul more profoundly (III:2,9). From a psychological perspective, however, her cutting comments provide a clue to another dimension of her own psychological structure. It seems that for her, what begins to emerge as the process of psychological healing progresses is what Kohut would call "archaic grandiosity." The person is depicted as feeling that she "has it all together" and can conquer the world--when in fact she remains immature and lacking in true self-control.

For Kohut, it will be recalled, the grandiose self--the aspect of the self that longs to be admired and "mirrored" perfectly--is a component of normal and healthy narcissism.[14] Just as with the idealizing self and its longing to be perfectly protected and embraced, the real issue with grandiosity is the degree to which it remains archaic and unintegrated. Mature and integrated grandiosity can fuel great achievements while being kept in check by gentle humor and wisdom. The smugness, brittleness, and barely disguised fantasies of perfection which Teresa attributes to those in the Third Dwelling Places, on the other hand, are signs of grandiosity that still has an archaic quality.

At this point we can pull together various clues provided by our study of the first three Dwelling Places and make a very brief preliminary statement about the probable structure of Teresa's self. While her conscious experience seems to be structured by an idealizing selfobject transference, there are also clear undertones of trauma in the area of the grandiose self. This is indicated by the repeated hints of

---

[14]See "The Concept of the Selfobject" and "The Nuclear Self and the Selfobject Transferences" in Chapter 8.

shame-propensity (i.e., self-belittling remarks) as well as by the great concern with humility, a seeming "reaction formation" against the desire for admiration.[15]

Teresa's primary healing process, then, employs the strength of the idealizing selfobject transference to work toward an integrated and cohesive self. The first sign of the success of this process is the emergence into consciousness of grandiosity, which had previously been split off and disavowed.[16] The next psychological challenge will be the full maturation and integration of this disavowed sector of the self. In Teresa's case, this occurs in the context of the beginnings of mystical transformation (in the "narrow sense").[17]

The Silkworm Transformed into a Butterfly

In the Third Dwelling Places, then, basic orderliness of life is achieved; in the Fourth Dwelling Places, Teresa says that "supernatural" or mystical experiences first appear. These Dwelling Places are basically transitional to the decisive change in the Fifth, when the soul first begins to experience transitory "unions" with God. It is when Teresa begins to discuss this period of decisive change that a new set of representations comes to the fore.

In V:2,2-8 Teresa describes the transformation of the soul from a fat, ugly silkworm into a beautiful butterfly. It is noteworthy, first of all, that the "foul-smelling worm" which was associated with filth and corruption has been replaced by the silkworm which, though fat and ugly, is the potential producer of something of great value. This in itself is a significant transformation of images, indicating that

---

[15]For textual citations and discussion, see "The King and the Worm" above.

[16]On "disavowal," see "The Transformation of the Self" in Chapter 8.

[17]On the distinction between the "broad" and "narrow" senses of mystical transformation, see "The Range of 'Mystics'" in Chapter 5.

transmuting internalization[18] has already progressed to the point where the psyche has united significant elements of the King's greatness and valuableness to the lowliness of the worm.

Yet Teresa goes much further. The silkworm will build itself a cocoon, "die," and be "raised up" as "a little white butterfly, which is very pretty" (V:2,2). This description is not in accord with the facts; what actually emerges from a silkworm's cocoon is a rather drab moth, not a beautiful butterfly. Yet for her psychological purposes, as well as her pedagogical ones, it was as important that the flying creature be a butterfly as that the worm be a silkworm; for at this point she wants to indicate the high value of both. Just as the silkworm is far more than a mere crawling thing, what emerges from the cocoon is far more than a mere moth.

At this point we must clarify again that our psychological interpretation is limited in that much of what Teresa intends by this set of images is beyond the purview of psychology. For her, this "death and resurrection" by which the worm is transformed into a butterfly is truly an action of God. She writes that when the worm begins to spin its silk cocoon, it is actually building "Christ," and that when it has done all it can in this work, "God will unite Himself, with His greatness, and give it such high value that the Lord Himself will become the reward of this work" (V:2,4-5).

For Teresa, then, the butterfly represents not only a transformation of the "natural" creature, but its union with that which is truly "supernatural." In the terminology developed in Chapters 4 and 5,[19] it is a transformation from "above downward" in that a higher and more comprehensive level of organization is mediated within the psychic level. Our analysis in this chapter, however, confines itself to what can be seen at the psychic level itself. We study the transformation at the

---

[18]On "transmuting internalization," see "The Transformation of the Self" in Chapter 8.

[19]See "'Below Upward' and 'Above Downward' Operations" in Chapter 4; also "The Specificity of Mystical Experience" in Chapter 5.

"natural" level for evidence of whether there is a positive direction of change and, if so, what known psychological dynamics may be at work in it.

In her own terms, then, Teresa is speaking here of the inbreaking of the mystical dimension. Viewed strictly from a psychological perspective, however, she is providing an image of the process by which the defective self is repaired and achieves a new level of integrated structure. The fact that henceforward Teresa emphasizes that the soul "now has wings . . . it can fly"[20] is particularly significant, given what we have previously hypothesized about the trauma that Teresa may have sustained in the area of the grandiose self.[21]

According to Kohut, the fantasy of being able to fly is "one of the most common ideational elaborations of the grandiose self."[22] Flying fantasies are escapist or dangerous when they remain archaic and split off from the integrated structure of the self. When they are integrated into the whole self, however, they can fuel great achievements. In a general comment on fantasy that arises from the grandiose component of the elf, Kohut observed that "Whether it contributes to health or disease, to the success of the individual or to his downfall, depends on the degree of its deinstinctualization and the extent of its integration into the realistic purposes of the ego."[23] Among the typical derivatives of the flying fantasy, he noted, are "ambitious strivings and the cognate

---

[20]This quotation, V:2,8. Throughout the remaining Dwelling Places the images of "butterfly" and "dove" recur frequently; see, for example, VI:2,1; VI:4,1; VI:6,1 and 4; VI:11,1; VII:2,5; VII:3,1 and 12-13. Teresa seems to make little distinction between these two; in V:4,1-2, for example, she uses "dove" to refer to the soul in one paragraph and "butterfly" for the same purpose in the next. For her what is most significant about these images seems to be their representation of the ability to fly.

[21]See above, "The Traumatized Grandiose Self."

[22]Kohut, "On Courage," p. 12. See also idem, *Restoration of the Self*, p. 112 n. 6.

[23]Kohut, "Forms and Transformations," p. 107.

self-expanding urge toward new discoveries . . . to move into new territories."[24]

The butterfly, with its beauty and its capacity for flight, is an image of the self as beautiful, capable and free. The transformation of images that we see here is an excellent example of what Kohut called "transmuting internalization."[25] In transmuting internalization, the functions which the selfobject has performed for the self are gradually incorporated into the self, with a corresponding shift in the self-image. When this process is progressing well the self does not take over the selfobject's qualities wholesale, but "transmutes" them in accord with its own structure and needs. Figure 1 schematizes the pattern of transmuting internalization in Teresa's case:

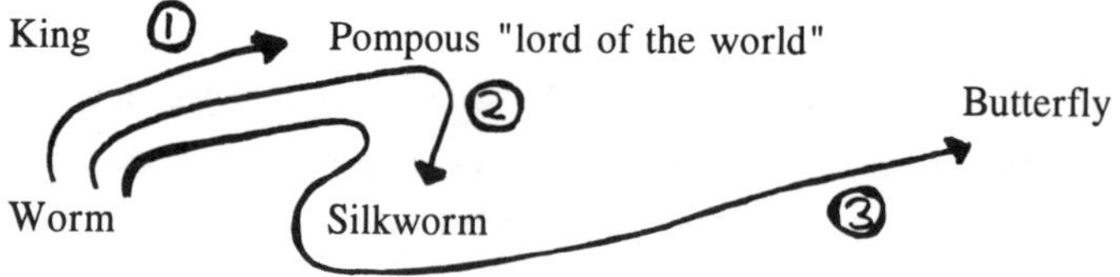

FIGURE 1

In a first move, the self (with a self-image of "worm") identifies with the selfobject (the "King") and, in a quite stilted and inadequate form, tries to take on the King's functions by becoming a pompous little "lord." In a second move, the self incorporates into its own structure some of the goodness and value of the King; now it images itself as "silkworm." In a third move, the self goes beyond identification and incorporation to a genuine transmuting internalization. The structure of the self undergoes a major process of repair and reorganization which

[24]Kohut, "Creativeness, Charisma, Group Psychology," p. 177.

[25]See "The Transformation of the Self" in Chapter 8.

is directed by the self's own preexisting structure (the "butterfly" is clearly a transformation of the worm, not of the King), yet involves a radical internalization of many of the King's qualities--freedom, goodness, power, joy, etc.

In the psyche, of course, this process does not occur in a lockstep or schematized fashion as a diagram such as this might suggest. Yet our analysis of the text of the *Interior Castle*--a text which, we must recall, is itself a schematization of Teresa's experience--finds strong evidence that this series of steps does take place.

It is noteworthy that Teresa herself described the transformative process in terms very reminiscent of "transmuting internalization," though she obviously did not have (nor was she interested in having) such technical vocabulary to work with. In her typical metaphorical language, she spoke of the "impression" of God's image and likeness on the soul, like a seal upon wax (V:2,12). Though her main point in this passage is to emphasize God's activity and the necessity of the soul's offering not resistance, at the psychological level the image aptly conveys the "taking in" of the God-image by the self.

The image of the wax and the seal might suggest that such a process of transformation is quite straightforward. The image of the transformation of the butterfly, however, includes representation of the fact that such a passage--whether in therapy, in ordinary life, or in spiritual discipline--involves repeated experiences of depression, depletion, and "death." The worm, says Teresa, must weave its cocoon and abandon itself to death before transformation can take place (V:2,5-6). This is a strong image of the experience of emptiness and loss that normally punctuates transformative processes.

Such experiences of depression and emptiness are part of the rhythm of every person's development, but they are intensified in the lives of those with greater or lesser degrees of pathology of the self. Indeed, Teresa's personality may well have shared some characteristics with those of certain persons with the type of pathology known as a "narcissistic personality disorder." Kohut describes how some such persons have a deep underlying level of chronic depression that has been walled off and covered over with a somewhat superficial "hypervitality." These persons are often "overly enthusiastic, dramatic, and excessively intense in their response to everyday events," and they tend to romanticize and eroticize their relationships in compensation for "a deep sense of uncared-for-worthlessness and rejection."[26] Such a disorder cannot be healed without the deeply painful experience of getting in touch with the emptiness and depression. On the psychological level, entering the cocoon to die is an image of this.

Writing from a more traditional psychological perspective, Afra Sinnige-Breed asserts that the young Teresa was characterized by a combination of intense vivaciousness and *desarraigo vital*--a term that means something like "fundamental uprootedness."[27] This psychological condition involves a deep distrust or even contempt for one's physical constitution. In compensation for this out-of-touchness with inner sources of vitality, says Sinnige-Breed, Teresa developed a great facility in attending to other people and responding to them as they would wish.[28]

This configuration of traits is close to what has traditionally been called the "hysterical character," which Freud's colleague Josef Breuer and various other commentators have attributed to Teresa.[29] Sinnige-Breed concludes, however, that Teresa should not be labeled an hysteric

---

[26]Kohut, *Restoration of the Self*, p. 5.

[27]Afra Sinnige-Breed, "Evolución Normal y Unitaria del 'Yo' Teresiano a la Luz de su Vida interior," *Revista de Espiritualidad* 22 (1963): 238-50.

[28]See the subsection entitled "Teresa's Milieu" in Chapter 6 for comments on Teresa's preoccupation with "honor."

[29]For a good description of these character traits, see Howard M. Wolowitz, "Hysterical Character and Feminine Identity," in Judith M. Bardwick, ed., *Readings on the Psychology of Women* (New York: Harper & Row, 1972), 307-14. For Breuer's comment, see Josef Breuer and Sigmund Freud, *Studies on Hysteria*, *Standard Edition* 2:232. Another classic study of Teresa's "hysteria" is G. Hahn, "Les Phénomènes Hystériques et les Révélations de Sainte Thérèse," *Revue des Questions Scientifiques* 12, 13, 14 (1883-84).

because her writings indicate that, coincident with the beginning of her "supernatural" experiences (Fourth Dwelling Places), she overcame her *desarraigo vital* and her narcissistic overconcern with other's opinions. She became integrated in body and psyche, and hence able to be open to the mystical dimension without pathology.

The self-psychological perspective suggests that the walled-off or disavowed[30] component of Teresa's psyche included much of what Kohut calls the "grandiose self." Hence, she experienced the unification of her psyche in terms of the liberation of this grandiosity--the image of the beautiful, free butterfly. If, indeed, this was a true unification of the psyche, this liberated grandiosity no longer operated in an archaic, narcissistic mode, as it had when it dominated the psyche unconsciously and made Teresa superresponsive to concerns of "honor" and to others' needs and opinions. In the unified psyche, "grandiosity" operates as the verve, ambition and creativity necessary to accomplish extraordinary works of innovation--such as those Teresa was called upon to do in her mature years.

Both Sinnige-Breed's analysis and my own self-psychological one suggest that Teresa's transition to "union" (Fifth Dwelling Places) involved a deep psychological unification. The self-psychological analysis also gives an account of the mechanism (transmuting internalization), experiences (getting in touch with walled-off depression), and dynamics (integration of disavowed sector of the self) involved in this passage.

---

[30]On disavowal, see "The Transformation of the Self" in Chapter 8; also above, "The Traumatized Grandiose Self."

C. Transitional or "Working Through"[31] Phase: The Spouse and the Betrothed

Another set of representations makes its appearance in the latter chapters of the Fifth Dwelling Places, which were written after Teresa had set the work aside for a few months. These are the images related to romantic love, courtship, and marriage. Many of the spiritual experiences contextualized within this set of representations are beyond the range of common psychological experience; they include unions, raptures, ecstasies, flights of the spirit, etc. Hence interpretation of the psychological implications of the images only touches upon one, relatively limited dimension of their meaning. Nevertheless, in the context of this study of maturing narcissism and intersubjectivity in relation to mystical transformation, this dimension is a crucial one.

In these texts God is still a "King," but now he is also "the Spouse."[32] The essential relational quality conveyed by the "espousal" images is that of an intensifying personal intimacy leading to a total and complete union. The "prayer of union" of the Fifth Dwelling Places is now seen as only a preliminary, like the pre-betrothal meetings of two who are eventually to be espoused. Yet even the very first such meeting, says Teresa, leaves the soul "more worthy for the joining of hands"--that is, it brings the soul closer to a relationship of mutuality with God (V:4,4).

In the "betrothal" experiences that begin in the Sixth Dwelling Places, Teresa writes, the soul experiences increasingly intense desire for God. Often this desire inflames the innermost depths of the soul with an extraordinarily intense pain that is nevertheless "delightful." She twice uses the image of an arrow piercing the soul to describe this experience (VI:2,4 and 11,2). Though the soul has not yet been brought

---

[31]On "working through," see above, footnote 2.

[32]For instances of the actual use of the title "Spouse" for God, see V:3:12; VI:1,1; VI:4,9; VI:5,11; VI:11,1. For examples of the emphasis on the regal nature of the One whom the soul is called to marry, see, in addition, VI:4,1 and VII:2:1-3.

into the Spouse's dwelling place, already "God carries off for Himself the entire soul, and, as to someone who is His own and His spouse, He begins showing it some little part of the kingdom that it has gained by being espoused to Him" (VI:4,9).

In this new set of representations we see another "transmuting internalization" of the idealized selfobject. Figure 2 attempts to schematize this shift:

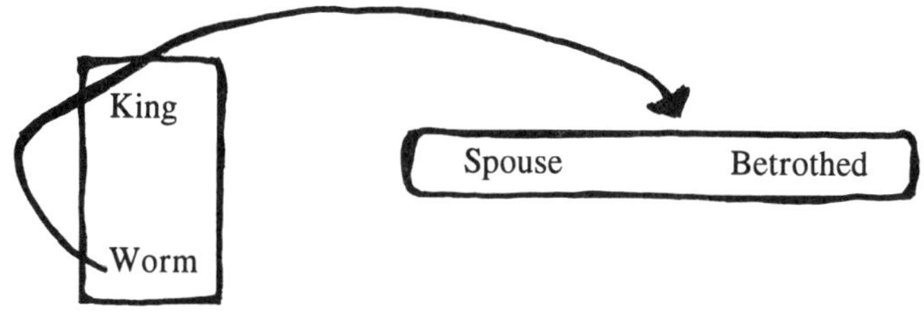

FIGURE 2

The essential move here is from a strongly vertical relationship, in which all liveliness, strength, love, goodness, etc. flow from the powerful King to the helpless worm, to an essentially horizontal relationship. The self, in imaging itself as "the Betrothed," has taken into itself the qualities of the Spouse-King. This goes even beyond the image of self as "butterfly," for that image did not internalize the relational qualities of the selfobject--its affection, its protective presence, its tender longing, etc.

The transmutation and internalization of these qualities. which are in fact among the most outstanding dimensions of the God-figure that Teresa depicts from the very beginning, herald the completion of the psychological process begun when the idealizing selfobject transference came into play. Now the self, too, is capable of genuine love. Henceforward, the relationship with the selfobject has characteristics not only of the idealizing and mirroring transferences, but also of the alterego transference--the sense of companionship with one "like oneself."

This transformation, however, is by no means as simple and straightforward as the above diagram and brief discussion might suggest. As the imagery itself indicates, this passage involves the transformation of sexuality--with all the freight of ambivalence and conflict that this dimension of human life normally carries.

Teresa's care to avoid "coarseness" and to emphasize the vast difference between everything involved in carnal romance and marriage and the process leading to "spiritual marriage" (V:4,3; VII:2,2-3) reminds us not to overinterpret the sexual connotations of her imagery. Yet respect for the mystical dimension does not require us to abdicate analysis of the psychological dimension in which the mystical is mediated. Psychoanalysis as Antonio Vázquez Fernández notes, rejects the notion that experiences and their corresponding imagery can be divided dualistically into "true" and "false," "objective" and "illusory," or "pure" and "impure." Rather, all experiences draw upon the same stock of overdetermined, "illusory" fantasy images--many of which are redolent with sexual connotations.[33]

When it comes to the religious use of sexual imagery, says Vázquez, a healthy set of representations is on that effectively sublimates human sexuality into a true openness toward and affection for other persons, while a pathological set of representations is one that merely displaces regressive or defensive libido from a primitive object onto a religious image. Also, the healthy religious/sexual representations show signs of the ongoing process of "working through"--the constant struggle to overcome the distorting effect of unconscious defense and resistance in favor of increasing capacity to love, to feel joy and meaningful suffering, and to utilize language appropriately.[34] A true religious

---

[33]Antonio Vázquez Fernández, "Notas para una Lectura de las 'Moradas' de Santa Teresa desde la Psicología Profunda," *Revista de Espiritualidad* 41 (1982): 482-5.

[34]Ibid., p. 485; see also p. 511.

transformation is indicated when human desire is progressively converted into a "religious love every more pure, yet without losing its sustaining roots in the imagistic level."[35]

Vázquez Fernández summarizes his own view of this dimension of Teresa's self-expression in the *Interior Castle*:

> In this perspective, the mystical process as it appears in the *Interior Castle* is the dramatic and living story of a long, winding, but ascending path by which Teresa of Jesus elaborated, with much joy and much sorrow, her human love and desire, transforming them into Christian love and desire . . . the amorous desire of Teresa of Avila is here with all the freight of her biographical and situational history, which from the beginning was an unrequited search for the longed-for, fascinating, "lost" primitive object. This history makes for a complicated contextual network where meanings are defensively displaced and substituted, but where there is also access to sublimated symbolism which detaches her desire from the primitive nutritive and sexual functions and renders it apt for enjoyment of and union with the other at more elevated and spiritual levels.[36]

It is not disrespectful, then, to examine Teresa's sexual imagery in terms of its roots in her own biography and, especially, as it indicates the "working through" of the essential human issues surrounding sexuality and intimacy.

The self psychological approach looks at successful working through less in terms of sublimation and more in terms of what Kohut calls the "firming of the self."[37] The foundational work of the repair of a defective self, which must precede this work of "firming," has already been discussed. At this stage the work is concerned with putting in place and elaborating a flexible yet stable set of representations that enable joyful, uninhibited, fruitful interaction with other persons and with the world.

---

[35]Vázquez Fernández, "Notas," p. 508; my translation.

[36]Ibid., p. 507; my translation.

[37]On "firming," see "The Transformation of the Self" in Chapter 8.

In Chapter 8 it was noted that in his clinical work Kohut had found that after narcissistic or "self" deficits had been healed at a basic level, patients very often experienced an "Oedipal phase" in which issues of sexual excitement and attraction, seductiveness, rivalry, etc. came to the fore.[38] In such cases the newly arising Oedipal transference does not seem to be a revival of childhood experiences, but rather a new and healthier way of interacting that the person did not have the capacity to experience before. Teresa's turn to imagery of romance and sexuality after the "union" of the Fifth Dwelling Places has created a basic wholeness in her self can be interpreted in similar terms.

The intimate, amorous dialogue that Teresa depicts between the soul and its Lord partakes of some of the Oedipal dynamics as Kohut describes them. The Lord, who began as a benevolent but somewhat distant "King" very reminiscent of an authoritarian father-figure, is transformed into the romantic Spouse who inflames the soul's desires, gives her gifts, pierces her heart, shares everything with her, and eventually will consummate marriage with her. The soul, meanwhile, does everything in its power to makes itself open, attractive, and willing. Yet all this takes place--as it would, according to Kohut, in a healthy childhood Oedipal phase, without inappropriate interest in obtaining sexual pleasure. The Lord, like a good parent, enters into the amorous play with the greatest delicacy and joy, focused mainly on affirming and building up the fragile self of the beloved.

This interpretation receives support from an article by Constance FitzGerald analyzing the series of visions that Teresa experienced over the years following her midlife conversion. The analysis shows how Teresa experienced her relationship with the Lord as a very concrete and intimate dialogue in which the Lord gradually led her "from confusion

[38]For discussion, see "The Transformation of the Self" in Chapter 8. Also Kohut, *Restoration of the Self*, pp. 220-48; idem, *How Does Analysis Cure?*, pp. 13-33.

of heart, inferiority and fear of abandonment" to "connectedness, mutuality and equality."[39]

Like the present inquiry, FitzGerald's study focuses on the transforming interplay between the image of Christ and Teresa's self-image. FitzGerald, however, studies the imagery--especially the visions--of all Teresa's writings, while this study focuses intensively only on the *Interior Castle*. FitzGerald shows the development and power of such images as the "hand of God" held out in support and finally given in marriage, the "beautiful face' of Jesus shining upon the soul like a mother's affirming gaze, and the"flaming arrow" that pierces the inmost heart and bring deep awareness of intersubjective union with the divine. She concludes,

> the emotional identification with . . . God that we see here is possible only because of the unity and wholeness of the self that have slowly developed in the life long relationship with Jesus Christ. Because her self-image had been purified, to some extent, of its sinful tendencies toward inferiority and excessive self-depreciation, Teresa could surrender to being loved and claimed by God.[40]

In the romantic and marital imagery of the last three Dwelling Places of the *Interior Castle*, then, we see represented the working through of the deepest human needs for relationality, intimacy, and self-giving. As FitzGerald puts it, "God does not violate our deepest needs, but fulfills slowly in our life situations our most profound desires for reassurance, unconditional love, tenderness and special regard."[41]

In the phase of primary healing, the soul had to be weaned away from its disordered desires and painstakingly trained to make choices on

---

[39]Constance FitzGerald, "A Discipleship of Equals: Voices from Tradition--Teresa of Avila and John of the Cross," in Francis A. Eigo, *A Discipleship of Equals: Towards a Christian Feminist Spirituality, Proceedings of the Villanova Theology Institute* 20 (1987), pp. 64-5.

[40]Ibid., p. 79.

[41]Ibid., p. 77.

the basis of higher values. This was not accomplished primarily by admonishing "detachment," but rather by fulfilling the self's deepest desire--that is, its longing to be held in safety and wholeness. What we see in this phase which we have termed "transitional" is the re-enlivening of the full spectrum of desire. This time, however, desire is spontaneously ordered toward the highest good, namely, relationship with the divine.

This phase is transitional because it is both the fulfillment of one process and the opening of another. The process which appears to be fulfilled here is the establishment of a healthy and cohesive self and the working through of the consequences of this basic transformation in the various sectors of the psyche. The process which is beginning is an experience of deep and living intimacy with the divine--that is, "mystical experience in the narrow sense."[42]

D. The Phase of Reconfiguration

In analyzing the imagery of this final phase, it becomes more difficult to confine ourselves to the strictly psychological perspective. In her discussion of such phenomena as "raptures," "visions," "mystical death," and "spiritual marriage," it is evident that Teresa is speaking of experiences that go beyond those normally encountered by psychological investigators. A strictly psychological analysis cannot do full justice to these experiences. It can, nevertheless, offer important insights.

The Death of the Butterfly

As the consummation of the spiritual journey nears, Teresa introduces yet another transformation of the worm-silkworm-butterfly imagery. She

[42]For the definition of this term, see "The Range of 'Mystics'" in Chapter 5.

says that "the little butterfly we mentioned dies, and with the greatest joy because its life is now Christ" (VII:2,5; cf. also VII:3,1).

The butterfly dies because its desire for union with God has become all-consuming (VI:11,1). Far from satisfying this desire, the raptures, ecstasies, visions, and other favors of the Sixth Dwelling Places only feed it. As a person nears the Seventh Dwelling Places, one undergoes an agonizing period in which:

> the soul sees that it is like a person hanging, who cannot support himself on any earthly thing; nor can it ascend to heaven. On fire with this thirst, it cannot get to the water; and the thirst is not one that is endurable, but already at such a point that nothing will take it away. (VI:11,5)

In Teresa's poignant description, all selfobject sustenance has disappeared. Neither the all-powerful "King" nor the all-loving "Spouse" reaches out to save the hanging one, and "no creature in all the earth provides it company, nor do I believe would any heavenly creature, not being the One it loves" (VI:11,5). The soul experiences a "strange solitude," bereft of all that it has previously relied on for support and entirely unable to reach that for which it longs.

While in this state of agonizing, unendurable desire, the soul experiences a "blow." Of this Teresa writes, "in my opinion, it isn't felt where earthly sufferings are felt, but in the very deep and intimate part of the soul, where this sudden flash of lightning reduces to dust everything it finds in this earthly nature of ours; for while this experience lasts nothing can be remembered about our being" (VI:11,2). This blow strikes at such a profound level of one's being that it puts one in genuine danger of physical death (VI:11,4 and 9).

Our previous analysis has suggested that the butterfly is an image of the self as healed and liberated. Our hypothesis has been that in Teresa's case the healing which she required particularly involved the acceptance and integration of the grandiose component of the self, with its typical psychological representation in the flying fantasy; hence the image of the newly cohesive and vital self was that of the freely soaring creature, whether butterfly or dove.[43] Her description of the agony of the butterfly's death as an experience of "hanging" corresponds to what Kohut calls the "obverse rendition of flying fantasies"--i.e., the utter terror of "falling" endlessly as one is left with no internal or external means of support.[44]

It seems that what Teresa is representing with the death of the butterfly is a "death of self" at a very profound level. What is meant by "death of self" must be carefully defined, however. In view of what is known about Teresa's life, it is clear that she was not suffering from the major psychological dysfunction that would typically be implied by the statement that someone lacks or has lost a self. The "death of self" at the end of the sixth dwelling places is not the psychotic experience of an "empty core," for in the case of the psychotic no self has ever developed; nor is it the borderline experience of panicky disintegration, for in the borderline personality the self has always been rudimentary and extremely weak.

Rather, in the spiritual transformation of which Teresa speaks all the *functions* of the self--i.e., the senses of cohesiveness, continuity, aliveness, centeredness, initiative--have reached maturity and have been exercised for some time with considerable efficiency. While the crisis Teresa describes as occurring at this point appears to threaten these functions at their root, ultimately it does not destroy them. It does, however, radically transform the subject's experience of these functions.

What seems to be happening is that the most foundational level of the unconscious self-representation, in which the self had invested its feeling of cohesiveness, centeredness, and so on, is undergoing a radical relativization. The "flash of lightning" that "reduces to dust everything it finds in this earthly nature of ours" (VI:11,2) is an image of the blinding light that reveals all that had seemed utterly central as mere

---

[43]For discussion, see above, "The Silkworm Transformed Into a Butterfly."

[44]See Kohut, *Analysis of the Self*, p. 87.

"dust."[45] In fact, the image of being reduced to dust suggests that it would not be too much to say that the root self-representation is essentially annihilated.

Here Kohut's distinction between the "narrow sense of the self" (the conscious and unconscious self-representation) and the "broad sense of the self" (the more fundamental, non-objectifiable center of initiative, cohesion, continuity, etc.)[46] takes on new relevance. It seems that in mystical transformation the self-representation can be exploded without dysfunction because the functions of the "self in the broad sense" continue to be fully operative in daily life. The mystical "death of self," then, is not a pathological disintegration of self, but rather a "post-mature" experience that can only occur when a deeply rooted functional stability is already in place.[47]

In order to distinguish between this genuine, "post-mature" experience of mystical disintegration and phenomenologically similar forms of pathological disintegration, one must include more in one's analysis than the inner experience alone. It is in study of the entire life-context and functioning of the individual claiming such a "mystical transformation" that one can discern its true character.[48]

---

[45]See Bernadette Roberts, *What is Self? A Study of the Spiritual Journey in Terms of Consciousness* (Austin, TX: Mary Goens, 1989), for a detailed discussion of the experience of the "loss of self" as the culmination of the spiritual journey. Although Roberts' framework of terms and relations is somewhat different from that developed here, I believe a credible correlation is possible.

[46]For further discussion, see "Kohut's Notion of 'the Self'" in Chapter 8.

[47]This does not necessarily mean that in order to be a mystic (in the narrow sense) one must first have a perfectly firm, integrated, pathology-free self. It does mean, however, that the pathways between the deepest levels of the psyche (the self in the broad sense) and the functions of daily life must be open and well-traveled enough so that the functions can continue even when the self-representation, which previously mediated between these two levels, undergoes radical change or even disintegration.

[48]Chapter 11 below is a preliminary approach to such a more comprehensive analysis.

Thus far, Teresa has spoken of two "deaths": the first in the Fifth Dwelling Places when the silkworm became a butterfly, and the second here in the Sixth Dwelling Places as the butterfly dies. Correlating these with our model of mystical transformation, the first "death" corresponds to the experience of bare consciousness and its immediate aftereffects, while the second "death" corresponds to the full blooming of mystical consciousness--that is, the mediation of the transcendent ground of consciousness in human consciousness.[49] What we see here is that, at the psychological level, these two death-experiences have quite distinct ramifications.

When Teresa describes the death of the silkworm, she barely mentions the fact that the worm must suffer in the process. Her whole focus is on anticipating the joy of the emerging butterfly. Of the worm she says only, "Let it die; let this silkworm die, as it does in completing what it was created to do!" (V:2,6). In our own analysis, we have suggested that the "worm" does indeed suffer; the process of overcoming pathology of the self and gaining a fully cohesive, vital, firm self often involves passage through deep experiences of pain, depression, and loss.[50] Yet in Teresa's imagery, the silkworm's final passage through "death" is not painful; it is more like falling asleep--and then awakening miraculously transformed.

What this seems to suggest is that, on the psychological level, "bare consciousness" itself is not terribly frightening or threatening to normal psychic functioning. It is more like "falling asleep"--and awakening to find that more and more of one's psyche has been "waked up" by a mysterious inflow of vitality. The catch is that among the sectors "waked up" will be those which have previously been traumatized or split off. It is in dealing with these that one may experience many intensely painful emotions. Teresa, however, does not focus on this painful dimension because her interest is in the entirely

---

[49]For review, see "A Schematic Review of the Proposed Model" in Chapter 5.

[50]See above, "The Silkworm Transformed Into a Butterfly."

positive context within which it occurs; namely, the coming into its own of the "butterfly"--the healed and liberated human self.

Bare consciousness, then, seems to have its first effect on an essentially "natural" level, setting in motion a process of healing, integration, and rejuvenation. This is in accord with our earlier finding that bare consciousness is the "asymptotic approach of human consciousness to its own ground" which, as such, can be acknowledged as a natural good whether or not one additionally affirms that it is the "bridge" to a special mediation of the transcendent ground of consciousness.[51]

When Teresa begins to speak about the second "death"--the death of the butterfly--she spends considerably more time discussing the pain and terror which the butterfly must undergo in the process of dying. It seems that on the psychological level, this second passage is far more consequential than the first. While the first "death" was really a passage to full integration on the psyche's own terms, the second "death" is a reorganization in terms that are not the psyche's own. In our model of mystical transformation, we have spoken of this as the passage to the state of "mystical intersubjectivity" in which the transcendent ground of consciousness is mediated at the level of one's own self-presence.

Kohut himself would probably have been quite uncomfortable with the suggestion made here that there is a "post-mature" state in which the normal self-structure is in some sense radically relativized or even dismantled. Yet his notion of cosmic narcissism does give such a state a possible location in his schema.[52] Kohut originally defined cosmic narcissism, one of the five characteristics of mature narcissism, as "a shift of the narcissistic cathexes from the self to a concept of participation in a supraindividual and timeless existence."[53] Though

---

[51]See "Developing a Model of Mystical Transformation" in Chapter 5.

[52]For discussion, see "The Self in the Face of Finitude and Death" in Chapter 9.

[53]Kohut, "Forms and Transformations," p. 119.

this definition remains somewhat vague, it does suggest that the developmental trajectory culminates in a movement beyond what has up to that time been experienced as the "self."

Whatever one's judgement on the value of the notion of "cosmic narcissism," it is significant that for Teresa the death of the butterfly is not the last step in the process of mystical transformation. This image of abandonment and disintegration conveys how at a certain level, the self and its selfobjects are illusions that must eventually be recognized as such; and yet in Teresa's schema, a yet more profound level of relatedness emerges from this radical loss.

Consummation

In order for the soul to attain the state imaged as the consummation of spiritual marriage, then, it must pass through the death imaged in the previous set of representations. Spiritual marriage, a state in which the soul "is called to enter into its center" (VII:1,5), is a union of God and human which is "like what we have when rain falls from the sky into a river or fount; all is water, for the rain that fell from heaven cannot be divided or separated from the water of the river" (VII:2,4). The butterfly has died; the soul "no longer is" (VII:3,1-2). While the faculties continue their outward functions, the center of the soul has dissolved into the utter silence and immovability of God (VII:2,9; 3,11; etc).

Now, says Teresa, God told her that "it was time that she consider as her own what belonged to Him and that He would take care of what was hers" (VII:2,1). This is a final and complete entrance into the center of the soul; God and the soul are now literally inseparable. Thus the spiritual marriage involves being brought onto God's own level--though in a very qualified sense. In a sense, there is a radical fulfillment here of all the selfobject needs: the need for the idealized caretaker, the need for the admiring mirror, and the need for the alterego companion.

In her first version of the manuscript Teresa three times compared this state to the consummation of human marriage, but in two of these cases she later altered her words to avoid the impression of coarseness. The allusion to "consummation" remains in the final version of VII:1,3, where she wrote "He brings [the soul], before the spiritual marriage is consummated, into His dwelling place, which is this seventh."[54] In VII:2,2 she originally wrote, "Between the spiritual betrothal and the spiritual marriage the difference is as great as that which exists between two who are betrothed and two who have consummated marriage," but later changed the last phrase to "those who cannot be separated."[55] In VII:2,3 she made a similar change in the statement, "[God] has desired to be so joined with the creature that, as with those who have consummated marriage, He doesn't want to be separated from the soul"; the clause became, "just as those who are married cannot be separated."[56]

Teresa probably had at least two good reasons for her ambivalence toward the metaphor of marital consummation. One was that comparing spiritual fulfillment with physical, sexual union was probably quite dangerous within her social context.[57] A second, even more compelling reason was that she herself felt the inadequacy of the metaphor. This final state of which she speaks is a union far more total than that of human lovers. The closest she could come to imaging it was in terms of the Christian notion of consummated marriage as "two in one flesh"; and yet even that did not quite satisfy her.

---

[54] ". . . primero que se consuma el matrimonio espiritual métela en su morada, que es esta séptima."

[55] ". . . entender que hay grandísima diferencia . . . del desposorio espiritual al matrimonio espiritual, como le hay entre dos desposados a los que ya no se pueden apartar."

[56] ". . . de tal manera ha querido juntarse con la criatura, qu ansí como los que ya no se pueden apartar, no se quiere apartar El de ella."

[57] See "The Life and Times of Teresa of Jesus" in Chapter 6 for review of some political and cultural factors which might make this the case.

Despite this ambivalence, it is significant that for Teresa the culminating image of transformation is a radically relational one. The shattering of the self (in the narrow sense), as imaged in the preceding set of representations, is not the last word; it was only for the sake of preparing the way for an infinitely intensified intimacy. Kohut described "cosmic narcissism" in the impersonal language of "participation in a supraindividual and timeless existence"; Teresa describes the culminating state in language more compatible with our own model of "mystical intersubjectivity" as a non-objectifiable intercourse with the divine at the level of the ground of one's being.[58] When the "self in the narrow sense" is shattered, the profundity of the foundational intersubjectivity of the "self in the broad sense" is revealed.

E. A Self-Psychological Overview of Teresa's Psychological Development

The following is an interpretation such as a psychoanalyst who had only the *Interior Castle* and some minimal biographical data might make of Teresa's "case history." As with any psychoanalytical interpretation, it is a construal of the data that must be held loosely; its usefulness can only be borne out in interaction with more complete data and the insights provided by other theoretical perspectives.

My hypothesis is that we can best understand Teresa's basic psychic configuration as involving a primary defect in the area of the grandiose self that was split off and disavowed at an early stage. Evidence for this in the text is the strong theme of shame propensity in the early Dwelling Places,[59] and the centrality of the emergence of

---

[58]Cf. the discussion of this state in Chapter 7 (at the end of the section on the Seventh Dwelling Places).

[59]See above, "The King and the Worm."

(healthy) grandiosity at the point of the consolidation of a cohesive self.[60]

Extratextual evidence also suggests that Teresa's "primary defect" may have been in the area of grandiosity. Teresa exhibited a lifelong propensity for seeking attention, affection and obedience from those around her. In childhood and youth, her need for approval and affection was so strong that it frequently dominated her better judgment. Always a leader and a person who attracted and fascinated others, Teresa had "charisma"--and she thrived on the attention paid to her.

Little is known about Teresa's early relationship with her mother, but it is known that Beatriz de Ahumada was a "sickly" women who bore eight children before her death at the age of 34. It is plausible to imagine that she had little energy for the kind of intensive interaction that best nurtures an infant's developing self. As Teresa--the only girl among a crowd of similarly-aged brothers[61]--grew into a toddler and a small girl, she came face to face with the hard facts of life in a thoroughly patriarchal society. An energetic, strong-willed little girl undoubtedly experienced many "narcissistic injuries" as her brothers received praise and privileges while she was strictly trained in the ways of ladylikeness.

Teresa's "pathology of the self," however, was not so severe as to prevent her from developing a self that functioned fairly adequately. Due to the original trauma in the area of the grandiose self, this was a compensatory self-structure built up by employing the idealizing line of development.[62] There is strong evidence, both in the text and in

---

[60]See above, "The Traumatized Grandiose Self."

[61]As noted in Chapter 6, Teresa's only sisters were her eldest sibling, who was nine years older than Teresa, and her youngest, who was thirteen years younger. Between these two, in addition to Teresa, were nine brothers.

[62]On "compensatory structures," see "The Nuclear Self and the Selfobject Transferences" in Chapter 8. For a discussion of a patient's use of an idealizing transference in the restructuring of a primary defect in the area of grandiosity, see: John M. Hall, "Idealizing Transference: Disruptions and Repairs," in Arnold Goldberg, ed., *Progress in Self Psychology* (NY: Guilford, 1985), esp. pp. 139-46.

biographical data, that the primary selfobject through which this self-structure was nurtured was Teresa's father. Evidence in the text is the strongly masculine, authoritative, protective qualities attributed to the idealized selfobject; evidence outside the text is the known fact of Teresa's deep attachment to her father, plus her lifelong propensity to seek relationships with authoritative, protective males.

A classical psychoanalytic approach would interpret Teresa's relationship with her father (and other male figures) in Oedipal terms. A self-psychological approach, however, interprets the Oedipal dynamics as real but secondary. The primary factor was the young Teresa's need for a sustaining selfobject with whom to structure a self; her father appears to have been the best selfobject available.

Oedipal dynamics naturally entered in as Teresa matured--especially since Teresa does seem to have been a "favorite" of her father. The death of her mother when Teresa was just reaching the crucial age of puberty undoubtedly gave these dynamics an added (and frightening) reality. Nevertheless, our analysis suggests that these dynamics do not provide the fundamental structure of Teresa's psychological development, and are not even a particularly significant factor until *after* the basic consolidation of the self has been achieved.[63]

At a psychological level,[64] a major motivating factor in Teresa's spiritual journey was an intense longing to heal the wound in the self.[65] The hope of being eternally cared for by the perfect idealized selfobject--namely, God--was probably central in her decision to enter religious life. When she began to work seriously on becoming "whole," her

---

[63]For discussion, see above, "Transitional or 'Working Through' Phase."

[64]As has been emphasized throughout this inquiry, the statement that there is a psychological dimension within a religious experience is not the same as reducing the spiritual dimension *to* the psychological. For further discussion, see "The Psychological Mediation of Mystical Transformation" in Chapter 5.

[65]See above, "The King and the Worm," for a note on how a psychological sense of "lack" may even be a *necessary* part of the motivation for the rigors of the spiritual search.

conscious mode of neutralization was intense rumination on God as the idealized selfobject. Underlying this, however, was the unconscious striving to be unique, special, and powerful (grandiosity).

Before Teresa could develop a fully cohesive self, therefore, the grandiose component of the self had to be freed and integrated. While the idealizing self-structure remained as a basic framework, the traumatized and disavowed grandiosity had to come into its own. Our analysis finds this process imaged as beginning in the Third Dwelling Places, when grandiosity emerges in archaic form,[66] and as completed in the Fifth, when the cohesive self is consolidated.[67] The "bare consciousness" experiences of the Fifth Dwelling Places are a significant factor in this process.

The full consolidation of the cohesive self requires the "working through" of the new capacities of the self in all dimensions of the psychic and behavioral life of the individual. It is at this point that the Oedipal dynamics come into their own, in what we have here termed the "transitional phase." Now the newly vitalized and firmed self is able to joyfully and freely "play" with the imagery of itself as involved in sexual attraction and romantic love. This sexual playfulness no longer has the aura of compulsion, lust, or fear that often accompany sexual arousal when the self is struggling with fragmentation.

In Teresa's case, there is some fairly good evidence that sexuality was a very problematic dimension of her life during her adolescence and young adulthood. Her very circumspect reports of her scandal-causing teenage dalliance with a cousin (*Life* 2,4-6) and her "vain" life as a young nun in the unenclosed monastery of the Incarnation (*Life* 7-8) have led some to speculate that Teresa was not a virgin.[68] Yet whether

---

[66]See above, "The Silkworm Transformed Into a Butterfly."

[67]See above, "The Death of the Butterfly."

[68]Victoria Lincoln, *Teresa: A Woman--A Biography of Teresa of Avila*, ed. with introductions by Elias Rivers and Antonio T. de Nicolás (New York: Paragon House, 1984), p. xiv.

she had explicit sexual experience or not, for our purposes the relevant point is that a young nun, vowed to celibacy, who spends much of her time and energy pursuing sexually-weighted relationships with men[69] is exhibiting a significant lack of psychological and spiritual integration. For Teresa, being able to "sublimate" her sexual passions, playing them out to the full in her imagery of herself in relationship with God while keeping her human relationships chaste, was a sign of a deep healing that had already taken place.[70]

According to our analysis, the final, specifically mystical phase of transformation involves a psychological experience that, phenomenologically, has elements in common with the kind of disintegration experienced in severe pathology of the self. One begins to lose one's grip on that which has been the foundation-stone of one's entire experience of oneself and the world, and there appears to be no bulwark against the terror of total disintegration. Teresa images this in terms of a "hanging" without support or companionship, a "blow" that reduces one to dust, and, finally, the death of the butterfly.

This experience differs from psychotic or borderline disintegration, however, in that the psyche does not fill the yawning void with attacking demons, disjointed and desperate lusts, or murderous rage. Instead of fragmenting, psychic energy becomes more and more intensely focused into an all-consuming thirst for complete union with the divine (VI:11,5).

This thirst is agonizing as long as it is not fulfilled, and yet it is also the first manifestation of an entirely new level of psychic unification. The painful relativization of the psyche's natural structure is its preparation for a final unification from "above downward," which Teresa images as the "spiritual marriage." Here, the psyche is

---

[69]This is Lincoln's claim. See Lincoln, *Teresa: A Woman*, pp. 22-41.

[70]Right up to her last days, Teresa continued to be attracted to men and to invest important energy in relationships with them. After her "second conversion," however, these relationships contributed to, rather than distracted from, the more fundamental commitments of her life.

organized by the transcendent ground of consciousness itself. In "mystical intersubjectivity," the individual's experience of self is at one with its experience of the divine.

CHAPTER 11

TRANSFORMED REPRESENTATIONS OF SELF, GROUP SELF, AND GOD

In Chapter 2, an hypothesis about mystical transformation was presented. In brief, that hypothesis was that mystical experience is the breakthrough into human consciousness of a transcendent, grounding "state of intersubjectivity," and that mystical transformation involves the mediation of this within interhuman intersubjectivity.[1] Part I of this inquiry developed this hypothesis into a model; Part II, so far, has tested that model by subjecting Teresa's *Interior Castle* to an interiority analysis of the operations of consciousness (Chapter 7) and a psychoanalytic study of intrapsychic structure (Chapter 10).

The use of the self-psychological framework for the study of intrapsychic structure has enabled us to find strong evidence that the mystic's intrapsychic "intersubjective field"[2] is transformed in the process of mystical transformation. Yet one task remains to be done before our hypothesis can be said to be even provisionally "verified."

---

[1]For a fuller presentation, see "Mysticism, Intersubjectivity, and Foundations: An Hypothesis" Chapter 2.

[2]Robert Stolorow and George Atwood have extensively developed this concept, which they define as "a system of differently organized, interacting subjective worlds." See their Structures of Subjectivity, p. 41.

This chapter will seek evidence giving insight into how the intrapsychic transformation correlative with mystical transformation can have an impact on *public* intersubjectivity.[3]

A. Introduction to the Analysis of the Castle/Dwelling Place Representation

Like Chapter 10, this section employs a self-psychological analysis. This section seeks to go beyond Chapter 10, however, to examine how Teresa's changing self-structure was also constitutively related to changes in her way of participating in groups. To study this we will have to attend to data which goes beyond that provided by the text of the *Interior Castle*. That text, nevertheless, will remain our central point of reference, for this analysis will focus on the text's central representation--the "interior castle" itself.

The Representation

The image of the human soul as "a castle made entirely out of a diamond or a very clear crystal, in which there are many rooms, just as in heaven there are many dwelling places" (I:1,1) encompasses the entire narrative of the *Interior Castle*. In doing so, it operates on a different level of the total network of images and representations than those studied in Chapter 10. Close study of this image and the related ones which make up the "castle/dwelling place representation" reveals that they support a remarkable conjunction of meanings from multiple levels

[3] Those with a particular interest in this aspect will find additional background provided in Appendix C, "Self Psychology and the Psychology of Groups."

of the spirit and psyche, as well as from numerous external and intersubjective sources.[4]

Our focus here is on the psychological and spiritual transformations evidenced in the development of this representation through Teresa's major writings. This section of the inquiry draws heavily upon important studies by Joseph Chorpenning[5] and Mary Coelho[6] which trace that development. These studies, in conjunction with insights from self psychology, suggest that the castle/dwelling place representation is closely related to the selfobject transferences that structured Teresa's psychic life and, therefore, her participation in the life of groups.

In this section I discuss five transmutations of this representation as it developed in Teresa's psyche. The probable basic structure of Teresa's psychic life was discussed in Chapter 10.[7] I hypothesize that each of the transformations of the castle/dwelling place representation involved a "transmuting internalization"[8] of relationships shaped by the basic idealizing selfobject fantasy and the subsidiary, but crucial mirroring and alterego selfobject fantasies.[9] The present section studies how Teresa actually worked through her selfobject needs as she changed

---

[4] See Appendix B, "Literary Sources and Influences on the Text," for further discussion.

[5]Joseph F. Chorpenning, "The Monastery, Paradise, and the Castle: Literary Images and Spiritual Development in St. Teresa of Avila," *Bulletin of Hispanic Studies* 62:3 (July 1985): 245-57.

[6]Mary Coelho, "St. Teresa of Avila's Transformation of the Symbol of the Interior Castle," *Ephemerides Carmeliticae* 38 (1987): 109-25.

[7]See "Basic Structure of Teresa's Self" in Chapter 10.

[8]On "transmuting internalization," see "The Transformation of the Self" in Chapter 8; also "The Silkworm Transformed Into a Butterfly" in Chapter 10.

[9]"Fantasy" as used here does not necessarily imply illusion or unreality. See Richard B. Ulman and Doris Brothers, *The Shattered Self: A Psychoanalytic Study of Trauma* (Hillsdale, NJ: Analytic Press, 1988), p. 9: "From a self-psychological perspective, we define a narcissistic fantasy as a representation of self (mental and physical) in relation to selfobject."

in her way of imaging self, local and global communities, and God. The following are the five versions of the castle/dwelling place representation which will be discussed in detail in this section:

TRANSMUTING INTERNALIZATIONS VIA THE CASTLE/DWELLING PLACE REPRESENTATION

1. From God/heaven as intangible idealized selfobject, to local community as tangible presence of this idealized selfobject.

2. From community as selfobject, to local community as group self firmed against threat to larger community.

3. From community as group self, to individual self as incarnating ideal qualities of group self.

4. From individual self as incarnating ideal qualities of group self, to individual self as structure grand enough for God to dwell in.

5. From individual self as structure within which God dwells, to radical mutual indwelling of God and individual.

Even more than was the case with the series of representations presented in Chapter 10, there are really no "clean breaks" between the various versions of the castle/dwelling place representation. Although they are presented here sequentially, with the suggestion that there was an element of progression in the way the images reorganized themselves at different stages of Teresa's journey, in fact all these organizations were to some degree present from the beginning and all are subthemes of the others even when one is clearly dominant. To some degree the sequential presentation is more a heuristic method than a claim of literal fact; on the level of psychic imagery development is never that neat.

Yet this presentation does provide evidence that development of imagery was taking place, even if not with the tidiness suggested by the sequential schema. Another possible way of organizing the material would be in terms of three interdependent and continuously interweaving streams of imagery--one of images of the self, another of images of the self-in-relation-to-groups, and a third of images of God--that coalesce in a variety of different ways at different times under different psychic and external pressures. What is most significant is that the final image as developed in the *Interior Castle* is a creative leap to a new level of integration of all the themes that play through the process of development. In the *Interior Castle*, the image truly makes concrete the integral mutual mediation of self, God, and community.

The Process of Transmuting Internalization

The development of the castle/dwelling place representation is here presented as a series of transmuting internalizations, each of which significantly reconfigures the self's "intersubjective field."[10] Transmuting internalization, as discussed in Chapter 8, is the process by which the self builds its own cohesiveness and strength by taking into itself (on its own terms) the qualities of the selfobject.[11] It is to be recalled that from the beginning the selfobject is, by definition, a part of the self's own world; the selfobject is structured as such by the self in order to provide the self with the support it requires in order to exist.[12] Thus, transmuting internalization is not the taking in of

---

[10]On the "intersubjective field," see above, footnote 2.

[11]For further discussion, see Chap. 8, "The Transformation of the Self."

[12]For discussion, see "The Concept of the Selfobject" in Chapter 8.

something external, but the shifting of qualities from one part of the self's world to another--that is, from the "side" of the selfobject to the "side" of the self.

Putting it that way, however, makes it sound deceptively simple. In the actuality of the psyche, the impact of such a shift is more like that of radically changing the *persona* of a character in a drama: the consequence is that all the interactions among all the characters have to be reconfigured.[13] Since this drama is not just an inner fantasy, but the structure of the individual's interaction with the concrete world, this reconfiguration of the intersubjective field is also a reconfiguration of behavior.

Before her "second conversion" experience in 1554,[14] Teresa undoubtedly already imaged God as a benevolent Father who would protect and care for her; but at that stage the idealized selfobject remained distant, vague, and intangible. At the time of the powerful experience before the statue of the wounded Christ, however, her consciousness was jolted into sharp awareness of the realness and tangibility of God's presence. A major reconfiguration of her intersubjective field was under way.

Before 1554, Teresa apparently did not envision herself as a reformer or foundress; but a mere eight years later, she was already living in the first monastery of her Carmelite Reform. In those years, she had to develop a new sense of herself as a capable teacher and leader, and of God as one who supported and stood with her in those endeavors. She also had to develop a new sense of the possibilities of community life, since her experience in her original religious community left so much to be desired.

In describing this process in terms of "transmuting internalization," we are saying that a major dynamic in these

[13]On the "psychic drama" metaphor, see "Images, Representations, and Structures" in Chapter 8.

[14]For a brief overview of Teresa's life, see "A Brief Biography" in Chapter 6.

reconfigurations of the intersubjective field was the transmutation and transfer of qualities of the idealized selfobject (that is, God) to other "characters" within the field. Like all psychic processes, this one is by no means univocal; it occurs over time, on several levels, and with various resonances in different dimensions of psychic and social experience. The following is an exploration of five versions of the castle/dwelling place representation, which are hypothesized to be pathways by which this process played itself out.

B. The Castle/Dwelling Place Representation In Relation to Self, Group Self,[15] and God

Local Community as Tangible Presence of the Idealized Selfobject

This first transmutation of the castle/dwelling place representation might almost be called a "transmuting externalization," for in it Teresa projected the formerly entirely interior, fantasy-imbued image of the idealized selfobject into a very concrete and practical form--namely, that of the idealized contemplative community which she would subsequently found at St. Joseph's in Avila.

The imagery upon which Teresa drew for this transmutation was not new to her. Before the conversion experience of 1554, she had already been a Carmelite nun for eighteen years. Despite the laxness of the community within which she lived, she had been deeply formed by the imagery and spirit of the monastic tradition. Among the central images of that tradition, Chorpenning notes, is that of the monastery as an imitation of heaven--a place of total and concrete intimacy with God.[16]

---

[15] Kohut hypothesized that groups of persons who are engaged with one another for sustained periods of time will develop a "group self" structure with functions and dynamics similar to those of the individual self. For a more fully developed discussion, see Appendix C.

[16] Chorpenning, "Monastery," pp. 246-47.

With her second conversion, the imagery of this tradition gelled for Teresa into a representation of a passionately-desired concrete manifestation of the idealized selfobject for which she longed. She began to pour her energy into the project of founding an ideal contemplative community. Teresa envisioned St. Joseph's in utopian terms, as an attempt to return to the purest traditions of monasticism, including asceticism, withdrawal from the world, imitation of the martyrs, and soldierly participation in Christ's battle against evil. She threw herself, heart and soul, into the work of bringing into being a community which would incarnate this ideal.

The monastic tradition commonly associated monastic life with the garden of paradise; the monks, in their enclosed monastic "garden," dwell with God. In the chapters added to the *Life* in 1565, after St. Joseph's had been in existence for just three years, Teresa called her maiden community "this little dwelling corner for God," "an abode in which His Majesty delights," "a paradise of delight for Him."[17] In the *Way*, written shortly after this, she added, "This house is a heaven, if one can be had on this earth" (*Way* 13:7). The famous allegory of the four ways of watering the garden (*Life*, chapters 11-22) is perhaps the most prominent resonance of this tradition in Teresa's early writings.

In this first transmuting internalization, then, Teresa's image of God (the idealized selfobject) combined with a variety of images from the monastic tradition to create a representation of a community which would serve as the tangible dwelling place of God and the ideal nurturing environment for the seeker of God. In this, we see the idealized selfobject moving more and more out of the realm of archaic fantasy.[18] Instead of a private dream of perfectly embracing love, there

---

[17]*Life* 35:12. In Spanish: "este rinconcito de Dios . . . morada en que Su Majestad se delita . . . paraiso de su deleite." See Chorpenning, "Monastery," p. 249.

[18]On the maturation of selfobject experience from archaic to "realistic," see "The Nuclear Self and the Selfobject Transferences" in Chapter 8.

is the willingness to enter into the down-to-earth struggle to create such an environment within the world.

The Group Self, Firmed and Expanding

Once St. Joseph's was securely established, Teresa became increasingly disturbed by reports of the inroads of the Lutherans against the Catholic Church. This concern had been in the back of her mind even during the activities of founding, but now it came into greater prominence. She drew upon the imagery of the *militia spiritualis* ("spiritual war"), which was also a part of the monastic tradition, as she began to speak more often of her little community as the fortress at the center of the whole Church. It is from this *militia spiritualis* tradition that the actual image of the castle moves into the center of her ruminations.

It is in the *Way* that the theme of the monastery as a fortified place where the nuns can do spiritual battle for the Church comes to the forefront. Speaking of the evils that she saw threatening the Church in her day, she wrote that in time of danger, a wise lord withdraws into a fortified city. She concluded,

> What we must ask God is that in this little castle [*castillito*] where there are already good Christians not one of us will go over to the enemy and that God will make the captains of this castle or city, who are the preachers and theologians, very advanced in the way of the Lord. (*Way* 3,1-2)

Here the monastery is envisaged as a "little castle" acting as a fortified stronghold at the center of the great castle or city which is the whole Church. The image of the monastery as a castle suggests that Teresa by this time had a strong sense of a firm "group self" at St. Joseph's. In this dimension of the process of transmuting internalization, we see more and more qualities of the idealized selfobject transferred into the structure of the group self. Now the group self is strong, cohesive, stable, capable, etc.

This group self, although centered in the local community, is clearly identified with the yet larger group self of the Church. In reaction to perceived threats which could lead to the fragmentation of the larger group self, Teresa counsels the firming of the local manifestation of the group self. Like a secure individual self, the group self of the new Carmelite Reform is able both to confirm its boundaries and to maintain an empathic sense of identification with the larger community of the Church. At the same time, Teresa begins to move toward the foundation of more Reformed monasteries.[19] The group self--and Teresa's sense of herself as a strong leader--is expanding.

The Individual Self Takes on Characteristics of Group Self

As Teresa's experience of life in community lengthened, she saw individuals as transformed by life in community. The imagery originally applied to the community increasingly was applied to the individuals within it.

Precursors of this version of the castle/dwelling place representation occur in the chapters of Teresa's *Life* which were composed in 1565. There, she occasionally applied the *militia spiritualis* imagery to the soul rather than to the community as a whole. In *Life* 18,4 she spoke of the soul as a "city" with a cowardly mayor who allows the enemy entrance; and in 20,22 she referred to the soul as a fortress with a custodian who "climbs, or is taken up, to the highest tower to raise the banner for God."[20] These texts, in context, are not particularly prominent; they are of interest mainly because they show that this link was already in the back of Teresa's mind.

---

[19]The second monastery for women (Medina del Campo) and the first monastery for men (Duruelo) were founded in 1567.

[20]Both of these texts clearly draw on precedents found in Ludolph, Osuna and Laredo as well as numerous other spiritual writers. On the influence of these writers on Teresa, see Appendix B.

Chorpenning discusses in detail how in both the *Life* and the *Way* Teresa increasingly applies the same images that she uses for St. Joseph's--a communal institution--to the individual soul. In the *Life*, the allegory of the watering of the garden subtly links the theme of the monastery/paradise with that of the soul/garden. In the *Way*, she explicitly calls the soul (rather than the monastery) a "fortified castle" (28,6) an "extremely rich palace" (28,9), and a "paradise" within which God dwells (29,4).

This transference of imagery from monastery to soul will reach its conclusion in the *Interior Castle*. Chorpenning summarizes,

> This transference illustrates how the soul is to appropriate the constitutive elements of the Teresian ideal and the effect of this process of appropriation upon the soul, namely, its progressive growth and development in beauty and grace.[21]

This transference of imagery is a classic example of transmuting internalization. The qualities present in the group self, which has functioned for its members both as a selfobject and as an auxiliary self-structure, gradually are taken more fully into the self. The individual now carries within herself the basic sense of cohesion, harmony, goodness, and vitality which formerly came only from the actual presence of the community.

In the context of this inquiry, a question that immediately arises is whether this internalization of the functions which the group formerly provided necessarily implies an emotional, or perhaps even physical, retreat from community. The self-psychological understanding would be that it is incorrect to say that the mature individual no longer needs the community, for selfobjects are a lifelong need regardless of one's level of maturity.[22]

---

[21]Chorpenning, "Monastery," p. 255.

[22]It is worth noting that the same applies to individual relationships as well. No matter how "transformed" Teresa was psychologically and spiritually, she never lost her need to form idealizing relationships with males. The relationship which she

With maturation and the development of internal structure, however, the quality and form of the need change significantly. As in a mature one-on-one relationship, self and group self can mutually exchange selfobject functions within a basic context of realistic assessment of one another's qualities and capabilities. In Teresa's case, she was clearly providing more and more selfobject functions within the expanding group self of the Carmelite Reform. At the same time, the group continued to function to supply many of her selfobject needs as well.

The Individual Self As Dwelling Place of God

This fourth transmutation of the castle/dwelling place representation also has to do with the self's internalization of the qualities of the idealized selfobject--in this case, God. At this point in our discussion of the various versions it becomes more evident why the "sequential" presentation is not entirely adequate. The transmuting internalization that occurs in the case of each version also impacts on each of the others. Thus, the experience of the local community as tangible presence of the idealized selfobject, the experience of the firm and expanding group self, and the experience of the firming of the individual self through relationship with the group are all integrally related to the development of the present version, in which the individual self is experienced as a dwelling place for God.

Insofar as there is a sequential trajectory working its way out here, however, we could say that the subtle transition from the third to the fourth is the most crucial transition of all; for it is here that the self truly begins to experience itself as "like God." No longer is the primary meaning of the castle that of a protected and nurturing place in which

---

developed with Jéronimo Gracián, for example, exhibits many of the qualities of the "idealizing transference of creativity" (cf. Appendix C); yet she did not even meet him until 1575, well after her "spiritual marriage" in 1572.

the self can dwell; now it also represents the self as glorious dwelling place for God.

Mary Coelho's 1987 article explores several issues relevant to the last two transmutations of the castle/dwelling place representation. Coelho notes that in her use of the image in Chapter 28 of the *Way*, Teresa already incorporates some of the most significant features of the later image of the *Interior Castle*. Teresa wrote:

> Well, let us imagine that within us is an extremely rich palace, built entirely of gold and precious stones; in sum, built for a Lord such as this. Imagine, too, as is indeed so, that you have a part to play in order for the palace to be so beautiful; for there is no edifice as beautiful as is a soul pure and full of virtues. The greater the virtues the more resplendent the jewels. Imagine, also, that in this palace dwells this mighty King who has been gracious enough to become your Father; and that He is seated upon an extremely valuable throne, which is your heart. (*Way* 28,9)

The "palace" here foreshadows the "castle" of the *Interior Castle* first in that the soul is symbolized by the glorious edifice of a palace or castle, and secondly in that God dwells at the center of the edifice. The idea of "many dwelling places" was probably also already in Teresa's mind.[23]

In Chapter 28 of the *Way* Teresa was teaching about active recollection. The main lesson she wants to convey in the text quoted is that God is within us, at the inmost center of ourselves, and that to join Him we must actively strive to withdraw into that inner sanctum. She emphasizes that this beautiful inner palace is something that we participate in building by all our acts of virtue as well as by our efforts in the prayer of active recollection.

Here we see the self-representation continuing to take on more and more of the qualities of the idealized selfobject. First the community was the benevolent, nurturing environment or "dwelling place" of the

---

[23]Coelho, "Transformation," pp. 4-5; see also *Way* 20,1.

self; now the self has fully transmuted and internalized these qualities so that it too has become a "dwelling place" for God. Along with this comes a shift from the intense focus on idealizing needs to a healthy balancing of these with mirroring and alterego needs. This is seen both in the emphasis on the enhanced status of being a dwelling place for God, and in the stress on the soul's capability to "build up" this dwelling place.

Radical Mutual Indwelling

The final and most profound transmutation of the castle/dwelling place representation--the one that perhaps occurred as the "vision" Teresa spoke of as inaugurating her writing of the *Interior Castle*[24]--integrates all that has been discussed in relation to the first four versions, plus another powerful stream of imagery.

Coelho's discovery is that, despite the basic similarities noted above, there is a crucially significant difference between the image of the palace in the *Way* (1566) and that of the castle in the *Interior Castle* (1577). The palace in the *Way* is made of "gold and precious stones," while in the *Interior Castle* the castle is made of "diamond or very clear crystal" (*Interior Castle* 1:1,1). Furthermore, the palace of gold and precious stones can be built up piece by piece by the "jewels" of virtuous acts, while the diamond or crystal castle emerges as a whole from God and is inseparable from him.

Coelho finds the key to this change in a text from Teresa's *Life*:

> Let us say, to make the comparison, that the Divinity is like a very clear diamond, much greater than all the world; or like a mirror, as I said referring to the soul in that other vision, except that it is a mirror in so sublime a way that I wouldn't know how to exaggerate this. And we could say that everything we do is visible in this

[24]The question of whether this was actually a "vision" or not has been much discussed. For review of these issues, see Kieran Kavanaugh, "Introduction to the *Interior Castle*," in *Collected Works*, vol. 2, pp. 266-69.

> diamond since it is of such a kind that it contains all things within itself; there is nothing that escapes its magnitude. (40,10)

Here it is God, who encompasses everything, who is "like a very clear diamond." It is only when this image coalesces with the castle/dwelling place representation that the final transmutation takes place. Another text from Chapter 40 of the *Life* (referred to in the preceding quotation as "that other vision") foreshadows the link:

> Once while I was reciting with all the sisters the hours of the Divine Office, my soul suddenly became recollected; and it seemed to me to be like a brightly polished mirror, without any part on the back or top or bottom that wasn't totally clear. In its center Christ, our Lord, was shown to me, in the way I usually see Him. It seemed to me I saw Him clearly in every part of my soul, as though in a mirror. And this mirror also--I don't know how to explain it--was completely engraved upon the Lord Himself by means of a very loving communication I wouldn't know how to describe. (40,5)

Here Teresa indicates how even before 1565 (when she completed the *Life*) she was experiencing a most intimate mutual "mirroring" between herself and God. At that time she was already well established in the unitive life (that is, the Fifth-Sixth Dwelling Places or spiritual courtship and betrothal). Thus, her discussion of active recollection in the *Way* is not in terms of God as separate from the self, but in terms of God as actually dwelling in greatest intimacy at the very center of the self. As discussed above, the self-representation at that stage already gave evidence of transmuting internalization of the qualities of the God-representation as well as of those of the community. In the stage of betrothal, then, the self recollected in its own center, while not identical with God, has already become the perfect "mirror" of God.

Yet at this stage (1565-66, the time of writing *Life* and *Way*) Teresa maintained a definite distinction between the way she represented this ultimate depth-dimension (God/the recollected soul) and that of the soul as active. While the soul as active appears in images drawn from the castle/dwelling place representation, only God and the recollected soul appear in the images of "mirror" and "diamond." It was only subsequent to the culminating experience of the spiritual marriage, which Teresa did not experience until 1572, that she was able to make the final synthesis of imagery, reflecting her own transformed consciousness. Then she could write:

> . . . we consider our soul to be like a castle made entirely out of a diamond or of very clear crystal, in which there are many rooms, just as in heaven there are many dwelling places. For in reflecting upon it carefully, Sisters, we realize that the soul of the just person is nothing else but a paradise where the Lord says He finds his delight. (I:1,1)

The two representations between which she had previously maintained a careful distinction have here melded into one: the soul is a castle made entirely out of the "diamond" which had formerly been the preserve of God. The totality of the soul--its active dimension as well as its recollected center--is imaged as at one with God.

The texts quoted from the Chapter 40 of the *Life* apparently refer back to a particular type of mystical experience which Teresa had had at least once before writing the *Life*.[25] She referred to this type of experience again in *Interior Castle* VI:10,2 when she wrote, "In this vision it is revealed how all things are seen in God and how He has them all in Himself," and in V:1,9 when she wrote that a sure sign that an experience was union is that "God so places Himself in the interior of the soul that when it returns to itself it can in no way doubt that it was in God and God was in it." What the "spiritual marriage" or Seventh Dwelling Place apparently meant for Teresa was that this reality became a permanent state. As Coelho put it,

> She is no longer seeking an inner, still separate, reality. She had found it. . . . The remarkable thing St. Teresa has done in the symbol of the interior castle for her last work is to offer a symbol that depicts

[25]See Kavanaugh and Rodriguez, *Collected Works*, vol. 1, p. 307 n. 6, for a list of references to the occasions of this experience.

> the mystery that God is both in us and we are in God or comprehended in God.[26]

In discussing the Seventh Dwelling Places Teresa wrote that "the soul, I mean the spirit, is made one with God" in such a way that the two cannot any longer be separated (VII:2,3-4). It seems that at the psychological level this state correlates with the culmination of the transmuting internalization of the God-representation, with the image originally used for God fully taken up into the self-representation. In her introduction to the *Interior Castle*, Teresa herself emphasized the likeness of "image" between God and the soul, even as she also stressed the remaining ontological difference.

> He Himself says that He created us in His own image and likeness. . . . [but] since this castle is a creature and the difference, therefore, between it and God is the same as that between the Creator and His creature, His Majesty in saying that the soul is made in His own image makes it almost impossible for us to understand the sublime dignity and beauty of the soul ((I:1,1)[27]

The "interior castle" image, then, brings into conjunction a remarkable richness of different levels of the psyche and spirit. The image was imbibed by Teresa through her participation in the intersubjective cultural network of the monastic tradition. Within her psyche it was gradually linked up with more and more dimensions of her experience of self, community, and God, until in the *Interior Castle* it emerged as the comprehensive symbol of the integral mutual mediation of all these dimensions.

---

[26]Coelho, "Transformation," p. [13].

[27]This passage is difficult to translate; some words may be missing in the manuscript. The Spanish text reads: "El mesmo dice que nos crió a su imagen y semejanza. . . . puesto que hay la diferencia de él a Dios que del Criador a la criatura, pues es criatura, basta decir Su Majestad que es hecha a su imagen para que apenas podamos entender la gran dignidad y hermosura del ánima."

C. A Self-Psychological Overview of Teresa's Active Life

The goal of the following brief discussion of aspects of Teresa's biography is to examine whether there is evidence in Teresa's public life of the kind of transformation of mediated intersubjectivity which we originally hypothesized would accompany mystical transformation. This review does not claim to be comprehensive, even in regard to the issues with which this inquiry is concerned. It is suggestive, however, of directions for further research.

The primary issue at hand in this section is Teresa's relationship with the various "group selves" in which she participated. As we will see, Kohut's insights in regard to the psychology of creativity and leadership are helpful in understanding Teresa's role in the group selves of her reform movement, the Church of her time, and the Church throughout history.

It has often been noted that Teresa's creativity (both literary and ecclesial) was not so much in the introduction of radically new images, ideas, or practices as in her capacity to transform and integrate a vast amount of pre-existing material, and then to communicate her insights with great simplicity and power. This is in harmony with Kohut's notion of the creative person and the leader as being able to tune in to the fears and struggles of the group self, and to respond in a way that enables the group self to move toward renewed cohesiveness.

Creative persons and leaders can do this, says Kohut, because they are personally experiencing the same threats; their creative response is as much a restructuring and firming of their own selves, as it is a gift to the group self. When the group and the individuals within it act as selfobjects for one another, the fragmentation or cohesion of one tends to produce a like experience in the other. The first question to ask about Teresa's life, then, is what kind of fragmentation she struggled with within her original familial and cultural context; for that struggle for a transformed personal cohesion was the primary resource she brought to the transformation of culture and Church.

As discussed in Chapter 10, it is not unreasonable to suspect that in childhood and youth Teresa experienced considerable "narcissistic injury."[28] There were surely significant deficiencies in her relationships with her parents, although these cannot be documented except--as we have done--through "reading backward" from Teresa's self-structure as mediated in her writings. Whatever "pathology of the self" Teresa was prone to as a result of her early familial nurture then came into conjunction with the continual subtle humiliation to which a girl was subjected within a patriarchal culture. The latter was probably aggravated by the presence of many male siblings who were being actively trained for leadership and adventure,[29] while Teresa--despite her gifts as a "natural leader"--was expected to prepare herself for the sedate, sheltered life of a *Doña* (lady).

Teresa was deeply attached to her home and family--especially to her father--and yet at age 20, against her father's wishes, she tore herself from that context to enter the convent. The pain and conflict that she experienced in making that choice is evidence that in it she was struggling with a deeply-felt lack of cohesion. She clearly did not see a future for herself in the boring, repressed existence of a noble's wife--the life for which family and culture had trained her. The fact that her older sister was trapped in a hellish marriage--she was what we would now call a "battered wife"--undoubtedly added to Teresa's conflictual feelings about marriage. It is likely that in her fantasies the religious life was embroidered with the imagery of the "holy war," pilgrimages, adventure, etc., from which her gender largely excluded her in the secular context.

---

[28]For discussion, see "A Self-Psychological Overview of Teresa's Psychological Development" in Chapter 10.

[29]Teresa grew up in the heart of Spain's "Golden Age." Almost all of her nine brothers either fought in the Moorish wars or went to the New World as *conquistadores*.

Thus, there was a fragility to Teresa's difficult resolution of her adolescent "identity crisis." Her subsequent illness,[30] near-death, and long period of being an invalid was almost too much for her; she was taken to the brink of distintegration, both physically and psychologically. Her physical recovery took many years, and was never really complete. As for her psychological health, she seems to have gradually returned to "normal" in the eyes of those who knew her. Yet the remaining years before her "second conversion" at age 39 were, in her own eyes, a time of unpeacefulness and mediocrity; she was in a holding pattern, waiting and searching for something without even knowing what it was.

It came, without warning, one day in 1554 as she knelt before an image of the bleeding, broken and crucified Christ. Seeing him (as if for the first time) in this state of disintegration--and yet also entirely whole in his love for her and all humanity--"something clicked"[31] and her experiences of herself, her God, and her Church were changed. In the image of the broken and yet resurrected Christ, she found the seed of a way to put herself--and the Church--back together at a new level of coherence.

We have conjectured that a key element of Teresa's "second conversion" (the 1554 experience) was a shift in the idealized selfobject from the realm of archaic fantasy to a more concrete level.[32] A movement had begun in which God would become increasingly more real and intimate to her; and correlative with that movement was an increasing concreteness and power in Teresa's participation in "group selves." The connection between the two, from a self-psychological

---

[30]As mentioned in Chapter 6, the latest research indicates that the genesis of the illness was primarily physical, not psychosomatic. There is always, however, a mutual interplay between physical and psychological health.

[31]This is the colloquial phrase that Kohut uses to describe what happens when a cohesive self suddenly comes into place, either in infancy or in a later adult transformation. See Kohut, "The Psychoanalyst and the Historian," p. 218; idem, "Civilization Versus Culture," p. 259.

[32]See above, pp. 330-31.

perspective, is the self's increasing cohesiveness and vitality through transmuting internalization of the qualities of the selfobject.[33]

The first fruit of this reconfigured self-structure was the development of Teresa's vision of a Reformed Carmelite monastery in which God would be more perfectly served--and the self would be more perfectly nurtured. This dream was realized in the foundation of St. Joseph's of Avila in 1562. Thus, Teresa's first vision of a solution to the problem of the potentially crumbling self (her own and the Church's) did not go far beyond the establishment of a single strong, nurturing local community. At that point her focus was probably as much on providing the environment that she herself needed as it was on contributing to a resolution of the Church's problems, although this was not absent from her thoughts.

As she developed as a leader, however, her identification with the group self of the Church increased and, building on her original empathy with its threatened situation, she expanded her vision both in word and in fact. Her writings spoke more frequently and more forcefully of the crucial role of the faithful little community within the threatened larger community. Eventually, this vision would lead her to spearhead the founding of seventeen more monasteries during her lifetime.

The religious order that grew from this beginning today numbers hundreds of monasteries and has representatives in almost every nation on earth. This is indication of the extraordinary power of the "group self" formed when Teresa strove to concretize her experience of God. In fact, Teresa is to this day a world-reknowned "leader," as is evident from the fact that millions throughout the earth still read her books and find therein sustenance for their own psychological and spiritual journeys. Furthermore, tens of thousands of these--i.e., those committed to the Carmelite spiritual path--regard her as one of the premier figures in their own "group self."

---

[33]For discussion, see "The Transformation of the Self" in Chapter 8 and "The Silkworm Transformed into a Butterfly" in Chapter 10.

The claim here is that this extraordinary intersubjective power is directly related to the intrapsychic processes which have been traced in this and the preceding chapter. Teresa was (and is) a leader in the sense Kohut described: she faced the deepest disintegrative crises of the self, and, in finding her way to a creative resolution, she created both a new vision of what the self is and a new "group self" within which others could tread the path she had trod.

In the context of the total inquiry, however, the key question is what relationship there is between the specifically *mystical* transformation that Teresa experienced, and the changes in her relationships with groups studied in this chapter. I would collate the findings of the preceding chapter and this one by saying that the first stage of "primary healing"--that is, the consolidation of a vital and cohesive self--seems to correspond to Teresa's "taking hold" as a dynamic leader within her immediate environment. She became able to serve as the focal point for a local "group self" that is a nurturing selfobject for herself and others.[34]

The specifically "mystical" phase of her transformation, on the other hand, seems to correlate with a radically new experience of the self as, in itself, a fundamentally intersubjective reality--that is, a "dwelling place" and a "spouse" for the divine Lord. The result of this is a massive expansion of both the inclusiveness and the power of the "group self." Even within her lifetime, Teresa became a nationally and internationally known teacher and leader, and her status in these roles has only increased as the centuries have passed.

Our conclusion, then, is that "mystical transformation in the broad sense"--that is, generic religious conversion--has the effect of enabling people to fulfill their potential as contributing members within their immediate intersubjective networks. "Mystical transformation in the narrow sense" may add a dimension to this by which the person can

---

[34]See "The Silkworm Transformed into a Butterfly" in Chapter 10; also above, "The Castle/Dwelling Place Representation in Relation to Self, Group Self, and God."

participate in creating intersubjective networks on a much broader and more profound scale. "Mystical intersubjectivity," then, is not only a transformed relationship between God and an individual; it is a transformation of that individual as an intersubjective being and, therefore, of all the relationships in which that individual participates.

CHAPTER 12

A CRITICAL REVIEW OF THE PROJECT

A. Introduction

In Chapter 1, we surveyed five sets of questions that modern and post-modern thought poses in regard to mystical phenomena. Viewed as criteria for a theory, these sets of questions ask:

1) Does the theory adequately acknowledge and account for the role of the subjective patterns of individual consciousness in mystical experience?
2) Does the theory adequately acknowledge and account for the reality of intersubjective dynamics in human life at all levels--psychological, social, political, and mystical?
3) Does the theory not only assert, but also explain, the reality of an integral relation between mystical experience and praxis?
4) Does the theory not only assert, but also explain, the traditional claim that mystical experience involves a "transcendent" or "supraworldly" dimension?

5) Is the theory fully and adequately explanatory? That is, doesit deal--insofar as is possible--with "things as related among themselves," rather than with "things as related to us"?[1]

The conclusion of the review in Chapter 1 was that these criteria have the greatest possibility of being fulfilled in a theory that, instead of seeking an objective context external to the human subject, takes the human subject her/himself as its basic "measure." We took as our position, therefore, that mysticism cannot be properly understood without insight into the general structures of the human subject. Knowledge of the human subject is to be pursued according to the three "canons of methodical analysis," which are "Be concrete; Be explanatory; Focus on acts, not words." The inquiry has been an experiment in carrying through this approach. Our contention is that this theory does fulfill the criteria spelled out in Chapter 1 and reviewed here. In the following review of the project we will focus primarily on its successes, but also point to areas that need further development.

B. A Review of the Project

Discussion of the Theory's "Prime Analogue"

A work of theory such as this one specializes in fidelity to the second canon of methodical analysis, "Be explanatory." One doing a work of theory needs to know the structures and limitations of the genre. A work of theory begins with an insight, a "hunch," a "bright idea" that seems to illuminate the basic structure of the phenomena under consideration. Essential to this insight is its image or "prime analogue." The theory develops by playing back and forth between the analogue and

[1]Lonergan, *Insight*, p. 291. See also the discussion of "criteria of objectivity" in Chapter 1.

the actuality; to take the analogue too literally is to fall into idealization, but to try to do without the analogue is to fall into incoherence.

Our "prime analogue," first presented in Chapter 2, compares the ground of consciousness to a "state of intersubjectivity." Where did the hunch to pursue this approach come from? Like most "bright ideas" it had multiple sources, including some that were intellectual and some that were more psychological or affective. The immediate concern that pushed it into the foreground of thought was a personal need to understand how contemplative spirituality--that is, the intensive pursuit of the interior life of prayer--is integrally related to human development in both the interpersonal and the social spheres. "Intersubjectivity" became a node-word, focusing insights and concerns from many levels of reflection. Once a bright idea is taken up into a theoretical project, however, it becomes subject to the rigors of that genre. It becomes necessary to justify the potential value of the analogue according to criteria of coherence, suitability, etc.

The first evidence offered in support of the selected analogue is that the ground of consciousness necessarily sublates subject-object structure, and yet must do so in a way that is "more than," not "less than," what it sublates. In a fundamental sense the ground is "transcendent" and so ineffable; on this basis we may demur from speaking of it on the grounds that all language is necessarily involved in subject-object structure and so inadequate. On the other hand, we can take the way of the theologians and speak of it in analogy. In speaking analogically we assert that all created things truly mediate something of their ground and, furthermore, that certain created structures (i.e., one's prime analogue--in this case, intersubjectivity) have a particular isomorphism with the ground and its most immediate mediations.

From there, the initial argument moves in two directions from the prime analogue. The first movement, a variation on the *via eminentiae*, is toward a clear assertion that the transcendent ground of consciousness is, itself, a "state of intersubjectivity" in a supereminent form. The second movement is toward the assertion that increase in awareness of the transcendent ground is a "mystical intersubjectivity" that will be mediated in positive changes at all levels of human intersubjectivity.

If the discussion were confined to this strictly abstract level, the theory presented here could be refuted in two ways. One would be to reject the adequacy of the prime analogue; the other would be to spell out weaknesses or *non sequiturs* in the application of the analogy to various dimensions of reality. The present project, however, is not conceived as resting its case with a strictly theoretical argument. In fidelity to the canons of concreteness and operations, the preliminary development of theory is seen as the sketching of an hypothesis to be tested.

The claim that mystical experience involves a state of mystical intersubjectivity, and that this is mediated in a transformation of psychological and social structures of intersubjectivity, has been investigated through the analysis of a concrete instance of mystical transformation. In that analysis, evidence has been found indicating that the original hypothesis is both plausible and--in a provisional sense[2]--verified. This means that a refutation of the theory not only must address any weaknesses it may have at the logical or philosophical level, but must also present evidence indicating why the analysis at the concrete level is inadequate.

Review of Steps Taken

The five chapters of Part I employed a transcendental method in the detailed development of a model of mystical experience and transformation. Chapter 1 indicated the general context of the choice of method, while Chapter 2 spelled out its theoretical grounds within the foundational methodology of Bernard Lonergan. Chapter 3 outlined Lonergan's phenomenology of the self-transcending subject, who has

[2]The verification is provisional because only one of many possible types of "intraworldly" analysis was carried out. For discussion, see "Concluding Discussion" in Chapter 7.

his/her ground in the non-objectifiable "subject-as-subject." Chapter 4 found the underlying theoretical structure of this phenomenology in the theorem of mediation, which articulates the general relation between a whole and its structurally coherent parts.

The most general statement of the theorem is that a whole is mediated in its structure, that is, its "terms and relations." The whole, as the "ground" of all the parts, always remains "more than" the sum of its parts. In the human being, the subject-as-subject is the ground of which the structured operations of intentional consciousness are the mediation. The dynamism of the subject-as-subject's mediation in intentional consciousness is termed "self-mediation." The importance of these chapters for our inquiry was that they provided the phenomenological and theoretical basis for understanding the specificity of mystical experience in terms of the ground of consciousness, and at the same time understanding its constitutive mediation in transformations of intentional consciousness.

Since the specific focus of the project is on the mediation of mystical transformation within human intersubjectivity, these chapters also strove to clarify the constitutive intersubjectivity of the subject. This included discussion of the subject's primordial intersubjectivity, which is a "presence-with" other subjects prior to subject-object differentiation, and mediated intersubjectivity, which is fulfilled in the existential subject's conscious and responsible contribution to the upbuilding of human community. The latter is an instance of "mutual self-mediation." Chapter 4 also included further examination of the concrete structures of psyche, spirit, and community within which intersubjectivity develops.

In addition, Chapter 4 studied how Lonergan's theoretical perspective resolves the problem of the relationship between a view of development based in the theorem of mediation, and a more classical "scientific" approach to the study of development. Empirical science views development from "below upward," as proceeding from lower levels of organization to higher ones; the theorem of mediation explains it from "above downward," as the stage-by-stage articulation of a pre-existing whole.[3] The two perspectives are complementary; the "above downward" perspective is more fully explanatory, but the "below upward" perspective is more adequate for tracing the concrete pathways of development.

The discussion of these issues in Chapter 4 was important for the present inquiry because it underlies the claim that there is an integral relationship between Part I and Part II. Part I takes the "above downward" perspective as normative and develops an explanatory theory of mystical experience and transformation. A theory remains only a "bright idea," however, unless it can be verified in the concrete phenomena which it purports to explain. For this reason the "below upward" approach of Part II is integral to the total project of the inquiry.

The explanatory model of mystical experience and transformation was explicitly developed in Chapter 5. The key to the model is the claim that the immediate ground of human consciousness is, in itself, a mediation of the transcendent ground of consciousness. Mystical experience is conscious awareness of this mediation. When this awareness occurs in intentional consciousness, it is "religious experience" or "mystical experience in the broad sense." When awareness of the mediation of the transcendent ground of consciousness occurs at the level of the immediate ground of consciousness itself, it is "mystical experience in the narrow sense." The latter is a state of "mystical intersubjectivity" in which the subject-object structure of intentional consciousness is radically transcended. Henceforward the mystic's intentional consciousness, which is a mediation of the ground of consciousness, is profoundly reconfigured. Chapter 5 concluded with a discussion of how this "mystical transformation" is mediated at the level of the mystic's psyche and spirit.

---

[3]To take a simple example: A "below upward" perspective on embryology focuses on the various developmental stages as they emerge; an "above downward" perspective focuses on the pre-existing genetic pattern by which the embryo is programmed to develop into an adult.

The six chapters of Part II developed an analysis of the *Interior Castle* of St. Teresa of Avila, which is a mystic's presentation of her mystical transformation. As noted above, such an analysis is an approach from "below upward"--that is, an approach that studies the process of stage-by-stage development as it occurs in the concrete. In keeping with the overall "above downward" theoretical structure of the project, however, this analysis proceeded in several steps. Following the introduction of the mystic and her text in Chapter 6, Chapter 7 studied the text for evidence of a series of changes at the level of "spirit"--that is, the way the operations of consciousness are configured.

This "interiority analysis" found considerable evidence that the model proposed in Part I is plausible as an explanation of mystical experience and transformation. First, it found that Teresa's presentation of the First through Third Dwelling Places correlates closely with Lonergan's views on "religious conversion" and with our previous discussion of "mystical transformation in the broad sense," in which the transcendent ground of consciousness is mediated within intentional consciousness and has the primary effect of increasing order, responsibility, and active love in daily life. Second, the transition Teresa describes in the Fourth and Fifth Dwelling Places correlates with our discussion of the shift to a "contemplative mediation" of the transcendent ground of consciousness, in which the operations of intentional consciousness are radically transcended. Third, Teresa's presentation of specifically mystical experience in the Fifth through Seventh Dwelling Places correlates well with our discussion of the mystical reconfiguration of consciousness as the transcendent ground is mediated directly in human consciousness.

The interiority analysis is quite successful in verifying that the proposed model is a plausible account of both the specificity of mystical transformation and its isomorphism with the general structure of religious conversion. It finds considerable evidence that the general intersubjective implications of religious conversion--i.e., increased harmoniousness, social responsibility, and love--are a constitutive dimension of mystical transformation in both its "broad" and "narrow" senses. The interiority analysis also provides evidence for the validity of employing the notion of a "state of intersubjectivity" as the prime analogue for "mystical experience in the narrow sense."

This kind of analysis, however, was less successful in showing how mystical transformation concretely transforms for the better the mystic's "intersubjective field"--that is, the way he or she enters into actual intersubjective networks in a way that enhances the building up of genuine community. Without this, the theory remains a plausible but unverified "bright idea." For this more concrete level of verification, a shift must be made to a yet more radically "below upward" perspective--namely, that of psychology.

In the context of this inquiry, what was required was a psychological perspective that is rigorously "empirical"--i.e., it deals only with intraworldly psychological factors[4]--but that also leaves a "space" for the specifically mystical dimension--i.e., it acknowledges the non-objectifiable "more" of the human person, of which psychological structures are the concrete mediation. This perspective was found in the psychoanalytic "self psychology" of Heinz Kohut. Chapters 8 and 9 presented the essential terms and relations of self psychology and made the case for the appropriateness of employing it in this inquiry.

Chapter 10 carried out a full-fledged self-psychological analysis of the imagery of the *Interior Castle*. It found evidence on the psychological level that Teresa's mystical transformation involved, first, the healing and integration of the self and, subsequently, its relativization as a yet deeper level of unification emerged. Chapter 11, finally, examined a broader level of evidence of the transformation of Teresa's participation in human intersubjectivity and correlated the stages of her mystical transformation with the expansion of her role within widening "group selves."

---

[4]The contrast here is with Jungian psychology, which often asserts the influence of psychological factors that cannot be accounted for by intraworldly dynamics. For discussion, see "The Self: A Reprise" in Chapter 8.

C. Discussion of Potential Implications

Implications for Theological Method and Foundations

In addition to its direct contribution to the debate on an adequate theory of mystical experience and transformation, the fruits of this project may also contribute to work on theological foundations and theological method.

In regard to theological foundations, the project aims to lay the groundwork for an argument that if mystical experience is correctly understood, it will necessarily be acknowledged to be at the very heart of the theological enterprise. To do theology is to seek to understand and articulate the mediation of the transcendent within human life. Theologians must be mystics at least in the "broad sense"; that is, they must be experiencing and appropriating that mediation as it transforms their intentional consciousness. Theologians have a responsibility to practice the disciplines (prayer, reflection, examination of consciousness, etc.) that foster this experience and appropriation.

Even with assiduous discipline, not all will become mystics in the "narrow sense." Yet it is these mystics who are gifted with the most profound insights into the subject matter of theology--namely, the living reality of the transcendent. This makes it all the more incumbent upon theologians to seek ways to understand the insights of the great mystics and to appropriate them within trained theological reflection. By developing an explanatory model of mysticism in terms of the general structures of the human subject, this inquiry provides a framework within which to do that.

In regard to theological method, the project also makes a creative contribution. Its methodological claim is that both transcendental and hermeneutical methods can be--in fact, ought to be--combined within a single, integral theological inquiry. While transcendental ("above downward") method is essential for grounding a fully critical and explanatory perspective, hermeneutical ("below upward") method is essential for studying the concreteness of the phenomena which one is purporting to explain.

In today's theological climate, the more controversial claim is that transcendental method is essential and perhaps even primary. Following Lonergan, we traced evidence that this claim is justified by the structure of the human subject, whose "ground" must be affirmed to be transcendent[5] to the subject-object structure within which hermeneutical method is ultimately confined. The project suggests that for the theologian, whose specific concern is with the mediation of the transcendent[6] within human life, this affirmation is not optional; it is the *sine qua non* of doing responsible theology.

Neverthless, the specific way this inquiry has combined the two components of method is not the only way. Instead of beginning with a transcendental analysis and then proceeding to the hermeneutical one, a theologian could begin with the hermeneutical analysis and build from that a case for the necessity of a transcendental analysis. To do this well would require a far lengthier process than the present approach, since in working from "below upward" one would have to consider all possibly relevant data and all possible explanatory configurations of the data before being able to claim the adequacy of one's specific "above downward" interpretation. This would be a worthy project--perhaps in some ways even more worthy than the present endeavor--but it would probably also require a lifetime's labor.

The present "short cut" approach is justified first of all in that it does offer a plausible and valuable interpretation of the data. A more fundamental justification, however, is that if the two components of method are really integral with one another, one will necessarily find

[5]Here, "transcendent" refers to the non-objectifiable, yet "natural" mystery of the human person; the only claim being made in regard to a "supernatural" dimension is that if such a dimension has reality, it is in relation to this "naturally transcendent" dimension of the human person that it will primarily be manifested.

[6]In this usage, "transcendent" includes what is classically called the "supernatural."

oneself employing both in a "scissors fashion" in any inquiry. The issue is not whether one uses both; the issue is whether one does so carefully and consciously, aware of the appropriate times and techniques of each.

Implications for the Psychology of Religion

In this project the study of religious psychology has been contextualized as an adjunct to the primary theological inquiry. Yet many readers--especially those who are uninterested in, or who disagree with, the theological approach employed in Part I--may find most value in the psychological portion of the study, even apart from its larger context.

The approach to psychological analysis developed here makes several contributions to the psychology of religion. The first is simply the in-depth exploration of the applicability of the principles of Kohut's self psychology to religious experience. The study provides evidence that Kohut's approach may offer a viable alternative to the predominant psychoanalytical interpretations of religion, namely, the Freudian approach, which tends to reduce religion to an epiphenomenon of intraworldly psychodynamics, and the Jungian approach, which tends to place religion in a supraworldly--and yet not, from a theological perspective, wholly "transcendent"--realm.

Self psychology, as interpreted here, offers a way to understand religion as a normal, growth-oriented dimension of human experience in mature phases as well as in primitive ones. For practicing psychologists, many of whom are religious agnostics, this interpretation offers a much more positive and helpful way of understanding their clients' religious experiences. Thus, the findings of the project can potentially have beneficial implications on the very practical level of psychotherapeutic praxis.

On the theoretical level, the inquiry goes on to develop the position that the notion of "self" in self psychology can serve as a bridge between the strictly empirical dimension of human personhood, and the explicitly transcendent dimension which is the preserve of theological reflection. Although the agnostics in the psychological community may be unable to affirm the reality of the transcendent dimension, they may nevertheless be able to accept this position as a framework for dialogue about the role, value, and dynamics of religious experience in human life. For religious believers, on the other hand, this position offers a way to allay fears of psychological reductionism while at the same time affirming that non-religious psychological exploration and insight has positive value for religious theory and practice.

Two contributions that this inquiry makes to the understanding of religious experience are especially noteworthy. One is the shift away from an individualistic focus. While accepting that depth psychology is necessarily a study of the intrapsychic dynamics of individual psyches, the project develops insight into how these dynamics are constitutively involved in "intersubjective fields" that reverberate on interpersonal, social and political levels. A second important contribution is psychological contextualization of the "bare consciousness" experience. By indicating how this experience stands at a transition-point, both psychologically and spiritually, the inquiry helps to clarify its value and role, as well as its distinction from phenomenologically-similar pathological experiences.

Implications for Spiritual and Pastoral Practice

For those whose concern is the practical one of fostering their own or others' spiritual growth, our analysis of the *Interior Castle* offers consoling insight into the full humanity of a great mystic. Knowing so well the mundane reality of the typical human interior life, these spiritual seekers and directors find great fascination in the exploration of how Teresa's unique world of psychological imagery, rooted in her familial, cultural and political experiences and structured (as every human psyche is) by deep affective and sexual dynamics, was the very material within which mystical transformation was mediated.

Yet, if the project has been successful, this insight into the mystic's humanness has been accomplished without in any way reducing the greatness and uniqueness of her special charism of mystical knowledge and union. By articulating an explanatory model of both the continuity and the distinction between general religious conversion and special mystical transformation, the inquiry provides a framework within which appropriate guidelines for all stages of the spiritual life can be developed.

Finally, perhaps the most significant pastoral implication of this project is its indication of the integral relationship between mystical transformation and social praxis. The transformation that mystics undergo, though deeply interior, reverberates profoundly through all the intersubjective networks in which they participate. The contemplative life need not be an individualistic or effete pursuit; rather, it may be an act of the highest social responsibility.

APPENDIX A

BACKGROUND TO THE NOTION OF MEDIATION

Lonergan's notion of mediation, says Martin Joseph Matustik, is "a more elaborate form of implicit definition."[1] A definition is an attempt to pin down or "fix" meaning. Lonergan distinguishes three types of definitions: nominal definition, which fixes meaning by clarifying the place of a sign within an established linguistic system; explanatory definition, which fixes meaning by setting forth the immanent structures of the objects referred to; and implicit definition, which "consists in explanatory definition without nominal definition."[2]

Implicit definition, in other words, moves completely away from any particular instanciation of the defined structure. "The significance of implicit definition," Lonergan wrote, "is its complete generality. The omission of nominal definitions is the omission of a restriction to the objects which, in the first instance, one happens to be thinking about."[3] What remains when the "matter" is thus eliminated is a "functional" expression, the primary analogate for which is the mathematical formula. This is an expression in which, as Matustik summarized, "the terms fix the relations and the relations fix the terms, and the function fixes both."[4]

This statement of Matustik's is a close paraphrase of a key sentence from Lonergan's *Insight*: "Let us say, then, that for every basic

---

[1]Matustik, *Mediation of Deconstruction*, p. 18.

[2]Lonergan, *Insight*, p. 12.

[3]Ibid., pp. 12-13.

[4]Matustik, *Mediation of Deconstruction*, p. 18.

insight there is a circle of terms and relations, such that the terms fix the relations, the relations fix the terms, and the insight fixes both."[5] Here Lonergan asserts an isomorphism between an insight--any insight--and implicit definition. Any insight, in other words, involves a grasp of a structure of being which *could* be expressed within the total generality of a functional expression. Insight occurs, of course, only as an insight into a particular existent; but its teleology is toward being itself.

An example may help to clarify this. An example of a mundane, common-sense insight is the sudden realization that the reason the checkout clerk is glaring angrily at you is because you have brought a full basket of purchases into the "ten items only" line. What are the terms and relations here? The terms are a full basket of purchases, a sign indicating that one may bring only ten items into this line, and a glaring clerk. The relations are a contradiction between the full basket and the required ten items, and a correspondence between this contradiction and the rise of anger in the clerk. One can say that in this situation the "terms fix the relations" in that these particular material realities are intrinsically related in these ways; and the "relations fix the terms" in that these relations (of contradiction and correspondence) define the sorts of things that will elicit this kind of situation.

To say that "the insight fixes both" is to say that the insight involves a sudden grasp of the terms, the relations among them, and the fact that these terms and relations mutually imply one another. As Lonergan put it, "All the concepts tumble out together, for all are needed to express adequately a single insight. All are coherent, for coherence basically means that all hang together from a single insight."[6]

In such a mundane situation, one would rarely (if ever) move from the common sense insight toward an effort to express it in the generality of a functional expression. If one did, however, one might come up with something like, "Breaking established rules makes the enforcers

---

[5]Lonergan, *Insight*, p. 12.

[6]Ibid.

angry"; or, still more abstractly, "The introduction of a contradiction within a structured system creates chaos." Perhaps it would even be possible to move to a mathematical expression of this insight.

Obviously, it would be quite counterproductive consciously to undertake such an abstracting process as a general procedure of daily life. The point, however, is that the insight itself already implicitly enacts this procedure. The insight is a grasp of a set of terms, a set of relations among them, and the fact that the terms and relations mutually imply one another. It is possible to articulate this in a nominal definition (i.e., in common sense language as related to this specific situation) or in an explanatory definition (in theoretical language as a general principle for this type of situation) or in an implicit definition (in a totally abstract functional expression). However, whether or how it is articulated is not really of the essence; what is essential is the dynamic, structured activity of self-transcendence--the "arc" between the concrete and the abstract. One might say that every insight enacts the implicit definition of implicit definition.

As Matustik noted, the notion of mediation is a yet more generalized form of the notion of implicit definition. Where Lonergan's notion of mediation goes beyond that of others is in integrally linking mediation as an explanatory principle of human knowing, and mediation as an explanatory principle of existence itself. The notion of implicit definition is derived from a grasp of the structures of the expressions of meaning, but the notion of mediation includes and sublates this within a grasp of the structures of being.

The link is made thus: human consciousness is intelligent and, through insight, can discern intelligible structure within concrete existents. Through self-appropriation, the conscious subject can gain "insight into insight" and discover intelligible structure within knowing itself. Human knowers, then, are both intelligible and intelligent: they are mediated (structured) and mediating (generative of structured knowledge, activity, etc.). The isomorphism between the structure of the knower and the structure of the known is verified principally in self-appropriation, when the knower *is* the known, and secondarily in other inquiries, through grasp of the isomorphism of implicit definitions.

Matustik concludes, "Literally, the what of one's nature is mediation (hence implicit definition) of the integral structure of the universe."[7] The center of immediacy is the subject-as-subject, which is mediated in the dynamic self-transcending activity of the operations of consciousness. This structure of immediacy and mediation is isomorphic with the structure of being. One cannot come to know either oneself or being directly, at the center of immediacy, but one can know both in the mediation of the operations of consciousness.[8]

The Transposition of Aristotle and Hegel

Lonergan developed his notion of mediation as a post-Hegelian retrieval of Aristotle's notion of mediation. Aristotle primarily understood mediation as a principle of logic; the middle term of a syllogism mediates between the subject and its attribute. The attribute is immediate in the middle term, but mediated in the subject. To understand a syllogism is to grasp its middle term, that is, to grasp the immediate premise or basic truth (i.e., a necessary structure of being) that is manifested immediately in the attribute and mediately in the subject.[9]

Syllogisms are concerned with relationships among definitions. In Lonergan's example, the syllogism is "All human beings are mortal." The middle term--that is, the definition that mediates between the terms of the syllogism--is compositeness, or the quality of consisting of parts. Compositeness is immediate in mortality, because what can come apart (die) has to consist of parts in the first place; it is mediated in human

---

[7]Matustik, *Mediation of Deconstruction*, p. 175.

[8]See ibid., pp. 59-65.

[9]See Aristotle, *Analytica Posteriora*, in *The Basic Works of Aristotle*, ed. Richard McKeon (NY: Random House, 1941), especially I,31--II,4.

beings, who (like all composite beings) do eventually come apart and die.[10]

For Hegel, mediation was the principle of the self-becoming of consciousness through its own objectification. He wrote:

> [M]ediating is nothing but self-identity working itself out through an active self-directed process; or, in other words, it is reflection into self, the aspect in which the ego is for itself, objective to itself. . . . The ego, or becoming in general, this process of mediating, is, because of its being simple, just immediacy coming to be, and is immediacy itself.[11]

In Hegel's system mediation, grasped as a principle of consciousness, becomes a principle of being. As an idealist, Hegel placed the emphasis on the concept or "Absolute Idea" (*Begriffe*) that functions teleologically to drive and define the entire process of self-mediating consciousness. "Consciousness is an activity which disengages universality from particularity"[12]--and universality is enshrined in concepts. As Lonergan summarized Hegel's position:

> Concepts are related immediately or mediately; everything reduces to concepts; therefore, everything is related immediately or mediately. Everthing aspires to the level of the *Begriffe*; consequently, the relations between concepts are found in an imperfect form on an inferior level in everything else, as processes toward the concept.[13]

Aristotle's notion of mediation represents the classical concern with necessary knowledge, while Hegel's represents the modern concern with the self-becoming of consciousness. Lonergan's claim is that Aristotle's

---

[10]Lonergan, "Mediation of Christ in Prayer," p. 1.

[11]G.W.F. Hegel, *The Phenomenology of Mind*, trans. J.B. Baillie (New York: Harper & Row, 1967), p. 82.

[12]Joseph L. Navickas, *Consciousness and Reality: Hegel's Philosophy of Subjectivity* (The Hague: Martinus Nijhoff, 1976), p. 21.

[13]Lonergan, "Mediation of Christ in Prayer," pp. 1-2.

notion contains the seeds of a modern, or even post-modern, conceptualization of mediation which can fully include and sublate the Hegelian perspective.

Much of Lonergan's thought actually draws heavily on basic Hegelian ideas, such as the self-mediation of consciousness, dialectic, and sublation. Lonergan acknowledged this,[14] but clearly distinguished his own position. Hegelian dialectic is "conceptualist, closed, necessitarian, and immanental," while Lonergan's position is "intellectualist, open, factual, and normative."[15] The heart of the difference is Hegel's inability to deal with the concrete and factual.[16] In terms of Lonergan's "canons of methodical analysis,"[17] Hegel is a master of the latter two ("Be explanatory" and "Focus on operations"), but completely fails to implement the first ("Be concrete").

The result is that Hegel's notion of mediation, while purporting to be an explanatory principle of all reality (rather than simply of logic), ends up reducing reality to concepts. Lonergan, by implementing his canon of concreteness (along with the other two canons), aims to develop the notion of mediation as an explanatory principle of the concrete operations of consciousness as actually knowing reality. To do this, he returns to Aristotle.

Aristotle, says Lonergan, really did not limit his formulation of mediation to the field of logic, that is, the field of the relations of subjects and predicates. He also sought to apply it to the more basic question of how we know the things themselves. Aristotle's answer to this question names the four causes, "end, agent, matter, and form." Form is the most important of these, because it is when we grasp a thing's form that we really know what the thing is.

---

[14]Lonergan, *Insight*, p. 374.

[15]Ibid., p. 421.

[16]Lonergan, *Insight*, pp. 372-74, 421-23; idem, *Understanding and Being*, pp. 309-11.

[17]See "The 'Canons of Methodical Analysis'" in Chapter 2.

In Aristotle's later works, Lonergan points out, the form is termed *to ti en einai* (form), not *to ti estin* (definition).[18] Lonergan believes that Aristotle was doing his best to get at the distinction between the insight--the implicit grasp of the structure of being--and the concept, in which all the terms and relations are explicitly spelled out. Aristotle did that by implicitly making an analogy: as the subject of a proposition is to its middle and its attribute, so a particular existent is to its form and its matter.[19] The being, then, is immediate in its form and mediated in its matter.

Aristotle, of course, did not work out the general form of the notion of mediation as a principle of being itself, nor did he grasp its implications on the levei of interiority. As Lonergan put it, "His expression was under quite different conditions. The reflective, introspective type of psychology and talk about self-appropriation were not yet possible."[20] Yet, in Lonergan's interpretation, Aristotle's notion of mediation is potentially more concrete than Hegel's because it is an "insight into insight." It required the impetus of Hegel's counterposition, which correctly identified the source of knowledge in the immediacy of consciousness but incorrectly identified the primary analogue of the mediated as the concept (rather than the insight), to press this Aristotelian "insight into insight" forward into the modern age.

Lonergan's position, then, is that mediation is a principle of being, the most adequate analogy for which is the dynamic operation of consciousness and its production of insights. Mediation is not to be understood, as in Hegel, in terms of the way each concept mediates all others and the totality of concepts, but in terms of the way the operations of consciousness mediate the structure of being itself. Matustik summarizes, "If Lonergan's notion of mediation is his transposition of both Aristotelian and Hegelian logic, and of their

---

[18]Lonergan, *Understanding and Being*, pp. 58-60.

[19]Aristotle, *Metaphysica*, in *Basic Works of Aristotle*; Books VI and VII.

[20]Lonergan, *Understanding and Being*, p. 60.

respective philosophies of nature, then self-mediation by operational development is his transposition of both Hegel's and contemporary phenomenology's self-mediation."[21]

[21]Matustik, *Mediation of Deconstruction*, p. 42.

APPENDIX B

LITERARY SOURCES AND INFLUENCES ON THE TEXT

Although Teresa was in many ways a highly original thinker, nearly every one of the similes and allegories through which she characteristically expresses her insights has multiple roots in the expressions of others. Here we will focus particularly on the direct and indirect sources of the main image of the *Interior Castle*, the "interior castle" itself. We will begin with the more diffuse cultural and literary sources, proceed from there to the textual sources which Teresa actually or probably read, and conclude with experiential sources.

General Sources and Influences

Women in sixteenth century Spain received little or no formal education, but those of the upper classes usually learned to read, write and cipher. Teresa says that she was an avid reader even as a girl, following her mother's "bad example" by devouring numerous *libros de caballería* (novels of chivalry--the "Harlequin romances" of the day; *Life* 2:1). These adventure stories were filled with florid imagery of castles and kings, soldiers and swords, battles and victories. When she wrote the *Interior Castle* it had been almost fifty years since she had read these, but the youthful shaping of her imagination, combined with the strong contemporary fascination with the trappings of kingship, war, and the exploits of the *conquistadores*, no doubt contributed to the ease with which she could elaborate her thought in these terms.

The young Teresa also read many lives of the saints (*Life* 1:4). When she entered the monastery, she continued to read widely among the spiritual books available in Spanish. These were what were called *los buenos libros*--devotional books, such as collections of edifying stories, the lives of the Saints, and treatises on asceticism.[22] As will be discussed below, certain books influenced her more deeply than others; but her broad familiarity with the whole milieu of spiritual writing means that multiple direct or indirect influences can often be hypothesized for any given image or idea.

Since she did not read Latin she could not read the bible or scholastic theology, which were not available to her in translation. Yet biblical phrases, images and doctrines pervaded her liturgical milieu and were daily expounded by preachers. Teresa valued scripture very highly, asserting (in regard to the Song of Songs) that even without understanding the Latin "my soul is stirred and recollected more than by devotional books written in the language I understand."[23] She herself alludes to the scriptural text "In my Father's house there are many dwelling places" (John 14:2) as a conscious source of her imagery of "dwelling places" (I:1,1).

Current theological insights were also constantly available through preaching and through conversation with those who did read Latin. Teresa adored conversation and was in turn much sought after in the parlor; at times this may have been a dissipating influence, but it also provided a forum for the mutual exploration of the spiritual questions of the moment. Teresa undoubtedly learned a great deal in these lively exchanges--both from those who were able to provide her with helpful new vocabulary and insights, and from those with whom she had to find a way to express her experience-based disagreement.

The more formal interchange with confessors--which, at that time, included what we would now term spiritual direction--was another forum within which Teresa received the benefit of others' learning. She had

---

[22]Hoornaert, *St. Teresa in Her Writings*, p. 107.

[23]Prologue to the *Meditations on the Song of Songs*, in Kavanaugh and Rodriguez, *Collected Works*, vol. 2.

a wide variety of confessors and advisors over the years, including Dominicans, Franciscans, Jesuits, *beatas*, and pious laity as well as Carmelites. Thus she was exposed to many different approaches to spiritual and theological issues. Despite her lack of formal education--which she always lamented--Teresa was a well-informed woman, deeply conversant with the cultural and theological milieu of her time.

One element of that milieu was the common use of architectural imagery for spiritual realities. Within Christianity, this imagery had roots as far back as the patristic period; among those who employed it were such diverse figures as Albert the Great, Hugh of St. Victor, and Henry Suso.[24] As Chorpenning summarizes, "The symbols most frequently employed were the city, the castle, the house, and the temple. The method of the medieval masters was to associate, say, each article of faith, or each stage of the spiritual life, with an appropriate part of the building."[25] This method was extremely helpful in organizing complex material for presentation, and it also assisted the process of implanting the material in the reader or hearer's memory.

The Islamic tradition also employed architectural imagery, some aspects of which are even closer to Teresa's imagery than that found in the Christian tradition. In a book entitled *Maqamat al-qulub* (Spanish translation: *Moradas de los corazones*), the ninth century Abu l-Hasan al-Nuri de Bagdad wrote of the soul in terms of seven concentric castles composed, respectively, of corundum, gold, silver, iron, copper, alum and adobe.[26] Later Islamic writers further developed the image.[27]

---

[24]On architectural imagery in general, see Henri de Lubac, *Exégèse médiévale: les quatre sens de l'Ecriture* IV (Paris: Aubier, 1964), pp. 41-60. On precedents to Teresa's use, see Robert Ricard, "Quelques remarques sur les *Moradas* de Sainte Thérèse," *Bulletin Hispanique* 42 (1945): 187-98. On its significance in the *Interior Castle*, see Joseph Chorpenning, "The Literary and Theological Method of the *Castillo Interior*," *Journal of Hispanic Philology* 3 (1979): 121-33.

[25]Chorpenning, "Literary and Theological Method," p. 124.

[26]See Luce López-Baralt, "Santa Teresa de Jesús y el Islam," *Teresianum* 23 (1982): 653-54.

Teresa would not have had direct contact with this tradition, but the pervasiveness of the Islamic influence in Spain was such that indirect influence--perhaps through conversation and preaching, even apart from the literary sources to be discussed below--is plausible.

Direct Textual Sources

Alfred Morel-Fatio, Rodolphe Hoornaert, and Gaston Etchegoyen have surveyed numerous examples of imagery similar or related to Teresa's "interior castle" image in literature with which she could have had contact.[28] Their general conclusion is that while related imagery was so widespread that it could be imbibed consciously and unconsciously from many sources, it is likely that the most significant direct sources are the *Vita Christi* of "el Cartuxano" Ludolph of Saxony;[29] Francisco de Osuna's *Tercer Abecedario Espiritual*; and Bernardino de Laredo's *Subida del Monte Sión*.[30]

Ludolph of Saxony's fourteenth century text was translated into Spanish as the *Vita Christi cartuxano romançado* early in the sixteenth century, and it was widely read and admired. Teresa refers to reading it in *Life* 38:9. There is evidence that its affective, image-filled meditations on scriptural vignettes influenced Teresa profoundly.[31] Ludolph did not employ architectural symbolism, but he did image the

---

[27]See Miguel Asín Palacios, "El símil de los castillos y moradas del alma en la mística islámica y en Santa Teresa," *Al-Andalús* 9 (1946): 263-74.

[28]Alfred Morel-Fatio, "Les Lectures de Sainte Thérèse," *Bulletin Hispanique* 10 (1908): 17-67; Rodolphe Hoornaert, *Sainte Thérèse écrivain*; Etchegoyen, *L'Amour divin*.

[29]Ludolphus de Saxonia, *Vita Christi: Selections, Latin and English on opposite pages* (Salzburg: Institut fur Englische Sprache und Literatur, 1973).

[30]Bernardino de Laredo, *The Ascent of Mount Sion*, trans. E. Allison Peers (New York: Harper, 1952).

[31]See Morel-Fatio, "Les Lectures"; also García de la Concha, *El Arte Literario*, pp. 57-62; Hoornaert, *Sainte Térèse Ecrivain*, pp. 340-44.

spiritual life in terms of a battle in which loyalty to the king, Jesus Christ, is all-important.

As noted above, Osuna's *Tercer Abecedario* was Teresa's spiritual reading at a crucial moment in her youthful conversion to contemplative prayer. Part 4, chapter 3 of this text compares the heart to a castle which must be carefully guarded against its enemies, the flesh, the world and the devil. The heart of the just, Osuna contines, is an earthly paradise in which the Lord dwells (*mora*) with delight. Teresa's copy of the *Tercer Abecedario* is extant, and this passage is marked with marginal crosses. Part 4 of Osuna's *Cuarto Abecedario*, which Teresa may also have read, does not use the castle image but does speak of the human body as a city which becomes the "city of God" when governed by love.[32]

Teresa encountered Bernardino de Laredo's *Subida del Monte Sión* at another crucial moment in her spiritual career. She recounts in *Life* 23:12 how, shortly after her second conversion (1554), she was having great difficulty explaining her prayer experience to her advisors and found help in this book. In chapter 46 of the 1538 edition Laredo waxes eloquent over the holy city Jerusalem, a city made of crystal and precious stones.[33]

Though all of the traditions and texts mentioned so far are likely to have contributed to the development of Teresa's imagination and reflection, there is no evidence that any of them served as a direct model for her "interior castle." In every case the point being made with the imagery is quite different, or it is developed in ways that have no parallels in the *Interior Castle*. Also, in each of the other texts the

---

[32]For discussion, see Ricard, "Le symbolisme," pp. 26-28. For a more general overview of Osuna's influence on Teresa, see García de la Concha, *El Arte Literario*, pp. 65-70.

[33]"un fino cristal, que es piedra clara y preciosa." For discussion of the influence of this text, see Ricard, "Le Symbolisme," pp. 28-30. For a more general overview of Laredo's influence, see García de la Concha, *El Arte Literario*, pp. 74-78.

architectural symbolism is only one among many images, while in the *Interior Castle* it is the basic structuring principle of the whole work.[34]

Experiential Sources

It has often been suggested that certain physical experiences were even more powerful than the literary reminiscences in forming Teresa's imagination. Miguel Unamuno was convinced that it was the vision of the walled city of Avila that inspired Teresa's "castle" imagery. Others have seconded his suggestion, although often allowing that this may be only one among many influences. Nicole Pelisson added the insight that the Cathedral of Avila, which forms part of Avila's wall and has numerous towers, is strikingly reminiscent of Teresa's description in I:1,3.[35] E.W. Trueman Dicken offers as an alternative the Castillo de la Mota in Medina del Campo, which is physically a somewhat closer parallel to Teresa's "castle."[36] It seems logical to assume that these visual and spatial experiences did help to shape Teresa's imagination, even though we must seek elsewhere for the roots of the meanings she attached to the images derived from these experiences.

Genre

Each of the preceding sections in this chapter has presented a single aspect or factor in Teresa's classic text, the *Moradas del Castillo Interior*. We have discussed its setting in history and in the author's life, its individual images, its doctrinal content, its cultural and literary

[34]Chorpenning, "Literary and Theological Method," pp. 125-26.

[35]For a review of the literature on this question, see Robert Ricard, "Le Symbolisme du 'Chateau Intérieur' chez Sainte Thérèse," *Bulletin Hispanique* 67 (1965), pp. 37-40.

[36]E.W. Trueman Dicken, "The Imagery of the Interior Castle and Its Implications," *Ephemerides Carmeliticae* 21 (1970): 198-218.

predecessors. It remains to look at what makes the text a whole--and what makes it a classic.

David Tracy has commented that a text claims our attention as a classic because "an event of understanding proper to finite human beings has here found expression."[37] The root of the classic is an extraordinary event of insight into meaning. Yet that event alone is not sufficient to make a classic; it also must find an expression that communicates the insight to many--perhaps potentially even all--other human beings. The structure of that expression in its distanciation from the original event is what is termed "genre."

Elaborating on the significance of genre, Tracy writes:

> Genre does not merely classify any more than the power or impetus behind it, the imagination, merely reproduces. Genre produces the meaning of the text. Genre accomplishes this not by remaining in the participatory understanding of the original experience. Rather, the ability to employ a genre distances the author from that original experience into an expression of its meaning by way of a production of a structured whole, a work, which allows the meaning to become shareable by provoking expectations and questions in the reader . . .[38]

The question of the genre of the *Interior Castle* has not been without controversy. While the mainstream tradition has usually classified it as an allegory, some, like Rodolphe Hoornaert, have insisted that Teresa's main genre was simply "direct exposition." Suspicious of the potential for illusion in symbolical and allegorical language, Hoornaert insisted that she "employs the image only for the sake of the idea" and uses allegory only to provide an overall framework for what is more fundamentally an expository treatise.[39]

---

[37]Tracy, *The Analogical Imagination*, p. 102.

[38]Ibid., p. 129.

[39]Hoornaert, *St. Teresa in Her Writings, p. 260.*

Hoornaert's claim was a response to the fact that most of Teresa's images are better classified as similes or allegories, rather than as metaphors or symbols. Whereas metaphors and symbols stand on their own as evocative imaginative expressions of meaning, similes and allegories are more closely tied to an effort to express intellectual and doctrinal meanings. While Hoornaert saw Teresa as beginning with ideas and then clothing them in images, most commentators see the opposite: she did not experience any facility or pleasure in dealing with ideas except in the form of images, which was in any case how they naturally occurred to her.

In his reluctance to classify the *Interior Castle* as an allegory, Hoornaert participated in the modern tendency to disparage allegory. His reasons, however, were the reverse of those of most moderns. While Hoornaert feared allegory as too imaginative, the more typical modern rationale for the rejection of allegory is the notion that it is a mere pawn of the intellect and so lacks the vitality and sophistication of a true imaginative figure.[40] Some recent studies of allegory offer an analysis that moves beyond both of these disparaging views and, at the same time, gives new insights into the communicative method of the *Interior Castle*.[41]

One of the pioneers of the new evaluation of allegory, Edwin Honig, summarized his definition of the genre thus: "We find the allegorical quality in a twice-told tale written in rhetorical, or figurative, language and expressing a vital belief."[42] The allegory is "twice-told" in that it typically takes an old or traditional story and retells it for a

---

[40]For a review of the modern critique of allegory, see Edwin Honig, *Dark Conceit: The Making of Allegory* (New York: Oxford University Press, 1966), pp. 3-9, 39-54; also García de la Concha, *El Arte Literario*, pp. 230-36.

[41]Important texts in the reevaluation of allegory, in addition to the one noted in the preceding footnote, include: Angus Fletcher, *Allegory: The Theory of a Symbolic Mode* (Ithaca, NY: Cornell University Press, 1970); Rosemond Tuve, *Allegorical Imagery* (Princeton, NJ: Princeton University Press, 1966); Gay Clifford, *The Transformation of Allegory* (London: Routledge and Kegan Paul, 1974).

[42]Honig, *Dark Conceit*, p. 12.

new purpose, seeking thereby to establish a new authority that is based in the authority of the tradition and yet carries its own power. It is "rhetorical" in that it uses a set of linguistic figures as tropes to speak about something else--often, something that cannot be spoken about in more direct language.

As for its function of "expessing a vital belief," Honig argued that allegory's motivation and structure are centered around an ideal that is envisioned as ordering the cosmos and establishing the boundaries and forms of human moral existence. The ideal is an expression of the innate human tendency to visualize and to seek a "state of uninterrupted happiness or perfection."[43] This ideal, in Honig's view, serves as "the constant aim of reference to which all portions of the text or the whole subject must be related."[44]

In all these aspects, elements of the *Interior Castle* fit the basic pattern of allegory. First, as the previous section has noted, Teresa drew nearly all of her images and even the main lines of her overall structure from traditional sources. Her creative retelling of this "old story" was a *tour de force* of integration and transformation of the old for a new time and a new need. The result was a text that has become, in every sense of the word, an "authority" in the Christian mystical tradition. Second, she employed her images figuratively to speak about the mystical life, for which she knew no other language. Thirdly, the whole narrative is motivated and structured by the "ideal" of radical union with God--a union which is placed at the beginning and foundation of the narrative with the inaugural image of the "diamond castle" and which further serves as the culminating denouement toward which the narrative builds, the "spiritual marriage."

It is also noteworthy how many similarities there are between the typical structure of allegorical narrative and the basic narrative structure

---

[43]Ibid., p. 149.

[44]Ibid., p. 29; cf. also pp. 13-14.

of the *Interior Castle*.[45] Each begins with a dreamlike or visionary "threshold symbol" (in the *Interior Castle*, the crystal castle) and continues with the "hero" journeying through many ordeals, always guided by a "beneficent intelligence that impels and even shares the hero's consciousness."[46] The adventures conclude with an "achievement of complete self-consciousness."[47]

Despite these similarities, there are certain difficulties with the classification of the *Interior Castle* as an allegory. Most literary allegories carefully build up their presentation of deeper meaning by the detailed elaboration of interconnected imagery with a definite story line and meaning on the literal level as well as on the "spiritual" one. While the images of the castle and of the movement toward its interior do provide the overall structure of the text, Teresa does not elaborate them in any detail. What is more, she often abandons them for chapters at a time. Even when aspects of this set of images are mentioned, they are often surrounded by a plethora of other images with no direct connection to the main allegory.

Helmut Hatzfeld describes this as a method of "image concatenation,"[48] in which one image spawns a whole series of new images and ideas, each of which in turn may set off a new series. Teresa's anacoluthic style pervades her narrative at every level, from sentence structure to paragraph structure to larger units. Hatzfeld likens it to "a mirror technique, . . . a theater within a theater, a picture within a picture. A great symbol develops a new imagery and this imagery

---

[45]Cf. Ibid., pp. 69-85.

[46]Ibid., p. 78.

[47]Ibid., p. 85.

[48]Helmut Hatzfeld, *Santa Teresa de Avila* (New York: Twayne, 1969), pp. 39-40.

proliferates into almost numberless new metaphors. The frame almost cannot contain this plethora of imagination."[49]

In his major study of the literary characteristics of Teresa's opus, Victor García de la Concha examines this paradox of scattering and coherence more deeply and concludes that Teresa's writing is structured by semantic "isotopes" in the form of a series of axial allegories which form richly interlinked networks of ideas and images at various levels. He concludes,

> If the value of a work is proportional to the density of relations that can be established among all the levels of its structure, there is no doubt that, regardless of their scanty development, independent of their origins and of their level of originality, despite, finally, their continual shifting in relation to the ideas, the teresian similes and allegories are generative axes of an extraordinary literary richness, manifested in a network of interdependencies.[50]

In the attempt to delineate the genre of the *Interior Castle*, it is necessary to acknowledge that while allegory is essential to both its narrative macrostructure and its imagistic microstructure, the forms and principles of other genres are operative as well. As Elias Rivers has noted, the genre most natural to Teresa was really the spoken one; "For her . . . writing is an inferior substitute for talking."[51] A conversationalist at heart, for the most part she did not consciously plan out her writings. What is more, beyond changing a word or a phrase here and there (usually for the sake of the censors), she did not

---

[49]Hatzfeld, *Santa Teresa*, p. 61. Note that Hatzfeld uses the terms "symbol" and "metaphor" loosely here.

[50]García de la Concha, *El Arte Literario*, p. 274; my translation.

[51]Elias Rivers, "The Vernacular Mind of St. Teresa," *Carmelite Studies* 3 (1984), p. 126. On Teresa's predilection for conversation, cf. also Hoornaert, *St. Teresa in Her Writings*, p. 111.

rewrite.[52] As a result, her texts are in many ways an unself-conscious creative synthesis of a variety of the genres which she had encountered in her own reading.

One of the genres which has been noted as most significant in the formation of Teresa's imagination is hagiography--the stories of the lives of the saints, which she read in great abundance as a young woman and continued to appreciate throughout her life. Commentator Joseph Chorpenning has proposed what he called "autohagiography"--that is, the story of the writer's life told according to the classical conventions of hagiography--as an alternative structuring principle for Teresa's writings.[53] In regard to the *Interior Castle*, he summarizes:

> While allegory may provide a structural principle for the [*Interior Castle*], it is the hagiographical pattern and point of view which unify its content and make it intelligible . . . . In the [*Interior Castle*] the spiritual life is charted from the viewpoint of the soul's friendship with God, and according to the hagiographical pattern of commonplaces, specifically demonology, favors, virtues, and the mystique of martyrdom and its substitutes.[54]

The "autohagiography" thesis must be taken with a grain of salt; Teresa certainly would not have consciously compared herself to the extraordinary saints. On the other hand, her task in writing the *Interior Castle* was a difficult one: to present her own experience--essentially, to write a spiritual autobiography--in entirely generic terms, never allowing

---

[52]Except, that is, when her confessors or advisors insisted upon it--not for literary reasons, but because of their doctrinal and ecclesial concerns. Their demands account for the existence of two versions of the *Life* and the *Way*. No such demands were made in regard to the *Interior Castle*.

[53]Joseph Chorpenning, "St. Teresa's Presentation of Her Religious Experience," *Carmelite Studies* 3 (1984): 152-88. For a fuller presentation of the "autohagiography" thesis, see Chorpenning's unpublished STL dissertation, "The Theological Method of St. Teresa of Avila's *Interior Castle*." See also Joseph Baudry, "Pédagogie thérésienne de l'imitation des saints dans le livre de la *Vida*," *Teresianum* 33 (1982): 587-618.

[54]Chorpenning, "St. Teresa's Presentation," p. 174.

the personal nature of the account to become explicit. Whether used consciously or unconsciously, the genres of the lives of the saints and of the classical accounts of spiritual development undoubtedly provided apt models for this endeavor.

This, however, does not take away from the fact that allegory appears to be the more significant overall genre. Joel Fineman has noted that "allegory seems regularly to surface in critical or polemical atmospheres, when for political or metaphysical reasons there is something that cannot be said."[55] Teresa, unable to speak directly about her mystical transformation for both political *and* metaphysical reasons, resorted to a form of linguistic expression designed for exactly this sort of circumstance.[56]

In a subsequent article Chorpenning himself strove to reconcile his discovery of elements of the hagiographical genre with the more traditional affirmation of allegorical structure. Drawing on recent research on Augustine's *Confessions*, he examines how allegory can function as an imagistic representation of autobiographical insight.[57] Thus, he argues, autohagiography and allegory as structuring principles of the *Interior Castle* are "neither in conflict nor mutually exclusive."[58]

The particular value of this work on elements of hagiography in Teresa's writings is that it gives insight into how her mind creatively synthesized the various "old stories" she had at hand into the "new story" which she was inspired to tell. The extraordinary authority of the

---

[55]Joel Fineman, "The Structure of Allegorical Desire," in Stephen J. Greenblatt, ed., *Allegory and Representation* (Baltimore, MD: Johns Hopkins University Press, 1981), p. 28.

[56]Cf. also García de la Concha, *El Arte Literario*, p. 236, where he quotes Gay Clifford's *The Transformations of Allegory* to the effect that allegory always communicates something that is "in some degree hermetic, too complex to be rendered in baldly prescriptive or descriptive language."

[57]Joseph Chorpenning, "St. Teresa of Avila as Allegorist: Chapters 11-22 of the *Libro de la Vida*," *Studia Mystica* 9 (Spring 1986): 3-22.

[58]Chorpenning, "St. Teresa of Avila as Allegorist," p. 16.

resulting text bespeaks the power of both her synthesis of the old and her creative leap to newness. Honig observes that allegory's struggle to create a new authority often arises in "periods of disrupted and changing forms," when a culture has a deep need to reformulate and re-create its own ideals.[59] Teresa's work, appearing just as the Church began to be directly confronted by the cultural revolution associated with the move into the modern age, is just such a re-presentation of the most fundamental "ideal" of Christianity.

A more definitive discussion of literary issues in regard to the *Interior Castle* is not possible within the limitations of this inquiry. Most significant for our purposes here is the insight this limited review has afforded into Teresa's extraordinary creativity and its significance within her intersubjective milieu. The body of the present text focuses on close study of the *Interior Castle* for evidence of how that creativity was manifested at the level of cognitive and psychological structures.

---

[59]Honig, Dark Conceit, p. 93.

APPENDIX C

SELF PSYCHOLOGY AND THE PSYCHOLOGY OF GROUPS

From a self-psychological perspective, it is not helpful to characterize persons who make special contributions to groups as "less narcissistic" than others, as is often implied by such notions as "selflessness," "unselfishness," "living for others," etc. In self psychology, "narcissism" and "intersubjectivity" are complementary, not contradictory; the essential insight of self psychology is simply that it is the human being's "self" that structures his or her experience of, and interaction with, others. As Kohut remarked after years of working on collaborative projects with others, narcissism can be

> a spur for constructive planning and collaborative action, if integrated with and subordinated to social and cultural purposes; . . . [or] a source of sterile dissension and destructive conflict, if in the service of unneutralized ambition or of rationalized rage.[60]

The appropriate question to ask is how a person's structures of narcissism--the structures of his or her self-world--are able to have a powerful and positive effect on the intersubjective field which they create with other persons. This shifts concern away from a simple scale of "more" or "less," acknowledging that a very wide variety of different personality structures can be making positive contributions in quite different ways. Before considering the specific case of Teresa, we must first consider the general psychology of groups.

---

[60]Kohut, "On Leadership," p. 51.

The Group Self

In Chapter 8 the self-psychological view of intersubjectivity was discussed in a strictly theoretical, experience-distant context. Kohut himself considered it in the more experience-near context of the "group self." Kohut postulated that when groups of persons experience a period of sustained mutual engagement, they may form a "group self" structure with similar function, patterns, and dynamics to those of an individual self.

The group self is formed out of the "sum total of those clusters of interconnected experiences of each individual that prevail in consequence of his temporary or continuous submersion into the group."[61] Once it is formed, the group self lives out its own trajectory with some degree of imperviousness to changes in personnel. Individuals who join the group at a later stage of the trajectory either are attracted by the established patterns and freely choose to enter into them, or are simply assimilated into them whether they like it or not.

Like the individual self, the group self is patterned primarily by an energic arc between ambitions ("mirrored *self*object greatness" and ideals ("admired self*object* perfections")."[62] The third major area of self structure, talents and skills reinforced by alter-ego selfobjects, is also important in group psychology. The point at which such a structure "gels" within a group often cannot be pinpointed exactly (as is also true in the case of the individual infant), but the group self can only be created and sustained within the context of a matrix of empathic selfobjects. The selfobjects of a group are its leaders and heroes, as well as the leading representatives of its culture--its "artists, political seers, prophets, historians."[63]

For Kohut, the healthiness of a group is largely a function of the maturity of its "group narcissism." Freud had suggested that groups are

---

[61]Kohut, "Self Psychology and the Sciences," p. 82.

[62]Kohut, "Self Psychology and the Sciences," p. 82.

[63]Kohut, "The Psychoanalyst and the Historian," pp. 218-19.

bonded together by a shared ego-ideal--a set of idealized values and standards held in common by all the individual members.[64] Kohut added that it is equally possible for groups to be held together by a shared grandiose self, manifested in common ambitions and in intense pride in group participation. Either type of bonding may be found in both constructive and destructive groups, although it is perhaps most common for very constructive groups to have the idealizing pattern of bonding and for very destructive groups to have the grandiose pattern of bonding. The really decisive factor in determining the constructive potential of a group, however, remains the degree to which narcissism is mature or remains archaic.

The maturity of a group's narcissism will be seen primarily in its relations with its selfobjects.[65] The group self may form either through "gross, archaic, essentially unstable identifications" with its selfobject-figures, or it may gain a more stable structure by gradual transmuting internalizations of selfobject sustenance offered by "the interpretative presence of many active and influential minds."[66] A weak group self is prone to self pathology in the form of empty depression, lack of vitality, fragmentation, and rage. These make the group vulnerable to archaic identifications and selfobject transferences to leaders who offer them instantaneous "healing," often through the promise of war and aggression (i.e., unrestrained narcissistic rage).[67]

The healthy group self, on the other hand, exists in a richly supportive environment where language, art, music tradition, etc. express and reinforce group cohesion, group ambition and group ideals.

---

[64]See especially Sigmund Freud, "Group Psychology and the Analysis of the Ego," *Standard Edition* 18:65-143.

[65]Kohut, "On Leadership," pp. 54-56.

[66]Kohut, "Self Psychology and the Sciences," p. 83.

[67]See Kohut, "On Leadership," pp. 56-68; idem, "'One Needs a Twinkle of Humor as a Protection Against Craziness,'" in Strozier, *Self Psychology and the Humanities*, pp. 246-47.

The real function of culture, says Kohut, is the support of the self.[68] As he put it:

> A healthy group self, as is the case for the healthy self of the individual, is continuously sustained in its course throughout time--during its life one can say--by ongoing psychological work that provides the cohesion and vigor of its changing yet continuous structure within a matrix of selfobjects who are in empathic contact with its changing needs. The sum total of the results of this work that must affect all layers of a people or at least the great majority of them . . . we call "culture."[69]

People who make especially powerful contributions to "group selves" often do so either by being uniquely creative or by being able to lead and influence others. Kohut studied both creativity and leadership in some depth.

The Creative Person in the Group

Throughout Kohut's career he frequently returned to the theme of creativity as a function of the maturation and liberation of the self. His interest was not only in those producers of creative products the value of which can be assessed by retrospective historical standards, but in the fulfilled creativity that can be seen in any life when the inner potentiality inscribed in the nuclear self is unleashed.[70]

For Kohut, creativity is of the essence of health--both for the individual and for the group self. He wrote:

> What moves society toward health is [the health] of creative individuals in religion, philosophy, art, and in the sciences concerned

---

[68]Kohut, "Civilization Versus Culture," in Strozier, *Self Psychology and the Humanities*, pp. 254-55.

[69]Kohut, "Self Psychology and the Sciences," p. 88.

[70]Ibid., pp. 74-75.

> with man (sociology, political science, history, psychology). These "leaders" are in empathic contact with the illness of the group self and, through their work and thought, mobilize the unfulfilled narcissistic needs and point the way toward vital internal change. It follows that during crisis and periods of regressive identification of the group self with pathological leaders there is an absence of creativity in religion, philosophy, art, and the sciences of man.[71]

Creativity, Kohut affirmed, is related to the "mobilization of formerly frozen narcissistic cathexes, in the area of both the grandiose self and the idealized parent imago."[72] The creative product has a function similar to that of a selfobject, whose presence and perfection is essential to the well-being of the self. In the act of creation the "I-you" barrier becomes indistinct and the outer world is in union with the self as, during the period of creative work, the creative person organizes all perception and all activity according to the structures of the self.[73] Thus, "Creative artists, and scientists, may be attached to their work with the intensity of an addiction, and they try to control and shape it with forces and for purposes which belong to a narcissistically experienced world."[74]

In his later writings Kohut clarified the distinction between creativity and productivity, asserting that

> all creative and productive work depends on the employment of both grandiose *and* idealizing narcissistic energies, but I think that truly original thought, i.e. creativity, is energized predominantly from the grandiose self, while the work of more tradition-bound scientific and artistic activities, i.e. productivity, is performed with idealizing cathexes.[75]

---

[71]Ibid., pp. 83-84.

[72]Kohut, *Analysis of the Self*, p. 308.

[73]Kohut, "Forms and Transformations," pp. 112-13.

[74]Kohut, "Forms and Transformations," p. 115.

[75]Kohut, "Creativeness, Charisma, Group Psychology," pp. 177-78.

Since both artistic and scientific work demand both elements, this distinction should be viewed as describing a continuum or tension arc in which energy is distributed throughout but more energy is concentrated at certain points.[76] Often the impetus for creativity is early frustration of narcissistic needs, which leads to an effort to find narcissistic response on a broader scale. If the early need for merger with a selfobject is frustrated, for example, the yearning for merger may gradually change into "a broad, sublimated empathic merger with the surroundings, [which] finally brings about the development of a keenly sensitive attitude toward the world."[77] When it can be channeled into socially communicative creative products, such potentially regressive tendencies can become a way for the individual both to find needed narcissistic affirmation and to contribute to the upbuilding of society.[78]

In such cases the creative person's tendency to merger cannot be said to be pathological;[79] it does, however, involve a lesser degree than usual of the buffering and neutralizing structures that normally protect the adult from psychic overstimulation.[80] Thus the creative person has a "fluidity of the basic narcissistic configurations" that often results in the alternation of periods of stability and steady work with periods of precreative emptiness followed by hypomanic creative activity.[81]

---

[76]Kohut, *Analysis of the Self*, pp. 309-12.

[77]Ibid., p. 315.

[78]Ibid., pp. 315, 323.

[79] See Kohut, "Creativeness, Charisma, Group Psychology," p. 196. Here Kohut acknowledges that creative persons may in fact have personality structures "ranging from normal to psychotic"; his concern is to emphasize that creativity itself is not a function of pathology, but rather is a healing and productive transformation of narcissism.

[80]Heinz Kohut, "Childhood Experience and Creative Imagination: Contribution to Panel on the Psychology of Imagination," in *Search for the Self*, vol. 1, pp. 272-73.

[81]Kohut, "Creativeness, Charisma, Group Psychology", pp. 189-90.

The fluidity of the creative person's self very often leads to what Kohut named the "transference of creativity." Although creative persons do not necessarily suffer from a deep, persisting lack of self-structure, they often do experience a decathexis of their self-structure during the period of precreative emptiness. As a result they are very prone, at those specific times, to form transferences that in some ways resemble the transferences of those with self-disorders. Upon examining the life stories of creative persons, very often one will find that during particularly creative periods they had a strangely "dependent" relationship with another person--a relationship that often ended or went into eclipse after the creative period was completed.

Kohut gives as the classic example the relationship of Freud with Wilhelm Fliess.[82] During the time when Freud was taking his first daring steps in his self-analysis--a creative act that would revolutionize the field of psychology and have vast reverberations beyond that field--he blatantly idealized Fliess, regarding him as a brilliant scientist and collaborator in Freud's own work. In point of fact, Fliess was an arrogant and rather flaky fellow who, among other things, believed that all psychopathology could be reduced to the chemistry of the sexual processes. After Freud had moved from the initial manic phase of exploration into a consolidating phase, he seems to have gained a more realistic insight into Fliess's character.

In the transference of creativity, Kohut summarizes,

> we are dealing with either (a) the wish of a self which feels enfeebled during a period of creativity to retain its cohesion by expanding temporarily into the psychic structure of others, by finding itself in others, or to be confirmed by the admiration of others (resembling

[82]For Kohut's discussion, see "Creativeness, Charisma, Group Psychology", pp. 180-83, 190-95; also idem, *Analysis of the Self*, pp. 316-17. For a more complete study of the relationship, see Ernst Kris's introduction to the Fliess correspondence in Sigmund Freud, *The Origins of Psychoanalysis: Letters to Wilhelm Fliess, Drafts and Notes, 1887-1902*, ed. by Marie Bonaparte, Anna Freud, and Ernst Kris, trans. Eric Mosbacher and James Strachey (New York: Basic, 1954); also Max Schur, *Freud: Living and Dying* (New York: International Universities Press, 1972).

> one of the varieties of the mirror transference) or (b) the need to obtain strength from an idealized object (resemblng an idealizing transference).[83]

Alter-ego transferences of creativity are also possible; Kohut cites work suggesting this operated in Picasso's life.[84] Kohut believed, however, that the idealizing transference of creativity is the most common.[85] This corresponds with his belief that prototypical creativity is largely fueled by the energies of the grandiose self. As the energies of grandiosity and of the search for "likeness" flow with great passion into the creative work itself, the idealizing sector of the self becomes depleted and in need of outside reinforcement.

The "individualism" of creative persons is also explained by this hypothesis. While sheer grandiosity without a capacity to idealize a group ideal--and so to participate in a tradition--would result in noncommunicative art and "rogue" science, Kohut wrote that "The channeling of the flow of a large part of the individual . . . narcissistic energies toward the group ego ideal creates psychological conditions unfavorable to creative activities that emanate from the grandiose self."[86] Thus, a total commitment of self-energies to the idealized group stifles creativity. In order for a tradition to remain alive and to be developed creatively, individuals within it must be able to strike a balance between their grandiose strivings and their idealizing needs.

At the same time, creative persons--and specifically great artists--have an essential role to play within group life. Kohut wrote:

> The great artists of any period are in touch with the currently preeminent psychological tasks of a culture. I call this the anticipatory function of art. The artist is thus ahead of the scientist

---

[83]Kohut, "Creativeness, Charisma, Group Psychology," p. 192.

[84]Ibid., p. 193.

[85]Ibid., p. 194.

[86]Ibid., p. 177.

> in responding to man's unfolding needs. Through his work he leads man to a dawning conscious awareness of a preconsciously experienced psychological conflict or of an only preconsciously experienced psychic defect. The artist prepares the way for the culturally supported solution to the conflict or for healing of the defect.[87]

Creative persons--especially artists--are empathically in tune with the needs and deficits of the cultural "group self," and they lead the way in the group's search for a way to overcome its traumas and achieve a new, more deeply rooted coherence and strength. Kohut concluded, "modern art is genuine when it is from the depths and describes a creative search for a reassembled self."[88] Art which is enduring has an "inner cohesiveness";[89] it is an expression, fueled by the deepest levels of human need and genius, of the unending search of the self for its own cohesiveness, continuity, participation, etc.

The Leader in the Group

Art and political action, notes Kohut, function more similarly than many realize. Speaking of the Nazi movement in Germany of the thirties, he wrote:

> The Nazi capacity to tune to large groups of the most diversified people and intuitively offer them an image of cohesion and strength, heal the fragmentation, the weakness, and the underlying depression, suddenly give people a sense that they are worthwhile, indeed better than others, had something truly artistic about it. Leni Riefenstahl, for example, captured this quality in her film of the Olympics or in the one of the party rally (*Triumph of the Will*) which has the plane

---

[87]Kohut, "Self Psychology and the Sciences," pp. 88-89.

[88]Kohut, "Civiliation Versus Culture," p. 259.

[89]Kohut, "On the Continuity of the Self," p. 243.

> coming out of the clouds with the Fuhrer in it. The film offered a perfect response to what the population needed.[90]

Leadership, like effective artistic creativity, is based in the leader's empathy with the deep needs of the group self of the people to be led. As the example of the Nazis illustrates, this empathy may be used for malignant purposes as well as for benign ones. As will be discussed below, in such cases the "empathy" involved is actually a malignant transformation of the leader's narcissism, as distinct from the healthy increase in the capacity for empathy that comes with the healing and expansion of the self.

The capacity for empathy--the ability to enter into another's experience--was discussed in Chapter 8 in the section on method in self psychology. In Kohut's view, empathy is based in a preverbal awareness of how the other self is affecting one's own self. On this basis one can (often still in a preverbal, almost instantaneous mode) imaginatively reconstruct what the other is actually experiencing, employing both one's own past experiences and one's assessment of what corresponds to one's present experience of the other in interaction with the self. Thus, empathy is a "way of relating to another person in a narcissistic mode."[91]

Kohut wrote, "The groundwork for our ability to obtain access to another person's mind is laid by the fact that in our earliest mental organization the feelings, actions, and behavior of the mother had been included in our self."[92] A high degree of empathic capacity is characteristic of mature transformed narcissism because it involves ready access to that level of "primary empathy," along with the ability to modulate it cognitively and to integrate it into well-organized ego functions.

---

[90]Kohut, "'One Needs a Twinkle of Humor,'"p. 246.

[91]Kohut, "Forms and Transformations," p. 117.

[92]Ibid., p. 116.

Certain types of leaders, however, are empathic in an untransformed, archaic mode. This may result from a shattering trauma these person experienced in the earliest period of the formation of the self.[93] The "superempathy" of this type of leader with him or herself is an in-tuneness with the archaic level of primary empathy that has never undergone gradual modification and integration with cognitive functions. These functions, meanwhile, have developed--often to a high degree of executive ability--on a parallel track that is totally lacking in normal empathy for other persons.[94]

Leaders of this type are geniuses at tuning in to what is happening in the group self at the archaic level. In extreme cases they have no restraints of compassion or concern to prevent them from exploiting weaknesses found there to meet their own needs. The two major types of these leader-personalities that Kohut discusses are the charismatic personality, who has totally identified with his or her archaic grandiose self and so has an absolutely unshakable (often bordering on delusional) self-confidence, and the messianic personality, who has totally identified with his or her archaic idealized selfobject and so has an absolutely unshakable sense of moral righteousness.[95]

Kohut's view seems to be that under "ideal" circumstances--that is, when the group self is essentially healthy, a supportive matrix of selfobjects is available, and no grave crisis threatens--leadership will be exercised by those of "modest, self-relativistic personality type"[96] within a culture characterized by "the interpretative presence of many active and influential minds."[97] In such a case the leaders' empathy

---

[93]Kohut, "Creativeness, Charisma, Group Psychology," pp. 201-2.

[94]See Kohut, "Creativeness, Charisma, Group Psychology," p. 198; idem, "Self Psychology and the Sciences," pp. 91-92; idem, "On Leadership," pp. 56-57.

[95]For discussion, see Kohut, "Creativeness, Charisma, Group Psychology," pp. 196-202.

[96]Ibid., p. 198.

[97]Kohut, "Self Psychology and the Sciences," p. 83.

with the needs of the group self operates on a continuum with cognitive insights such as those expressed in the cultural products of art and intellectual life.

Since such ideal conditions are not in actuality the norm, however, leadership very often is taken by those with a greater or lesser degree of the self pathologies Kohut has described. Although the charismatic and messianic forms of self-structure are essentially pathological, Kohut points out that under certain circumstances such leaders may function in ways that are beneficial for those they lead. The circumstances in such cases usually involve an external threat to the group self and a leader whose pathology is not of the most extreme variety. He gives as an example Winston Churchill's relationship with the British people during World War II. Churchill's charismatic personality structure, characterized by "unshakable belief in his and, by extension, the nation's strength," gave the group self strength to maintain coherence and hence to survive a crisis of the gravest proportions. When the crisis was past, however, Churchill's style of leadership was no longer appropriate and the nation turned to others.[98]

Another example of the potentially benign functioning of charismatic or messianic personalities is in the transference of creativity described above. Most often, says Kohut, such transferences are idealizing ones involving a charismatic personality. The creative person whose self-energies are off balance due to the passionate storm brewing in the area of the grandiose self seeks to idealize someone who exhibits utter self-confidence and calm. As in the case of the group self, after the crisis has passed the creative person sees the idealized person in a more realistic light and the relationship ends or decreases in importance.

---

[98]Kohut, "Creativeness, Charisma, Group Psychology," pp. 198-99. For discussion of Churchill's personality structure, see also idem, "Forms and Transformations," p. 110; "On Courage," pp. 12-13; "'Stranger, Take Word to Sparta,'" pp. 268-69.

The following quotation summarizes Kohut's view of the narcissistic dynamics of powerful leaders and of their relationship with the group self.

> During crucial moments of self survival--not just biological survival but *self* survival--something fundamental is threatened. At such moments, the gifted and successful leader experiences danger on the personal level but can realize and express that danger on the group level. He experiences it at a personal level because he himself lacked the sustenance of selfobjects as a child. He is threatened by disintegration and goes through phases of near fragmentation frequently in late adolescence or early adulthood, then reassembles himself with a set of creative ideas that happen to fit the overall needs of the group. He and the group then become each other's selfobjects. They come to form a unit that is exhilarating and full of vitality. The self that was fragmented clicks firmly back into place. It is for these experiences that people will gladly die.[99]

[99]Kohut, "Civilization Versus Culture," p. 259.

BIBLIOGRAPHY

I. PRIMARY SOURCES

A. Bernard J.F. Lonergan

"Christ as Subject: A Reply." In *Collection*, 153-84.

"Christology Today: Methodological Reflections." In *Third Collection*, 74-99.

"Cognitional Structure." In *Collection*, 205-21.

Collection, 2nd ed. Edited by Frederick E. Crowe and Robert M. Doran. Toronto: University of Toronto Press, 1988.

"Dimensions of Meaning." In *Collection*, 232-45.

"*Existenz* and *Aggiornamento*." In *Collection*, 222-31.

"First Lecture: Religious Experience." In *Third Collection*, 115-28.

Grace and Freedom: Operative Grace in the Thought of St. Thomas Aquinas. Edited by J. Patout Burns, with introduction by Frederick E. Crowe. New York: Herder and Herder, 1971.

"Healing and Creating in History." In *Third Collection*, 100-109.

Insight: A Study of Human Understanding, 3rd ed. New York: Philosophical Library, 1970.

Lectures on Education. Lectures given at Xavier University, Cincinnati, OH, August 1959. Transcription available from The Lonergan Center, Boston College, Chestnut Hill, MA 02167.

"The Mediation of Christ in Prayer." *Method: Journal of Lonergan Studies* 2 (1984): 1-20.

"Metaphysics as Horizon." In *Collection*, 188-204.

Method in Theology. London: Darton, Longman & Todd, 1971.

"Method: Trend and Variations." Lecture given at Austin College, Sherman, TX, March 1974. Transcription available from The Lonergan Center, Boston College, Chestnut Hill, MA 02167.

"Natural Right and Historical Mindedness." In *Third Collection*, 169-83.

"Existentialism." Notes on lectures given at Boston College, Boston, MA, July 1957. Montreal: Thomas More Institute, 1957. Mimeographed edition.

On the Ontological and Psychological Constitution of Christ: A Supplement Prepared by Bernard Lonergan, S.J., for the Use of his Students. Translation of *De Constitutione Christi ontologica et psychologica supplementum confecit Bernardus Lonergan, S.J.* (Rome: Gregorian University, 1956). Translated by Timothy P. Fallon, 1973. Copyright, 1979. Photocopy available from Lonergan Research Institute, 10 St. Mary St., #500, Toronto, ON M4Y 1P9.

"Openness and Religious Experience." In *Second Collection*, 209-30.

Philosophy of God and Theology: The Relationship Between Philosophy of God and the Functional Speciality, Systematics. London: Darton, Longman & Todd, 1973.

A Second Collection: Papers by Bernard Lonergan, S.J. Edited by William F.J. Ryan and Bernard J. Tyrrell. London: Darton, Longman & Todd, 1974.

"The Subject." In *Second Collection*, 69-86.

A Third Collection: Papers by Bernard J.F. Lonergan, S.J.. Edited by Frederick E. Crowe. New York: Paulist, 1985.

"Third Lecture: The Ongoing Genesis of Methods." In *Third Collection*, 146-65.

Understanding and Being: An Introduction and Companion to Insight. Edited by Elizabeth A. Morelli and Mark D. Morelli. New York: Edwin Mellen, 1980.

B. Heinz Kohut

The Analysis of the Self: A Systematic Approach to the Psychoanalytic Treatment of Narcissistic Personality Disorders. Monograph Series of the Psychoanalytic Study of the Child, no. 4. Madison, CT: International Universities Press, 1971.

"Beyond the Bounds of the Basic Rule: Some Recent Contributions to Applied Psychoanalyis." In *Search for the Self*, vol. 1, 275-303.

"Childhood Experience and Creative Imagination: Contribution to Panel on the Psychology of Imagination." In *Search for the Self*, vol. 1, 271-74.

"Civilization Versus Culture." In *Self Psychology and the Humanities*, 254-60.

"Creativeness, Charisma, Group Psychology: Reflections on the Self-Analysis of Freud." In *Self Psychology and the Humanities*, 171-211, and *Search for the Self*, vol. 2, 793-843.

"Discussion of 'The Self: A Contribution to Its Place in Theory and Technique' by D.C. Levin." In *The Search for the Self*, vol. 2, 577-88.

"Forms and Transformations of Narcissism." In *Self Psychology and the Humanities*, 97-123, and *Search for the Self*, vol. 1, 427-60.

How Does Analysis Cure? Edited by Arnold Goldberg with the collaboration of Paul E. Stepansky. Chicago, IL: University of Chicago, 1984.

"Introspection, Empathy, and Psychoanalysis: An Examination of the Relationship Between Mode of Observation and Theory." In *Search for the Self*, vol. 1, 205-32.

"Introspection, Empathy, and the Semicircle of Mental Health." In *Empathy*, edited by Joseph Lichentberg, Melvin Bornstein, and Donald Silver, vol. 1, 81-100. Hillsdale, NJ: Analytic Press, 1984.

"On Courage." In *Self Psychology and the Humanities*, 5-50.

"On Leadership." In *Self Psychology and the Humanities*, 51-72.

"'One Needs a Twinkle of Humor as a Protection Against Craziness.'" In *Self Psychology and the Humanities*, 244-53.

"Psychoanalysis and the Interpretation of Literature: A Correspondence with Erich Heller." *Critical Inquiry* 4 (1978): 433-50.

"The Psychoanalyst and the Historian." In *Self Psychology and the Humanities*, 215-23.

"Religion, Ethics, Values." In *Self Psychology and the Humanities*, 261-62.

"Remarks About the Formation of the Self: Letter to a Student Regarding Some Principles of Psychoanalytic Research." In *Search for the Self*, vol. 2, 737-70.

The Restoration of the Self. Madison, CT: International Universities Press, 1977.

The Search for the Self. 2 vols. Edited by Paul H. Ornstein. New York: International Universities Press, 1978.

"The Self in History." In *Self Psychology and the Humanities*. 161-70, and *Search for the Self*, vol. 2, 771-82.

Self Psychology and the Humanities: Reflections on a New Psychoanalytic Approach. Edited by Charles B. Strozier. New York: W.W. Norton, 1985.

"Self Psychology and the Sciences of Man." In Strozier, *Self Psychology and the Humanities*.

"'Stranger, Take Word to Sparta: Here We Lie Obeying Her Orders.'" In *Self Psychology and the Humanities*, 263-69.

"Thoughts on Narcissism and Narcissistic Rage." In *Self Psychology and the Humanities*, 124-60, and *Search for the Self*, vol. 2, 615-58.

C. St. Teresa of Avila

The Collected Works of St. Teresa of Avila. 3 vols. Translated and edited by Kieran Kavanaugh and Otilio Rodriguez. Washington, DC: Institute of Carmelite Studies, 1976-85.

The Letters of Saint Teresa. 2 vols. Translated and annotated by the Benedictines of Stanbrook. London: Thomas Baker, 1926.

Santa Teresa de Jesús: Obras Completas. 3 vols. Edited by Efrén de la Madre de Dios. Madrid: Biblioteca de Autores Cristianos, 1951-59.

II. SECONDARY SOURCES

Albrecht, Carl. *Das Mystische Erkennen*. Bremen, Germany: Carl Schuenemann Verlag, 1958.

-----. *Psychologie des mystichen Bewusstseins*. Bremen, Germany: Carl Schuenemann Verlag, 1951.

Aristotle. *Analytica Posteriora*. In *The Basic Works of Aristotle*, edited by Richard McKeon. New York: Random House, 1941.

------. *Metaphysica*. In *Basic Works of Aristotle*.

Asín Palacios, Miguel. "El símil de los castillos y moradas del alma en la mística islámica y en Santa Teresa." *Al-Andalús* 9 (1946): 263-74.

Atwood, George E. and Robert D. Stolorow. *Structures of Subjectivity: Explorations in Psychoanalytic Phenomenology*. Hillsdale, NJ: Analytic Press, 1984.

Augustine. *The Confessions of St. Augustine*. Translated by John K. Ryan. Garden City, NY: Image Books, 1960.

Aumann, Jordan. *Spiritual Theology*. Huntington, IN: Our Sunday Visitor, 1980.

Bache, Christopher M. "A Reappraisal of Teresa of Avila's Supposed Hysteria." *Journal of Religion and Health* 24, no. 4 (1985): 300-15.

Barron, Frank. "The Creative Personality: Akin to Madness." In *Understanding Mysticism*, edited by Richard Woods, 312-20.

Baudry, Joseph. "Pédagogie thérésienne de l'imitation des saints dans le livre de la *Vida*." *Teresianum* 33 (1982): 587-618.

Baxter, Ian F.G. "Justice and Mysticism." *Revue Internationale de Philosophie* 17 (1963): 353-80.

Becker, Ernest. *The Birth and Death of Meaning*. 2nd ed. New York: Free Press, 1971.

Blinkoff, Jodi. "St. Teresa of Avila and the Avila of St. Teresa." *Carmelite Studies* 3 (1984): 53-68.

Breuer, Josef and Sigmund Freud. *Studies on Hysteria*. Vol. 2, *The Standard Edition of the Complete Psychological Works of Sigmund Freud*. Translated and edited by James Strachey. London: Hogarth Press and the Institute of Psychoanalysis.

Buckley, Michael J. "Atheism and Contemplation." *Theological Studies* 40 (1979): 680-99.

Carballo, Juan Rof. "La Estructura del Alma Humana Según Santa Teresa." *Revista de Espiritualidad* 22 (1963): 413-31.

Chorpenning, Joseph. "The Literary and Theological Method of the *Castillo Interior*." *Journal of Hispanic Philology* 3 (1979): 121-33.

------. "The Image of Darkness and Spiritual Development in the *Castillo Interior*." *Studia Mystica* 8 (1985): 45-58.

------. "The Monastery, Paradise, and the Castle: Literary Images and Spiritual Development in St. Teresa of Avila." *Bulletin of Hispanic Studies* 62:3 (July 1985): 245-57.

------. "St. Teresa of Avila as Allegorist: Chapters 11-22 of the *Libro de la Vida*." *Studia Mystica* 9 (Spring 1986): 3-22.

------. "St. Teresa's Presentation of Her Religious Experience." *Carmelite Studies* 3 (1984): 152-88.

Clifford, Gay. *The Transformation of Allegory*. London: Routledge and Kegan Paul, 1974.

Cocks, Geoffrey, and Travis L. Crosby, eds. *Psycho/History: Readings in the Method of Psychology, Psychoanalysis, and History*. New Haven, CT: Yale University, 1987.

Coelho, Mary. "St. Teresa of Avila's Transformation of the Symbol of the Interior Castle." *Ephemerides Carmeliticae* 38 (1987): 109-25.

Crookall, R. *The Interpretation of Cosmic and Mystical Experiences.* London, 1969.

Crowe, Frederick E. *Old Things and New: A Strategy for Education.* Atlanta, GA: Scholar's Press, 1985.

Deikman, Arthur J. "Bimodal Consciousness and the Mystic Experience." In *Understanding Mysticism*, edited by Richard Woods, 261-69.

------. "Deautomatization and the Mystic Experience." In *Understanding Mysticism*, edited by Richard Woods, 240-60.

Delacroix, Henri J. *Études d'histoire et de psychologie du mysticisme: les grands mystiques chrétiens.* Paris: F. Alcan, 1908.

de Lubac, Henri. *Exégèse médiévale: les quatre sens de l'Ecriture*, 4 volumes. Paris: Aubier, 1964.

Dicken, E.W. Trueman. *The Crucible of Love.* London: Darton, Longman & Todd, 1963.

------. "The Imagery of the Interior Castle and Its Implications." *Ephemerides Carmeliticae* 21 (1970): 198-218.

Doran, Robert M. *Subject and Psyche: Ricoeur, Jung, and the Search for Foundations.* Washington, DC: University Press of America, 1977.

------. *Psychic Conversion and Theological Foundations: Toward a Reorientation of the Human Sciences.* AAR Studies in Religion, no. 25. Chico, CA: Scholars Press, 1981.

Dunne, Tad. *Lonergan and Spirituality: Towards a Spiritual Integration.* Chicago: Loyola University , 1985.

Efrén de la Madre de Dios and Otger Steggink. *Tiempo y Vida de Santa Teresa.* Madrid: Autores Cristianos, 1968.

Egan, Harvey D. *What Are They Saying About Mysticism?* New York: Paulist, 1982.

Egido, Teófanes. "The Historical Setting of St. Teresa's Life." Translated by Steven Payne and Michael Dodd. *Carmelite Studies* 1 (1980).

Eliade, Mircea. *The Two and the One*. Translated by J.M. Cohen. London: Harvill, 1965.

Ennis, Phillip H. "Ecstasy and Everyday Life." *Journal for the Scientific Study of Religion* 6 (1967): 40-48.

Erikson, Erik H. "The Dream Specimen of Psychoanalysis." *Journal of the American Psychoanalytic Association* 2 (1954): 5-56.

Etchegoyen, Gaston. *L'Amour divin: Essai sur les sources de Sainte Thérèse*. Bordeaux-Paris: Féret et Fils, 1923.

Fineman, Joel. "The Structure of Allegorical Desire." In *Allegory and Representation*, edited by Stephen J. Greenblatt, 26-60. Baltimore, MD: Johns Hopkins University Press, 1981.

Fischer, Roland. "A Cartography of the Ecstatic and Meditative States." In *Understanding Mysticism*, edited by Richard J. Woods.

Fittipaldi, Silvio E. "Human Consciousness and the Christian Mystic: Teresa of Avila." *Journal of the Academy of Religion and Psychical Research* 3, no 2 (1980): 94-104.

FitzGerald, Constance. "A Discipleship of Equals: Voices from Tradition--Teresa of Avila and John of the Cross." In *A Discipleship of Equals: Towards a Christian Feminist Spirituality*, edited by Francis A. Eigo. *Proceedings of the Villanova Theology Institute* 20 (1987): 63-97.

Fletcher, Angus. *Allegory: The Theory of a Symbolic Mode*. Ithaca, NY: Cornell University Press, 1970.

Forman, Robert K.C., ed. *The Problem of Pure Consciousness: Mysticism and Philosophy*. New York: Oxford University, 1990.

Freud, Sigmund. "On Narcissism: An Introduction." In *Standard Edition* 14:73-102.

------. "Group Psychology and the Analysis of the Ego." *Standard Edition* 18:65-143.

------. *The Origins of Psychoanalysis: Letters to Wilhelm Fliess, Drafts and Notes, 1887-1902.* Edited by Marie Bonaparte, Anna Freud, and Ernst Kris, translated by Eric Mosbacher and James Strachey. New York: Basic, 1954.

Frohlich, Mary. "Politics, Mysticism and Liturgy: Schillebeeckx on Prayer." *Liturgy* 5, no. 3 (Winter, 1986): 35-39.

Galilea, Segundo. *The Future of Our Past.* Notre Dame, IN: Ave Maria, 1985.

------. "Liberation as an Encounter with Politics and Contemplation." In *Understanding Mysticism*, edited by Richard Woods.

García de la Concha, Victor. *El Arte Literario de Santa Teresa.* Barcelona: Editorial Ariel, 1978.

Gracián, Jerónimo de la Madre de Dios. *Espíritu y revelaciones y maner de proceder de la Madre Ana de San Bartolomé, examinado por el P., su confesor.* Edited by Silverio de Santa Teresa. *Biblioteca Mistica Carmelitana* 17 (1933).

Greenacre, P. "The Childhood of the Artist: Libidinal Phase Development and Giftedness." *Psychoanalytic Study of the Child* 12 (1957).

Gregson, Vernon, ed. *The Desires of the Human Heart: An Introduction to the Theology of Bernard Lonergan.* New York: Paulist, 1988.

Grof, Stanislav. *Realms of the Unconscious.* New York: E.P. Dutton, 1976.

Hahn, G. "Les Phénomènes Hystériques et les Révélations de Sainte Thérèse." *Revue des Questions Scientifiques* 12, 13, 14 (1883-84).

Hall, John M. "Idealizing Transference: Disruptions and Repairs." In *Progress in Self Psychology*, edited by Arnold Goldberg, vol. 1, 109-46. New York: Guilford, 1985.

Hart, Kevin. *The Trespass of the Sign: Deconstruction, Theology and Philosophy.* New York: Cambridge University, 1989.

Hartmann, Heinz. "Comments on the Psychoanalytic Theory of the Ego." In *Essays on Ego Psychology*, 113-41. New York: International Universities Press, 1964.

Hatzfeld, Helmut. *Santa Teresa de Avila.* New York: Twayne, 1969.

Haught, John F. *Religion and Self-Acceptance: A Study of the Relationship Between Belief in God and the Desire to Know.* Washington, DC: University Press of America, 1980.

Hegel, G.W.F. *The Phenomenology of Mind.* Translated by J.B. Baillie. New York: Harper & Row, 1967.

Helminiak, Daniel A. "Human Solidarity and Collective Union in Christ." *Anglican Theological Review* 70 (1988): 34-59.

Hood, Ralph. "Differential Triggering of Mystical Experience as a Function of Self Actualization." *Review of Religious Research* 18 (1977): 264-270.

------. "Gender Differences in the Description of Erotic and Mystical Experiences." *Review of Religious Research* 21 (1980): 195-207.

------. "Knowledge and Experience Criteria in the Report of Mystical Experience." *Review of Religious Research* 23 (1983): 76-84.

Honig, Edwin. *Dark Conceit: The Making of Allegory.* New York: Oxford University Press, 1966.

Hoornaert, Rodolphe. *Saint Teresa in Her Writings.* Translated by Joseph Leonard. New York: Benziger Brothers., 1931.

------. *Sainte Thérèse écrivain, son milieu, ses facultés, son oeuvre.* Paris: Desclée de Brouwer, 1922.

Hügel, Friedrich Von. *The Mystical Element in Religion, as Studied in Saint Catherine of Genoa and Her Friends*, 2 vols. London: J.M. Dent, 1908.

Husserl, Edmund. *The Crisis of European Sciences and Transcendental Phenomenology.* Translated by David Carr. Evanston, IL: Northwestern University Press, 1970.

Huxley, Alduous. *The Perennial Philosophy.* New York: Harper & Bros., 1945. Reprint, Harper Colophon Books, New York: Harper & Row, 1970.

Ignatius Loyola. *The Spiritual Exercises of St. Ignatius: A Literal Translation and A Contemporary Reading*. Translated and edited by David L. Fleming. St. Louis, MO: Institute of Jesuit Sources, 1978.

James, William. *The Varieties of Religious Experience*. New York: Modern Liberary, 1902.

John of the Cross. *The Living Flame of Love*. In *The Collected Works of St. John of the Cross*, translated by Kieran Kavanaugh and Otilio Rodriguez. Washington, DC: Institute of Carmelite Studies, 1973.

Johnson, R.C. *Watcher on the Hills*. London, 1959.

Kant, Immanuel. *Critique of Pure Reason*. Translated by Norman Kemp Smith. New York: St. Martin's, 1965.

Katz, Steven T., ed. *Mysticism and Language*. New York: Oxford,

______, ed. *Mysticism and Philosophical Analysis*. New York: Oxford University, 1978.

------, ed. *Mysticism and Religious Traditions*. New York: Oxford University, 1983.

Keller, Joseph. "Mysticism and the Implicate Order." *Studia Mystica* 7, no. 4 (1984): 28-36.

------. "Mysticism and Intersubjective Creativity." *Studia Mystica* 8, no. 4 (1985): 36-46.

Kelly, Anthony. "Is Lonergan's *Method* Adequate to Christian Mystery?" *The Thomist* 39, no. 3 (1975): 437-70.

Kereszty, Roch. "Psychological Subject and Consciousness in Christ." *Communio* 11 (1984): 258-77.

Kidder, Paul. "Lonergan and the Husserlian Problem of Transcendental Intersubjectivity." *Method: Journal of Lonergan Studies* 4 (1986): 29-54.

King, Sallie B. "Two Epistemological Models of the Interpretation of Mysticism." *Journal of the American Academy of Religion* 56, no. 2 (1988): 257-79.

Klee, Robert L. "Micro-Determinism and Concepts of Emergence." *Philosophy of Science* 51 (1984): 44-63

Klein, G. *Psychoanalytic Theory: An Exploration of Essentials*. New York: International Universities Press, 1976.

Kohut, Thomas A. "Psychohistory as History." *American Historical Review* 91, no. 2 (1986): 336-54.

Lamb, Matthew L., ed. *Creativity and Method: Essays in Honor of Bernard Lonergan*. Milwaukee, WI: Marquette University Press, 1981.

------. *History, Method and Theology: A Dialectical Comparison of Wilhelm Dilthey's Critique of Historical Reason and Bernard Lonergan's Meta-Methodology*. AAR Dissertation Series 25. Missoula, MT: Scholars Press, 1978.

Laredo, Bernardino de. *The Ascent of Mount Sion*. Translated by E. Allison Peers. New York: Harper, 1952.

Laski, Marghanita. *Ecstasy*. Bloomington, IN: Indiana University, 1962.

Lawrence, Fred. "Gadamer and Lonergan: A Dialectical Comparison." *International Philosophical Quarterly* 20 (1980).

------. "Method and Theology as Hermeneutical." In *Creativity and Method*, edited by Matthew L. Lamb, 79-104.

Lehmann, Karl. S.v. "Transcendence." *Encyclopedia of Theology: The Concise Sacramentum Mundi*, edited by Karl Rahner, 1734-42. New York: Crossroads, 1986.

Leuba, James H. *The Psychology of Religious Mysticism*. New York: Harcourt, Brace, 1925.

Lincoln, Victoria. *Teresa: A Woman--A Biography of Teresa of Avila*, edited with introductions by Elias Rivers and Antonio T. de Nicolás. New York: Paragon House, 1984.

Lobkowicz, Nicholas. S.v. "Theory and Practice." *Marxism, Communism and Western Society: A Comparative Encyclopedia*, edited by C.D. Kernig, vol. 8, 160-72. New York: Herder and Herder, 1973.

López-Baralt, Luce. "Santa Teresa de Jesús y el Islam." *Teresianum* 23 (1982): 653-54.

Ludolphus de Saxonia. *Vita Christi: Selections.* Latin and English on opposite pages. Salzburg: Institut fur Englische Sprache und Literatur, 1973.

Mallory, Marilyn May. *Christian Mysticism: Transcending Techniques.* Amsterdam: Van Gorcum Assen, 1977.

Maréchal, Joseph. *Studies in the Psychology of the Mystics.* Translated by Algar Thorold. London: Burns, Oates & Washbourne, 1927. Reprint, Albany, NY: Magi, 1964.

Matustik, Martin J. *Mediation of Deconstruction: Bernard Lonergan's Method in Philosophy: The Argument from Human Operational Development.* Lanham, MD: University Press of America, 1988.

McDargh, John. "Beyond God as Transitional Object." Paper presented at the Psycholgy and Religion Section of the College Theology Society, Los Angeles, CA, May 1988.

------. *Psychoanalytic Object Relations Theory and the Study of Religion.* Lanham, MD: University Press of America, 1983.

McGinn, Bernard. *The Foundations of Mysticism: Origins to the Fifth Century.* New York: Crossroad, 1991.

Meissner, William. *Psychoanalysis and Religious Experience.* New Haven, CT: Yale University, 1984.

Melchin, Kenneth R. *History, Ethics and Emergent Probability: Ethics, Society and History in the Work of Bernard Lonergan.* Lanham, MD: University Press of America, 1987.

Metz, Johann Baptist. *Faith in History and Society: Toward a Practical Fundamental Theology* Translated by David Smith. New York: Seabury, 1980.

Morgan, C.L. *Emergent Evolution.* London: Williams and Norgate, 1923.

Morel-Fatio, Alfred. "Les Lectures de Sainte Thérèse." *Bulletin Hispanique* 10 (1908): 17-67.

Morelli, Mark. "Reversing the Counter-Position: The *Argumentum Ad Hominem* in Philosophic Dialogue." In *Lonergan Workshop*, edited by Fred Lawrence, vol. 6, 195-230. Atlanta, GA: Scholars Press, 1986.

Morón-Arroyo, Ciriaco. "'I Will Give You a Living Book': Spiritual Currents at Work at the Time of St. Teresa of Jesus." *Carmelite Studies* 3 (1984): 95-112.

Navickas, Joseph L. *Consciousness and Reality: Hegel's Philosophy of Subjectivity*. The Hague: Martinus Nijhoff, 1976.

Neumann, Erich. "Mystical Man." *Eranos Jahrbuch* 30 (1968): 375-415.

O'Callaghan, Michael. "Rahner and Lonergan on Foundational Theology." *Creativity and Method*, edited by Matthew L. Lamb, 123-40. Milwaukee, WI: Marquette University, 1981.

Ornstein, Robert E. "Two Sides of the Brain." In *Understanding Mysticism*, edited by Richard Woods, 270-85.

Osuna, Francisco de. *Tercer parte de libro llamado Abecedario Spiritual*. Madrid: Escritores misticos espanoles, 1911.

Pepper, Stephen. "Emergence." *Journal of Philosophy* 23 (1926): 241-45.

Price, James R. III. "Contemplation and Mediation: Mysticism, Philosophy and Social Responsibility." *Journal of Religion* (forthcoming).

------. "Lonergan and the Foundation of a Contemporary Mystical Theology." *Lonergan Workshop* 5 (1985): 163-95.

------. "The Objectivity of Mystical Truth Claims." *The Thomist* 49, no. 1 (1985): 81-98.

------. "Transcendence and Images: The Apophatic and Kataphatic Reconsidered." *Studies in Formative Spirituality* 11, no 2 (May 1990): 195-201.

Prince, Raymond H. "Cocoon Work: An Interpretation of the Concern of Contemporary Youth with the Mystical." In *Understanding Mysticism*, edited by Richard Woods, 338-54.

Pseudo-Dionysius: The Complete Works. Translated by Colm Luibhéid. New York: Paulist, 1987.

Quitslund, Sonya A. "Elements of a Feminist Spirituality in St. Teresa." *Carmelite Studies* 3 (1982): 19-50.

Rahner, Karl. *Foundations of Christian Faith: An Introduction to the Idea of Christianity*. Translated by William V. Dych. New York: Crossroad, 1982.

------. "The Individual in the Church." In *Nature and Grace*. New York: Sheed and Ward, 1964.

------. "The Logic of Concrete Individual Knowledge in Ignatius Loyola." *The Dynamic Element in the Church*. New York: Herder & Herder, 1964.

------. "Mystical Experience and Mystical Theology." *Theological Investigations* 17 (1973).

------. "On the Significance in Redemptive History of the Individual Member of the Church." In *The Christian Commitment*. New York: Sheed and Ward, 1963.

------. "On the Theology of the Ecumenical Discussion." *Theological Investigations* 11, translated by David Bourke. London: Darton, Longman & Todd, 1974.

Randall, Robert L. "The Legacy of Kohut for Religion and Psychology." *Journal of Religion and Health* 23, no. 2 (1984): 106-14.

------. "Soteriological Dimensions in the Work of Heinz Kohut." *Journal of Religion and Health* 19, no. 2 (1980): 83-91.

Ricard, Robert. "Quelques remarques sur les *Moradas* de Sainte Thérèse." *Bulletin Hispanique* 42 (1945): 187-98.

------. "Le Symbolisme du 'Chateau Interieur' chez Sainte Thérèse." *Bulletin Hispanique* 67 (1965): 25-41.

Ricoeur, Paul. *Interpretation Theory: Discourse and the Surplus of Meaning*. Fort Worth, TX: Texas Christian University Press, 1976.

------. *Freud and Philosophy: An Essay on Interpretation*. Translated by Denis Savage. New Haven, CT: Yale University Press, 1970.

Ritter, W.E. *The Unity of the Organism*. Boston: The Gorham Press,1919.

Rivers, Elias. "The Vernacular Mind of St. Teresa." *Carmelite Studies*3 (1984): 113-29.

Rizzuto, Ana-Maria. *The Birth of the Living God: A PsychoanalyticStudy*. Chicago, IL: University of Chicago, 1979.

Roberts, Bernadette. *What is Self? A Study of the Spiritual Journey in Terms of Consciousness*. Austin, TX: Mary Goens, 1989.

Romano, Catherine. "A Psycho-Spiritual History of Teresa of Avila: A Woman's Perspective." In *Western Spirituality: Historical Roots, Ecumenical Routes*, edited by Matthew Fox. Santa Fe, NM: Bear, 1981.

Sandler, J. and B. Rosenblatt. "The Concept of the Representational World." *The Psychoanalytic Study of the Child* 18 (1962): 128-45.

Schafer, R. *A New Language for Psychoanalysis*. New Haven: Yale University Press, 1976.

Schepers, Maurice. "Human Development: From Below Upward and From Above Downward." *Method: A Journal of Lonergan Studies* 7 (1989): 141-44.

Schillebeeckx, Edward. *Christ: The Experience of Jesus as Lord*. New York: Crossroad, 1980.

Scholem, Gershom. "Mysticism and Society." *Diogenes* 58 (Summer 1967): 1-24.

Schur, Max. *Freud: Living and Dying*. New York: International Universities Press, 1972.

Sellars, R.W. *Evolutionary Naturalism*. Chicago: Open Court, 1922.

Seris, Homero. "Nueva genealogía de Santa Teresa." *Nueva Revista de Filologia Hispanica* 10 (1956): 365-84.

Sinnige-Breed, Afra. "Evolución Normal y Unitaria del 'Yo' Teresiano a la Luz de su Vida Interior." *Revista de Espiritualidad* 22 (1963): 238-50.

Smart, Ninian. "Interpretation and Mystical Experience." In *Understanding Mysticism*, edited by Richard Woods, 78-91.

------. *The Phenomenon of Religion*. New York: Herder & Herder, 1973.

------. *The Religious Experience of Mankind*. New York: Scribner, 1969.

------. "Understanding Religious Experience," in *Mysticism and Philosophical Analysis*, edited by Steven T. Katz, 10-21. New York: Oxford University, 1978.

Smuts, J.C. *Holism and Evolution*. New York: Macmillan, 1926.

Spence, D. *Narrative Truth and Historical Truth*. New York: Norton, 1982.

Spero, Moshe Halevi. "Transference as a Religious Phenomenon in Psychotherapy." *Journal of Religion and Health* 24, no. 1 (1985): 8-25.

Sperry, Roger W. "Discussion: Macro-Versus Micro-Determinism." *Philosophy of Science* 53 (1986): 265-70.

------. "Structure and Significance of the Consciousness Revolution." *Revision* 11, no. 1 (1988): 39-56.

Stern, Daniel N. *The Interpersonal World of the Infant*. New York: Basic, 1984.

Stolorow, Robert D. and George E. Atwood. *Faces in a Cloud: Subjectivity in Personality Theory*. Northvale, NJ: Jason Aronson, 1979.

-----, Bernard Brandchaft, and George E. Atwood. *Psychoanalytic Treatment: An Intersubjective Approach*. Hillsdale, NJ: Analytic Press, 1987.

Straus, Roger A. "The Social-Psychology of Religious Experience: A Naturalistic Approach." *Sociological Analysis* 42, no. 1 (1981): 57-67.

Streeter, Carla Mae. *Religious Love in Bernard Lonergan as Hermeneutical and Transcultural*. Unpublished Th.D dissertation. Toronto: Regis College, 1986.

Streng, Frederick. "Language and Mystical Awareness." In *Mysticism and Philosophical Analysis*, edited by Steven T. Katz, 141-69.

Strozier, Charles B. "Heinz Kohut and the Historical Imagination." In *Advances in Self Psychology*, edited by Arnold Goldberg, 397-405. New York: International Universities Press, 1980.

Theophilus, Fr. "Mystical Ecstasy According to St. Teresa." In *St. Teresa of Avila: Studies in Her Life, Doctrine and Times*, edited by Fr. Thomas and Fr. Gabriel, 139-53. Westminster, MD: Newman, 1963.

Tracy, David. *The Analogical Imagination: Christian Theology and the Culture of Pluralism*. New York: Crossroad, 1981.

------. *Blessed Rage for Order: The New Pluralism in Theology*. New York: Seabury, 1978.

Tuve, Rosemond. *Allegorical Imagery*. Princeton, NJ: Princeton University Press, 1966.

Wolowitz, Howard M. "Hysterical Character and Feminine Identity." In *Readings on the Psychology of Women*, edited by Judith M. Bardwick, 307-14. New York: Harper & Row, 1972.

Ulman, Richard B. and Doris Brothers. *The Shattered Self: A Psychoanalytic Study of Trauma*. Hillsdale, NJ: Analytic Press, 1988.

Underhill, Evelyn. *Mysticism: A Study in the Nature and Development of Man's Spiritual Consciousness*. New York: Meridian, 1958.

Valera, J. Eduardo Perez. "The Structure of Christian Prayer and Its Integration with the Sciences." Paper given at the Lonergan Workshop, Boston College, June 1988.

Varela, Avelino Senra. "La Enfermedad de Santa Teresa de Jesús." *Revista de Espiritualidad* 41 (1982): 601-12.

Vázquez Fernández, Antonio. "Notas para una Lectura de las 'Moradas' de Santa Teresa desde la Psicología Profunda." *Revista de Espiritualidad* 41 (1982):

Wapnick, Kenneth. "Mysticism and Schizophrenia." In *Understanding Mysticism*, edited by Richard Woods, 321-37.

Welch, John. *Spiritual Pilgrims: Carl Jung and Teresa of Avila*. New York: Paulist, 1982.

Wilber, Ken. *The Atman Project*. Wheaton, IL: Quest, 1980.

------. *The Spectrum of Consciousness*. Wheaton, IL: Quest, 1977.

------. *Up From Eden*. Garden City, NY: Doubleday, 1981.

------, Jack Engler, and Daniel P. Brown, eds. *Transformation of Consciousness: Conventional and Contemplative Perspectives on Development*. Boston, MA: Shambhala, 1986.

Winquist, Charles E. *Epiphanies of Darkness: Deconstruction in Theology*. Philadelphia: Fortress, 1986.

Woods, Richard, ed. *Understanding Mysticism*. Garden City, NY: Doubleday, 1980.

Zaehner, R.C. *Mysticism Sacred and Profane*. Oxford: Oxford University Press, 1961.